A GOVERNMENT OF INSIDERS

A GOVERNMENT OF INSIDERS

The People Who Made the
Affordable Care Act Possible

WILLIAM GENIEYS
Translated by MELANIE MAUTHNER

 JOHNS HOPKINS UNIVERSITY PRESS | *Baltimore*

This book is an adaptation and revision of a work originally published in French as *Gouverner à l'abri des regards: La réussite de l'Obamacare.* © Presses des Sciences Po, 2020.

Johns Hopkins University Press
2715 North Charles Street
Baltimore, Maryland 21218
www.press.jhu.edu

Library of Congress Cataloging-in-Publication Data is available.

A catalog record for this book is available from the British Library.

ISBN 978-1-4214-4768-1 (paperback)
ISBN 978-1-4214-4769-8 (ebook)

Special discounts are available for bulk purchases of this book. For more information, please contact Special Sales at specialsales@jh.edu.

For Laure Kié,
My Lovely Writer

CONTENTS

Foreword, by Larry Brown   ix

Acknowledgments   xv

List of Tables   xvii

Acronyms and Abbreviations   xix

Introduction   1

PART I.   **The Custodianship of State Policies: A Government Out of Sight**   9

1.   A Government of Insiders: Unelected Governmental Elites Acting as Custodians of State Policies   13

2.   Variations in the Custodian Role: From the NHI Project to the Clinton Plan   30

PART II.   **The Making of Long-Term Health Insiders**   53

3.   Mapping the Unelected Governmental Health Coverage Policy Elites   59

4.   The Clinton Plan Veterans: Career Paths Marked by a Collective Failure   81

5.   From Late Clintonism to Obama: Shared Career Paths?   110

PART III.   **The Hidden Origins of the Affordable Care Act: Elite Configurations and Programmatic Changes**   143

6.   The Clinton Plan: Programmatic Fragmentation and Divided Elites   147

7.   The Impossible Government of "Strangers"   165

8. The George W. Bush Years: Clinton Plan Veterans Make the Next Reform Possible   184

9. Behind the Congressional Votes: Custodianship and the Politics of Accommodation   209

   Conclusion   243

Appendix 1. Methodology: A Programmatic Elite Framework   255
Appendix 2. Interviews for the OPERA (2009–2012) and PRoAcTA (2018–2021) Research Programs   261
Notes   265
Bibliography   285
Index   297

Exhibit A for the alleged exceptionalism of US health care policy would seem to be the Affordable Care Act (ACA) of 2010. One basic element—the individual mandate—is shared by some other Western health care systems, to be sure, but the rest of the package—expansion of insurance for a means-tested lower-income population, a ban on preferred risk selection by insurers, health care "marketplaces" in which a delimited set of citizens buy subsidized private insurance, and a potpourri of new speculative initiatives and institutions aimed at cost containment—adds up to a construct that could only be "made in America." The process that gave birth to the ACA, moreover, seems to have been as peculiarly American as the product: a weak state offering front-end concessions to powerful interests (pharma, hospitals, insurers, and physicians); the crucial role of "unorthodox lawmaking" (notably centralized Democratic party leadership within each of two legislative chambers whose powers are formally separated from one another and from those of the executive); and the determination to effect redistribution of health care resources without saying so out loud. Understandably, most accounts of the politics of the ACA portray its success as a distinctively American blend of luck and skill.

In one little-noticed respect, however, the process that gave rise to the ACA bears a marked resemblance to health-policy patterns observed in France and other nations in Western Europe—namely, the central role of policy elites in shaping the contents of policies (reform and other kinds) and in steering them politically. Taking issue with Hugh Heclo's famous characterization of the upper echelons of the American state as a "government of strangers," William Genieys, in a remarkable sociological examination of the origins and enactment of the ACA, traces the crucial contributions of custodians of health coverage policy—that is, cadres of "inside, long-term" appointed officials (in both the executive branch and in Congress) who combine (1) deep expert knowledge of the substance of health care policy, (2) extensive experience and savoir faire in the political and practical workings of health care policy, (3) a shared vision of policies (programmatic orientations) that are both desirable and feasible, and (4) the resolve and capacity to work collectively to promote that vision. Genieys's meticulous account of the imprint of these custodians puts into place a piece of the explanatory puzzle of the ACA that has heretofore been left largely on the analytical margins.

Autopsies of failed twentieth-century reform projects underscore both the seeming intractability of the obstacles to reform—securing agreement within Congress and between Congress and the executive branch, crafting a workable model for a better system, assuaging the concerns of interest groups, and addressing cost concerns in ways that neither dodge the issue nor terrify the electorate—and the magnitude of the accomplishments of the ACA's creators, who painstakingly crafted a plausible and politically acceptable policy package. Interviews with key protagonists and detailed biographical accounts of their careers furnish a rich and broad empirical foundation for Genieys's account of the who, the how, and the why behind the custodians' construction of a far-reaching health care reform that, ironically, was widely viewed as imprudent if not impossible in the middle of the great recession that dogged the proposal's formative years.

For Genieys, the roots of the ACA lie in the unhappy fate of the Clinton plan in 1993–1994. That reform project was an authentic case of governance by strangers: long-term insiders, who argued for a play-or-pay approach, were sidelined by entrepreneurial outsiders infatuated with a comprehensive, systematic overhaul within the framework of managed competition, a supposedly ingenious synthesis of government and market, regulation and competition, left and right. When this approach, having failed to gain traction, was buried in 1994, the entrepreneurial outsiders mostly left government or moved on to other projects. By contrast the spurned insiders (some then still in, some then out of government) regrouped and went back to work along three lines. Structurally they put their heads together in think tanks, universities, and an expanding set of nonprofit centers and institutes, mainly but not only in and around Washington, DC, to dissect the disappointments of 1993–1994 and ponder what to do for an encore. Analytically they identified and evaluated the (myriad) ways in which the Clinton reform had gone off the rails. And prescriptively they began to elaborate ends and means that might work better next time. Their work was "custodial" in character because (as noted above) it drew on the participants' wide policy knowledge, their hard-won understanding of the rules of the political game, their shared vision of a more equitable and efficient system, and their collective determination to avoid the fragmentation among supporters of reform that had doomed so many previous reform efforts.

The "next time" for which they prepared came into view in 2006. In that year the state of Massachusetts enacted a reform package that embodied the major ingredients on which the custodians had converged: an individual mandate, expansion of Medicaid, a health exchange in which a portion of the population could use subsidies to buy private insurance, and the prohibition of preferred risk selection by insurers. Moreover, elections in November 2006 returned control of both houses of Congress to Democratic majorities, whereupon leaders on congressional committees embraced and embroidered on the policy handwork the custodians had been designing for a decade. The custodians themselves were increasingly involved in and central to these policy deliberations in a mix of roles: "institutional migrants" (who serve over time in both the legislative and executive branches), "technocratic translators" (who move in and out of a single branch), and "policy bureaucrats" (experts who enjoy civil-service status within a single branch of government). Genieys carefully traces the scope and the depth of their penetration and influence in and across the House Committee on Ways and Means; the Senate Committees on Finance and Health, Education, Labor, and Pensions; the Congressional Budget Office (CBO); the Office of Management and Budget (OMB); the assistant secretary for planning and evaluation (ASPE); the Health Care Financing Administration (HCFA) and other units of the Department of Health and Human Services (HHS); and the White House staff. There they were, ready to go—expert, politically astute, visionary, and bent on forging consensus.

The fine-grained sociological lens through which Genieys examines the ACA illuminates the politics of policy in several original ways. First, it brings to center stage a set of players whose contributions to the design and advancement of the ACA have been too little acknowledged in previous accounts of the reform. Second, it enfolds the particular players in this cast of characters into a broader and more general category—custodians of state policies—that challenges familiar propositions about governance of and by "strangers" as a normal feature of the weak American state. Third, it invites policy studies to deploy the custodian construct in comparative inquiries across arenas both within and across political systems. Perhaps, for example, the US state is weaker in some policy domains (income redistribution, say) than in others (health policy, defense) and weaker in some facets of health policy (regulation of prices) than in others (promotion of biomedical research). And the intriguing parallels between patterns of custodianship in, say, US and French health care policy suggest that the United States may not be the only political system in which the strengths and weaknesses of state intervention and direction vary by policy arena.

Finally, Genieys's work takes—and invites—a fresh look at the role of elites in American government. Present-day populist polemics bewailing the baleful role of elites serve mainly to raise the heat and pitch of longstanding antagonisms that drive the right to denounce elites as the denizens of a deep bureaucratic state bent on usurping prerogatives of the popular will, while the left condemns them as public agents of the economically powerful. The sociopolitical history of the ACA lends support to neither image. As Genieys shows, in this case an elite, custodial cadre, drawing strength from expertise (both substantive and governmental), commitment to a coherent and carefully crafted vision of reform, and group cohesion around the means to achieve that vision, proved to be indispensable to the success of a huge democratic breakthrough that secured health insurance for more than twenty million (largely lower-income) Americans whom the political system had heretofore failed to protect. In this case the elite insiders who steered the design of the ACA, far from constituting a threat to democracy, were central to correcting what S. H. Beer termed "pluralist stagnation" and to putting state power in the service not of Wall Street or K Street but of the people. In this profound book, William Genieys has thrown fresh light on the largest domestic US policy reform of the last half century and has used this case to refresh and expand deliberations (both academic and popular) on why and how savvy insiders, working in the shadows in the back offices of policy, may make government—and democratic politics—serve the public interest.

LARRY BROWN
Mailman School of Public Health
Columbia University

The thesis put forward in this book has its origins in two research programs that I coordinated which analyzed American government and policy. The first program was "Operationalizing Programmatic Elite Research in America (1988–2010)" (OPERA). The second program was "Programmatic Action in Times of Austerity: Elites' Competition and Health Sector Governance in France, Germany, the UK (England) and the US (2008–2018)" (ProAcTA). These two programs have allowed us to carry out important empirical research into the unelected governmental health coverage policy elites in the United States and were made possible with the involvement of senior researchers from the Université de Montpellier Marc Smyrl and Jean Joana. A special mention also goes to my close friend and collaborator Saïd Darviche, who accompanied me during these long years of research.

A team of academic experts, whom I would like to thank, was set up to monitor the OPERA research program. It was composed of Gary Adams (American University, Washington, DC), Larry Brown (Columbia University, New York), John Higley (University of Texas at Austin), Ezra Suleiman (Princeton University), Joseph White (Case Western Reserve University, Cleveland, Ohio), and André Mach (University of Lausanne, Switzerland). Larry Brown, professor at the Mailman School of Public Health at Columbia University, has become a close friend and collaborator.

This book also owes much to the help of my French colleagues: Pierre Birnbaum, Patrick Hassenteufel, Bruno Palier, Philippe Bezès, Olivier Rozenberg, Jean-Claude Thoenig, and Cyril Benoît. I extend a special mention to the unfailing intellectual support of my friend Patrick Le Galès. Additionally, the final English adaptation and revision of a book originally published in French by the Presses de Sciences Po (*Gouverner à l'abri des regards: La réussite de l'Obamacare*, 2020) owe much to the financial support provided by Florence Haegel, director of the Centre for European Studies and Comparative Politics at the Institut d'études politiques de Paris (Sciences Po) and the translation work of Melanie Mauthner. A big thank-you also goes to Robin Coleman, my editor at Johns Hopkins University Press, who helped me to improve this version of the book.

Last but not least, I would like to thank my friend François Balmelle, who was kind enough to host me at his home in Brooklyn during my research stays in the United States.

2.1. Social background and career paths of "old" SI elites and "new" health coverage policy elites 50

II.1. Typology of long-term insiders' career paths 55

3.1. Population of health coverage policy elites 62

3.2. Gender balance among unelected governmental elites 63

3.3. Highest qualification obtained among health coverage policy elites, 1988–2010 65

3.4. Fields of study among health coverage policy elites 66

3.5. Universities where undergraduate degrees were obtained 67

3.6. Universities where postgraduate degrees were obtained 68

3.7. Universities where JDs, MDs, and PhDs were obtained, 1988–2010 69

3.8. Age when first post was obtained, 1988–2010 70

3.9. Profession held immediately prior to post being studied 73

3.10. Length of time spent in post being studied, 1988–2010 76

3.11. Length of time spent in public sector, 1988–2010 77

3.12. Exits from administration (senior appointees) and Congress (staffers), 1988–2010 78

3.13. Worked in administration (senior appointees) or Congress (staffers), 1988–2010 78

3.14. Principal reform projects initiated by policy entrepreneurs 79

5.1. Comparison of long-term insiders' career-path subtypes 140

8.1. Comparison of Clinton plan veterans' recommendations 201

A.1. Number of positions held for longer than six years: Population of health coverage policy elites, 1988–2010 258

ACRONYMS AND ABBREVIATIONS

ACA   Affordable Care Act (2010)

AEI   American Enterprise Institute

AHA   American Hospital Association

AHCPR   Agency for Health Care Policy and Research (1996–, approximate equivalent previously named AHRQ)

AHRQ   Agency for Healthcare Research and Quality (1989–1996, approximate equivalent subsequently named AHCPR)

AHSR   Association of Health Services Researchers (1981–1998, subsequently named Academy Health)

AMA   American Medical Association

ASPE   assistant secretary for planning and evaluation

BBA   Balanced Budget Act (1997)

BPC   Bipartisan Policy Center

CAP   Center for American Progress

CBO   Congressional Budget Office (Congress)

CBPP   Center on Budget and Policy Priorities

CCIIO   Center for Consumer Information and Insurance Oversight (previously named OCIIO)

CEA   Council of Economic Advisers (White House)

CMS   Centers for Medicare and Medicaid Services (agency within HHS, 2001–, approximate equivalent previously named HCFA)

CWF   Commonwealth Fund

DRG   diagnosis-related group

GAO   General Accountability Office (Congress)

HCFA   Health Care Financing Administration (agency within HHS and HEW, 1977–2001, approximate equivalent subsequently named CMS)

HELP   US Senate Committee on Health, Education, Labor, and Pensions

HEW   Department of Health, Education, and Welfare (1953–1979, approximate equivalent subsequently named HHS)

HHS   Department of Health and Human Services (1979–, approximate equivalent previously named HEW)

HIAA   Health Insurance Association of America

HMO   health maintenance organization

HPA   health policy alternatives

HSA   health system agency

HSR   health services research

KFF   Kaiser Family Foundation

MCCA   Medicare Catastrophic Coverage Act

MedPAC   Medicare Payment Advisory Commission (1997–, approximate equivalents subsequently named PPAC and PPRC)

MMA   Medicare Prescription Drug, Improvement, and Modernization Act, 2003

NCHSR National Center for Health Services Research (1968–1989, approximate equivalent subsequently named AHCPR)

NIH National Institutes of Health

OCIIO Office of Consumer Information and Insurance Oversight (renamed CCIIO in 2011)

OMB Office of Management and Budget (White House)

OTA Office of Technology Assessment (Congress)

PAD program associate director (at OMB)

PPAC Prospective Payment Assessment Commission (1984–1996, approximate equivalent subsequently named MedPAC)

PPBS program planning and budgeting system

PPRC Physician Payment Review Commission (1986–1996, approximate equivalent subsequently named MedPAC)

PPS prospective payment system

PSRO professional standards review organization

RWJF Robert Wood Johnson Foundation

SCHIP State Children's Health Insurance Program

SSA Social Security Administration (1946–, approximate equivalent previously named Social Security Board [1935–1946])

A GOVERNMENT OF INSIDERS

Introduction

T
HIS BOOK considers the people who made the Patient Protection and Affordable Care Act[1] possible, out of sight of the public. It aims to highlight the key role of unelected governmental elites in the failure and ultimate success of the last great health insurance reform projects in the United States. The words of one of the ACA's architects reveal the nature of the intellectual challenge: "Those who are 'real insiders' will never write a book about their experience. One shouldn't write about what goes on in secret, behind closed doors."[2] As disclosed by this habitué of the government's back offices, political decision makers' advisers operate within a shared culture of discretion that makes it difficult to grasp their political role. Compelled not to speak their own minds publicly, these individuals nevertheless contribute to government activities on a daily basis by influencing policy formulation or even drafting bills. In his autobiography, Louis Brownlow, executive adviser to Franklin D. Roosevelt during the New Deal, underlined these professionals' "passion for anonymity" (1958). For these reasons, these insiders remain largely ignored by history, whereas they are often the unelected elites who, out of sight, sway the decision-making process.

Despite some recent efforts both in the United States and in France, the study of the political role played by these unelected governmental elites has barely begun (Vaughn & Villalobos, 2015; Whipple, 2017). American political culture—built around the myth of an antidespotic society (Mann, 1993), where democratic pluralism gradually freed itself from the hold of Washington's elite in the early nineteenth century (Young, 1966) and later from that of an omnipotent "Power Elite" (Mills, 1956)—leaves little space for this type of inquiry (Genieys, 2015). Critical sociology tends to reduce the role of these individuals either to that of the ruling elite's "useful idiot" (Domhoff, 1990, 1996) or to that of the "flex group's" auxiliary who form a "shadow elite" acting on behalf of private interests (Wedel, 2009). These interpretations unexpectedly overlap with the research of Hugh Heclo, whose brilliant interpretation of the formation of "a government of strangers" (1977) implicitly corroborated the argument for the weakness of the US federal government.

Furthermore, Heclo noted that the Washingtonian executive power, despite its dual structure composed, on the one hand, of political appointees with a technocratic profile, and on the other hand, of administrative elites with a bureaucratic profile, resembled European state elites in its modus operandi (1984: 12–13). Robert Putnam (1977) has shown how, at the end of the 1970s, technocratic elites acquired an esprit de corps based on a technical and occupational identity that was capable of modifying their power relations with elected officials and politicians. Subsequent research studies confirmed the way that American administrative elites have increased their hold over policy programs (Aberbach, Putnam & Rockman, 1981; Aberbach & Rockman, 2000; Aberbach, 2003).

Several reasons explain the weakness of this critical gaze cast upon the role of unelected governmental elites in shaping the health insurance system. First, Theda Skocpol and her team's sociohistorical research on the different sector reforms conducted during the New Deal established the link between the creation of "strong state islets" and the action of sector-based elite groups (Skocpol & Finegold, 1982; Skocpol & Ikenberry, 1983; Skocpol & Weir, 1985). Other studies of the Great Society program developed during the 1960s by President Lyndon B. Johnson pointed to the importance of the role played by leaders in the sector-based administrations concerned (Derthick, 1979). In his study of the creation and implementation of health maintenance organizations, Larry Brown establishes a clear link between the change in health policy orientation and the emergence of a policy-entrepreneur profile (1983a,b; 1985). Research on the social background, career path, and role of unelected governmental elites acting at the apex of the American state has remained marginal in studies of American politics.

By privileging the structuring influence of existing policies on political innovation, historical neo-institutionalism strongly curtailed researchers' interest in technocrats' and other elites' role in changing policy (Steinmo, Thelen & Longstreth, 1992). In this way of thinking, it is owing to the weight and complexity of political institutions ("It's the institutions, stupid!") and not that of actors (that of elites) that the establishment of a national health insurance system based on the European model repeatedly failed in the United States (Steinmo & Watts, 1995; Steinmo, 2010). Vague attempts among governmental elites to bring about reforms, insofar as political decision makers' actions and that of policy elites or bureaucrats advising them allow, often tend to be stymied by their path dependencies on institutional procedures (Pierson, 1994, 2001). Jacob Hacker (2002) even goes as far as to suggest that any reform project upsetting the traditional division of social work in health care coverage between the public and the private is doomed from the outset. Other researchers blame the recurring failure of the grand national health insurance system on stakeholders and sector-based interest groups' capacity to always turn the mechanisms of political institutions to their own advantage (Quadagno, 2004, 2005).

In a similar perspective, there is a shared view that the American state develops strong policies without the explicit mediation of its unelected governmental elites (King & Lieberman, 2009). Starting from the idea that the institutions resolve problems of collective action by modifying the context in which individuals devise their strategies, these authors minimize the role of unelected governmental policy elites. In a partial exception to this trend, scholars in the field of American political development have pointed out that eras of strong state interventionism favored the inclusion of more actors in the political process, notably the progressivists' experts and bureaucrats (Orren & Skowroneck, 2004). Throughout the twentieth century, the development of the policy state, from Progressive Era to Great Society, was built in a variety of sectors marked by the creation of new rights and benefits such as the New Deal and the Great Society (Orren & Skowroneck, 2017). These authors point to the role of the "officials in action" but without mobilizing the issue of elites. Health policy experts, however, focus on relevant political variables to explain how the health system has evolved.[3] Centered on the Medicare program, these studies analyze various political arrangements underpinning it and the gradual change in their composition (Marmor, 1970; Oberlander, 2003). Jacob Hacker (1997), examining in minute detail the link between the different reform projects and the groups of individuals involved, finally plumps for the weight of political divides when accounting for the defeat of the Clinton plan. The success of the Affordable Care Act can essentially be explained by Washington politicking (Jacobs & Skocpol, 2010; Starr, 2013). Sociologist Mark Mizruchi (2013) is the only one to link the fracturing of the American corporate elite, the major health sector groups, and its diminishing power during negotiations.

This book will provide a deeper understanding of the interactions between elites and the development of the US policy state in the health sector. For Heinrich Best and John Higley, political elites are "individuals and small, relatively cohesive, and stable groups with disproportionate power to affect national and supranational political outcomes on a continuing basis" (Best & Higley, 2018: 3). We will focus on a subtype of political elites—the nonelected—by studying, beyond the short term of electoral cycles and the renewal of elected officials, the long-term role of unelected governmental elites on the policy-making process (Linz, 2006: 104–109). We qualify these elites as "long-term insiders." Our hope is to establish a link between the making of new unelected governmental elites and the reform process of the ACA. Drawing on their shared experience of the Clinton defeat, these insiders' can be characterized by specific social backgrounds[4] and career paths. These unelected governmental health coverage policy elites are skilled with a specialist knowledge of governmental affairs, which they often put to advantage by moving within the two branches of power. Indeed, they possess a thorough understanding of (1) the particular issues at stake in health policy (policy issues) and (2) the mechanics of the policy-formulation[5] process aimed at facilitating political decision-making (achievement). This elite group is driven by (3) a shared programmatic orientation "to extend health insurance to the greatest number by taking on cost containment and acknowledging the preexisting system." To bring this collective endeavor to fruition, these unelected governmental elites develop (4) the role of custodian of state policies. In exercising this role, they embody a particular vision of the reform project (programmatic orientation). As a result, in the decision-making context, they favor marginalizing potential rivals such as policy entrepreneurs or academic experts whom they consider "strangers" to governing policy.

This argument will begin with a study of the historical and cultural context that favored the making of custodianship of state policies out of sight in the health insurance domain (part I). In order to test empirically the issue of the transformation of the unelected governmental elites' social background and career path, an in-depth sociographic study of the people who took part in the process of health coverage policy formulation during the Clinton and Obama administrations is proposed (part II). This will be followed by the study of changes in elite configurations and programmatic orientations (part III). Taken together, these reflections will enable us to focus on the hidden springs of success of a "far-reaching reform" that became the ACA.[6] Taking this premise in earnest, we shall set out the following counterintuitive argument: the "weakness" of the American policy state promotes the development of custodians' policy role (chapter 1). In the US, this role is endorsed by unelected governmental elites at the apex of executive power (political appointees) and of legislative power (congressional staffers). Following on from Giddens (1972: 366), these elites are able to shape policy formulation (decision-making process), even though they do not wield any actual political authority to decide upon this (decision-taking process).[7] In France, the study of the transformation of the social background and career path of the state elites (i.e., high-level civil servants) in different sectors in the early twenty-first century has enabled researchers to examine the making of the role of custodian of state policies in strategic sectors for the French state, such as defense and health insurance (Genieys, 2010; Genieys & Darviche, 2023). In the United States, government interventionism and the force of policy in these sectors varies according to the party in government: the Republicans tend to privilege the defense sector, whereas the Democrats tend to privilege health (Genieys & Joana, 2017; Jacobs, King & Milkis, 2019).

The sociohistorical exploration of the development of the health care insurance system via the prism of unelected governmental elites' transformation and the development of the role of custodian of state policies will lead us to consider how the American policy state evolved from a different perspective, from the national health insurance project to the Clinton plan (chapter 2). The New Deal prompted a group of progressivist elites from Wisconsin to advocate a new programmatic orientation that would create a universal and egalitarian national public health insurance system inspired by European models. The National Health Insurance (NHI) project set up by the Roosevelt and Truman administrations fostered the emergence of a generation of Social Insurance elites. Despite their successive failures, these elites became more specialized within the Social Security Administration and reassessed their strategy of instituting a universal health insurance system by devising two public coverage programs that initially would target all vulnerable citizens, before being extended thereafter to every single citizen. The Medicare program (for the elderly and the disabled) preceded Medicaid, which was added at the last minute (for marginalized mothers and children from poor families).[8] Launched in 1965 during President Johnson's Great Society initiative, their formulation led to the bureaucratization of the "old" Social Insurance elites who had initiated them. Faced with these programs' rapidly increasing costs and the accompanying rise in power of pressures trying to limit these, the Social Security Administration custodian role was challenged during the 1970s through the 1990s.

The second part of this book offers a close reading of changes that occurred in the social backgrounds and career paths of health coverage policy elites from the Clinton administration through the Obama administration.[9] We will consider the first stage of the programmatic elite framework through the lens of a sociographic study of the unelected governmental elites who held occupational positions of power in the health sector between 1988 and 2010 (chapter 3). Our focus will be on those elites (n=151) who held long-term positions of power (for six years or more) and were able to influence health insurance policy formulation.[10] We mapped the social background of these elites through a statistical analysis of age, gender, type and level of educational qualifications, occupation, career path (appendix 1, Methodology, table A.1). This analysis reveals specific sociological characteristics, such as a large number of women, a high level of educational qualifications, an expertise in health policies, a long-term career path, a mobility in and out of the profit and nonprofit sectors, and a capacity to take advantage of the revolving-door effect. The second step of the programmatic elite framework renders an "in-depth" study of the career paths of these long-term insiders. We will start by studying the Clinton veterans' career paths that began before or during the Clinton plan (chapter 4). Then we will interpret career paths of Republican health insiders during George H. W. Bush's administration and those of the Democratic newcomers who started afterward during the second Clinton term or under the George W. Bush administration and lasting up to the Obama administration, highlighting the formation of unelected governmental health coverage policy elites who shared a particular professional knowledge base and a strong potential to wield the decision-making process (chapter 5).

In the third part of this book, we will study the correlations between the transformation of elite configurations and the change of reformist programmatic orientations. Studying the health coverage policy elites' involvement in the struggles over programmatic orientations during presidential and midterm election campaigns, while the reform project was placed on the decision-making agenda, shows how the insiders' identity was given substance as their role of custodian around a specific programmatic orientation: "play-or-pay" (chapter 6). In September 1994, the withdrawal of the Health Security Act reform bill confirmed the failure of the Clinton administration's health elites. Some of them mobilized the lessons of the failure and formed the Clinton Plan Veterans (chapter 7). During the George W. Bush administration, the Clinton plan veterans along with the Democratic newcomers and some Republican long-term insiders initiated collaborative working practices in the think tanks, foundations, and other Washington nonpartisan and nonprofit organizations (chapter 8). These health coverage policy elites considered that the necessary political consensus for such a reform to be successful was to take into account how attached certain American citizens were to the preexisting health insurance system (health insurance provided by their employer and the Medicare and Medicaid programs) and to take into account the issue of budgetary costs.

Having returned to the back office of power following the Democrats' 2006 victory in both houses of Congress, the health coverage policy elites positioned themselves first and foremost at the head of congressional committees and even at the Congressional Budget Office in order to transpose their new programmatic orientation into a preliminary project for reform (chapter 9). Taking advantage of President Obama's launch of the reform project, these insiders, by colonizing nearly all the strategic posts within the executive (at the White House and the Department of Health and Human Services), formed an unprecedented elite configuration. This strategy of conquest at the apex of government by these elites who had endorsed the custodians of state policies role rendered a government of "strangers" improbable. These people thus paved the way for a far-reaching reform of the health coverage system—the ACA.

PART I

The Custodianship of State Policies

A Government Out of Sight

The first part of this book aims to demonstrate the value of an elite approach to policy change and state reconfiguration (Genieys & Darviche, 2023). In order to attain this objective, one must consider the relevance of the role of unelected governmental elites in the process of the transformation of modes of governing in the United States, where traditionally they work out of sight of public scrutiny (Balogh, 2009; Sheingate, 2009). Accordingly, their capacity for action is barely visible to citizens but also to social science research, and it is accordingly presumed to be weak. The concept of state elites or governmental elites constitutes a relatively polymorphous and little-used category for analyzing political power (Genieys, 2010). For some researchers, state elites are inextricably linked to the development of "despotic power" under absolutist monarchies (Mann, 1984, 1993). Michael Mann underlines how the nineteenth century coincided with despotic state power being transformed into power based on infrastructure and a state's burgeoning capacities to act on civil society and trigger political decisions within its realm (Mann, 1984: 213).

For others such as Hans Daalder, when in nineteenth-century Europe these same elites were faced with uncertainty on the looming democratic horizon, they appropriated the role of "custodian of the State" by allying themselves with the military elites to establish authoritarian regimes, such as occurred in Germany (Daalder, 1995: 125). By contrast, in France, the "hauts fonctionnaires" (high civil servants) gradually established itself as a foundation stone upon which a "strong" state was erected (Birnbaum, 2001). In Europe, two types of political development coexisted for individuals who served the state: an "ethos of service to the state" (authoritarian regime) and an "ethos of service to the public" (democratic regime) (Ertman, 2005: 178–179). Owing to the absence of any legacy of feudalism upon its political development, but also because of a determined political preference, the founding fathers of the United States opposed establishing any form of centralized bureaucratic power (Young, 1966). Taking up Pierre Birnbaum's (2001) distinction between a strong state and a weak state, other researchers have drawn attention to how significant elites remained in decision-making with regard to New Deal policies in the United States (Skocpol & Finegold, 1982). Other Anglo-American researchers dismiss this opposition, however, and remain skeptical of the supposed "weakness" of the American state in enacting strong policies (Lieberman, 2002; King, 2005; King & Lieberman, 2009).

Based on an implicit comparative analysis, the first chapter will lay the theoretical groundwork for revisiting the relationship between elite types and state types by showing why and how it is relevant to analyze the correlation between the transformation of the structure of elites (social background and career path), long term policy change, and state reconfiguration (chapter 1). The policy state would seem to have developed without a hidden role of elites embodying the action of the public authority (Orren & Skowroneck, 2017). To complicate matters, the crisis of the welfare-state model at the end of the 1980s eroded the legitimacy of elites embodying the government's action (Leca, 2012). In the United States, this has led to the development of the policy state being seen as illegitimate by the Republicans, a process set in motion under President Reagan, for whom "government is not the solution to our problem, government is the problem," a statement given credence by Donald Trump's victorious brand of populism.

Yet in order to understand how in the United States, as in most other Western democracies, the capacity for action as well as the structure of unelected governmental elites who actually participate in policy formulation have been subjected to a major restructuring, it is necessary to explore these changes over time. Let us recall that since the end of the 1970s, the Keynesian substratum of policy has been the object of a concerted attack that has gradually spread to the majority of Western democracies (Prasad, 2006; Fourcade, 2009). Thus, the Reagan administration and the Thatcher government in the United Kingdom launched, albeit in different ways, policies to increase public spending in order to dismantle their welfare-state regimes (Pierson, 1994). In a similar move, the Swedish social-democratic model, initially supported by the administrative elites, was reassessed by conservative governments (Blyth, 2001). If, for the vast majority of political scientists and sociologists, this paradigm shift in budgetary spending led to the fading away of Keynesian rhetoric to the benefit of neoliberal discourse, thereby carrying along in its wake the very elites who were its advocates (Blyth, 2013), for a minority of researchers, ourselves included, it prompted certain Keynesian technocrats to rethink the context of their action around policies incorporating the rationalization of budgetary decisions (Genieys & Smyrl, 2008b; Genieys & Joana, 2017; Brookes, 2021). It is this second path that we hope to investigate.

From this perspective, we will conduct a sociohistorical detour to first highlight the making of unelected governmental elites at the time of the Progressive Era in the health sector and in social welfare, including those individuals who developed a long-term commitment to promoting the project of setting up a national health insurance system (i.e., Social Insurance elites, as we discuss in chapter 2). Reassured over the long term in their role of custodian of state policies, these SI elites after the Truman administration's failure opted for welfare programs targeting certain demographic groups. At the end of the 1990s, the Social Security Administration's bureaucratic elites witnessed their own decline, despite inheriting the legacy of the national health insurance project and being the guarantor of the well-managed Medicare and Medicaid programs. Their demise, which benefited a new type of unelected governmental elites in the health policy domain who were trained to manage financial constraints, constitutes the most tangible proof of this. The policy of rationalizing budgetary choices (Planning, Programming, and Budgeting System [PPBS] in the United States), which came into being more than twenty years later (Enthoven & Smith, 1971), fostered the rise of these new elites at the apex of government in the Clinton administration.

CHAPTER 1

A Government of Insiders

Unelected Governmental Elites Acting as Custodians of State Policies

UNLIKE IN European countries, the development of centralized power in the United States during the twentieth century often failed, even during the 1930s, when the New Deal introduced Keynesian policies (Skocpol & Finegold, 1982). Yet the debate provoked by the historical institutionalism concerning the relationship between the "weak" state and "strong" policies (Lieberman, 2002; King & Lieberman, 2009) constitutes an invitation to seriously consider those who design such policies. To deepen our knowledge of this issue, we will focus on the analysis of the role of unelected governmental elites in the political work of government. Indeed, can one imagine the development of strong policies in certain domains of state activities without questioning the unelected governmental elites who support them? Can one really consider how the "policy state" (Orren & Skowronek, 2017) arose without realizing that it would foster the making of elite groups that promote or defend policies?

In order to address these issues, we need to dispel a certain number of assumptions that are specific to research on unelected governmental elites in the United States (Genieys, 2015). While most research studies on the executive branch or Congress acknowledge the making of a new type of policy elites (Heclo, 1978, 1984), few among these draw any general conclusions about the ongoing restructuring at the apex of power. In the case of France and other European countries, however, the making of "long-term" elites that are strongly anchored in certain sectors of government activity reflects these ongoing changes (Genieys, 2010; Hassenteufel et al., 2010).

What about the situation in the United States? A "government of strangers," characteristic of the transitional administration of President Jimmy Carter, constitutes the general rule when it comes to governmental elites' weak structural power (Heclo, 1977). Other scholars interpreting the profound transformation of Washington's expertise in the health sector since the 1970s have advanced the idea of the formation of a veritable in-house proto-administration in the US capital (Lepont, 2014). How could these transformations have avoided affecting, more or less comprehensively, the way in which policies are formulated? Does the institutionalization, since the 1980s, at the heart of the decision-making process by newly qualified professionals equipped with skills and knowledge—the so-called policy wonks or policy czars—not reveal how profoundly the unelected governmental elites have been restructured? What reasons might explain why these elites' actions have remained ignored by political scientists?

Policy Wonks, Policy Czars, Policy Advisers: Early Signs of Change?

It is worth recalling that, as Putnam (1977) and Heclo (1978) noted, a considerable number of terms such as "issue experts," "technical officials," "policy technicians," "policy specialists," and "policy activists," among others, confirm the existence of these new types of unelected governmental elites that constitute a kind of proto-administration that would bring a new impetus to the process of policy formulation during the 1980s. For Heclo, these new "policy specialists" would gradually form a senior informal bureaucracy whose members over time moved from post to post within the back offices of power as well as in the many non-governmental organizations inside the Beltway. Their increasing power gave rise to a critique of Washington's increasingly technocratic government as cut off from American political reality. This tendency to castigate the establishment's influence remains a political argument often wielded by the Republicans ever since Ronald Reagan's presidency, and it reached a new level of intensity during Donald Trump's 2015–2016 presidential campaign.

Nevertheless, if we limit ourselves to existing research studies on the transformation of the health insurance policy-making system, it would seem that the historical weight of the administrations has greatly diminished, namely, that of the Democrats' "reformers" who proposed and led the Great Society's health insurance initiative (Medicare and Medicaid), paving the way for a new kind of unelected governmental elites, that of the political appointees with their far less bureaucratic sociological features (Brown, 1983b, 1985). Equipped with their professional expertise regarding sector-strong policies and their temporary status, these elites gradually took over the back offices of both the executive and the legislative branches of power (Heclo, 1984, 1987; Aberbach, 2003). Empirical research on the soaring number of political appointees shows that since the end of the 1980s, both their Washington-based education profile and the time they spent in Washington research institutions such as universities and think tanks constitute key indicators of this change (Fisher, 1987: 28–29; Pfiffner, 1987). Other scholars have observed how the total number of employees in both branches of power more than doubled from the end of the 1970s (Mackenzie).

Moreover, studies on the changes that affected the bureaucratic structure of the executive branch and Congress during the 1970s and 1980s show how bringing political appointees and congressional staffers into teams would transform the sociological features of American unelected governmental elites: here were individuals with professional policy savoir faire acquired through specialized university courses and training in the newly formed schools of public policy (Wildavsky, [1979] 2001; Allison, 2006). When schools of public policy were set up at eight universities in September 1975, this was at the Ford Foundation's instigation to launch a new training program: its aim was to modernize the training of unelected governmental elites by broadening their horizons with new knowledge based on policy analysis. The training's practical and theoretical content focused on a "cost/effectiveness" approach to policy as well as on quality-of-life and social-justice issues. These universities' unofficial motto was "to dream up ways to make the world a better place."[1] The schools of public policy, which today include more than forty institutions, have underpinned the growth of the new unelected governmental elites whose professional legitimacy stems from their policy knowledge.

In fact, some political scientists contend that if "new policies create new politics," this is because new "policy specialists"—that is, elites with sociological characteristics similar to those of issue experts—have gradually made their presence felt in Washington's decision-making power structure (Brown, 1983a,b; Heclo, 1984, 1987). Heclo also notes that this gradual transformation of unelected governmental elites corresponds to how "the growing ranks of graduate programs in public policy and management of think tanks and Washington-headquartered interest groups and law firms are providing a constituency and source of supply for this regime of political technocrats" (1987: 215). It would seem that we are witnessing the ascent of a new generation of unelected governmental elites at the apex of American state, elites who have been trained in the Washington, DC, area's universities to assess and evaluate policies (Genieys, Darviche & Epperson, 2022).

Drawing on their solid social background, these new unelected governmental elites would, within certain sectors, gradually form public policy networks where people possessing the same professional know-how, language, and grammar found it easier to create a shared policy vision in a particular domain of state activities (Medvetz, 2012: 40). This competence-based knowledge has fostered the rise of new policy figures in Washington—whom the political media refer to as "policy wonks"[2] or sometimes as "policy czars,"[3] alluding to their considerable influence within the Executive Office of the President (EOP). Often considered as a media invention, the term "czar" has recently been the object of attempts by the political scientists Vaughn and Villalobos (2015) to define it. Starting from the principle that this term aims to refer to an empirical reality, these scholars stress that in most instances, it refers to individuals responsible for coordinating government action between an administrative sector and Congress for a particular policy area and policy problem (11–12). From the perspective of decision-making regarding policies specific to the American system, one can well imagine that the czars' actions can lead to either a government of strangers or an insider government. Yet some public administration experts, observing the phenomenon during President Obama's administration, noted when a domestic policy consultant was being hired, there "were more czars than under the Romanovs" (Saiger, 2011). On the other hand, James Pfiffner noticed how President Obama wished to surround himself with "many White House 'czars' who were supposed to 'coordinate' administration policy. His designation of these 'czars' signaled that he would continue the trend of centralizing policy making" (2011: 76). More recently still, Chris Whipple has shown how successive presidential chiefs of staff gradually asserted themselves as the "gatekeepers" of most policies by actively participating in defining the presidential style of government (2017). On the other hand, these studies tend to privilege the action and role of a single person, whereas, as we will show further on, these individuals belong to a group of unelected elites whose members are interchangeable and are well connected to one other. This allows them to succeed each other and to hold positions of responsibility in both branches of power.

To hypothesize that unelected governmental elites—understood as those groups of technocrats who, in the back offices of government, act as policy-formulation professionals—actually exist compels us to simultaneously consider those individuals who are appointed to the head of the executive branch of power as well as to congressional committee staffers' posts. It is vital to investigate their career paths beyond the academic distinction separating presidential and executive studies from legislative studies. Regarding executive power, the historian Arthur Schlesinger Jr. has shown how the growing number in and role of the president's cabinet (the EOP) constitutes one aspect of an incontestable "imperial presidency" (1973). Pfiffner has drawn attention to the crucial role of those White House political advisers who at the end of the 1980s were tasked with launching policy change in the relevant departments and agencies (1987).

The success of these presidential advisers depended on two conditions: first, the speed with which the new programmatic orientation was initiated during the transition between two presidential administrations; and second, that these unelected governmental elites needed some practical policy experience to ensure a certain continuity, thereby avoiding the sense of a "government of strangers" (Pfiffner, 1987: 151–152). The failure of President Clinton's health reform project can partly be explained by strong divisions among various clans of policy experts (Hacker, 1997) but also by the Clinton administration's new health elites, the sector agencies, and the administration of the Department of Health and Human Services (HHS)[4] that had been "republicanized" since Reagan (Michaels, 1997: 284). On the other hand, the alignment of political advisers' views with executive-branch and congressional policies during President Obama's time in office, which facilitated the success of health insurance reform, can perhaps be explained by the arrival in political control of a homogeneous group of unelected governmental elites.

Since the 1970s professional staffers in Congress have asserted themselves as true policy advisers insofar as they have been able to direct the elected incumbent toward rational choices in terms of policy (Price, 1971, 1978). Their expert knowledge in a realm of public action had a crucial influence on decision-making within congressional committees (Kingdon, 1981). Research on how the congressional committees operate illuminates the way in which staffers play a central role in formulating and gathering information, as well as discussing and assessing it (Whiteman, 1995: 294). In his careful study of the congressional health committee staffers' skills, David Whiteman points out that these key players have extensive training and sectoral expertise that leads them to form strong friendship ties and promote a "community of health people" (1987). Well connected and informed about health issues, members of these committees are seen as health policy professionals in the eyes of those for whom this field remains distant.

Generally, these new policy advisers, who are working in the realm of public policy for the president or as a staffer for a representative or senator, monopolize key positions in the back offices of government and have unique professional skills. Acting in the heart of the executive and legislative branches of power and moving sometimes for professional reasons between both of these, they develop, as we shall illustrate in the case of health coverage policy, long career paths inside the Beltway, despite to-ing and fro-ing between the public and private spheres.

For these reasons, they are far beyond the remodeled technocratic profile cautiously evoked by some American researchers and are closer to that of the French elites acting out of sight as custodians of state policies (Genieys, 2010; Genieys & Darviche, 2023).

Why Are Some Unelected Governmental Elites Out of Sight?

Ever since Mills via Adams, research on power in Washington, DC, has emphasized both the continuity of an "iron triangle" existing between interest groups, the administration, and Congress in the defense policy sector (1982) and the revolving-door effects on the formation of a "shadow government of individuals available for political appointments" tightly linked to the world of business, law, and think tanks (Fischer, 1987: 29). With the "weak" state perspective, the very idea of the existence of unelected governmental elites with a capacity to act autonomously seems inconceivable (Domhoff, 1990, 1996). Janine R. Wedel's study on the role of the "shadow elite" within George W. Bush's administration confirms the pervasiveness of this argument (2009). She shows how we are witnessing increasing prioritization of government work owing to the private elite coteries' consolidating power and reach, such as that formed by the neoconservatives (Paul Wolfowitz, Richard Perle, Douglas Feith, etc.) whose friendship ties and habit of working together would have enabled them to devise a shared alternative project for defense and foreign policy (2009). The argument for privatizing the action of the US government is founded on the fact that two-thirds of these unelected governmental elites are not senior career bureaucrats but political appointees, and that by moving between the public and private realms (lobbies, think tanks, and the media), they could insist on programmatic orientations that would benefit private interests. Located within an anthropological framework, Wedel's argument leans toward the Domhoff perspective in which a ruling elite hovering on the margins of the government seizes the moment when certain favorable political conditions arise—such as the advent of a Republican administration—in order to push through its own interests. On the other hand, Hacker and Pierson in their "winner-take-all politics" argument consider the power of the "powerful" who are capable of influencing the "cost-price" of policy programs from outside the government (2010). In sum, despite their various intellectual approaches, these scholars reject the very idea of governmental elite groups acting autonomously in the policy-formulation sphere.

Yet since the failure of the Carter administration's "policy planning groups," which fell into the *Government of Strangers* trap (Heclo, 1977), most empirical studies on the summits of the executive power reveal that attachment to public policy is a common characteristic among Washington's unelected governmental elites, which manifests itself empirically by the growth of long-term career paths built upon policy issues. Judith Michaels asserts that "the shadow government model involves what Heclo terms 'political careerist,' who may be a congressional staff member, academic, career civil servant, or employed in think tanks or consulting firms who is tapped for temporary government service (model only dominant at the Department of Defense). They are people who build their careers around problems of public policy" (1997: 105). Some studies underline the fierce attachment seen among these new elites who frequently move between the public and private domains, formulating and implementing those policy programs that they prize. Michaels reminds us that 80% of presidential appointees confirm having a professional preference for devising new policies to solve public social problems (277). Indeed if "too many recruits arrive from the private sector who are totally unfamiliar with their work as political executives," it is these very same elites who "finally . . . must immerse themselves in the substance of the programs over which they have jurisdiction" (Pfiffner, 1987: 143–44).

Similarly, Heclo recalls that the weak competence of the political appointees who move between the public and private sectors is largely compensated for by their training and their career path which reflects their thorough understanding of policy issues (1987). James Pfiffner reveals how the policy advisers of the Executive Office of the President, moving within academic institutions (such as the National Academy of Public Administration) or certain think tanks (such as the American Enterprise Institute [AEI], the Brookings Institution, and the Heritage Foundation), rally around policy teams built ad hoc to drive through reform projects during presidential campaigns and then develop them further in the advent of an electoral victory (1987). Moreover, despite the high mobility between positions inside the government and moves into the private sector, Pfiffner could observe how meetings were organized and negotiations carried out between the president's advisers, the political appointees in the department and the congressional staffers on programs and reforms. Pfiffner also notes that these elites generally are familiar with the unofficial rules regulating the "smooth" functioning of the policy decision-making process.

Other researchers have emphasized that career longevity within both branches of power, just as much as mobility between the executive and legislative branches, during a transition administration between two presidents allows a relationship of trust to be established, which is necessary for a new presidential administration formulating a reform program. The experience gained over long careers may have a greater influence in the policy domain, where technical know-how is more complex. During the Reagan administration, the professor of medicine Robert J. Rubin, who became assistant secretary for planning and evaluation (hereafter ASPE) at the Department of Health and Human Services, explained that this highly technical and financial sector, with its need to formulate programs over a three-year cycle, justified recruiting experienced political appointees (Light, 1987: 160). Moreover, the latter, having enjoyed long careers in Washington including spells in the private sector, enjoy a greater ability to influence the content of the favored policies than the sector-based bureaucratic elites. This observation leads us to relativize the weak ability of political appointees to formulate policy because, all too often, they are considered to be neophytes arriving directly from civil society who plan their careers by equalizing time spent in the private and public sectors (chapter 3). Despite the revolving-door system, establishing long-term career paths in those policy domains at the summit of power remains an underestimated phenomenon that can prevent directing our attention to the governmental work of these insiders.

The development of professional long-term specialist careers in a policy domain remains stronger still in Congress. Indeed, career staffers who are attached to prestigious congressional committees and who are generally fairly senior, display their professional knowledge during hearings as well as their shared vision of future policies (Price, 1978). This shared policy orientation is sustained by strong long-term friendship ties. Quite paradoxically, when David Whiteman questioned the health committee staffers about their own perceptions of their professional world, they declared not having the impression of belonging to a "health community" (Whiteman, 1987, 1995). The reason for this gap between an externally observable empirical reality by the sociologist and the key players' own experiences can certainly be explained by the common perception in the US of the government's "janus-faced" dimension (Sheingate, 2009). Indeed, the presumed weakness of the state might impede not only citizens from measuring the pertinence of its capacity to act (Steinmo & Watts, 1995; Steinmo, 2010) but equally those key players from perceiving themselves as elites.

Therefore, we will observe what happens in the shadow of elected officials and take another look at the actions of those unelected governmental elites who, because of the acquisition over time of a deep knowledge of policy and the functioning of federal government, are tremendously influential on policy formulation. Furthermore, this analysis will show that the ideal type of unelected governmental elite is not limited to those senior career bureaucrats and their techno-bureaucratic ethos. We intend to demonstrate empirically that this ideal type can encompass other elites fostering the role of the custodian of state policies.

Revisiting Selznick's "Custodian of Policy": Acting as Custodians of State Policies

Whatever one's preferred picture, unelected governmental elites are not mere "ingredients" in the making of policy, the presence, absence, or involvement of which may be adjusted in the manner of seasoning in a recipe; rather they are intrinsic to and inseparable from policymaking processes. In Western nations, the twentieth century saw (and the twenty-first century continues to see) a steady growth in statutory and regulative interventions of government in the economy and society. Those interventions have called attention to a special and, as it were, specially concentrated type of elites, which the sociologist of organizations Philip Selznick called "custodians of policy," whose shared values, elaborated by means of policy, assure the institutional integrity of organizations, both public and private (1957). Custodians of policy, then, are elites, both inside and outside government, who combine political and substantive expertise in service of a commitment to preserve, protect, perpetuate, and promulgate "their" programs. This type of unelected governmental elites differs from "experts," "entrepreneurs," "advocates," and other promoters of policy, who come and go with bright ideas. Their distinctive feature is persistence and longevity in policy roles that may find them in or out of government but recurrently involved in shaping policies in their chosen arenas.

We have analyzed the unelected governmental elites who developed the role of "custodian of state policies" in defense and social-insurance domains and have examined their characteristics and behavior in France (Genieys, 2010; Genieys & Darviche, 2023). At this point, we should recall that we consider the development of the role of custodian of state policies as a means to restore the action of governmental elites when they are in the situation to sustainably influence the decision-making process (Genieys, 2010: 9–10). Exploring this role enables us to ascertain the correlation between the development of long sector-based career paths inside the back offices of government where policies are shaped and the advocacy of programmatic orientations in policies that aim to strengthen public authority. In the United States, because of the weakness of the policy state and an "out of sight" government practice, the interpretation of their activity remains invisible. By focusing on the unelected governmental elites who are part of the appointees' and staff members' entourages and who, by virtue of their positions and unique professional knowledge gained in office, are potentially capable of formulating or defending a policy agenda, we will shed light on this neglected aspect of the research on state reconfiguration (King & Lieberman, 2009; King & Le Galès, 2017).

Applied to the case of the US policy state, our elite approach is based on the programmatic elite framework (PEF), which weaves an in-depth sociographical analysis of the elites that govern health coverage policies with a study of changes in the programmatic orientations (see appendix 1, Methodology). The PEF avoids restricting the scope of study to merely what the potential unelected governmental elites "are" insofar as it also touches upon what they "do" when they contribute to the process of policy-making and decision-making (promoting or upholding a public action program). Our sociographic study of American unelected governmental elites during a given period (1988–2010), as we shall see further on (chapters 3, 4, and 5), will allow us to assess their social backgrounds and career paths. As we examine the competing programs during the grand health coverage reform projects, the Clinton plan (1993–1994) and the Affordable Care Act (2008–2010), we will interpret the transformation of the role of custodian of state policies.

Furthermore, unelected governmental elites as custodianship should be understood as the reverse image of a "government of strangers" in the Carter administration, as described by Heclo (1977). For this reason, this elite configuration corresponds solely to those individuals whose long-term career paths unfold in the back offices of government in a policy domain despite the political effects of "the in-and-outers" system (Mackenzie, 1987). Despite being obliged to move into the private sector during the transition between two political administrations as occurs with most unelected governmental elites in the United States, these individuals considered as potential insiders tend on the whole to return to decision policy-making. Their capacity to leave and return to policy work over the long term illustrates how these insiders act (Genieys, Darviche & Epperson, 2022). As mentioned above, their career paths differ from that of the vast majority of political appointees who generally spend a short spell in their posts and are known as "short-timers" (Heclo, 1987). Meanwhile, these long-term insiders benefit from this mobility by spending temporary stints within the numerous nongovernmental organizations in Washington when they are working far from the core of power. Moreover, it is important to see from a new perspective the professional sector-based paths of these elites as shaped by a system of political appointments (i.e., the in-and-outer system) that generates high mobility between the public and private sectors linked to short-term contracts, and which often require mastering a considerable set of skills and knowledge about policies, as well as the art of governing.

On the basis of these initial considerations, it is possible to imagine inductively how, as in the French context where this elites group benefits from the status of high-level civil servants (Genieys, 2010), these elites can form stronger attachments to upholding the government than those who remain in office for only a short time. Our diachronic study of the Obama and Clinton reforms explored further on will allow us to ascertain how the health coverage policy elites—the long-term insiders (part II)—have a propensity to organize themselves collectively during the decision-making process and resist attempts by external "policy entrepreneurs" or interest groups. The interpretation of the decision-making process through the balance of power between insiders and strangers—making a fleeting passage through the upper echelons of power—allows us to understand the failure of the Clinton plan as well as the success of Affordable Care Act (part III). Owing to the lack of any unelected governmental elites whose status would "naturally" let them endorse the role of custodian of state policies as in the French case (Genieys, 2010), it is mainly political appointees and members of the congressional committees hired under private legal contracts (which can therefore be terminated at short notice) who are likely to play this role. For Heclo, this is one reason why in the United States, these individuals form an informal governmental elite, since their career path is not based on the European high-level civil servant but rather on a series of private-sector contracts in government and nongovernmental organizations in Washington. In this particular context where contract-breaking is the norm, it is important to identify in which kind of private organizations they will work once they leave the sphere of political power (both the executive and Congress). On this point, the critical sociology of elites tends to consider work for a private body as "private sector mobility" while showing no interest in the company's social mission.

For this reason, it is necessary to distinguish clearly between those unelected governmental health coverage policy elites who decide to make a professional change from government affairs to for-profit lobbying and law firms, and those who opt for a career in nonprofit organizations. This distinction is fundamental to understanding why several Democratic health coverage policy elites justify taking on a job in the nonprofit private sector once they cease working for the federal government. The plethora of foundations, think tanks, and schools of public policy or health policy in the Washington, DC, area means that they can feasibly move inside the Beltway without working for a business firm. In addition to their transitory professional role, especially during transitions from one administration to another, these institutions play a "proto-administration" role where the new programmatic formulations are discussed and amended (Lepont, 2014). Benefiting subsequently from the change in political majority in the presidency or Congress, these elites who are likely to be making health policy and have deepened their knowledge and widened their networks during the time spent in these para-state institutions soon find themselves in extremely advantageous positions for rejoining one of the two branches of federal government.

Finally, as we imagine the role of custodian of policies, if we pursue Philip Selznick's line of argument (1957), this also compels us to take into account the shared ideas and values promoted in the institutions where these unelected governmental elites work. In certain Western democracies, studying the growth of this role among this type of elite has led to ties being forged to promote programmatic orientations that reinforce the state's capacity in a given sector (Genieys & Smyrl, 2008b). This decision sets our research apart from those arguments that consider the withdrawal from the state's sphere of intervention as a "victory" on the part of neoliberal policies over the many different types of Keynesian states (Blyth, 2013; Brookes, 2021). The growth of the role of custodian of state policies is seen as a response to the way in which the Keynesian technocrats' mode of action has been challenged by the conservative or neoliberal revolutions. In fact, the general consensus seems to be that the constraints that policy programs have been subjected to since the successive establishment of retrenchment policies, in terms of public spending and policies inspired by the new public management, have led to a long-term weakening of the power of unelected governmental elites (Pierson, 1994; Suleiman, 2003). While some scholars have demonstrated that these elites have abandoned the Keynesian approach as a hegemonic discourse, others have suggested that the elites have benefited from these in order to better circumscribe the state's sphere of influence (Prasad, 2006; King & Le Galès, 2017).

In the case of France, this phenomenon has led sector-based elites in some strategic areas of government action such as national defense or health care insurance to reinvent their discourse on cost-containment policies (Genieys & Joana, 2017). In the health care insurance sector, it was the elites in the Directorate of Social Security, a central administrative unit, who lay claim to the role of custodian of state policies by creating their own vision of cost containment in health policy, thus freeing themselves from the minister of finance's political grip (Genieys & Hassenteufel, 2015; Genieys & Darviche, 2023). In France, it is a group of high-level civil servants working in health policy, pursuing long careers at the top of the executive branch and ensuring that the issue of cost containment became their cause, who have developed the role of custodian. By collectively contesting the dismantling of the state's authority, and fiercely identifying with the state's long-term ability to regulate spending, they enacted reforms that met their own objectives. Therefore, it seems certain that the health care insurance sector, whose cost for the public purse in the United States as much as in France has not ceased to increase since the 1980s, will allow us to examine how the new health coverage policy–endorsed custodianship, which over two decades steered reform projects under the Clinton and Obama administrations, has reclaimed the debate around financial pressures.

This is the reason, for the purpose of thinking through the transformation of the unelected governmental health coverage policy elites' structure and reframing the custodian role, we will need to thoroughly consider the cost-containment issue surrounding the competing programmatic orientations' content for reforming the health care insurance system. It is well known that the 1990s were a decade when public-spending budgets experienced considerable pressure. In fact, the prospective assessments conducted by the Congressional Budget Office (CBO) on the financial sustainability of competing reform projects during the Clinton and Obama administrations played a crucial role in the former's failure and the latter's success (Hacker, 1997; Joyce, 2011). On this basis, we can presume that the budgetary issue, which in health policy translates as a cost-containment issue, probably affected the formulation of programmatic orientations to reform the health system, and equally transformed the sociological characteristics of health coverage policy elites who aspired to shape and formulate policy. From this perspective, as we study those career paths, we will attend in particular to individuals who were sent as political appointees to organizations involved in controlling the costs of policies, such as the Office of Management and Budget (OMB), the Health Care Financing Administration (once the HCFA, it is now the Centers for Medicare and Medicaid Services [CMS]), the Congressional Budget Office (CBO), the Office of the Chief Actuaries, and even the financial and budgetary committees in Congress. Ascertaining someone's professional knowledge of budgetary challenges and their grasp of the cost-containment argument will be treated as a criterion to help us distinguish among professionals who, for example, have been affected by rivalry among the unelected elites inside the government competing with one another to devise health policies. At this point, we should mention that the budgetary cost-containment argument lay at the heart of struggles among groups of elites when health reform was discussed during both the Clinton and Obama eras.

By adopting the same counterfactual reasoning we applied to the French case, we will endeavor to test the hypothesis according to which the cost-containment issue and the quest for a political arrangement, often presented as an insurmountable obstacle to the progressive comprehensive reform of health care insurance sought by the Clinton administration, would be transformed by the action of new health coverage policy elites in terms of resources, so that the far-reaching reform of the Affordable Care Act could be adopted by Congress. More generally, taking seriously the role of unelected governmental elites in health system reforms allows us to interpret the reconfiguration of the US policy state in a new light.

CHAPTER 2

Variations in the Custodian Role

From the NHI Project to the Clinton Plan

I N THIS chapter, we will apply our elite approach to the social insurance domain—from the National Health Insurance Project to the Clinton plan.[1] The historical perspective of the development of the US policy state allows us to observe the variations in the custodian's role between an older and a newer generation of governmental elites. The first generation was the one that carried the national health insurance project during the Progressive Era. The second emerged when the Clinton administration launched its health reform project, the so-called Clinton plan. The nature of the US political system and of the policies it produces—comparatively small and few public programs of social protection; a heavy reliance on means-tested programs run by the fifty states; limited trust in the good intentions and competence of government, including its experts; aggressive penetration of political appointees into public bureaucracies; a revolving door conveying public officials in and out of a government of "strangers"—might suggest a system that precludes or forestalls by definition the types of custodianship found in other Western nations (Heclo, 1977). Yet in the OPERA research program, we have identified a sizable corps of US health coverage policy elites who have endorsed the custodian role toward state policies. They combined, over the course of often lengthy career paths, political and substantive expertise, in a reasonably cohesive and concerted fashion, to protect and advance specific policy programs in the defense and health care sectors, thus displaying patterns with some substantial resemblance to those seen in Europe (Genieys, 2010; Genieys & Joana, 2017; Genieys & Darviche, 2023).

A question arises at the outset; namely, what *is* the health care policy over which custodianship might be asserted? After all, no major health care policies emerged from the US federal government until after the end of World War II, and while other nations were building and implementing systems of national health insurance (NHI) that remain the centerpieces of their health care systems, the United States, deadlocked on this front, set about developing the supply side, not the demand side, of its system by means of the National Institutes of Health (which promoted biomedical research) and the Hill-Burton Act (which authorized federal grants to the states for the planning and construction of new hospitals). Unable to make NHI a pillar of the limited programs of social protection it adopted, and thrown into disarray by the fragmentation that besets both its public and private health care systems, the US policy state would seem to offer inhospitable terrain for elites playing the custodian of state policies role.

The sociohistorical perspective on the evolution of the social insurance system points to the notion that elites and their custodianship played a key role in the development of the US health care system during the twentieth century. As well, our inquiry throws light on the dynamics—sometimes competitive, sometimes cooperative, sometimes accommodative—that have shaped custodianship over time. Depending on the era, however, we will distinguish between the "old" and "new" generations of elites with variations in their custodianship. The old generation of social insurance (SI) elites was committed to the creation of a national health insurance system to supplement social security under the F. D. Roosevelt administration. These SI elites increasingly gave way to the new generation of health coverage policy elites, who shared with their forebears a firm commitment to universal health insurance but who were obliged by political circumstances from the 1990s to draw on their command of health coverage policy issues in order to craft eclectic strategic tools that not only protected social insurance but also resorted to means-testing to expand coverage, to seek to contain health care costs, and to indulge proponents of market forces.

Progressive Era: The Rise of Social Insurance Elites

Social insurance (the financing of benefits with sums accrued in public trust funds from contributions by workers and their employers at specific rates over the course of a worker's employment) has been a prominent force in US health care politics since the early 1900s. In particular, the state of Wisconsin and the University of Wisconsin at Madison cultivated both the progressivism of Robert La Follette and the "Wisconsin idea," which extolled public service and the duty of universities to lend expertise to the work of government. Scholars, especially John R. Commons and Richard Ely, who fused historical research with institutional and labor economics at the university in Madison, shaped a common training and career path for a generation of SI elites.

Edwin Witte, for example, earned a PhD in economics under Commons in 1927. Wilbur Cohen got his bachelor's degree in Madison in 1934 with Commons, Ely, and Witte, for whom he then became a research assistant when Witte was named director of President F. D. Roosevelt's Committee on Economic Security later that year (Berkowitz, 1995). Arthur J. Altmeyer, a specialist in labor policy (workers' compensation and unemployment insurance) earned a PhD in economics at Wisconsin in 1931. In 1933 Altmeyer went to work in Washington for Roosevelt's secretary of labor, Frances Perkins, and would author FDR's message on economic security, which heralded what became the Social Security Act. Aspiring reformers in the Progressive Era scrutinized innovations in Europe that extended social protections—notably pensions and health care coverage—to all or part of the citizenry by means of social insurance programs, and sketched how the United States might follow suit (Rodgers, 1998). This movement's momentum was dissipated by World War I (which put the United States into conflict with Germany, the pioneer of social insurance in Europe) and by the Russian Revolution of 1917 (which threw suspicion on anything vaguely socialist). On the eve of Roosevelt's election in 1932, the strategy of contributory social insurance had made little headway. Several states had enacted pensions for the needy elderly, but these were tax funded and means tested. Health reform agendas, state and national, featured a miscellany of proposals—building more hospitals, pushing for prepaid group practice, and expanding the roles of the Public Health Service, for instance—among which the funding of health coverage by social insurance was by no means the most notable.

The Great Depression of 1929 and the election of Roosevelt to the presidency in 1932 brought social insurance to the forefront of policy once again. As governor of New York, Roosevelt had helped to make that state "the cockpit" of battles over social insurance in the United States (Rodgers, 1998: 438). Now, at the national level, amid what Rodgers calls "the intellectual economy of catastrophe," a "quiet, structural, behind-the scenes institutionalization of European-acquired social insurance knowledge in the key university economics departments and policy centers" supplied the expertise policy-makers demanded (Rodgers, 1998: 438). This first generation of SI elites is characterized by a common training and career path.

The New Deal and the Emergence of the Custodian Role

The New Deal triggered a convergence between the rise of a new governmental social insurance elite in DC and the emergence of the custodian's role. The promotion of the social security program, including the project of founding a national health insurance, was the ground on which this role was built. The year 1934 found the above-mentioned core of SI elites hard at work in Washington, as evidenced by the study of their career paths. While Altmeyer collaborated with Frances Perkins to design what would become Social Security, Witte directed the President's Committee on Social Security, with the assistance not only of Wilbur Cohen but also of Edgar Sydenstricker, who had earned a PhD in economics at the University of Chicago and had become a leader of statistical surveys at the Public Health Service, and I. S. Falk (who had earned a PhD in public health at Yale in 1923). Falk worked as an associate director of the Committee on the Costs of Medical Care (1927–1932) before joining Sydenstricker at the Milbank Memorial Fund, which then lent both men to the federal government. Their common objective, aptly summarized by Altmeyer in 1943, was a "unified comprehensive system of contributory social insurance" that would "cover all major economic hazards" to which workers are subjected.[2] The Social Security program, which used contributory mechanisms to fund pensions for most Americans over age sixty-five, was enacted in 1935, and that legislative success spurred proponents of social insurance, who were numerous and articulate within the councils of the New Deal, to urge a similar approach to national health insurance, which they viewed as the most important missing pillar in the New Deal's portfolio of social protections (Social Security, Unemployment Compensation, and Aid to Dependent Children) that the administration and its Democratic majorities in the Congress had seen through to enactment. Roosevelt, uncertain how much political capital would be required to defeat the opposition of the American Medical Association (AMA), demurred and consigned SI to be studied—and then studied again—by a series of commissions and task forces (Starr, 1982; Blumenthal & Morone, 2009).

Roosevelt's death in 1945 left the social insurance program in limbo, but this first generation kept in mind its reform project. Although Witte returned to the University of Wisconsin as chair of its economics department in 1936, he remained active as an adviser to social insurance proponents in Washington (and in Wisconsin) for two decades thereafter. Altmeyer served either as chair of the three-member Social Security Board or commissioner of the Social Security Administration (SSA) from 1937 to 1953. Cohen deployed his vast substantive expertise and legislative skill as Altmeyer's assistant until 1953 and then headed the SSA's research branch until 1956 (Berkowitz, 1995). Falk directed the Division of Research and Statistics at the Social Security Board (from 1940 to 1946) and at the SSA (from 1946 to 1954). Oscar Ewing, a lawyer and luminary in national Democratic politics, helped to design Harry Truman's Fair Deal and then headed the Federal Security Agency in 1947. Robert Ball, a New Jersey native who joined a field office of the new SSA in 1939, rose rapidly within that federal agency (Berkowitz, 2005). These elites then acted as custodians of their principal progeny, Social Security, and awaited a political opening that would permit them to extend that approach to health coverage (Rodgers, 1998: 442–443).

The accession to the presidency by Harry Truman, an unapologetic proponent of SI, seemed to offer that opening. Truman's efforts to move the measure through Congress (where social insurance was embodied by the Wagner-Murray-Dingell Bill, a proposal that enjoyed substantial but far from majoritarian support) made little headway against the concerted opposing forces of organized medicine, big business, and the lobby of insurance entities (both non- and for-profit) that had filled the vacuum left by federal inaction on health coverage in the 1930s. When Dwight Eisenhower, a moderate Republican with little taste for bigger government, won the presidency in 1952, SI elites looked dead, at least for the next four, and perhaps for the next eight, years.

From Social Insurance Failure to Medicare: A Programmatic Adaptation

Republican control of the White House for the first time in twenty years saw the immediate departure from the federal government of some SI elites—Oscar Ewing returned to the private practice of law in 1952, for example—and the eventual exit of others. Altmeyer left government in 1953; Falk exited in 1954; and in 1956 Cohen decamped to academia, returning to federal service as assistant secretary of health, education, and welfare in 1961 under John F. Kennedy. One prominent retention was Robert Ball, who had held various positions in the SSA since 1939, then left in 1945, but returned in 1949 and served as commissioner of that agency from 1962 to 1973. Whether in or out, however, this generation of elites retained both their commitment to a social insurance–based version of NHI and to finding a political path by which it might be realized. That path, they concluded, needed to be incremental—instead of continuing the quest for a universal program created in one fell swoop, they would enact a program for a subgroup of the population, show that this approach worked, and then push to extend it to other subgroups (Marmor, 1970; Orberlander, 2003). The group with which to start, they concurred, was the aged, who had left the workforce (hence could seldom be covered by private employer-based insurance), faced higher than average health care needs and costs, and were already familiar with and grateful for the benefits of Social Security, which constituted a real-world model for how the new health coverage would be funded. Indeed, the outlines of such an approach had been unveiled in the last days of the Truman administration by Ewing, head of the Federal Security Administration, whose plan, crafted by Cohen and Falk, proposed federal hospital insurance for beneficiaries of Social Security (Orberlander, 2003: 23).

Throughout the 1950s, the SI elites—most notably Ball in the SSA and Cohen, then in academia—allied with outside supporters, such as Nelson Cruikshank, director of the Department of Social Security of the American Federation of Labor and Congress of Industrial Organizations (AFL-CIO), and union leader Walter Reuther of the United Auto Workers, to build support for what came to be called Medicare, a program funded by social insurance contributions to cover the hospital expenses of Americans aged sixty-five and over. This proposal, like its more comprehensive forebear of the Roosevelt-Truman years, inflamed opposition by the AMA and other conservative interests—opposition that liberal Democrat John F. Kennedy, elected president in 1960, and his legislative allies were unable to surmount. Then events external to health policy per se—namely, the assassination of Kennedy in 1963 and the nomination of archconservative Senator Barry Goldwater as the Republican opponent to President Lyndon B. Johnson in the presidential election campaign of 1964—triggered an electoral landslide that returned Johnson, an ardent supporter of Medicare, to office and brought a surge of new liberal Democrats into the House and Senate. In 1965, Medicare became law.

With this great reform, the SI elites gradually adapted their custodian's role to these new programmatic orientations. Medicare covered solely the aged; its Part A (hospital insurance) was funded by social insurance, but Part B (for physician services) drew instead on the premiums of beneficiaries and the general revenues of the federal government.

Moreover, Medicare came accompanied by a sister program, Medicaid, for some of the poor—a means-tested, state-run program funded by state and federal general revenues that encapsulated precisely the features of a "poor people's program" that the SI elites anathematized. They, however, looked on the bright side: after decades of deadlock, the forces supporting SI and Medicare had defeated the AMA and were now well positioned to move along the incrementalist continuum to Medicare for more—and in due course, for all.

The Fall of "Old" SI Elites

The SI elites' optimism was soon dashed. Even as events in 1963–1964 had created the political conditions in which Medicare became law, so too did domestic turmoil over issues having little to do with health policy—notably, the war in Vietnam and the domestic War on Poverty— derail the plans of Johnson's Great Society and then usher Republican Richard Nixon into the White House in the 1968 election. To the new administration, Medicare was one of many products of Johnson's relentless overpromising and excessive centralization, and a particularly worrisome one at that because the financial costs of the program were growing all too clear. For the first time, the federal budget was responsible for a sizable share of the nation's health care bill, which was rising much faster—an average of 40.2% in 1968 and 1969—than its sponsors had predicted (Oberlander, 2003: 47).

Semantic innovations told the tale: the term "uncontrollable spending" (on programs that could not be trimmed by the annual appropriations process) grew prominent in Washington's budgetary lexicon, and the word "entitlement," lately used admiringly to denote programs that "belonged" to beneficiaries by virtue of the social contract embodied in the contributory principle of social insurance and therefore could never rightfully be "taken away" by government, quickly came to connote "runaway" spending on government "giveaways" to grasping beneficiaries of questionable need and desert (Oberlander, 2003: 7). These critiques soon found welcoming homes in proliferating right-wing think tanks—for example, the Heritage Foundation (created in 1973), the Cato

Institute (launched in 1974 as the Charles Koch Foundation and renamed in 1976), and the American Enterprise Institute (an organization that dates from 1938 and unveiled its Center for Health Policy Research in 1974). In the short interval between 1965–1966 and 1969–1970 the old SI elites had been forced to abandon the imminent promise of incremental expansion for defensive maneuvers in a new and disquieting ideological era.

Arthur Hess, who in 1965 became Medicare's first "head" as director of the Bureau of Health Insurance in the Department of Health, Education, and Welfare (HEW) and was later a founding member of the National Academy of Social Insurance, recalled in 1996 how in the Social Security program, Wilbur Cohen's "baloney slicer" kept working: "Everything they took on got bigger and bigger" (Berkowitz, 1996). Assuming that Medicare could likewise be "the first step," however, misread a situation that "had changed completely" because "private insurance had expanded so much," a trend that shaped "the political implications of the objections to the government moving in and taking over a field that had been carved out of private insurance, and that is people were working for whom premiums could be paid." Perhaps first among other important sources of ambivalence or opposition was organized labor, some of the constituent unions of which "had better health contracts and tax implications for the individuals than you could have gotten out of a tight Medicare program" (Berkowitz, 1996).

The Nixon team had no illusions about the political fallout certain to accompany any effort to take away Medicare's new coverage, but it was both compelled by fiscal angst not merely to sit there but rather to do something and at a loss to know what to do. Retrenchment on Medicare invited political retribution; combining tough systemic cost controls with some version of SI risked handing to the Democratic Congress (and especially to Senator Edward M. Kennedy of Massachusetts, a leading proponent of SI who was expected to challenge Nixon in the 1972 presidential election) an opportunity to take control of legislative action. Slapping regulatory controls on Medicare's prices risked antagonizing medical providers and conservative purists who detested heavy-handed public regulation. The costly Medicare program had to be fixed, but how to do it by means that were both substantively plausible and politically acceptable?

The Making of Policy Entrepreneurs

The figure of policy entrepreneur (Kingdon, 1984; Mintrom, 2019) emerged, on the Washington field of health governmental affairs, at the beginning of 1970 through the years of the Clinton plan. Paul Ellwood, a physician and policy expert, chanced to meet with a special assistant to the undersecretary of HEW, and the two brainstormed about the health policy conundrums with which the administration struggled. (This account of health maintenance organizations follows Brown, 1983a.) Ellwood offered his diagnosis: health care costs in Medicare, as in the system as a whole, ran too high because the system foolishly conjoined fee-for-service delivery of care with third-party payment for it, thus ensuring the predominance of faulty, incorrect incentives: the more providers did, the more they got paid, while both consumers and providers blithely passed along the costs to others. Ellwood then followed this diagnosis with a prescription: prepaid group practices (PGPs), exemplified by the Kaiser Permanente plans familiar to numerous Californians during the Nixon administration, embodied correct incentives by combining in one integrated organizational structure both financing and provision of care (doing away with third-party payment) and delivering care solely by salaried physicians who worked full-time for the plan (thus averting fee for service). This strategy enabled Kaiser and other PGPs to provide reasonable access to good quality care at costs below those of the traditional sector.

To be sure, the Kaiser plans in California were large million-member entities that could hardly be replicated to scale across the United States. But ingenious policy-makers could adopt, as it were, the organizational and financial skeleton of a PGP and give the new streamlined creations an appealing name: health maintenance organizations (HMOs). The strategy could be (and soon was) introduced throughout the health care system at large; but the place to start was Medicare, and the first step would be to create within it a new Part C that allowed beneficiaries to enroll in HMOs for their coverage. In short, market forces—competition among plans and providers to win beneficiaries, now blessed with new choices—would save Medicare from the illogical and perverse incentives its benighted creators had built into it. This proposal, which launched in 1970 the managed care strategy that has, for better or worse, heavily shaped US health care policy to the present day, appealed strongly to the Nixonites. It reduced no benefits, entailed no expensive SI gambits, and relied very little on new regulations. Quite the contrary: it worked by means of enlightened incentives (consumers would access all their care within an "integrated" plan); gave consumers choices among such plans and between them and their costlier traditional counterparts such as Blue Cross; and trusted that competition between the older and newer forms of coverage would drive costs down. The HMO proposal, in short, inaugurated the fascination of US policy-makers, as well as a generation of policy entrepreneurs, with market forces as a means of repairing the faults in the system.

Resolved to move ahead with a legislative initiative for HMOs, the administration dutifully circulated its plans to HEW for comment, and reviewers registered various objections. The SI elites, Arthur Hess, at the time deputy commissioner of the SSA, noted, for example, that the plan gave no sense of "how to get from here to there in any reasonable period of time" (Feder, 1977: 130–133; Brown, 1983a: 209). The Nixon team discounted these comments as the parochial grousing of bureaucratic holdovers from previous Democratic regimes, who were wedded to the programmatic arrangements they had forged and who therefore reflexively resisted innovation. Authorization for federal support to create HMOs made its way slowly through Congress, which finally assented in December 1973. Medicare enrolment in Part C, the guiding notion that put the show on the road, ironically made little headway because congressional critics pressed the above-mentioned arguments that the approach was not consistent with the Medicare statute. Nixon officials had long since concluded, however, that HMO-building should advance on a scale far beyond Medicare itself.

Managed care and market forces complicated the calculations of SI elites, whose ranks were steadily shrinking within the executive branch but who continued to await opportunities to resume their push for national health insurance. The market innovations also underscored and accentuated the health care exceptionalism of the United States with respect to both policy and process. The peculiarity of the policy—the faith the US policy-makers put in competition, choice, and the rest of the marketist package as a strategy for health care reform, which had then no counterpart among the nation's Western peers—can be attributed largely to the comparative eccentricity of the process. The managed care initiative was concocted by interplay between policy entrepreneurs outside government and policy generalists within it, with little contribution by program specialists, including of course the old SI elites who had shaped US health care policy in the Roosevelt, Truman, Kennedy, and Johnson administrations.

Policy Entrepreneurs and Health Economics Advisers

By the mid-1970s the declining fortunes of a social insurance–based model of reform and the ascendance of market forces applied in and beyond Medicare might seem to suggest that the policy entrepreneurs promoting market forces were on track to emulate, indeed to supplant, the custodianship of SI elites behind the creation of Medicare. Market forces, after all, drew plausibility and legitimacy from succinct staples of economic theory (incentives, choice, competition) and were, as the adoption of HMOs demonstrated, "culturally conceivable" as well (Dobbin, 1994: 228). The basic challenge was how to embody the diffuse enthusiasm for market forces programmatically. In other words, having passed legislation promoting HMOs, what might marketists do for an encore? Even in the United States, enamored culturally (if not practically) with laissez-faire economics, free markets, and individual entrepreneurship, there was no evident formula for making health care markets behave as "normal" markets do.

Although the presence and voice of economists had grown steadily during and after the New Deal and the war (a Council of Economic Advisers was installed in the Executive Office of the President in 1946, for example), health as a distinct policy field generated little interest within that intellectual tribe. Indeed in 1963 Kenneth Arrow published in the *American Economic Review* his seminal article explaining how the welfare economics of medical care departed widely from the features of "classic" markets (Arrow, 1963). By the time Medicare was enacted, however, the development of "health economics" was on the rise. Eli Ginzberg's studies of "conservation of human resources" increasingly included health care concerns. In 1963 economist Seymour Harris published *The Economics of American Medicine*, and in 1965 Herbert Klarman's *The Economics of Health* appeared. Rashi Fein, who had served on the staff of Truman's Committee on the Health Needs of the Nation in 1952, and later worked on Medicare on the senior staff of Kennedy's Council of Economic Advisers and then as an adviser to Lyndon Johnson, published his study of the nation's alleged doctor shortage in 1967 and in 1968 joined the Harvard Medical School as a professor of the economics of medicine.

On the whole, however, the economics discipline remained ill-suited to steer health policy reforms. Many academic economists disapproved on principle of extensive government "interference" in private sector pursuits such as medicine. Economic advisers inside government tended to greet proposed expansion of public coverage with alarm over costs so much so that Blumenthal and Morone elevated the shutting-up of economics as one of a handful of crucial preconditions to presidential leadership in health policy (2009: 413–415). The preferred tool of economists outside government was more "skin in the game"—greater cost consciousness among consumers, a strategy that of course lacked appeal to political leaders under pressure to ease the burden of health care costs on the voting public. And anyway, as Arrow had adroitly demonstrated, the fundamentals of the health care system, including but not limited to widespread third-party payment, branded that market as more or less intrinsically abnormal. On the eve of Medicare, in short, market forces looked as much like problems as solutions.

The creation of Medicare and Medicaid soon set these issues in a fresh context. Rising health care costs were not only a collective problem for society but also a threat concentrated on and within the budgets of the federal and state governments. Policy-makers demanded advice on how to contain these costs, and their demands triggered a growing supply of attention from economists and from market-minded enthusiasts outside that profession to the theoretical and practical challenges posed by the health care sector. To be sure, the highly advertised HMO development strategy, initiated five years and authorized eight years after Medicare passed, owed its political appeal, at least in Washington, to its promotion of market forces—incentives, choice, and competition. But this unapologetic endorsement of market reforms carried an element of paradox: among the leading policy entrepreneurs who promoted HMOs in the 1970s, only one—Alain Enthoven, who held a PhD in economics from MIT—was an economist. Ellwood, as noted above, was a physician, Clark Havighurst a professor of law, and Walter McClure a physicist, then working with Ellwood at InterStudy.

To be sure, HMO development put market forces squarely on multiple private and public agendas—including that of Medicare managers in the Bureau of Health Insurance (BHI) and its successor in 1977, the Health Care Financing Administration (HCFA). Robert Derzon and Leonard Schaeffer, heads of BHI and HCFA under Jimmy Carter, dutifully touted HMOs, as did Carolyn Davis and William Roper, their counterparts under Ronald Reagan. For all four of these officials, however, economics was, as it were, a second language; Derzon and Schaeffer were seasoned health care managers, Davis a professor of nursing, Roper a physician, and neither the Carter nor the Reagan administration made managed care and competition a major, much less predominant, programmatic focus of their health care initiatives. Indeed both regimes pushed ambitious regulatory reforms: Carter proposed a national cost cap on hospital prices (crafted by two highly regarded economists, Henry Aaron and Karen Davis), which failed in Congress. Reagan successfully sought to move Medicare from retrospective payment of actual costs to hospitals to a new prospective payment system based on diagnosis-related groups, a reform overseen by another health economist, Stuart Altman, who had worked on issues of coverage and costs as assistant secretary for planning and evaluation at HEW under Nixon and Ford—and then under Reagan and Clinton, he chaired the federal Prospective Payment Assessment Commission from 1984 to 1996 (Altman & Shactman, 2011).

These economist luminaries-in-government were, on the whole, mainly of the traditional, pragmatic "markets are good for some things, not so much for others" persuasion and therefore were not inclined to use their public-sector savvy and status to promote transformative visions and build networks in support of market-based health care reforms (Pierson, 1994). Given the limits of the professional economists' numbers and influence, the advancement of market forces in the Carter, Reagan, and Bush Sr. years came mainly from three sources: policy managers (in HCFA and elsewhere in government) parroting the rhetoric of political leaders; business leaders and consultants seeking to make money by getting in on the ground floor of a future managed care "revolution;" and some academic economists who believed as a matter of theoretical conviction that increased competition in virtually any market could not fail to be a good thing. In short, support for broad-ranging market-based reform of health policy was too diffuse to generate the cohesive custodial elites that nurtured social insurance and refined it into Medicare. Support was not entirely diffuse, however. Commissioned by Carter to devise a cost-effective approach to universal coverage, Alain Enthoven, a strong advocate of HMOs as noted earlier, presented in 1978 and 1979 a "consumer choice health plan," later called "managed competition," that envisioned not the piecemeal infusion of more market dynamics into local communities but rather a national reform that would forge the fractured pieces of US health care and health care policy into a genuine "system" in which each part bore a rational relation to the others (Enthoven, 1980). Enthoven's career path is that of policy entrepreneur. It is built around regular interventions to advise the presidential administration in the formulation of policies. He is also characterized as a distinguished economist, former occupant of an important federal position, bearer of a bold and detailed vision of a better health care system, and center of a network of like-minded actors in and out of government. But as we will see in a following chapter, the experience of the Clinton plan will make Enthoven fall definitively on the side of the policy entrepreneurs embodying the government of strangers (see chapter 6).

Through the 1980s, however, Enthoven's vision made little headway. One problem was that Reagan et al. were attracted to the competition

Enthoven's plan honored but repelled by the "managed" part—the framework of government rules without which, Enthoven insisted, markets could not be relied on to work well. Second, the plan, which expected competition to squeeze wasted dollars from the bloated US system, complicated the pecuniary aspirations not only of providers and insurers but also of managed care entrepreneurs, who sought market opportunity not public discipline. And third, the premise of the plan—that competition per se was only half the story of market reform, that unregulated competition among managed care (and other) plans could yield market failure—did not sit well with health economists who were congenitally leery of regulation by big government. At the end of the 1980s support for managed competition, a policy that promised to overcome the dysfunctional diffusion of competitive forces, was itself succumbing to diffusion.

Elites and Custodianship Revisited: The Medicaid Program

To borrow Weber's famous terms, the allegiance of old SI elites and the adaptation of the custodianship to the "ethic of conviction" seemed to cede the "ethic of responsibility" to another vehicle of coverage—namely, Medicaid. As early as 1994, when prospects for the Clinton plan looked increasingly dim, staff in the White House, HSS, OMB, and Senate began planning for expanded coverage for children, among other incremental reforms (Sardell, 2014: 75). And in 1997, seeking to salvage something from the ashes of the failed plan, reformers crafted the State Children's Health Insurance Program (SCHIP), a Medicaid look-alike which (like its model) made federal matching funds available to states offering new coverage to children in families that lacked private health insurance but were not poor enough to qualify for Medicaid. In doing so, policy-makers not only built on successes already registered by that program but also laid the foundations for expansions of coverage to come in 2009–2010.

When eleventh-hour deliberations in Congress brought forth Medicaid alongside Medicare in 1965, the old SI elites were ambivalent. On the one (principled) hand, Medicaid incorporated all the elements of a "poor people's program" they most despised. It was means-tested, linked to eligibility for public assistance ("welfare"), funded by general revenues (a "handout" from "the taxpayer" instead of an earned benefit), and subject to extensive discretion by the fifty states. On the other (pragmatic) hand, it was a way to get coverage to populations that neither Medicare nor any other program then on the books or contemplated would reach, and it might (as Wilbur Mills had hoped) secure Medicare and its social insurance base by mitigating pressures to expand that program to populations beyond the aged. Moreover, supporters of universal coverage could not help but find it unsettling that Medicare, unquestioned social triumph though it was, tilted the nation's public health coverage markedly in favor of the elderly, while doing little for children and the non-aged poor.

By the time Reagan entered the White House, it had become clear that this species of "welfare medicine in America" had burst its bounds as a program for low-income mothers and children on public assistance (Stevens & Stevens, 1974). Some states availed themselves of federal matching funds (which ran between 50% for the richest states to 76% for the poorest) to extend coverage to "optional" groups and services. And Medicaid had become the prime source of coverage for a range of disadvantaged groups—the disabled, the mentally ill, people with AIDS, low-income seniors (who were also eligible for Medicare), and not least important, formerly middle-class Americans who had "spent down" their assets on long-term care in order to meet the requirements for Medicaid benefits—thereby amassing formidable support among constituencies of beneficiaries and providers of care (Brown & Sparer, 2003). When, in the Reagan–Bush Sr. years, the prospect of extending Medicare to new groups was remote at best, some within the camp of new health policy elites began looking to Medicaid as the next best obtainable thing.

Whereas Medicare's elites emerged from powerful currents in social insurance, organized labor, and public health, those promoting Medicaid were heavily represented by advocates for the needs of children and by anti-poverty attorneys, a nascent specialty within the US legal profession. Prominent among them were Marian Wright Edelman, who founded the Children's Defense Fund (CDF) in 1973; Sara Rosenbaum and Kay Johnson (who worked at the CDF on health policy issues and forged extensive connections with Congress and advocacy groups); and staff at the National Governors' Association, among other sources of influence (Sardell, 2014: 26–30). Rosenbaum and Andy Schneider had law degrees. And another notable Medicaid elite, Diane Rowland, earned a doctoral degree in public health at Johns Hopkins University (see chapter 4 for the analysis of their career paths).

Beginning in the mid-1980s these stalwarts seized each chance to expand coverage by the incrementalist strategy that Medicaid (unlike Medicare) invited—namely, raising the thresholds of eligibility among income groups, clinical conditions, and other "categories" (Smith & Moore, 2008). In the Reagan–Bush Sr. years, Rosenbaum, Johnson, and their allies worked with staff such as Rowland and Schneider on committees headed by supportive congressmen (most notably Henry Waxman—dubbed Mr. Medicaid—plus George Miller in the House and Lloyd Bentsen in the Senate) who had perfected techniques for including in omnibus reconciliation budget bills mandates and options that markedly increased the program's enrolment (Sardell, 2014: 32). As will be discussed below, however, these new Medicaid elites, unlike the old SI elites, will become part of the new generation of unelected governmental health coverage policy elites at the turn of the 1990s. Less attached to the implementation and defense of "their" program and converted to the virtue of policy analysis, this new generation promoted a different approach to the reform of the US health care system.

Elites and Custodianship: A First Historical Assessment

Social insurance–based health coverage was proposed but deferred, leaving coverage for most of the population in the hands of health insurance plans (some for-profit, some nonprofit) in the private sector. Checkmated at the midpoint of the twentieth century, SI elites downsized their designs into Medicare, celebrated its enactment in

1965, envisioned incremental expansion toward universal coverage, and then, disappointed in this expectation, settled into defensive maneuvers to protect Medicare from a growing corps of critics who relentlessly derided the alleged vices of this "government monopoly" (and of course its proposed extension into a universal single-payer program). This shift from an expansionist to a defensive agenda by the SI elites left the policy terrain open to alternative programmatic orientations, two of which—expansion of Medicaid and reorganization of the system by means of market forces—came to the fore. As these policy blueprints gained ground, the SI elites adapted their custodian role by pragmatically accepting accommodations that were in many ways antithetical to their social philosophy—embracing, for example, the non-universal, means-tested, state-run Medicaid program and the insertion of mini versions of managed competition within Medicare.

Our elite approach to policy and state reconfiguration applied to the historical development of the social insurance system reveals some evidence. The unelected governmental elites, SI elites (1932 to 1980), and the health coverage policy elites (1980 to 2010) examined here combine subject-matter expertise, political seasoning and savvy, a programmatic agenda that convincingly relates means to ends, and the taste and capacity for a cohesive pursuit of that agenda (see table 2.1).

First, the governmental elites studied here display very high levels of subject-matter expertise. Training at the graduate schools of prestigious private universities, Ivy League or otherwise (old SI elites), is declining in favor of schools in the Washington area (new health coverage policy elites; see part II). Similarly, degrees in social economics from schools of administration where government and administrative sciences were taught are giving way to degrees from schools of public policy and public health. But that expertise is not entirely academic. Its application to policy requires a sophisticated comprehension of laws and rules, of settled understandings, of accommodations within the federal system, of budgetary terms and processes, of implementation conundrums, and of ripple effects that changes in one program may cause in others. That this comprehension constitutes practical knowledge should by no means obscure its arcane, indeed sometimes Talmudic, character.

Second, their savoir faire demands much more than simple policy skill, as in the case of policy entrepreneurs. As the vignettes above show, custodianship is a social as well as intellectual calling, involving the ability to work cooperatively laterally and hierarchically, to persuade and negotiate with stakeholders and with Congress, and often to explain and defend proposals and policies to constituents, the media, and the public at large. If the old SI elites favored careers within the executive branch of power (the Committee on Economic Security at the White House and the SSA), the new ones will organize themselves within the HCFA and on the congressional committees (such as Finance, and Ways and Means). In addition, the new elites are able to move professionally between the two branches of government as insiders.

Third, these insiders constitute a kind of purposive community whose members share a broad policy mission and a more or less coherent vision relating means to ends. In the United States, the most prominent mission and vision combinations are universal health care coverage by means of social insurance; expanded health coverage for lower-income groups by means of categorical, means-tested federal-state programs; and a more efficient and cost-effective system achieved by the installation of market forces. Though seldom given their due in lists of preconditions for the success of policy initiatives, community and cohesion were essential to the creation of Medicare, Medicaid, and the ACA (see part III)—even as the failure to attain them amid protracted squabbling by proponents of market forces is fundamental to explaining the collapse of the Clinton plan and the failure of the marketists to extend their visions beyond programmatic orientations and pieces of public policies (see table 2.1).

Small government notwithstanding, the story of US health care policy since World War II prominently features steady (and correlative) institutional as well as intellectual growth of government—more programs, more agencies, more units within those agencies, more national commissions and advisory boards, more staff, more public resources, and more constituencies of beneficiaries and stakeholders. Present-day incubators of new health coverage policy elites' commitment include foundations of diverse pedigree (the Robert Wood Johnson Foundation,

TABLE 2.1. Social backgrounds and career paths of "old" SI elites and "new" health coverage policy elites

Social background	Social insurance elites (1970 to 1990)	Long-term insiders as health coverage policy elites (1990 to 2010)
Educational institution (graduate diploma)	Ivy League (Yale, Harvard, Columbia) and University of Wisconsin	Washington, DC, area universities and state universities (public)
Field of study	Economics or law, PhD	School of public policy, MPP, MPA, MP health, PhD, JD
Type of education	Political economics and comparative social law	Policy analysis and health policy
Career path types and length of appointment	Long sectoral career, duration: between 6 years and 20 years	Long-term insiders, duration: between 6 years and 20 years
Revolving-door effect on career paths	Weak effect of back-and-forth system; specialization in governmental agencies	Weak effect of back-and-forth system with weak mobility to private sector (NPOs, think tanks, foundations)
Career path inside branches of power	Low circulation between the two branches of power Remain on Committee on Economic Security and within the Social Security Administration	Strong circulation between government and Congress; passage in institutions with financial control (OMB, HCFA [CMS], CBO, and Finance, Budget, and Ways and Means Committees)
Dominant professional skill	Technocratic and bureaucratic	Specialized in policy issues and cost-containment strategies
Values and goals	Defense of ethics of ultimate ends	Promotion of ethics of responsibility
Policy style	Interventionist and bureaucratic	Market regulation and policy accommodation
Social policy learning	Medicare program development	Health Care Security Act failure (Clinton plan)
Approach to programmatic change	From SI to Medicare and Medicaid programs	From Massachusetts plan to Affordable Care Act

SOURCE: OPERA Research Program

the Commonwealth Fund, the Heritage Foundation, and the Kaiser Family Foundation, among others); think tanks (the Brookings Institution, the Cato Institute, the American Enterprise Institute, the Center for American Progress); programs and centers within universities, some in or near Washington, DC (Johns Hopkins, Georgetown, George Washington, American), others within easy reach of the capital by plane or train; institutions such as Academy Health, which mobilize the recipients of federal money for health services research to demand more of it; and the flourishing law and lobbying firms on and around K Street, increasingly populous now that erstwhile government insiders are said to be more loath to leave Washington and go back to what used to be home (see part II). "Almost no one leaves here [Washington] anymore," remarks Leibovich (2014: 44).

The new health coverage policy elites were obliged to revisit both ends (universal coverage versus coverage for more of the disadvantaged) and means (Medicare for all versus Medicaid for more). The Clinton plan is a privileged moment to understand how the role of custodians of state policies will be recomposed by the health coverage policy elites (see part II). Indeed, as we will see below, the internal confrontations within the Democratic administration between the pro-market forces and the heirs of the SI elites turned into a major political fiasco (see part III). After the 1980s, the unelected governmental health elites were then deeply divided, not only on the policy formulation process but also between "insiders" (Washingtonians) and "strangers" (policy entrepreneurs). It is around this double cleavage line that the role of the new custodians will progressively be redefined. At the same time, our elite approach to the transformation of the health care system sheds new light on the development of the US policy state.

The Making of Long-Term Health Insiders

The second part of this book aims to map Washington's unelected governmental elites in charge of health coverage policy from the administration of George H. W. Bush (1988) to that of Barack Obama (2010). An in-depth sociographic analysis—the first strand of the programmatic elite framework (appendix 1, Methodology)—unveils the elites' structural transformation. Because of the balance of powers particular to American democracy, the positions of power that we concentrate on have been selected from the back offices of government (Congress and the executive branch). We holistically investigate salient elements of continuity and discontinuity in social background and career path of the elites since the late 1980s. The results will confirm or challenge our hypothesis about the formation of a government of insiders in the health coverage policy domain. For this purpose, we will compare the health coverage policy elites' sociological characteristics with those of the bureaucratic elites of the Social Security Administration, the "old" SI custodians.

Chapter 3 proposes a mapping of health coverage policy elites in Washington, DC, from 1988 to 2010. It proposes a study of these unelected governmental elites. They have been selected because of their long careers (six years or more) in positions of government where health care coverage policy was formulated at the heart of the executive branch (the White House and the Department of Health and Human Services) and in Congress (the House of Representatives and the Senate [n=151]).[1] The mapping will allow us to assess their university background and type of degree, their mobility to and from the private and public sectors, and their capacity to take advantage of the revolving-door system by returning more than once to government back offices. Looking at this group as a whole will also illustrate a clear trend toward the greater presence of women in charge. Comparing these results with those obtained in other studies of unelected elites in the executive branch and staffers in Congress will enable us to show that the long-term insiders, because of their career longevity, have a unique professional savoir faire in policy decision-making (Fischer, 1987; Mackenzie, 1987; Aberbach & Rockman, 2000).

Some scholars might identify a certain incongruity insofar as, in the United States, rules concerning professional careers of congressional staffers and political appointees are somewhat different from French senior civil servants (chapter 1). From the inductive perspective adopted here, our goal is to ascertain the making or not of an elite group that organizes itself within the process of policy formulation in both branches of the federal government. Our elite approach focuses on the correlation between social-background and career-path transformation of these unelected governmental insiders and changes in health coverage policy programmatic orientations. Mapping the circulation of these long-term insiders reveals that a significant number of them shape their career paths by moving from the executive to the legislative branch or vice versa, and we refer to them further on as "institutional migrants" (table II.1). This factor has a particularly heuristic dimension insofar as it allows for a different perception of the revolving-door effect (MacKenzie, 1987). As we shall see for the health sector, far from being a constraint, this movement between both branches of power became a political resource for a minority of individuals who remained for a very long time in charge. Indeed, this is one of the reasons why, in some cases, the long-term insiders possess the professional resources needed to monopolize key positions in health governmental affairs.

TABLE II.1. Typology of long-term insiders' career paths

Institutional migrant	Technocratic translator	Policy bureaucrat
Horizontal circulation between the two branches (administration and Congress)	Absence of horizontal circulation: career anchored in only one of the two branches	Absence of horizontal circulation: career anchored in only one of the two branches
Vertical circulation and occupation of strategic decision-making positions	Vertical circulation and occupation of strategic decision-making positions, always in the same branch of government	Vertical circulation and occupation of strategic decision-making positions, always in the same branch of government
Career in executive agencies or congressional committees focused on financial oversight of policies	Career in executive agencies or congressional committees focused on financial oversight of policies	Career in executive agencies or congressional committees focused on actuarial or fiscal issues and advantages of a civil service career
Time spent working for the inside-the-Beltway private sector: interest groups (Rep.) or nonprofits (Dem.)	Time spent working for the inside-the-Beltway private sector: interest groups (Rep.) or nonprofits (Dem.)	Employment in inside-the-Beltway interest groups but only after the end of a long public-sector career
Strong interpersonal network at the heart of legislative and executive centers of power	Strong interpersonal network, and strong expertise and direct role in transforming the programmatic orientations of legislation	Strong technical knowledge of policy (statistical, accounting, legal)

SOURCE: OPERA Research Program

Our in-depth sociographic study of long-term insiders' career paths will consist of sketching about fifty sociological portraits[2] of elites to point out the making of health coverage policy elites (chapter 4 and chapter 5). This study of career paths encompasses (1) the length of their career paths in policy formulation; (2) the process of acquiring health coverage policy skills thanks to involvement in reform forums (think tanks, foundations, and academic departments)—and for the Democrats, a temporary appointment to a school of public health; (3) the time spent in a public budget-control agency (the Health Care

Financing Administration and the Congressional Budget Office) or on House committees focused on issues of cost-containment; (4) putting the revolving-door effect into the private sector to strategic use or ensuring that a spell there was correlated to health policy issues; and (5) their shared experience in decision-making struggles. Drawing on the intersections between issues of circulation and acquiring skills regarding policy formulation processes, we shall examine the distinctiveness of the long-term insiders' professional mobility according to three career-path subtypes: institutional migrants, technocratic translators, and policy bureaucrats (table II.1).

The institutional migrant subtype corresponds to a career path marked by circulating between a position in the executive branch and one in Congress (or vice versa). This type of occupational mobility occurs when one successively holds key positions in institutions where health policy is shaped in both branches of government (e.g., at the CBO, OMB, HCFA [CMS], GAO, or on specialized House committees). The institutional migrants possess an extensive knowledge of the issues, a high level of expertise (especially regarding financial matters), and a powerful partisan political network. The circulation of institutional migrants when the process of decision-making begins, as much as the positions of power they are committed to, often leads to those interest groups opposed to the reform being neutralized or to political negotiations between the White House, Congress, and HHS being favored.

The technocratic translator subtype describes those insiders whose long careers unfold within one of the branches of power as they hold successive posts as top policy advisers. This type of career path is often built upon a specialist university health or law degree.[3] Equipped with a "special technical subject matter expertise," these individuals directly participate in formulating policy issues by formulating policy tools and instruments. As this interviewee explained: "It's my job to be almost a translator, that I get a level of expertise on certain kinds of subject matter."[4] When presidential administrations turn over, technocratic translators tend to improve their skills, expanding their personal network through a position at one of the many think tanks, foundations, or even a school of public policy at a Washington, DC, area university. Then they return in charge to the governmental back offices, bringing their knowledge to formulate health coverage programmatic orientations.

Lastly, the policy bureaucrat subtype corresponds to senior civil servants or some career staffers on congressional committees who establish long-term stable career paths in policy-evaluation and control organizations within the executive or legislative branches of government. With respect to the executive branch, this subtype describes senior officials who are appointed to a policy-monitoring position in a health administration. They generally enjoy a protected status known as "senior executive service" (Aberbach, 2003). Concerning Congress, this subtype refers to those who, because of their long-standing expertise in health care issues, have secured the specialized role of chief fiscal adviser on certain congressional committees. Congressional policy bureaucrats possess impressive technical, often legal or fiscal, policy-related skills. Similar to technocratic translators, they may be called upon to play a critical role during reform by providing input on the financial viability of these policies. An in-depth study of the three subtypes of career paths reflecting the shared comprehensive policy expertise and deep knowledge of governmental work in Washington, DC, will confirm the making of long-term insiders.

We will also examine the political learning process of the distinctive career paths of long-term insiders from a historical perspective by separating those who held policy-making positions during the battles over the Clinton plan from those who held those positions after the plan's political defeat. This choice explains the effects of this political experience on the identity of the new custodians of health coverage policy. We will thus differentiate the career paths of the Clinton plan veterans from those of the others (chapter 4). Their study over time will make it possible to identify very precisely the role of those of them who returned to governmental affairs in order to formulate a new health insurance reform project as soon as the Democrats returned to power, first in Congress (110th legislature, 2006), then under the Obama administration (2008–2010). Our study compares these career paths with those of long-term Republican insiders, highlighting their similarities and differences (chapter 5). Finally, analyses of the career paths of Democratic newcomers, whose careers took place under the late Clinton period (Balanced Budget Act [BBA], 1997), the two G. W. Bush administrations (Medicare Prescription Drug, Improvement, and Modernization Act [MMA], 2003), and the Democrats' return to power (2006–2008), will allow us to see whether these newcomers followed the same career paths and developed the same programmatic vision of health coverage reform as the Clinton plan veterans. The rejection of a government of "strangers" and the adoption of an ethic of responsibility by defending the principle of consensual reform open to market forces will then be discussed. These sociological characteristics are the basis for our hypothesis of the formation of a government of long-term insiders.

CHAPTER 3

Mapping the Unelected Governmental Health Coverage Policy Elites

O
UR MAPPING of the elites in the executive and legislative branches of power explores the changing social backgrounds and career paths of unelected governmental health coverage policy elites. It stems from a sociographic study of a sample of individuals who held positions of power between 1988 and 2010 for at least six years. We should make it clear that during these twelve legislatures and six presidential administrations, there was considerable mobility among these unelected governmental elites. Over more than twenty years, there was also an increase in the number of influential posts in both branches of power. In the executive branch, presidential appointments grew from 286 during President Kennedy's administration to 914 under the Clinton presidency (Lewis, 2008: 222). In Congress, since 1980 the already significant number of staffers—12,000 individuals to which were added 3,000 health professional staffers in the 1980s (Grupenhoff, 1983: 1)—has doubled, thus bringing the current figure to almost 30,000 individuals.[1]

For the health sector, if we limit ourselves only to the studies available on the increase in political-appointee posts at HHS, for the preceding period, we can see that their number grew from 139 under the Reagan presidency in 1981 to 156 posts under the George H. W. Bush presidency in 1991 (Michaels, 1997: 35). It is worth noting this context of tremendous mobility and growth of staff who populate the back offices within the executive and legislative powers, even if at this stage there is no indication whether this factor influences the length of elite career paths in Washington.

The empirical dimension regarding the first component of our programmatic elite framework (see appendix 1, Methodology) first lets us identity a sample of individuals who held those positions of power during health care reforms and then lets us note those who remained there long-term. To control for the revolving-door effect, I take a long career path to be that of an individual who held one or more positions of power for at least six years, not necessarily continuously, during the period under investigation in our empirical study (transition from the big N to the small n). The positions of power concerning the executive were selected in the White House (the president's health adviser and the program associate director [PAD] at the OMB; the director and deputy director of the agencies within HHS and of HHS itself) and in Congress (health subcommittee career staffers). Individuals who hold these positions for an unusually long period will be considered the target population for our mapping study of health coverage policy elites. Before we describe this population in greater detail, it is incumbent upon us to outline in broad strokes the sociological features of the elites at the apex of power in the United States.

As a reminder, the staff employed in the executive and legislative branches are drawn from two distinct fields of study: on the one hand, the political appointees and the senior career bureaucrats[2] (Aberbach & Rockman, 2000); and on the other, the congressional staffers.[3] Traditionally studied as two separate groups, the elites who occupy posts in the two branches of power nevertheless share several sociological characteristics which the mapping study will highlight. On the whole, the elites in the executive tend to be highly qualified individuals (Aberbach, Putnam & Rockman, 1981; Aberbach & Rockman, 2000), and they share this characteristic with those staffers attached to House committees (Hammond, 1984; Henschen & Sidlow, 1986; Romzek & Utter, 1996). Other more recent studies point out that these elites have gradually become politicized since the 1970s—apparent from their increasing partisan affiliation (Ingraham, 1995; Lewis, 2008)—and that they share a high level of professional mobility between the public and private sectors, as well as relatively brief careers at the apex of power (Heclo, 1977; Salisbury & Shepsle, 1981; Mackenzie, 1987; Lewis, 2008).

All these features indeed reflect an American government whose destiny was to lie in the hands of either the "birds of passage" (Heclo, 1977, 1978) or the "short-timers" (Mackenzie, 1987), who use and abuse the revolving door[4] to flit between the administration and the private sector (Lewis, 2008). This situation applies without a doubt to the vast majority of senior appointees (SA) in the executive branch but also to those congressional staffers who remain in a post no longer than two or three years (Salisbury & Shepsle, 1981; Fischer, 1987; Romzek & Utter, 1996). Research studies on congressional staffers reveal a minority among them, the committee staffers who remain in a post longer than five years and are considered to be "veterans"; they often will establish careers on committees to obtain those highly sought-after posts such as chief of staff or general counsel (Salisbury & Shepsle, 1981; Romzek & Utter, 1996). The culture of the out-of-sight government, however, does not encourage any research nor take account of any potential existing minority of individuals able to establish long-term, sector-based career paths in the executive.

This is the reason why we will map the health coverage policy elites in the two branches of power in Washington, DC. To identify these individuals, we selected those positions of power that were able to influence the process of shaping health care insurance policy during the 1988–2010 period. This provided an initial sample of 944 executive and legislative individuals who we studied as one large cohort (see table 3.1). In order to identify long-term career paths, we reduced this baseline population using a criterion of career length in these posts lasting at least six years. We also defined a subpopulation of 151 respondents comprising the health coverage policy elites. Within the executive branch, we found 88 SAs[5] who corresponded to this profile type among an initial population of 538 respondents (16.3% of the entire baseline population). In Congress, there were 63 committee staffers out of 406 respondents who established this type of career (15.5% of the baseline population). At

TABLE 3.1. Population of health coverage policy elites, 1988–2010

	Baseline population	Health coverage policy elite insiders	
Senior appointees	538	63	16.3%
Staffers in Congress	406	88	15.5%
Total	944	151	16.8%

SOURCE: OPERA Research Program

this stage, it is worth mentioning that almost exactly the same proportion of health coverage policy elites (16.3% and 15.5%) can be found within the legislative and executive powers; this is most certainly because these individuals experienced the dramatic impact of the revolving-door system following an electoral defeat.

Furthermore, it is important to note that if the health coverage policy elites—with sociological characteristics of long-term insiders—constitute a minority compared with the majority of short-term insiders, this difference stems from the significant number of respondents (n=151) who, owing to their long careers in the health care insurance sector, might have played a significant role in formulating policies. Before we discuss this key aspect of our in-depth analyses of health coverage policy elites' social backgrounds and career paths (chapter 4 and 5), we should examine some general sociographic characteristics of this population. With this in mind, we will address the following issues: What level of qualifications do they have; which universities did they obtain their degrees from; and what field was their early career in? What makes their career paths in those institutions of power distinctive? What is the average length of their career paths? What kind of mobility shapes their career paths? And what professions will they enter once they cease to work for the federal government?

"Mothers" in Charge of Health Coverage Policy?

It is a well-known fact that women in the United States have played a central role in establishing the social welfare system (Orloff, 1991), from war widows in the mothers' pensions movement, so dear to Theda Skocpol (1992), to the more recent "poorer mom and kids" movement pleading for Medicaid's scope to be broadened (Sardell, 2014). Our mapping study allows us to appreciate the extent to which women are in charge in the sector today. Looking at gender and how it affects the population of health coverage policy elites confirms those great trends regarding the gradual increasing number of female staffers and administrative elites observed by other scholars in their research. In the mid-1980s Grupenhoff's research into staffers on health committees and subcommittees (1983: 3) revealed how present women were in this sector. Indeed, women represented 35% of the Senate and 46% of the House in 1977; in 1982 they held, respectively, 58% and 57% of staffers' posts.

Women's access to the administrative elite arises from a different historical situation—one owing to their structural underrepresentation amid senior career bureaucrats. The first studies carried out by the Brookings and National Academy of Public Administration on political appointees (table 3.2) shows relatively little progress in terms of women's presence, increasing from 0.7% during the 1933–1965 period to 7.9% in the years 1964–1984. Aberbach and Rockman's (2000) more recent research spanning the decades between 1970 and 1990 shows a very different picture. Indeed, under the Nixon administration, women held 3% of political-appointee posts and 2% of senior bureaucrat posts, and 13% of those posts during the Reagan years in both categories; but during the George H. W. Bush administration, women occupied 27% and 20% respectively (61) of those posts. Results of our research on health coverage

TABLE 3.2. Gender balance among unelected governmental elites (%)

	Political appointees, 1933–1965	Political appointees, 1964–1984	Health coverage policy elites, 1988–2010	
			Senior appointees	Staffers
Men	99.3	92.1	68.2	56.5
Women	0.7	7.9	31.8	43.5

SOURCES: 1933–1965: Stanley, Mann & Doig (1967); 1964–1984: NAPA Appointee Data Base (Fischer, 1987: 4–5); 1988–2010: OPERA Research Program policy elites reveal, however, that various policies combatting discrimination have continued to strengthen women's presence. The number of women is growing: more than a third of SAs and nearly 44% of staffers are women. It is interesting to note that a study of French health social insurance elites reveals the same phenomenon (Genieys, 2010: 55–59). The sociographic approach in the strict sense indicates that a higher number of women only exists in the back offices of government in the health care insurance sector, not in other policy domains. Nevertheless, our fine-grained study of elite career paths explored in the following chapters will allow us to highlight the central role played by a large number of women in the various projects concerned with health coverage policy. They were present and yet divided regarding the programmatic orientations that should be pursued during the Clinton administration; the role of women who held positions of strategic power would be crucial in part in establishing a consensual style of decision-making that contributed to the success of the reform known as the Affordable Care Act (see part III).

A Washington-Based Education Focused on Policy

We know, in the wake of the first empirical study devoted to the level and type of qualifications held by the unelected governmental elites, that they possess a high level of education compared with that of average American citizens (Stanley, Mann & Doig, 1967). A rise in educational attainment has remained constant since the 1970s. Indeed, Prewitt and McAllister stress the increase in numbers of both law degrees and PhDs among administrative elites (1976: 118–119). Aberbach and Rockman have more recently shown that the high level of educational qualifications of the administrative elites—of whom more than 93% are postgraduates—render this type of elite the "best and brightest" in American society, ahead of economic elites (Aberbach & Rockman, 2000: 68). Pfiffner emphasizes that 34% of staff who are political appointees have a law degree, or a juris doctor (JD) degree (1987: 143), while other scholars corroborate the increasing presence of the doctorate (Michaels, 1997: 197). Furthermore, research on staffers' academic background during the 1971–1972 legislature indicates that 93% of staffers had a bachelor of arts degree, while also noting the strong preponderance of law degrees (Hammond, 1984: 279). Ever since the 1980s, several research studies have revealed that the vast majority of staffers (93%) hold a university degree, and more than a quarter of them have obtained a master's degree (Hammond, 1984: 279). This trend is corroborated by a later study where it transpired that at least 64% had a BA, and 22% had a master's (Romzek & Utter, 1996: 425).

Our study reflects the extremely high level of academic training that the health coverage policy elites have (table 3.3). They all attended university. The minority hold a bachelor of arts or a master's degree. The majority possess a doctorate (JD, MD, or PhD) with, however, a higher percentage of PhDs among senior appointees (66.2%) than among congressional staffers (50.9%). Moreover, although the health coverage policy elites share with the majority of administrative elites from the executive branch or even with Congress staffers a very high level of education, they differ in their tendency to privilege qualifications favoring a sector-based specialism regarding health policies, often acquired in one of the many schools of public policy or schools of public health (chapter 4 and chapter 5). Apart from their main training, these health coverage policy elites cement their knowledge of health policies by occupying university posts in this academic discipline in the Washington, DC, area.

As far as the general scope of these research studies is concerned, the decline of traditional disciplines such as the humanities, as they have

TABLE 3.3. Highest qualification obtained (%) among health coverage policy elites, 1988–2010

Degree	Senior appointees	Staffers
BA/BS/equivalents	10.8	12.7
MA/MS/equivalents	23.1	36.4
JD	26.2	38.2
MD	18.5	0
PhD	21.5	12.7
No university education	0	0
n	65	55

SOURCE: OPERA Research Program

become subsumed by the social sciences, is clear. Whereas the former prevailed as disciplines privileged by unelected governmental elites between 1933 and 1965, now they are experiencing an irreversible decline linked partly to the new academic prestige of certain social-science departments (Burris, 2004). Our study corroborates the relative demise of legal training (table 3.4), particularly within the executive branch of the health sector (i.e., in 1970, 35% of political appointees held a law degree, but only 26.6% of health coverage policy elites [SAs] from 1988 to 2010 did). Although legal training is on the wane, law degrees, especially the JD, remain very popular for congressional career staffers insofar as they remain a privileged prerequisite for accessing the prestigious status of chief counsel and staff director. On the other hand, we see the pure sciences gradually encroaching in the training programs for senior appointees. The growth in number of social-science graduates, however, has remained constant for the health coverage policy elites (37% of SAs and 50% of staffers). The higher proportion of social-science graduates in Congress can certainly be explained by the strong need on health committees for experts in policy analysis. The relatively heavy presence (29.7%) of the pure sciences among senior appointees probably stems from their expertise in health care (i.e., among practitioners or medical researchers).

TABLE 3.4. Fields of study among health coverage policy elites (%)

	Political appointees, 1970	Political appointees, 1986–1987	Political appointees, 1991–1992	Long-term insiders, 1988–2010	
				Senior appointees	Staffers
Law	35	27	26	26.6	42
Humanities, including history	6	10	12	6.3	4
Social sciences	47	39	52	37.5	50
Natural sciences and technology	12	24	10	29.7	4
n	49	51	42	64	50

SOURCES: 1970, 1986–1987, 1991–1992: Aberbach & Rockman (2000: 72); 1988–2010: OPERA Research Program

Historically, American unelected governmental elites were educated at the Ivy League colleges (Stanley, Mann & Doig, 1967; Prewitt & McAllister, 1976; Fischer, 1987). Aberbach and Rockman estimate that since the 2000s, it is the elites of the business world rather than the administrative elites who obtain a degree from the Big Three or the Ivy League. Regarding undergraduate and postgraduate qualifications, the data obtained for the health coverage policy elites (including the Ivy League and other prestigious private institutions) corroborate our earlier observations (table 3.5 and table 3.6). We note, however, that the proportion of doctorates (PhDs), still in large part obtained from the main private universities, exceeds 30% (table 3.7).

The relative decline of time spent studying in the great private universities with their impressive historical traditions can be explained, however, by the rise in power of the role played by the Washington, DC, area as a training ground. Our study illustrates the significant role played by university institutions in Washington, DC, for training the policy-formulating elites: 21.4% for the senior appointees and 31.3% for

TABLE 3.5. Universities where undergraduate degrees were obtained (%)

	Political appointees, 1970	Political appointees, 1986–1987	Political appointees, 1991–1992	Long-term insiders, 1988–2010	
				Senior appointees	Staffers
Harvard-Yale-Princeton	13	8	7	11.5	15.4
Other Ivy League institutions	4	2	2	6.6	7.7
Other prestigious private institutions	20	18	11	4.9	13.5
Main state universities	11	7	5	19.7	11.5
Sector institutions in Washington, DC	7	3	5	14.8	7.7
Other institutions	46	63	71	42.6	44.2
n	56	62	44	61	52

SOURCES: 1970, 1986–1987, 1991–1992: Aberbach & Rockman (2000: 67); 1988–2010: OPERA Research Program

TABLE 3.6. Universities where postgraduate degrees were obtained (%)

	Political appointees, 1970	Political appointees, 1986–1987	Political appointees, 1991–1992	Long-term insiders, 1988–2010	
				Senior appointees	Staffers
Harvard-Yale-Princeton	15	8	13	14.3	12.5
Other Ivy League institutions	12	6	3	12.5	6.3
Other prestigious private institutions	24	16	19	8.9	10.4
Main state universities	7	12	7	17.9	12.5
Sector institutions in Washington, DC	12	8	10	21.4	31.3
Other institutions	30	50	48	25	27.1
n	41	50	31	56	48

SOURCES: 1970, 1986–1987, 1991–1992: Aberbach & Rockman (2000: 67); 1988–2010: OPERA Research Program

the career staffers (table 3.6). For the latter, the phenomenon is even more pronounced because of the system of financing professional training that Congress offers to its employees. With this financial support, they can often consolidate their university curricula via specialized MBA, MPA, MPH, or even JD and PhD degrees from the American University, Georgetown University, the George Washington University, or Johns Hopkins University (table 3.7). Indeed 46.4% of long-term insider staffers prolong their university training in the Washington, DC, area.

In sum, the high level of educational qualifications, the discipline specialism (law, political science, and public health), as well as having completed their training in the political and administrative capital of the United States, constitute a set of factors that brings the health coverage policy elites in American health closer to the sociological characteristics of the social insurance policy elites identified in the French context (Genieys, 2010; Genieys & Darviche, 2023).

TABLE 3.7. Universities where JDs, MDs, and PhDs were obtained (%), 1988–2010

	Senior appointees	Staffers
Harvard–Yale–Princeton	12.2	7.1
Other Ivy League institutions	12.2	7.1
Other prestigious private institutions	7.3	17.9
Main state universities	22	3.6
Sector institutions in Washington, DC	22	46.4
Other institutions	24.4	17.9
n	41	28

SOURCE: OPERA Research Program

Tracking Careers: Early Entry into Governmental Back Offices

The issue of age when embarking on their career does not have the same import when we compare congressional staffers to political appointees in the executive. Two reasons at least can explain this structural difference. The first is linked to their possible commitment level as mere congressional staffers for these young, ambitious, newly qualified under-30-year-olds (Romzek & Utter, 1996). The second is a reminder of how rare it is to embark upon a career path within the executive branch before the age of 40 (Aberbach & Rockman, 2000). Moreover, research studies on this issue mention the average age of staffers employed on congressional committees as 40 (Fox & Hammond, 1977: 44) and 32 for the entire group of staffers (Romzek & Utter, 1996: 430). A study focusing on those staffers appointed to health committees illustrated this trend, showing that 60% are under 29 and 95% are under 40 (Grupenhoff, 1983: 2). For the political appointees, Linda Fischer observed that between 1964 and 1984 (NAPA Survey, 1985), the average age was 47 when individuals were appointed to a post by the president (1987).[6] Aberbach and Rockman's study on the entire group of administrative elites shows that their average age was 47.7 in 1970, 49.3 in 1986–1987, and 45.9 for the period 1991–1992; while for the same time frames, for the senior career bureaucrats, they were respectively 51.7, 48.4, and 52.3 (2000: 74).

Regarding the age when individuals obtained their first position of power, our mapping analysis of the population of health coverage policy elites shows that the same type of discrepancy is prevalent according to the branch of power. Indeed the age when first appointed to a position of power differs between congressional staffers and senior appointees in the executive branch. Our analysis shows 68% of staffers obtain their posts before the age of 40 (table 3.8) while among senior appointees on the other hand, only 30% of them obtain their posts before the age of 40, and 70% before the age of 50. As we will make clear further on when we explore their career paths in detail (chapter 4 and chapter 5), however, their relatively advanced age when they secure a position of power is compensated for in practice by their early commitment to the health sector as they take on less prestigious roles, for example as personal staffers. It is often the case with senior appointees, however, that they take advantage of an intermediary step out of government as part of the revolving-door system, and these elites become known as long-term insiders when, after a change in political power on Capitol Hill, they return to power.

TABLE 3.8. Age when first post was obtained (%), 1988–2010

	Senior appointees	Staffers
Age 25–29	7.4	10.6
Age 30–34	9.3	31.9
Age 35–39	13	25.5
Age 40–44	18.5	14.9
Age 45–49	20.4	6.4
Age 50–54	16.7	8.5
Age 55–59	3.7	2.1
Age 60 and above	11.1	0
n	54	47

SOURCE: OPERA Research Program

Presence in Public Affairs Before Policy Governance

Research on government elites regarding the profession has found differences linked to the congressional staffers on the one hand and the administrative elites on the other. If a staffer's professional experience can be the preamble to a career that leads to them being appointed to the executive, an appointment as an SA is more than the cherry on the cake—it's like being crowned for an already successful career (Aberbach & Rockman, 2000). Investigating the health coverage policy elites' professions before they secure these positions of power shows that the majority of them began their careers in the public sector. This observation confirms that elites exist within the American government who, while not being senior bureaucrats, nevertheless spend several spells during their career in public affairs.

Regarding congressional staffers, Romzek and Utter mention that these generally young, ambitious individuals with an excellent set of university qualifications see their time in Congress as a stepping stone toward a high-flying professional career (1996: 421–422). These staffers benefit from this occupational experience to gain knowledge, competencies and specific skills, to learn how to work as part of a team, and to build a solid network that will be useful for furthering their career path in Congress, joining the executive branch of power, or switching to the private sector (Salisbury & Shepsle, 1981). Romzek and Utter also note that their motivations (their interest in public affairs), much like the way of working or the knowledge and skills that the staffers acquire, in many respects resemble those of the political appointees in the executive branch (1996). By exploring this structural similarity, Salisbury and Shepsle showed that the staffers easily moved from one professional role to another owing to posts on offer on congressional committees (1981: 385).

The first study on the political appointees' professional origins for the 1933–1965 period already showed a fundamental difference between their initial occupation of entry and that held once the individual was appointed to the executive: the first was generally private, the second public

(Stanley, Mann & Doig, 1967: 32). The observation that more than 70% of political appointees had some experience in public affairs prior to being appointed has often been confirmed by more recent research studies. These highlight the relative decline of political appointees coming from the business world in favor of those coming from spheres of expertise (think tanks and universities, for example) or from Congress (Mackenzie, 1987). The NAPA 1985 study showed that more than 57.5% of political appointees had first experienced the public sector before being appointed, among whom 31.7% were appointed within the federal government even though they were not career bureaucrats, compared with only 9.5% who were appointed while being career bureaucrats.

We should also mention that the percentage of political appointees who come straight from the teams of staffers in Congress (3.4%) and from universities or research (10.6%) complement the trend of those who can acquire some experience that will benefit their new role (NAPA Appointee Data Base, Fischer, 1987: 15). While those who have obtained university degrees or spent time in think tanks generally possess a high level of policy expertise, however, they do not necessarily have the knowledge of how government or policy formulation works in practice in order to carry out their role (Pfiffner, 1987: 145). For Fischer (1987), those coming straight from the private sector are often recruited either from the world of business and banking (14.6%) or from law firms (10.8%). Lawyers are generally equipped with an ability to negotiate, linked to their professional practice, making it easy to switch to a temporary post in policy formulation.[7] Their prior experience before being appointed by the president to one of these policy adviser roles plays a crucial part in determining the ensuing choice. Their high level of training and recognition of their brilliant professional career path constitute necessary requirements. Nevertheless, this does not completely guarantee their ability to formulate new public action programs.[8] For some scholars such as Frederic V. Malek, who was assistant director of the OMB under Nixon and Ford, the political appointees' lack of preparation constitutes a form of "hidden tragedy" of central government.[9] The making of health coverage policy elites career paths that combine policy knowledge and lengthy experience in government affairs constitutes in the particular case of the health sector some form of antidote to the tragic plight of inexperience (chapter 4 and chapter 5).

The profession practiced by health coverage policy elites immediately before they held the post explored in this study was on the whole in the public sector, especially for senior appointees, with 78.5% of them having performed various public activities, especially at the level of the federal state (46.2%); whereas 12.3% had held posts as congressional staffers (table 3.9). Later in our detailed study of their career paths, we will show that this professional migration between the two branches of power is often linked to changes in political majority and to placing a reform project on the decision-making agenda (chapter 4 and chapter 5). In the private sector, the rarest professions practiced were in the world of business

TABLE 3.9. Profession held immediately prior to post being studied (%)

	Political appointees, 1933–1965	Political appointees, 1964–1984	Long-term insiders, 1988–2010	
			Senior appointees	Staffers
Public sector	70	57.5	78.5	69.1
Reappointment		4.6	4.6	
Federal, state, local		6.4	1.5	9.1
Member of Congress		1.2		
Congress staffer		3.4	12.3	47.3
Non-career federal employee	54	31.7	3.1	10.9
Career federal employee	7	9.5	46.2	
Public service in general			7.7	
Other public sectors	9	0.7	3.1	1.8
Private sector	30	42.5	21.5	30.9
Business	13	14.6	1.5	7.3
Lawyer in a private law firm	11	10.8	1.5	7.3
Think tanks		1.6		
Teaching, research		9	10.8	3.6
Science, engineering		1.5		
Political party		1.4	4.6	3.6
Other private sectors	6	3.6	3.1	9.1

SOURCES: 1933–1965: Stanley, Mann & Doig (1967); 1964–1984: NAPA Appointee Data Base (Fischer, 1987: 15); 1988–2010: OPERA Research Program (especially for the SAs) and the most common occupations were in nonprofit organizations (for example, in teaching and research, for a political party, or elsewhere in the private sector). This phenomenon especially affected the senior appointees (86%) and remains significant for the staffers (52%). We should note the relative importance of SAs emerging from teaching and research (10.8%) and staffers coming from not-for-profit organizations (described as "other private sector," 9.1%). The in-depth sociographic study of health coverage policy elites' career paths will illustrate how the decision to choose a professional post in the private not-for-profit sector constitutes a unique phenomenon characterizing the democratic elites (see chapter 4 and chapter 5). In sum, one can wonder whether the development of this trend of prior professional socialization in the public sector typical of the population of health coverage policy elites does not tend to minimize the difference observed with the example of countries where the weight of the senior civil service is structurally heavier (Heclo, 1987; Aberbach, 2003).

Taming the Revolving Door

As a reminder, the revolving-door phenomenon affects the careers of political appointees and senior civil servant status quite differently. In contrast with the latter, the average length of time that political appointees spend in their post is only 2.3 years (Fischer, 1987: 22).[10] As the number of appointments to these positions of power at the summit of the executive has continued to grow, thereby reinforcing the possibility of moving between positions of power,[11] the OPERA study shows how a minority of elites have devised career paths in this new context. The increase in the number of posts available as a political appointment, while reinforcing the "musical chairs" trend specific to the summit of American executive power, has led in a logical and fortuitous way to an emerging minority of unelected governmental elites. It is on this basis of career paths being established in the back offices of government over the last few decades that the health coverage policy elites would reinvent their custodian's role (part III).

We also find a similarity between the growth of legislative and executive careers in terms of their length even if staffers' careers do not conform to the same hierarchical pressures as that of the political appointees (Romzek & Utter, 1996).[12] Romzek and Utter's study (1996) of the staffers in the 104th Congress (in 1995) mentions that 69% of them had been in their post for the previous two years or less, thereby corroborating those studies that showed the average length of time spent in the role as being between two and three years.[13] Salisbury and Shepsle (1981) in their study explain the staffers' high mobility by the lack of career path, the difference between working for a House representative or being appointed to a congressional committee, the continuous growth of the number of employees in Congress as much as in the executive, and the frequent change of political majority.[14] For these reasons, it seems that the vast majority of staffers who do not secure the long-term status of a staffer's post on a congressional committee can remain "birds of passage," forever willing and available to be considered candidates who are ready to make a professional move into the private sector or to other governmental posts (i.e., in the executive or Congress).

Furthermore, this high professional mobility is underpinned by a mutual support system for switching posts unique to Congress, based for example on certain university-funded courses. Nevertheless, this high mobility into the private sector in no way prevents some individuals among them from specializing in a particular area of public policy, in the health coverage sector for instance, or from extending their career on a congressional committee in the other house of Congress (the House of Representatives or the Senate). Our mapping study also shows that in contrast with the 1980s, when staffers leave their positions of power, they tend to switch to professional employment in Washington, DC.

Our mapping of health coverage policy elites shows that lengthy professional pathways became established in the executive as much as in the legislative branch, thereby limiting the effects of the revolving-door system. These abnormally long career paths in charge inside governmental health affairs—often lasting between ten and twenty years—typically include less mobility (and are punctuated with returns) and a later switch into the private sector. Indeed, when a brief spell in the private sector between two posts is not excluded, it generally ends with a return to the initial institutional base or the other branch of power. In addition, I will explore further on and in greater detail, via several individual career paths, examples of how elites choose different areas in the private sector (for profit versus not for profit). Some health coverage policy elites move between both branches of power after having spent a short spell in the private sector (the institutional migrants) while others prefer the legislative or the executive branches, where they can acquire specialist competencies regarding one aspect of health care insurance (the technocratic translators).

The senior appointees (75%) remain in positions of power for on average nine years in the health sector (table 3.10). These employees' careers tend to last four times as long as those of the majority of the elites working in the executive branch of power. Similarly, the senior appointees can boast of pursuing their career under at least two successive presidential administrations. Moreover, the length of their careers in the back offices of power is remarkable in that, for nearly 31.8% of SAs and 28.3% of staffers, it lasts thirty years or longer (table 3.11). Congressional staffers have a strong propensity to remain in their posts. Nearly 50% of them remain in a post between ten and fourteen years. Similarly, almost 30% of them remain in a post in their sector for thirty years or more (table 3.11).

Lastly, we should focus on the fact that these long careers in positions of power do not exclude the practice of coming and going from profes-

TABLE 3.10. Length of time spent in post being studied (%), 1988–2010

	Senior appointees	Staffers
6–9 years	75	40.3
10–14 years	18.2	50
15–19 years	3.4	4.8
20–24 years	2.3	3.2
25 years or more	1	1.6
n	88	62

SOURCE: OPERA Research Program

TABLE 3.11. Length of time spent in public sector (%), 1988–2010

	Senior appointees	Staffers
6–9 years	16.7	2.2
10–14 years	6.1	19.6
15–19 years	16.7	19.6
20–24 years	9.1	21.7
25–29 years	19.7	8.7
30 years or more	31.8	28.3
n	66	46

SOURCE: OPERA Research Program

sional public and private spheres, exclusively in the field of health affairs, in the interlude between two appointments to positions of power. In this instance, the revolving-door phenomenon enables certain health coverage policy elites to scale echelons that are unique to a career in the back offices of government or to spend time—out of financial choice or because of constraints (a change of political majority)—in the worlds of business, not-for-profit organizations, academia, and think tanks. Considering the number of exits from their main institution (the executive or Congress) allows us to show that the majority of health coverage policy elites left their post at least once before returning to policy matters: 67.8% of senior appointees and 85.5% of staffers (table 3.12).

Finally, the issue of mobility between both branches of power is another sociographic aspect of the health coverage policy elites' career path: 52.8% of staffers had worked in administration, whereas 25% of senior appointees had spent time in Congress (table 3.13). Certainly, from a strictly statistical perspective, it is difficult to privilege the significance of this kind of mobility among unelected governmental elites in the health sector in both branches of power. It is important to mention here that legislative studies as well as administrative studies have neglected the issue of the effect of the elites' mobility between the executive branch and Congress. Further on, based on numerous examples of individual career paths corresponding to the institutional migrant type, we will show that this mobility can bring together perspectives with different

TABLE 3.12. Exits from administration (senior
appointees) and Congress (staffers) (%), 1988–2010

	Senior appointees	Staffers
0	32.2	14.5
1	57.6	56.4
2	10.2	23.6
3		5.5
4 and above		
n	59	55

SOURCE: OPERA Research Program

TABLE 3.13. Worked in administration (senior
appointees) or Congress (staffers) (%), 1988–2010

	Senior appointees	Staffers
Yes	24.6	52.8
No	75.4	47.2
n	61	53

SOURCE: OPERA Research Program

competing programmatic orientations in Congress, as much as in the executive branch of power, when a policy reform is put on the agenda (chapter 9).

Our mapping of population health coverage policy elites' features leads us to highlight specific sociological characteristics. Firstly, it allows us to point to the existence of a significant minority of these elites who, despite the systemic effects of the revolving-door phenomenon, manage to establish long-term career paths in charge of policy formulation within both branches of power—and this despite repeated changes of political majority. Apart from unusually long career paths, these elites share a similar academic background (higher education qualifications), having often specialized in the social sciences. Time spent in schools of public policy or university departments of public health, often in the Washington, DC, region or its outskirts, is another element attesting to their public-policy and health expertise. The increasing number of women in health care governance cannot but act as a reminder of the historic role

TABLE 3.14. Principal reform projects initiated by policy entrepreneurs

Models and initiators	General project orientation of failed reforms
Single payer National Public Insurance system (Ted Marmor)	Comprehensive health care insurance coverage depends on a single unique public payer. It was inspired by the health care insurance system that is managed by the public sector in Canada.
Managed competition Market regulated by the public sector (Alain Enthoven)	The managed competition option offers strong market regulation and a strengthening of competition between health care providers needing to contain and lower costs and extend insurance coverage.
Public option Public offer in competition with the market (J. Hacker and H. Halpin)	The public option is a health care insurance model managed by the government that individuals and companies could choose instead of a private insurance model.

SOURCE: OPERA Research Program

played by "mothers" to establish a "maternalist" social welfare system (Skocpol, 1992). Lastly, the specificity of the health coverage policy elites' career paths is a testimony to the presence of a group of long-term insiders who remain durably in policy formulation and, because of this, differ from Heclo's famous "birds of passage."

Our study of health coverage policy elites distinguishes them from other professionals such as policy entrepreneurs (Kingdon, 1984; Medvetz, 2012). While policy entrepreneurs share with these elites the wish to influence the policy-formulation process by proposing policy solutions to shape policy content, they have very different career paths and approaches to reform. Policy entrepreneurs, like many academic experts, often independently establish ambitious policy reform models (big pictures), which their names become associated with. This has been particularly notable in the case of health care reform projects since the end of the 1970s, when the names of policy entrepreneurs coming from several disciplines became associated with the reform projects (table 3.14). The best known were the medical doctors Abraham Bergman (who created the National Health Service Corps) and Paul Ellwood (HMOs); health economists Alain Enthoven and Paul Starr (managed competition); Jonathan Gruber (the individual mandate in the Massachusetts plan); and the political scientists Ted Marmor (single payer)[15] and Jacob Hacker (public option).[16] As a general rule, their career paths in health governance were short or ephemeral. Their advisory policy role was mainly an unofficial one. Their actual presence in governmental affairs was short-term (less than two years), unlike the long-term insiders who remained in charge for more than six years. Generally, policy entrepreneurs preferred to return to the academic and research world. Long-term insiders' academic credentials, however, cannot compensate for their weak learning in the practices of the governmental decision-making process. This is one reason why their influence on policy can be confused with Heclo's "birds of passage" (1977). On the contrary, long-term insiders establish durable career paths that put them in charge of the policy-formulation process.

CHAPTER 4

The Clinton Plan Veterans

Career Paths Marked by a Collective Failure

THIS CHAPTER is devoted to a detailed study of the sociological portraits of the unelected governmental health coverage policy elites who occupied positions of power during the Clinton reform (1992–1994). These portraits characterize the Democratic long-term insiders (in Congress and the administration) who participated in the Clinton plan battle. Some of these individuals began their career paths inside government affairs prior to the Clinton administration. Only a few of them remained after the failure of the reform. A handful of them would return to the issue from key posts once President Obama launched a new health reform in 2008. Some research studies have already discussed the impassioned conflict among the Democratic health coverage policy elites between those who were entrenched in Washington's spheres of power—known either as the "blueberry donut group" (Johnson & Broder, 1996: 70) or the "Washington advisory group" (Hacker, 1997: 110)—and the "prominent policy experts or policy entrepreneurs,"—temporary presidential advisers (Lepont, 2014). It is indisputable that their strategy of amending the initial project opened the door to a divided configuration of elites, weakening the chances of the reform succeeding before Congress (Starr, 1994; Glied, 1997).

The choice of a systematic study of unelected governmental elites who remain in office for more than six years in Congress or the administration allows for a more thorough sociological interpretation of the "Clinton veterans" (Hacker, 2010; Jacobs & Skocpol, 2010; McDonough, 2011). Often put forward as one of the factors explaining the success of the Affordable Care Act, these studies on the Clinton plan veterans reveal little regarding their sociological characteristics. Why did some of them become key players in the formulation of the new reform agenda or in the decision-making process under the Obama administration?

The programmatic elite framework answers this question by developing, through sociological portraits (social background and career path), an in-depth study of long-term insiders. Clinton plan veterans are identified as individuals who developed a career path initiated during the Clinton years.[1] Some of them extended their career paths to the Obama health care reform bill. These elites who began their careers with the Clinton reform were joined by individuals identified in "key informant" interviews as highly influential on health insurance policy during the reform era.[2] Their portraits should allow us to verify the hypothesis of the formation of a group of long-term insiders, the Clinton plan veterans, who shared common social-background and career-path features. They enable us to identify career paths forged over the long-term in health policy formulation and governance. We have shaped these portraits through a series of criteria: the role of an initial high-level university education furthered by a subject specialization (in health or law) in Washington, DC;[3] the involvement in the bipartisan congressional committee known as the Pepper Commission, which looked at the health system's future; appearing before the Clinton task force; and moving to the nonprofit private sector (characterized by an appointment under contract to universities, in think tanks, or in foundations). These sociological portraits will highlight the specificity of the career paths of the veterans who took part in and witnessed the Clinton reform project's defeat from inside the back offices of power.

More precisely, the professional and institutional dimensions of career paths during and after the Clinton administration reform will be studied through the empirical investigation of three subtypes of long-term career paths: the institutional migrant, the technocratic translator and the policy bureaucrat (see table II.1). All these elements will enable us to ascertain whether and how the long-term insiders remained connected to each other over time, especially when they migrated to the margins of power in Washington and participated in activities organized by various reform forums (the Alliance for Health Reform, the Bipartisan Policy Center, the Center on Budget and Policy Priorities, etc.) during periods when the Republicans had returned to power, both in Congress and the presidency. Thus, their strong sector base in Washington, DC, and their specialized knowledge base in policy formulation made these individuals strong candidates with great potential for returning to health governance when a future political majority would arise. For this reason, namely by making a reality of their return to the health policy formulation issue, they differ from those who after a brief stint in government turned toward lucrative careers in the private sector. From this perspective, studying the Clinton plan veterans' career paths will allow us to distinguish between those who returned to the back offices of the Obama administration and those who remained active but on the margins of power in Washington, DC.

Institutional Migrants Circulating across the Two Branches of Power

The institutional migrant's career path reveals the existence of individuals who successively experienced the process of policy-making decisions in the executive branch of power (the White House or HHS) and then in one of the two houses of Congress, or the other way around. To study the Clinton plan veterans' mobility, we distinguish between those who were involved in the genesis of the new health insurance reform project but did not return to government under the Obama administration[4] and those who did return to the back offices of power.[5]

Clinton Plan Veterans on the Margins of the Obama Administration

The first sociological portrait is that of Judy Feder, an institutional migrant who remained on the margins of power during the Obama reform. An emblematic figure of the Democratic health coverage policy elites in Washington, DC, during the Clinton administration, she was acknowledged as one of the major advocates of the "play-or-pay" project (chapter 6), which the great majority of Washington's Democratic health elites fell in line behind (Johnson & Broder, 1996: 109–111; Skocpol, 1996: 40; Hacker, 1997: 103; Blumenthal & Morone, 2009: 358–359). A political scientist by training, Feder obtained her BA from Brandeis University and her MA and PhD in government from Harvard University. In the early 1970s, she pursued research on public health issues, studying the relationships between Congress and the Social Security Administration regarding the Medicare program. She then wrote a book on this issue, *Medicare: The Politics of Federal Hospital Insurance* (1977). In her post at the Brookings Institution, and then at the Urban Institute, Feder collaborated with health economists in order to combine the study of politics with policies—namely, the issue of the cost of social insurance coverage.[6] In 1984, she became codirector of the Center for Health Policy Studies at Georgetown University School of Medicine in Washington, DC. During this first stage of her career path, she published several articles on health policy in *Health Policy, Health Affairs*, and the *Journal of Health Politics, Policy, and Law*.[7] Benefiting from a solid reputation in Washington's health policy world, in 1989 Feder became committed to a career as a congressional staffer, with the aim of furnishing the Democratic Party with arguments for the creation of a public health coverage system.[8] Soon after, she took on the leadership of young Washington experts tackling the challenges surrounding health care by directing the work of a bipartisan congressional commission—1990's so-called Pepper Commission. The ensuing report proposed a reassessment of the public health insurance system that advocated what became known as "play-or-pay."

During Bill Clinton's presidential campaign, Feder became the spokesperson for this reform project. As director of health affairs in President Clinton's transition team, she was appointed to a strategic post as assistant secretary for planning and evaluation (ASPE) at HHS from 1993 to 1995. With other Washington Democratic health advisers, she set up the "blueberry donut group"[9] to defend the reform option set out in Congress by the Pepper Commission. In this capacity, she took part in the Clinton task force, where her programmatic orientation was rejected for an option blending the public and the private (chapter 6). In 1995, at the end of the first Clinton administration, Judy Feder left once and for all the back offices of government and resumed her academic career. A well-known health policy expert, she participated in the creation of the Georgetown Public Policy Institute (known since 2013 as the McCourt School of Public Policy) and was its dean from 2001 to 2008. She remained very involved in forums such as the Alliance for Health Reform[10] and the Kaiser Commission on Medicaid and the Uninsured, defending the need to formulate a new health coverage reform project. It was thanks to her Clinton veteran status within the Democratic forums on the margins of the Obama administration that she became involved in formulating a new programmatic orientation that would serve as the foundation for the Affordable Care Act.

The second institutional migrant portrait illustrating how Clinton plan veterans shouldered the Obama reform from outside government is that of Diane Rowland. After obtaining a master's of public affairs from UCLA, she joined the Carter administration in early 1976 to take up the post of special assistant to health economist Karen Davis, then ASPE at HEW. During this apprenticeship, Rowland learned "how to write recommendations to policy-makers" on health issues.[11] After her work with Davis, in 1990 Rowland joined the department of health policy and management at Johns Hopkins University in Baltimore to work on a doctorate looking at how to limit the cost of public health insurance. During her doctoral research, she worked from 1991 to 1994 as a part-time staffer in charge of health issues on the Energy and Commerce Committee for Henry Waxman, a progressive congressman. On this committee, Rowland established close long-term ties with influential members of Waxman's staff, future Clinton plan veterans. These include Brian Biles (Rowland's future husband), Karen Nelson, Tim Westmoreland, Michael Hash, and Phil Schiliro—all of whom have had careers as institutional migrants. Others such as Andy Schneider and Ruth Katz would emerge as technocratic translators in Congress.

Rowland's work with the Pepper Commission widened her network, notably by introducing her to Judy Feder and Chris Jennings. It was alongside Feder that Rowland would form the "Washington insiders' health care team" (Jennings & Lambrew, 2003: 15),[12] a group whose mission was to establish links between Congress and the new administration during the transition period just prior to the Clinton presidency.[13] Following the failed Clinton reform project, she left the realm of Democratic health political advisers to take up a post as manager at the Henry J. Kaiser Family Foundation "to get involved in promoting and communicating new policy ideas in a non-academic style."[14] Following Feder's example, Rowland would put her health policy expertise to use devising a new reform project that marshaled the powerful resources of the foundation she led and contributed to the Alliance for Health Reform's communications strategy. Although her role meant that she was involved in the Kaiser Foundation's work, she stayed on the margins of the Obama administration.

The third institutional migrant portrait is that of Brian Biles (Diane Rowland's husband). Trained as a medical doctor, he took advantage of his move to Maryland, near Washington, DC, to obtain a specialized master's degree in public health at the esteemed School of Public Health (known since 2001 as the Bloomberg School of Public Health) at Johns Hopkins University.[15] In 1983, he began his career in health administration with the State of Maryland. Biles then started a career path as a committee staffer, which stretched for more than twenty years. During his long staffer career in health policy, he moved across both houses of Congress, advising members of Congress William Roy, Pete Stark, and Henry Waxman in the House of Representatives, as well as Senator Ted Kennedy. Biles served as a policy adviser in the Pepper Commission's work on the American health insurance system. After these long years of experience in Congress, in 1993 he was appointed deputy assistant secretary for health at HHS during the Clinton presidency in order to drive the administration's reform project.

From 1996 to 2003, Biles returned to the House of Representatives to lead the Health Subcommittee on the influential Energy and Commerce Committee, then led by the Democrat Henry Waxman. Following several back-and-forth moves between Congress and the executive branch of power, Biles joined the School of Medicine and Health Sciences at the George Washington University as a professor of public health. Although he kept a low profile and avoided government back offices, he would play a crucial role alongside other Clinton plan veterans at the Alliance for Health Reform, such as Chris Jennings, David Nexon, Karen Pollitz, and Dean Rosen, organizing several seminars dedicated to drawing up an inventory of reasons the Clinton reform failed (Biles, 2008: 18–20). The road map outlined then made the case for certain Clinton plan veterans—"namely, those of the Waxman staff on the Energy and Commerce Committee"—to return to both branches of power in order to optimize the launch of the Obama reform.[16]

Other portraits of Clinton plan veterans such as David Nexon and Tim Westmoreland illustrate how institutional migrants' career paths involved them in the making of the Obama reform while not, officially at least, returning them to the back offices of government. David Nexon, the first case, hailed from Chicago and obtained his bachelor's degree in government from Harvard College; he went on to receive a master's and a PhD in political science from the University of Chicago, where he then taught from 1970 to 1977. Always displaying a "strong interest for politics and policy . . . but unhappy as a university lecturer,"[17] Nexon joined the OMB as bureau chief in the health division in charge of the Medicare and Medicaid program budgets under the Carter administration.[18] In 1983 he left the executive and joined Senator Ted Kennedy's staff, where he worked for more than twenty-five years as director of the health office at the Labor and Human Resources Committee (from 1983 to 2008). His long career as a committee staffer led him to receive the accolade of "dean of health policies of the American Senate" (McDonough, 2011: 53). As director of the health office, Nexon initiated a change of strategy in the recruitment of staffers to the Health Subcommittee. He decided to surround himself with individuals who had a "doctorate or even a social policy master's" in order to increase the collective capacity of expertise on the issue of extending health insurance. As Senator Kennedy's representative, he took part in the Pepper Commission's work and contributed to the Clinton task force in 1993. In 2005 Nexon moved into the private sector to take up a post as executive vice president of Advanced Medical Technology. In 2007, however, during the rallying of the Democratic health policy elites in Washington, Nexon took part in the memory work organized by Clinton plan veterans to analyze their experience of defeat—work which was published by the Alliance for Health Reform for the Robert Wood Johnson Foundation (see chapter 8) as "Recommendations: Nine Lessons Learned from the Health Reform Debate of 1993–1994" (see table 8.1).

For his part, Tim Westmoreland, who obtained a BA from Duke University and a JD from Yale Law School, began his university teaching career on a part-time basis in 1979 so he could also work as assistant counsel, and later as counsel, on the House of Representatives' Health and Environment Subcommittee, led at that time by Henry Waxman.[19] Between 1979 and 1995, Westmoreland developed his career on the committee staff as an assistant and then as an adviser on legislative matters. Within the Waxman staff, Westmoreland worked alongside other institutional migrants such as Diane Rowland and Brian Biles. Thereafter, he became active as a public health policy adviser on the Clinton-Gore administration's transition team from 1992 to 1993. Like the great majority of members of Henry Waxman's health staff, Westmoreland contributed to the Clinton task force's work. Respected in the sector for his legal and budgetary knowledge regarding health insurance policies, he moved to Georgetown University's law school as a senior policy fellow in 1995, while also contributing to the nonprofit Henry J. Kaiser Family Foundation. Between 1999 and 2001, toward the end of the second Clinton administration, Westmoreland resumed his activities in the executive branch when he was appointed strategic director of the Health Care Financing Administration. When George W. Bush arrived in the White House, Westmoreland became a "visiting professor of law and research professor of public policy at Georgetown University, while keeping 20% of his work time to continue working as an adviser to Henry Waxman."[20] Like the vast majority of Clinton plan veterans during the 2000–2010 years, Westmoreland contributed to the work of the Alliance for Health Reform.[21]

Before turning to the cases of the Clinton plan veterans who returned to fill posts to formulate policy during the gestation of the Obama reform, it is appropriate to comment on Christopher (Chris) Jennings's emblematic career path (Starr, 2013: 176–177). He was one of those rare Washingtonians who, for more than thirty years, moved in ten-year periods across the three spheres where policies are shaped in the American political system—the administration, Congress, and private interests—before returning in July 2013 as health policy coordinator and strategist to work within the Obama administration on the implementation of the Affordable Care Act.[22] In his 2010 OPERA interview just after the ACA was enacted, Jennings presented himself as follows: "I am a twenty-seven-year veteran in health care and aging policy . . . with a rich and fulfilling career. . . . That's what I'm known for in DC."[23] Certainly, Jennings could not claim to have a specialist degree in public health or to have spent time in a prestigious university on the northeast coast. For his BA, he studied philosophy, political science, and gerontology at the University of Miami.[24] It was during his long career in Washington in both branches of power that he built his reputation as a health insurance policy figure. Jennings entered the Senate as a staffer attached to the Committee on Aging and worked successively with three Democratic senators. His contribution to the work of the Pepper Commission from 1989 to 1990 on a new health reform project was the X factor that led him to join the network of Washington health policy advisers that was being established.

Working closely with Hillary Clinton, Jennings took on the liaison role between the White House and Congress, and "prepared [Clinton] for hundreds of meetings with members of Congress" during the negotiations regarding the health reform project (Jennings & Lambrew, 2003: 7). He also took part from 1993 to 1994 in the preparatory work of the Clinton task force. By his own admission, he did not really consider himself a "policy person" then. It was only after his long experience as a special health adviser at the White House from 1995 to 2001 when he took part in elaborating bipartisan legislation, such as the State Children's Health Insurance Program and the Balanced Budget Act, both from 1997, when he felt that his professional role changed. Following that experience, Jennings truly became a "policy wonk," a political person able to translate ideas developed by policy experts to policy-makers. Regarding this point, Jennings continued: "You know, very few people are able to do this translation. Often, the two worlds are independent from each other and don't communicate well. So, if you ask me who am I, the best answer I can give is I am a translator."[25] It is important to mention that the definition of "policy wonk" proposed by Jennings differs from that put forward by Thomas Medvetz, who describes this role as tied to academic knowledge and qualifications, and who mistakenly leaves aside all the political work carried out by the people who are in charge in the back offices of government (2012: 40). For Jennings, this is the role of the translator: adapting the academic model of social policies to the empirical reality of political action.

The argument developed here is central for understanding the thesis of the government of insiders. Indeed it enables us to see that behind the contrasting roles in the world of health policy experts and elected officials are individuals in charge of translating "policy big pictures" into plans compatible with the political decision-making process. With the inauguration of President George W. Bush, Chris Jennings went into the private sector and created an eponymous consulting agency, Jennings Policy Strategies, to defend those private interest groups (for-profit and nonprofit) at risk of conflicting with the new orientation given to health policies by the Republicans. This niche work gave Jennings tremendous visibility in Congress and enabled him to advise the Kaiser Family Foundation and the Robert Wood Johnson Foundation, while he simultaneously contributed to the Alliance for Health Reform's communications work. In 2007, absorbing one of the lessons from the Clinton defeat (i.e., the absence of political consensus regarding the reform), he launched the Bipartisan Policy Center, the aim of which was to devise a new health coverage reform project (McDonough, 2011: 57), and he became "wholeheartedly" involved in preparing the work of the Obama administration. From July 2013 to January 2014 Jennings would return to the White House as a special adviser to President Obama focusing on reducing health care costs and implementing the ACA.

Clinton Plan Veterans Involved in the Obama Administration

Studying the career paths of institutional migrants among the Clinton plan veterans who helped health governance when the ACA was put on the political agenda, we see how these portraits indicate the role played by Clinton plan veterans in the success of the ACA decision-making process. These institutional migrants filled nearly half the available key posts in both branches of power during the negotiation process of the reform.[26] Further on, we will observe that they were accompanied in this task by other Clinton plan veterans with technocratic translator career paths (table II.1).

Wendell Primus is one of the Clinton plan veterans who joined the Obama administration, and we will draw his portrait here.[27] The *Washington Post* described this long-time policy adviser to House Speaker Nancy Pelosi as "a quiet liberal lion."[28] One of our interviewees described Primus's career path as "an interesting story. Wendell Primus has been around for a very long time in office. He was always on staff on the Budget Committee and Ways and Means Committee, just before joining the House Speaker's staff. But he has worked for the House of Representatives for a very long time, but during the Clinton administration, he went over to HHS, where among other things, he worked on our welfare program, cash assistance for poor people."[29] Returning later to Congress to devise a new reform project, Primus's career path illustrates the portrait of the institutional migrant. With a PhD in economics from the University of Iowa and his experience as a lecturer at that university, Primus then went to Georgetown University as an assistant professor at the same time as he began working as a part-time staffer on the Committee on Agriculture in the House of Representatives from 1974 to 1977 (Berkowitz, 2002). Soon after, he shifted his staffer career to the Human

Resources Subcommittee of the Ways and Means Committee, where he held various posts, including that of senior staff economist from 1977 to 1987); he then became chief of economic staff (1987–1991) and then of director of staff of the Health Subcommittee (1991 to 1993). Primus acknowledges that during this first long stretch as a staffer, he grew closer to the "historical" staff on the Waxman staff, such as Karen Nelson and Andy Schneider, whom he maintained very good relationships with, professionally and personally.[30] As a specialist in the budgetary approach to policies for wages and childhood, he then played a central role in the negotiations between the Ways and Means Committee and the CBO on these issues (Howard, 2007: 103; Joyce, 2011: 130).

In 1993 Primus was appointed to the strategic post of ASPE. In 1996 he resigned following a personal conflict with Rahm Emanuel, who at that time was Bill Clinton's political adviser, owing to the lack of "liberal" orientation in the welfare reform's focus. From 1997 to 2003 Primus temporarily left the arena of power and moved to the nonprofit private sector, where he became research director of the bipartisan liberal think tank the Center on Budget and Policy Priority, the aim of which was to devise a new health coverage reform project. Primus also worked alongside many Clinton plan veterans as a mediator for the Alliance for Health Reform and for the Kaiser Family Foundation. Toward the end of 2003, however, he headed back to the House of Representatives, initially as staff director of the Economic Committee. In 2005 he became senior policy adviser on budgetary and health issues for Nancy Pelosi while she was a minority Democratic leader; he retained the post while she was Speaker of the House from 2007 to 2012 (Bai, 2009: 10). In this role, Primus resumed the fight with Rahm Emanuel, who was then President Barack Obama's chief of staff, regarding the health project's scope: comprehensive versus incremental reform.[31] The option that Congress finally retained with the Affordable Care Act was the far-reaching reform that the long-term insiders envisioned, despite the fears and reticence expressed by certain top Obama advisers.

William Corr is another good example of a Clinton plan veteran moving time and again not only between both branches of power but also between the House of Representatives and the Senate.[32] With a JD from

Vanderbilt University Law School in Nashville, he settled in Washington in 1977 and worked as a "lawyer staffer" for Henry Waxman on the Energy and Commerce Committee in the House of Representatives. After eleven years in that role, Corr joined the Antitrusts, Monopolies, and Business Subcommittee, where he stayed from 1989 to 1993, first as chief counsel and then as staff director. In 1993 he was appointed to HHS, where he stayed until 1998. Within the executive branch, Corr held several political posts as policy adviser to the health secretary. He then returned to Congress—but this time to the Senate—as policy director on Tom Daschle's staff (from 1998 to 2000). With the return of the Republicans to power, Corr left public life to take up a post as executive director for a private nonprofit foundation, working on an antismoking campaign and youth protection. Because of his long experience at the apex of power, in both branches of power, and his impressive political network in the Democratic party, Corr was appointed during the Obama administration to be deputy to the secretary of health, who at the time was Kathleen Sebelius.[33]

Karen Pollitz's portrait illustrates in a different light the institutional migrant career path. With a master's degree in social policy from the University of California at Berkeley, Pollitz began her career as a legal assistant on several committees in the House of Representatives, moving from the Subcommittee on Compensation and Employee Benefits to the influential Ways and Means Committee from 1984 to 1989, while at the same time becoming a health specialist.[34] Pollitz then joined the staff of Senator J. D. Rockefeller IV, who was a stalwart of the Pepper Commission from 1990, as well as the founder and chairman of the Alliance for Health Reform in 1991. While working on the Pepper Commission, Pollitz became close to another future Clinton plan veteran, Judy Feder; the two later co-published a series of articles on health policy issues.[35] At the same, Pollitz was also pursuing a part-time academic career in health policy at Georgetown University. From 1993 to 1997 she held posts as deputy director of the HHS's legal section and contributed in this capacity to the work of the Clinton task force. The following decade, Pollitz left the policy-formulation sphere for a post as assistant professor at the Institute for Health Care Research and Policy at Georgetown University in Washington, DC. Her research there was on links between private insurers and health insurance system reform. She regularly presented results of her academic work to forums at the Kaiser Family Foundation and the Alliance for Health Reform, and started defending the idea of a mixed programmatic orientation combining public and private interests. When the Obama reform was being steered through, Pollitz returned to health governance in a post at HHS as director of administration in charge of relations with the insurance system.

Lastly, to give even more weight to the in-depth study of the Clinton plan veterans with an institutional migrant career path, we will examine simultaneously the portraits of "historical" pillars of Democratic Congressman Henry Waxman's staff: Karen Nelson, Michael Hash, and Phil Schiliro. Apart from the fact that the three circulated among both branches of power over several years, they also have in common the fact that they returned to key positions in the decision-making process during the Obama administration.

With a bachelor's degree from Cornell University, Karen Nelson's extremely long career began in federal administration at the Justice department from 1965 to 1966. Nelson then moved to the OMB at the White House (1966–1970) and continued at HHS, where she was office manager in charge of health policy planning and evaluation. In 1974 Nelson moved to the House of Representatives, and in 1978 she became Waxman's special adviser. She then spent more than thirty-five years scaling the echelons of a committee staffer's career. She contributed to the Clinton task force as a supporter of comprehensive reform of the health insurance system. Later, when the Obama reform was being launched, Nelson took on the role of coordinator in the House of the Tri-Comm (a group of three committees: Energy and Commerce, Ways and Means, Education and the Workforce), charged with shaping the reform project on that side of Congress (McDonough, 2011: 72). According to Democratic lobbyist Richard Tarpling, "Karen Nelson is the heart and soul of the health team [referring to Henry Waxman's team], and for others, [she is] a towering figure in health care circles around town who knows more about the collection of health care policy issues than anybody in town and, as importantly, knows where all the bodies are buried on each issue."[36]

In a similar vein, Michael M. Hash's career path reveals a long-term commitment to the outcome of health insurance system reform. A postgraduate in political science from Vanderbilt University in Nashville, Hash began his career as an administrator with the American Hospital Association and in different agencies in the hospital sector from 1973 to 1990.[37] From 1990 to 1995 Hash worked as part of Waxman's staff on the Subcommittee for Health and Environment at the House of Representatives. A Medicare legislation specialist, Hash was involved in the Clinton reform project by contributing to the task force as Waxman's representative. In this role, Hash became close to another future Clinton plan veteran, Chris Jennings, as well as to the Republican Tom Scully (see chapter 5). Subsequently Hash went into the private sector to work for Health Policy Alternatives Inc. (HPA) before returning to work on social issues and take up a strategic role in policy formulation as deputy director of the Health Care Financing Administration during the end of Bill Clinton's second term (1998–2000). One OPERA interviewee pointed out that HPA was not a think tank: "It is a consulting firm with about forty clients from all across the health care stakeholders' spectrum . . . The health policy community is very small and filled with many smart people who used to work for government or on the Hill and, even though they are now working in the private sector as lobbyists or consultants, still give advice to those of us working on the Hill."[38]

During the George W. Bush administration, Hash returned once again to HPA as a consultant. He then worked alongside Liz Fowler, a new Democratic figure in health policy (chapter 5); within the Bipartisan Policy Center and the Alliance for Health Reform, Hash pleaded with Fowler for a consensual approach to reform. Drawing on a professional background typical among Clinton plan veterans, during the genesis of the Obama reform, Hash was appointed senior health adviser to the White House (2009–2011) and then director of the Office of Health Reform at the HHS (2011–2014). This career path is emblematic of that of the Clinton plan veterans who would find themselves at the heart of the decision-making process when the ACA reform project was going through Congress.

Finally, Phil Schiliro's career path confirms the ability of Waxman's staff, specialists in health policy challenges, to come and go across both branches of power but equally to move across both houses of Congress.[39] With a BA in political science from Hofstra University in Long Island, New York, and a JD from Lewis and Clark Law School, Phil Schiliro began his committee staffer career at the House of Representatives in 1981. From 1983 until 2004 he worked on the Waxman staff as legislative director then as chief of staff on the Health and Environment Subcommittee. Originally working on environmental legislation, Schiliro gradually oriented himself toward the challenges linked to health insurance reform. His time on the Senate side of the House as part of Senator Tom Daschle's staff—an experience that led Barack Obama to believe Daschle would make a good health secretary—led him to become a health policy specialist who could take on the field's particular challenges. In 2006, when a Democratic majority returned to the House of Representatives, Schiliro rejoined the Waxman staff to take up the post of chief of staff for the House Committee on Oversight and Government Reform in order to initiate within Congress some new thinking around health insurance reform. After working on Barack Obama's presidential campaign, Schiliro was appointed as White House adviser to serve as liaison with Congress on the health reform issue (Brill, 2015: 118). This final example of an institutional migrant endorses the Clinton plan veterans' collective strategy once they had returned to the back offices while the Obama administration was settling in—namely, their intentions to monitor the new reform project in the two branches of American power.

It's important to point out that, apart from the central issue of "returning to business" under the Obama administration, the institutional migrants' career paths illustrate how the vast majority of them had appointments at the Health Care Financing Administration (named CMS since 2001), honing policy skills which the bureaucratic elites in the health sector at that time did not possess. This observation confirms the decline of the SI elites' features (chapter 2) and the emergence of a health coverage policy elite promoting a new programmatic orientation based on the issue of cost containment.

Technocratic Translators Focused on Congress and the Executive Branch

Next we will study the portraits of Clinton plan veterans who fall into the technocratic translator subtype. This subtype corresponds to a career path built over time in Washington within one of the two branches of power (table II.1). It corresponds to individuals who, although they moved into the private sector as administrations alternated, returned once or twice to the back offices of one of the two branches of power.[40] Drawing on their subject-matter expertise in health policy, these individuals took into account political and policy issues in order to shape future reform. Being in charge and aware of what that entailed in relation to the political elites they advised, these individuals generally tended to prioritize negotiation and accommodation with the aim of establishing a consensual programmatic orientation.

In Congress: Career Paths Determined by Health Subcommittees' Leadership

The first examples of technocratic translator career paths are in Congress. Personal and professional attachment to great figures of Congress who fought to reform the health system constitutes a singular characteristic of the Clinton plan veterans' career paths. Congressman Henry Waxman and Senator Ted Kennedy, both great defenders of successive projects to transform the American health insurance system since the end of the 1970s, enabled the development of this type of career path within their professional entourage. First, we will examine the portraits of technocratic translators who built this type of career path within the House of Representatives. Let us initially focus on the cases of three Clinton plan veteran staffers—Andy Schneider, Ruth Katz, and Philip Barnett—who led the work of the health committees on behalf of California Congressman Henry Waxman. According to some of the Clinton plan veterans with an institutional migrant profile, they shared a convivial family spirit as the "Waxman team." According to one of our interviewees, every year at Christmas, all the Waxman team members, past and present, met up in Washington, DC, to cement their relationships: "No, it's just a celebration. I mean [Waxman] is conservative Jewish, so he doesn't celebrate Christmas. So we don't have a Christmas party, we have a holiday party, and we get together every year, and I cook the kosher turkey."[41]

Andy Schneider was a legal adviser on health policy for Waxman for forty years; he retired in 2011, one year after the Obama reform was enacted.[42] After getting a BA from Princeton University and a JD from the law school at the University of Pennsylvania, Schneider started his career as a legal adviser on health at the National Health Law Program in Los Angeles from 1974 to 1979. From 1979 to 1994 Schneider worked as Waxman's health counsel on the Health Subcommittee within the House Committee on Energy and Commerce. A specialist in Medicaid policies and budgetary issues, Schneider first played a role in the bipartisan elaboration of two bills, the Medicare Catastrophic Coverage Act (1988) and the Medicaid Voluntary Contribution and Provider-Specific Tax Amendments (1991), alongside the new health coverage policy elites who advocated to extend the scope of Medicaid (chapter 2).[43] He contributed to the Clinton task force on reform alongside another historical pillar of the Waxman staff, institutional migrant Karen Nelson, to advocate for extending health coverage. After the defeat of the Clinton reform, Schneider acted as an adviser for Medicaid policy on the Oversight and Government Reform Committee (1995–1996).

From 1997 on, Schneider worked in the nonprofit private sector as a health adviser at the pro-reform Democrat think tank the Center on Budget and Policy Priorities. In this role, Schneider collaborated with another Clinton plan veteran, institutional migrant Wendell Primus, with whom Schneider developed a long-term friendship.[44] Moreover, like many other long-term insiders, he held other simultaneous posts, such as that of associate professor at the School of Public Health and Health Services (called the Milken Institute School of Public Health since 2014) at the George Washington University. He then ran his own consulting firm, Medicaid Policy, from 2000 to 2007. In addition to these positions, Schneider remained involved in bipartisan reform forums such as the Alliance for Health Reform and the Kaiser Family Foundation, where he coordinated the work of forums devoted to the future of the Medicaid program. In 2007, with the return of a Democratic majority in Congress, he returned to the House of Representatives as chief health counsel for Medicaid on the Oversight and Government Reform Committee. In 2009 Schneider rejoined the Waxman staff as chief health counsel; he then played a key role, with the support of the "Waxmanian" institutional migrant Tim Westmoreland, in adapting and extending the scope of Medicaid insurance when the second version of the ACA was being drafted (McDonough, 2011: 144).

The example of Ruth Katz, another eminent member of the Waxman staff, brings out another career-path facet of the technocratic translator subtype. With a solid academic background—a BA in history from the University of Pennsylvania, a JD from Emory University in Atlanta, and a master's in public health from Harvard University—Katz practiced for a short time as a lawyer.[45] In the early 1980s, she decided to become a health legislative adviser on the Waxman staff on the Energy and Trade Committee from 1982 to 1995; in this capacity, she contributed to the Pepper Commission's work. In favor of a comprehensive reform of the health insurance system, Katz worked with Andy Schneider and the "Waxmanian" institutional migrants Karen Pollitz, Michael Hash, and Tim Westmoreland on the preparatory work for the Clinton task force's reform project. Following the reform project's defeat, Katz worked as director of public health programs in the nonprofit health sector at the Henry J. Kaiser Family Foundation. Anticipating the moment when the Republicans would hold political power in Washington, DC, she entered academia as an assistant professor and as deputy administrative director of the medical school at the prestigious Yale University (1997–2003). Later, with Andy Schneider, Katz was recruited as a public health professor to the school of public health at the George Washington University. In 2008, when President Obama launched the new reform project, she was recalled by Waxman to take up the post of public health counsel in charge of legislative health issues related to the reform.

Finally, the career path of "Waxmanian" Philip Barnett resembles in many respects that of Ruth Katz. Holding a BA from Princeton University and a JD from Harvard Law School, he worked in the legal field before joining the Waxman team as a young staffer on the Health and Energy Subcommittee in the Energy and Commerce Committee (1989–1992).[46] In 1993, in the midst of conflict surrounding the Clinton reform project, Barnett opted for a career as a committee staffer and took the post of health counsel. He then followed Andy Schneider as chief adviser and staff director of the Oversight and Government Reform Committee from 2003 to 2006. After the Democrats' 2006 victory in Congress, Barnett led the Waxman staff and then prepared the ground for future negotiations regarding the new health reform project.[47]

In the Executive: Career Paths Leading to Top Posts

Looking at other portraits of technocratic translators, we can understand the aspects of these careers that led the long-term insiders of the executive branch to conquer top decision-making posts at HHS and at the Executive Office of the President (EOP) in the White House. These career paths are characterized by one of three kinds of appointment: (1) at the OMB as a program associate director; (2) at HSS as assistant secretary for planning evaluation; or (3) as an administrator or deputy administrator at the Health Care Financing Administration (CMS since 2001) of HHS. This type of appointment is also common among the institutional migrant subtype (table 5.1). Three examples illustrate the career paths of Clinton plan veterans who became technocratic translators in the executive branch of power: Bruce C. Vladeck, Nancy-Ann DeParle, and Carolyn M. Clancy.

Bruce C. Vladeck's portrait highlights the influence of technocratic translators' career paths on health policy formulation change (chapter 2). As a reminder, a technocratic translator's career path is distinct from that of the generic figure of the policy expert not only because of their long spell in charge of policy formulation issues but also because of their involvement in creating new policy instruments. Indeed Vladeck's professional trajectory is built at the crossroads of academia, health administration, and hospital lobbying. A graduate of Harvard University, he entered the University of Michigan to pursue a PhD in political science under the supervision of John Kingdon (Berkowitz, 2002: 168). After a brief stint at the RAND Corporation in New York, Vladeck became an assistant professor in public health and political science at Columbia University from 1974 to 1978 and made contact there with the political scientist Ted Marmor and the institutional migrant Judy Feder.[48] Vladeck wrote a book, *Unloving Care* (1980), criticizing the poor quality of nursing homes in the United States (Brown, 1985). He was then appointed director of the resource development service and health planning at the Department of Health for the State of New Jersey, where he developed a new payment system for medical care (1979–1982).

Vladeck then spent a brief spell as vice president of the Robert Wood Johnson Foundation before spending ten years as president of the United Hospital Fund of New York. He then initiated actions in advocating for AIDS patients and the homeless. Considered a "visionary"[49] by his peers and a supporter of grand health reform, Vladeck contributed to the Clinton task force before President Clinton appointed him in 1993 to the HCFA, an agency within HHS.[50] He then managed to instigate a culture change of this key HHS institution by placing the recipient of care at the heart of the policy formulation process. During President Clinton's second term, along with Chris Jennings, another Clinton veteran, Vladeck played a central role in devising two bipartisan reforms: the American Health Insurance Portability and Accountability Act (1996) and the Balanced Budget Act (1997). In 1997 Vladeck left the department for a post at the National Bipartisan Commission on the Future of Medicare (Oberlander, 2003: 187). In contrast with most Clinton plan veterans, he stepped back from public affairs, initially as professor of public health at Mount Sinai's school of medicine in New York, before entering the private sector as a health consultant, first at Ernst and Young and then at the New York Hospital Association.

Nancy-Ann (Min) DeParle is the most representative portrait of the technocratic translator career path for Clinton plan veterans. She returned during the Obama administration to the Executive Office of the President to take over the decision-making process of the reform. A first-rate university student, after obtaining her history BA in Tennessee, she entered Harvard University's prestigious law school. She was awarded the highly competitive Rhodes scholarship, a student exchange program,[51] and studied at Balliol College at the University of Oxford, where she obtained a second BA in politics, philosophy, and economics (Berkowitz, 2002: 189). DeParle then returned to Harvard Law School to earn her JD in 1983. After working for a federal judge in Nashville from 1987 to 1989, she was recruited by the governor of Tennessee to be commissioner in charge of the Department of Health for two years; in this role she took part in setting up TENN care, a program aiming to extend health insurance to the noninsured. She then returned to practicing law before settling in Washington, DC. She initially refused to join the Clinton-Gore transition team owing to her attachment to her profession as a lawyer. In the midst of the debate on the health insurance reform project, in February 1993 she accepted the post of associate program director for health issues at the OMB at the White House; in the aftermath she became heavily involved in the Clinton task force's work as part of a "small group of eight people who work ten hours a day alongside Ira Magaziner on the reform project."[52] DeParle then collaborated with institutional migrants Chris Jennings and Alice Rivlin, and the technocratic translator Bruce Vladeck, whom she would succeed as HCFA administrator, to put in place the policy of the Balanced Budget Act (1997–2000).

Once the Republicans returned to power, DeParle went to the private sector, where she held numerous posts from 2000 to 2008. DeParle also worked as an associate researcher at Harvard's Institute of Politics at the John F. Kennedy School of Government. In 2009 President Obama appointed her special adviser for health reform in the White House, following a request from Rahm Emmanuel, Obama's chief of staff.[53] As soon as she took up the post, DeParle drafted a briefing memo for the White House outlining the main programmatic orientations of the future health coverage reform.[54] Drawing on her experience in the Clinton defeat, she quickly made her presence felt among President Obama's advisers as the "health czar,"[55] playing a key role in navigating the political obstacles faced by the reform project. "Acknowledged as the most brilliant thinker among her generation in health policy circles,"[56] and known as a phenomenal negotiator, DeParle played a determining role with newcomers Peter Orszag and Jeanne Lambrew (see chapter 5), and with the support of previously mentioned Clinton plan veterans Mike Hash and Phil Schiliro, in smoothing the way for the decision-making regarding the ACA within the executive branch of power. The experience of the Clinton plan failure, which she shared with some of these close colleagues, would lead her to defend, whatever the cost, the quest for the most consensual possible reform and the least costly, in federal budget terms (chapter 9).

Contrary to policy entrepreneurs who spent a short time in charge while the content of new reform was being outlined, the long-term insiders who were technocratic translators took action over the long term at the apex of executive power. Like the institutional migrants, these Clinton plan veterans often held the same strategic posts, following in each other's footsteps either within prestigious congressional committees or at HHA (ASPE, HCFA), or even at the White House (OMB). These insiders spent periods of time under Republican majority in the private sector but tended on the whole to opt for the nonprofit private sector. Several of them opted for the status of assistant professor in public health schools at the George Washington University and Georgetown University. The long-term insiders participated collectively in the preparatory work for reform carried out in think tanks such as the Center on Budget and Policy Priorities and the Alliance for Health Reform (chapter 8). Clearly the technocratic translator subtype took on an original hybrid form in the case of Sherry Glied.[57] Indeed Glied, known for her excellent book *Chronic Condition: Why Health Reform Fails* (1997), which details the Clinton defeat based on her personal experience in the administration, often moved backward and forward from academic posts (in the school of public health at Columbia University and as dean of the Wagner School of Public Service at New York University) to the executive branch, where she was appointed in 2010 to be ASPE at HHS.

Policy Bureaucrats Focused on Policy Oversight

The policy bureaucrat subtype calls to mind the senior civil servants who developed long-term career paths in the organizations that control health policy at HHS and in Congress. Owing to their status, policy bureaucrats did not gravitate toward the private sector until the end of their careers. Often committed to their regulatory responsibilities (budgetary and actuarial) or sector specialty (law), their professional trajectories tend to be consolidated in those institutions examining the viability of policies, which leads them to make pronouncements regarding the financial sustainability of health insurance reform projects. In the executive branch of power, this type includes the career bureaucrats who make the decision to accede—via a political appointment—to positions of power that confer the protected status of senior executive service (SES). In Congress, this designation applies to those individuals who have managed to develop long-term career paths by accessing the post of senior administrative officer in legal and financial bodies regulating laws. The number of long-term insiders conforming to this subtype is relatively high owing to their initial selection of positions of power that were captured in the context of the OPERA study.[58] The prerequisite of the programmatic elite framework resides in the large selection of posts, and consequently of individuals, subsequently needing to be gradually reduced by harnessing criteria linked to these insiders' presumed influence on formulating the programmatic orientation toward and their involvement in the decision-making process. From this perspective, we will see that the individuals whose portraits fit into the career path of policy bureaucrat, while being "in charge," play a less decisive reforming role than the institutional migrants or the technocratic translators.

Senior Bureaucrats Controlling Health Spending

Most policy bureaucrats can be found in institutions controlling or studying health policies. Richard (Rick) S. Foster is an emblematic case. For nearly forty years, he was a senior bureaucrat at the Office of the Actuary, the agency within HHS that analyzes the financial impact and risks of social insurance plans.[59] With a degree in applied mathematics from the University of Maryland, in the 1980s he started his administrative career as an actuary. Heavily involved in the actuarial professional world (Society of Actuaries, American Academy of Actuaries), as well as in administration (Senior Executive Association), this senior bureaucrat enjoyed a high-flying career at the Office of the Actuary, holding posts as deputy head (from 1982 to 1995) and then head (from 1995 to 2012). Under his leadership, more than one hundred people worked in this agency to produce reports for the administration and Congress; this experience reinforced Foster's independent judgment regarding public policies. One of our interviewees, the director of the CBO during the Clinton presidency, explained, "Rick Foster, the chief of actuary at CMS, is very independent, but it is because of his position."[60] This independence turned Foster into an "exceptional" senior bureaucrat, who in 2004 did not hesitate to question the validity of the financial assessment of the Medicare program proposed by the Republican institutional migrant Tom Scully (see below), health adviser to George W. Bush (Joyce, 2011: 106–107). Despite being a Democrat, when the ACA was being drafted, Foster was one of the rare non-Republicans to point out the probable increase in public spending that the reform risked incurring (McDonough, 2011: 246–247). Beyond these responsibilities, his professional activism led Foster to publish several academic articles (e.g., in *Health Care Financing Review*) and give "more than two hundred presentations on Medicare and Social Security issues."[61]

In a similar vein are the career paths of the policy bureaucrats pursuing careers at the Office of the General Counsel at HHS, for example, such as June Gibbs Brown, Lewis Morris, Andrew Hyman, and David Cade. Their portraits allow us to consider this type of career path from another angle. These policy bureaucrats generally hold a JD from a law school. If they sustain long careers and attain SES status,[62] they essentially act in a legal regulatory capacity for HHS's public action programs. Some of these policy bureaucrats, such as June Gibbs Brown, who arrived from the Department of Defense, and Lewis Morris, focused their careers on fighting fraud in the Medicare and Medicaid programs. Some of them, however, such as David Cade and Andrew Hyman, made a similar decision as that of the majority of Clinton plan veterans—that is, to firmly commit to extending health insurance coverage by contributing to the Clinton task force's work. David Cade served in the Office of General Counsel at HHS and advocated for a new more integrated system of health care. He worked there until 1998, when he became director of programs for childhood and family, and headed the financial section of HHS. He then returned to take up the post of deputy director at the Office of General Counsel from 1999 to 2009. Andrew Hyman started his career as a special assistant at the Office of General Counsel in the early 1990s during the Clinton administration. He remained there during the George W. Bush administration. Having become aware in practical terms of "the failure" of the health insurance system, Hyman joined the Robert Wood Johnson Foundation in 2006 to contribute to the new bipartisan reform project to extend health insurance.[63]

Other policy bureaucrats' career paths, like those of Barry Clendenin and Thomas G. Morford, unfurled in the financial administration of HHS. Equipped with a PhD in history from the University of North Carolina at Chapel Hill, Barry Clendenin started his career at the OMB at the White House, where he was responsible for the financial evaluation of health programs. Between 1993 and 1994, during the first Clinton administration, he worked at HHS as head of financial administration; he then worked with Clinton plan veterans DeParle and Jennings. In 1995 Clendenin joined the OMB and became program associate director, a post he would occupy until 2008. Then he opted for academia and became an associate professor at the school of public policy at George Mason University in Arlington, Virginia. Thomas Morford's path exemplifies this type of long administrative career path dominated by a spell in the financial-regulation sector. After Morford arrived in 1971 at the Department of Health, Education, and Workforce to work in financial administration, he held several posts there for more than thirty years. In 2001, when the Republicans arrived in power, Morford became a professor of public health in the Urban Health Institute at Johns Hopkins University; he stayed until 2010 when, to back the Obama reform, he joined HHS.

Tax Experts' Rise in Power in Congress

We can also find examples of career paths conforming to the policy bureaucrat type in Congress. These individuals are committee staffers who occupy posts as specialist clerks or counsels. Often holding a status similar to that of senior administrative officers, these policy bureaucrats sometimes become involved in the policy formulation process. The most representative portrait of this type is without a doubt that of Janice A. May. Holding a JD from the University of Georgia in Athens, in 1975 May began her career as a chief tax counsel on the staff of the Ways and Means Committee in the House of Representatives. She then furthered her specialist training by obtaining a master's in taxation law from Georgetown University. In 1981 May became director of staff of the chief tax counsels for the Democrats on this committee. She would hold this post for nearly thirty-six years. Although she worked within the legislative branch, May said, "Mine was a public service career," and under the minority Democratic periods, "I directed a staff of twenty-six people to analyze and prepare the taxation policy that applies to Social Security and Medicare."[64] She refused to capitalize on her knowledge and skills in the private sector, despite very lucrative offers, because she "always believed in the state [government, in the American sense], [and she] thinks that the government can help the people." According to POLITICO, a news site covering politics and policy, her long career as a staffer beyond the reins of power in Congress makes her "a fixture in all discussion of taxes and health care."[65] Early in the Clinton administration, May became aware of the need for comprehensive reform of the health insurance system's taxation and saw in extending health insurance a means to control the rise in costs. This was the reason she became involved in developing an argument in favor of the ACA.

Other instances of long-term insiders from Congress include Maria Curpill, Adrienne Hallet, Peter H. Rutledge, and Erik Fatemi, who established careers on the health subcommittees of Congress. These career paths also correspond to the policy bureaucrat type. The existence of insiders' career paths with policy bureaucrat features therefore confirms the presence of individuals who, in their professional trajectories, display an attachment to government's capacity to regulate policy while controlling public spending—which does pose a severe challenge. These career paths, however, are distinct from the Clinton plan veterans, including both the institutional migrant and the technocratic translator types, owing to their lesser commitment to defining new reforms.

To conclude the study of different types of career paths of long-term insiders, it is appropriate to highlight the sociological characteristics of these health coverage policy elites, who over time would become so-called Clinton plan veterans (table 5.1). Apart from their long-term careers, these insiders share a career path based in Washington, DC. This is often due to their initial training in one of the region's schools of public health or because they become a professor with one of these universities. Some of these insiders, especially those close to Waxman, committed themselves in the 1980s to the strategy of extending Medicaid (see chapter 2). They then went on to join the new Medicare specialists and contribute to the prospective work of the Pepper Commission (in Congress) on the future health insurance system. Others rallied within the executive branch on the Clinton task force to prepare that administration's reform plan (chapter 7). Moreover, the Democratic long-term insiders in large part opted for professions in nonprofit organizations after they temporarily left public life. We can therefore distinguish their mobility outside of government affairs from that of Republican insiders who favor the lucrative private sector (chapter 5). These Clinton plan veterans prolonged their reform activism in Washington, DC, think tanks (the Bipartisan Policy Center, the Center on Budget and Policy Priorities) and in the Alliance for Health Reform's communications forums, pooling their shared learning from the failed health reform with Democratic newcomers (chapter 8).

The mobility of these insiders shows how they targeted certain key positions in the policy formulation process—positions in which they succeed each other during a change of political majority. Far from being anodyne, these shared career-path choices display their wish to influence the formulation of policies within both branches of power (chapter 5, table 5.1). In Congress, it is on the health subcommittees of prestigious committees such as Ways and Means in the House of Representatives, and on the Committee on Health, Education, Labor, and

Pensions on the Senate side, where the influence of Democratic leaders Henry Waxman and Ted Kennedy was strong. Similarly, the Congressional Budget Office played an important role in the learning process regarding the financial constraints. In the executive branch, an "iron triangle" of positions of power seems to have emerged during the studied period. Initially, it included the posts of assistant secretary for planning and evaluation at HHS, where the programmatic orientation of policies was orchestrated, and the role of director of the Health Care Financing Administration (HCFA, later CMS), where the budgetary viability of policies was discussed. The third pillar was program associate director at the OMB, a position in charge of following up health policy budgets at the White House. This role was often held by an individual known as the health policy czar (chapter 1).

Our in-depth sociographic study of the portraits of the Clinton plan veterans highlights the salient sociological features of the career paths of Democratic health coverage policy elites. Indeed, Gail Wilensky, a Republican health policy figure and former director of the HCFA during the George H. W. Bush administration, described the change in these terms: "Democrats historically have been much more interested in health care policy. . . . [In] the Clinton administration, you had a lot of centers of expertise in the department and various individuals in the White House who were knowledgeable and recognized in various aspects of health care policy and financing. That tends to be less true for the Republican administration; the implication for me when I was there was that there were not many people in other parts of HHS, the White House, or OMB, who had a very well-developed background in health care financing or policy."[66] Moreover, when these elites left the sphere of government during the Republican presidency of George W. Bush, they remained strongly connected to each other and became involved collectively in bipartisan reform forums, such as the Alliance for Health Reform and the Center on Budget and Policy Priorities. It is for these reasons that Clinton plan veterans—namely, those whose career paths fit the institutional migrant type, although some also fit the technocratic translator type—would return in force to both branches of power when President Obama launched the next reform project.

CHAPTER 5

From Late Clintonism to Obama

Shared Career Paths?

T HE STUDY of long-term health insiders' portraits during the period following the defeat of the Clinton plan (the Health Security Act was withdrawn from Congress on September 26, 1994) and up to Obama's accession to the presidency (in 2008) further confirms the transformation of unelected governmental elites' social backgrounds and career paths. After having studied the portraits of the Democratic long-term insiders, it behooves us to concentrate on the health coverage policy elites who followed them in those same positions of policy-making after the Clinton plan failure. By taking this new period into account, we can compare the portraits of Democratic long-term insiders, referred to here as "newcomers" in the back offices of government under the late Clinton era, with those of the Clinton plan veterans. Studying them over time also enables us to look at the newcomers' social backgrounds and career paths, those that continued once the Democrats returned to power, first in Congress (in 2007's 110th legislature) and then in the presidency (in 2008). This will allow for an empirical discussion of the issue of continuity and discontinuity in these career paths, while highlighting their potential correlations to the further development of health insurance reform. This historical analysis also lets us make comparisons with Republican insiders who formulated health policy during President George W. Bush's two terms (2000–2008) and in Congress (1997–2007).[1]

In the wake of research carried out by Martha Derthick (1979), Larry Brown (1983b, 1985), and more recently Ulrike Lepont (2014), we know how the policy elites who advocated for government's growing role in managing the health insurance system were mainly of a Democratic persuasion. Our interviews confirmed that "many of the Democrats may know or think they know more particular details about how to send a payment policy or how to decide what treatments should be covered or not, and that goes back to their underlying philosophy, which is that government can make better decisions. Republicans don't need to know exactly some of those details, because they believe their job is to set the policy and set the acceptable parameters, and then let the people in the health care field do their job."[2] This particular phenomenon can be explained by historical factors which, following the New Deal and until the Great Society project, strongly linked SI elites and their heirs to Democratic administrations (Roosevelt, Truman, and Johnson). Nevertheless, in the period we investigated, we observed some instances of Republican long-term insiders who, after fiercely opposing the Clinton plan in Congress, then contributed to devising George W. Bush's health policy[126] while at the same time, at least for some of them, being involved in bipartisan work on the future health coverage reform project.[3] We will apply the subtypes of career paths (institutional migrant, technocratic translator, and policy bureaucrat) defined for Clinton plan veterans to the cases of Republican insiders and Democratic newcomers.

Republican Long-Term Insiders: Superficial Resemblance in Career Paths?

The population of Washington's health coverage policy elites studied over time (1988–2010) allows us to explore a number of cases of prominent Republican individuals with long-term insiders' characteristics (more than 50 cases in a sample of 151). Some of them established unusually long career paths within both branches of power. Generally, these sector-based career paths began during President George H. W. Bush's administration and continued during both of President George W. Bush's terms. Moreover, a small number of them, who often acted in the name of sector-based interest groups in Congress, launched a fierce opposition to the reform project driven by the future Democratic Clinton plan veterans (chapter 7). Paradoxically, while having established their professional legitimacy by torpedoing the Clinton plan, from the year 2000 on, some of the Republican long-term insiders would decide to envisage a new bipartisan health coverage reform project. The study of their social backgrounds and career paths partly explains this major strategic realignment.

Institutional Migrants: Inevitable Mobility to the Lucrative Private Sector?

Within the population of long-term insiders, more than a dozen examples illustrate the subtype of the Republican institutional migrant's career path.[4] These elites formed a small nucleus with strong health governance expertise acquired by moving between the executive and Congress following George H. W. Bush's presidency. The Republicans possessed advanced qualifications, which they had obtained from prestigious universities just as their Democratic counterparts had. Republicans, however, preferred to attend law schools (for a JD), to the detriment of a more specialized policy training. From the outset, the Republicans did not benefit from the same resources and political networks as the Democrats did in order to be recruited for a spell within the many university health departments in the Washington, DC, area. More inclined to defend the interest groups (private hospitals, insurance companies) where they preferred spending time during political changes, the Republicans showed themselves to be committed to market forces regulating the health insurance system. Having acted as veto players at the time of the Clinton project, these insiders, once they had returned to power during the George W. Bush administration, would try to angle health coverage policy toward the individual-mandate model.

The portrait of Joseph (Joe) R. Antos illustrates the fairly marginal career path of a Republican long-term insider that corresponds to the institutional migrant subtype—someone who moves to the nonprofit private sector (which includes think tanks). With a BA in mathematics from Cornell University and an MA and PhD in economics from Rochester University, Antos joined the Office of Research and Evaluation—part of the Bureau of Labor Statistics within the US Department of Labor[5]—as a senior economist. In 1983 under the Reagan administration, Antos held the post of program associate director at the OMB before being appointed chief of staff for the Council of Economic Advisers (CEA) at the White House. Between 1987 and 1995, he steered his career toward HSS by successively holding the posts of administrator of the HCFA and assistant director of the Office of the Actuary. In this role, Antos contributed to the work of the Clinton task force.[6] But with the return under the 104th Congress (1995–1997) to a Republican majority, he crossed over to the congressional side and joined the CBO (1995–2001) as assistant director in charge of health insurance policy.

Antos acknowledged that after twenty-five years of service in administration, and "a salary that no longer increases, and the routine work of evaluating Medicare and Medicaid expenses at the CBO,"[7] he decided to take a position as an associate professor at the school of public health at the University of North Carolina, which he held from 2001 to 2003. He then went on to secure a research chair in public health issues at the American Enterprise Institute (AEI), a conservative think tank. During this period, Antos established himself among Republicans as one of the important thinkers regarding health coverage policy. Boosted by this legitimacy—and certainly convinced before the end of George W. Bush's presidency that the health insurance system needed to be reformed—Antos contributed to the work of the Health Policy Consensus Group in order to outline a bipartisan reform project (Lepont, 2014). He regularly contributed to the communications work of the Clinton plan veterans in the bipartisan Alliance for Health Reform forum (chapter 8).

David Abernethy's portrait illustrates one difference from the Clinton plan veterans in terms of career path circulation toward private-sector interest groups during changes in political power. With a history BA and public health MA from Yale University, Abernethy started out in 1978 as a young staffer at the Health and Environment Subcommittee in the House of Representatives. During this period, he cowrote a series of works on the issue of cost containment in hospital settings.[8] In 1981 he moved to the State of New York's Health Department as an assistant commissioner for policy planning, where he stayed for six years. In 1987, just before the Democrats returned to power, he rejoined the House of Representatives as chief of staff on the Health Subcommittee of the Ways and Means Committee.[9] During the following decade, he established himself with his colleague Chip Kahn (see below) as one of the leaders of the young Republican guard who specialized in health policy and, while acting on behalf of sector-specific lobby groups, torpedoed the Clinton plan when it was brought before Congress (Johnson & Broder, 1996: 399–400). Nevertheless, unlike several of his colleagues, owing to his experience in hospital administration, Abernethy was not an inveterate partisan of the free market.[10] For this reason, for a time he was asked to support the Canadian single-payer model so dear to the Democrats.[11] Abernethy realized that health policy planning was the only way to stem the endemic costs of the American health insurance system. In spite of this, in 1996 he moved to the private sector as vice president of the Health Insurance Plan (HIP) insurance group, where he was responsible for the group's relationships with government and the states. Yet, although he was working for this lobby, he remained open to negotiating with the Democrats and became involved with the Alliance for Health Reform's bipartisan communications strategy for a new project to extend health insurance (chapter 8).

The portrait of institutional migrant Charles "Chip" Kahn III confirms the Republican long-term insiders' affinity for partisan policy and for defending the health sector's interest groups.[12] Born in New Orleans, Kahn had a politically active mother. When he was sixteen, he took part in his first electoral campaign with Republican Newt Gingrich, who went on to be a congressman and later Speaker of the House. During his long career, Kahn would consider Gingrich as the "big brother I never had."[13] When Kahn attended Johns Hopkins University in Baltimore to study history and political science, he continued to take notes for his political mentor and to actively work on Gingrich's electoral campaigns. At the end of the 1970s, realizing that he needed to specialize in public policy in order to remain connected to the political world, Kahn decided to pursue a three-year public health master's degree at Tulane University in New Orleans. He developed a real interest for this subject and became an agency director at the Association of University Programs in Health Administration (AUPHA) in Washington, DC. In 1983, he became Senator Dan Quayle's health adviser. And a year later, he became Senator David Durenberger's senior health adviser on the Finance Committee's Health Subcommittee, where he was known as a formidable health policy finance expert. Hoping to pave the way toward a committee-staffer career in Congress, Kahn moved to the House of Representatives and joined the Health Subcommittee of the Ways and Means Committee, initially holding the post of health legal adviser. In 1993, in the midst of the embattled Clinton plan, Congressman Willis D. Gradison—who had just become president of the powerful private insurance lobby the Health Insurance Association of America (HIAA)—recruited Kahn with the aim of sabotaging the reform project (Johnson & Broder, 1996: 199). To this end, Kahn devised a winning communications strategy centered on the "Harry and Louise" ad campaign that denounced the arrival of a socialist health insurance system (McDonough, 2011: 52; Brill, 2015: 87).

Basking in the glow of this victorious strategy and fortified by the Republicans winning a majority in the 104th legislature (1995), Chip Kahn inched closer to his mentor, Newt Gingrich, who was then Speaker of the House of Representatives, with a post as staff director on the Health Subcommittee in the Ways and Means Committee. Kahn then became actively involved in drafting two important bills during the second Clinton term: the Balanced Budget Act (1997) and the Health Insurance Portability and Accountability Act (1996). In early 1998, Kahn decided to move into the private sector, first as executive vice president of the private insurance HIAA lobby, and later in 2001 as president of the influential private-hospital lobby, the Federation of American Hospitals

(FAH). In 2005 Kahn was appointed for a year as commissioner in charge of the American Health Information Community program by the Republican secretary of health, M. Leavitt, before taking up once again his lobbyist role. In 2008 Kahn, a cautious backer of the bipartisan approach who always claimed to defend the virtues of the market and free enterprise, showed his support for the future reform because "all the lobbies sensed that something was going to happen, and so it was necessary to be part of the process in order to alter it from the inside."[14]

The study of Thomas A. Scully's portrait illustrates from another angle how a Republican institutional migrant moved between both powers and sector-specific interest groups. As soon as he finished his BA at the University of Virginia, Scully went to Washington, DC, to work for Senator Slade Gorton as his personal staffer (1981–1985).[15] After this first experience as a staffer, Scully studied law, obtained his JD, and practiced as a lawyer for a few years in a legal office. In 1988 Scully campaigned for the Bush-Quayle presidential and vice-presidential ticket before being recruited as program associate director (PAD) at OMB in charge of human-resources policies, veterans, and work and labor issues. He was one of the rare political appointees by President George H. W. Bush who contributed to the work of the Pepper Commission in Congress (1990) (Feder, 2007: 4). At the end of the George H. W. Bush administration, Scully was simultaneously the president's adviser and PAD at the OMB. During the transition to the Clinton administration, he befriended the future Clinton plan veteran, Democrat Nancy-Ann DeParle and worked with the Clinton task force. In 1993 Scully returned to the private sector, first to a prominent legal firm in Washington and then as director of the lobby for American private hospitals (the Federation of American Hospitals [FAH]) (Johnson & Broder, 1996: 588). In 2001, during George W. Bush's administration, Scully was appointed to HHS as director of the Centers for Medicare and Medicaid Services (formerly HCFA) to rationalize the health programs' costs (Blumenthal & Morone, 2009: 398).

Between 2003 and 2004 conflict pitted the chief of actuaries in Congress against policy bureaucrat Richard Forster (chapter 4), who reproached Scully for having transmitted erroneous information to Congress about the Medicare program's budget costs (Joyce, 2011: 104–107). Following this scandal, Scully left as head of health administration to resume his private part-time activities in a legal firm lobbying for the health sector. According to one Democratic Clinton plan veteran: "Scully is a back-and-forth player. As far as I know, he has gone back and forth between OMB, being a lobbyist, and HHS," just like Chip Kahn, who "was the chief Republican person in the House on health as a staff person, and then left and became first a lobbyist for the for-profit hospitals, and then became a lobbyist for the insurance industry—a lobbyist for the insurance industry, and he is still a lobbyist."[16]

The study of Republican long-term insiders' portraits which resemble the institutional migrant subtype career path confirms that mobility within the back offices of both branches of power over time constitutes a characteristic they shared with the Democratic Clinton plan veterans. This homology in Democrats' and Republicans' social backgrounds and career paths constitutes a sociological factor that made it easier during the 2000s to put in place a bipartisan reform strategy. Indeed, when the programmatic orientations were being reformulated, it was these Republican insiders who would launch this initiative with their Democratic peers (chapter 8). On the other hand, the appeal that work in the lucrative private sector held for them once they left the public sector, especially work for sector-based interest groups, constituted a real difference from the Democratic insiders.

Technocratic Translators: For a Bipartisan Approach to Health Reform?

The sample of Republican long-term insiders included approximately twenty individuals whose career paths qualify as the technocratic translator subtype.[17] In order to provide as complete an overview as possible, we will analyze four portraits in the following order: an example of a pathway focused on the executive power (Gail Wilensky); a second route focused on the Senate (Mark Hayes); a third path focused on the House

of Representatives (Howard Cohen); and lastly, an example that strad-
dles both Houses (Chuck Clapton).

Gail Wilensky is an example of a technocratic translator's career
path closely resembling the same type among Clinton plan veterans.
After obtaining her PhD in economics from the University of Michigan,
Wilensky launched her career path as executive director and adviser to
the governor of the state of Maryland on budget and taxation issues
(1968–1971).[18] Next she concentrated on researching issues around the
cost of health care, initially at the Urban Institute and later on as a visiting assistant professor at the University of Michigan. In 1975 Wilensky
joined HEW where for seven years she codirected a research program
on citizens' behavior and the health care system for the National Center
for Health Services Research. In 1983 she left the Reagan administration,
whose approach to programmatic orientation, social care, and the welfare system she did not espouse. She then contributed to developing the
Center for Health Affairs and its eponymous journal at the Project
HOPE foundation (Health Opportunities for People Everywhere) (Lepont, 2014: 231–233). Buoyed by her health policies[19] research path,
Wilensky joined HHS in 1989 as HCFA administrator to oversee the financing and management of the Medicare and Medicaid programs.

Later she worked at the White House as President George H. W. Bush's
deputy assistant and led the team responsible for developing a comprehensive health reform program (Hacker, 1997: 71; Blumenthal & Morone,
2009: 342). At the start of the Clinton administration, Wilensky became
president of the Physician Payment Review Commission set up by Congress to evaluate rising health costs and the outcomes of the Medicare
and Medicaid programs, an activity that she continued with a new commission of experts (the Medicare Advisory Commission, or MEDPAC)
until the Republicans regained power. During the George W. Bush administration, Wilensky joined a task force that strove to improve the
health system for veterans, and she then moved to the Defense Department to implement this policy (2001–2003). While still a senior fellow
working on the HOPE project, she produced several articles, organized
conferences, and generated controversy with her Democratic colleagues

on the issue of the content of the future reform of the health care system. And so confident in her independent judgment of these policies, she was one of the rare Republican experts to defend until the bitter end a bipartisan approach to the Affordable Care Act, which garnered sharp criticism from her own supporters (Lepont, 2014).

The portrait of Republican Mark Hayes shows how the career path of a technocratic translator evolved within the Senate. After obtaining his bachelor of science with a specialty in pharmacology from the University of Kansas City–Missouri, he was recruited as a personal staffer from 1989 to 1999 by the Republican senator for Missouri, Christopher S. Kit Bond.[20] In 1996 Hayes left the Senate to become a lobbyist for the Hoffman-LaRoche pharmaceutical company. From 1996 to 2000 he worked with Senator J. Danforth to lead a nonprofit organization that aimed to regenerate Missouri's St. Louis area. In 2001 Hayes returned to the Senate to take up the post of health policy adviser, initially for Senator Olympia Snowe and then for the chairman of the Finance Committee, Senator Charles Grassley. While pursuing his committee-staffer career, and in order to secure the post of chief health counsel, Hayes obtained a juris doctor from the American University's law school in Washington, DC. During this long collaboration with Senator Grassley during the George W. Bush administration, Hayes played a key role with Democratic health coverage policy newcomers Cybele Bjorklund and Liz Fowler (see below) in promoting a bipartisan approach to the new policy for the Medicare Prescription Drug, Improvement, and Modernization Act (MMA, 2003). This instance of collaboration between Democratic and Republican career staffers served as Hayes's political apprenticeship as he nurtured interpersonal ties that crossed the partisan divide. As an extension of this bipartisan collaboration, Hayes emerged as a leader among the health staffers who were involved with the Republican "Gang of Six" senators (McDonough, 2011: 68) and who between 2006 and 2010 would develop a bipartisan approach to the new health coverage reform project with both the Clinton plan veterans and the Democratic newcomers (Beaussier, 2012). When the Obama reform was passed, Hayes left Congress to work as a lawyer for the Greenberg Traurig firm.

Overlapping somewhat with that of Mark Hayes, the technocratic translator career path of Howard Cohen centered on the House of Representatives. With a BA from the University of Illinois, a PhD in psychology from the University of Massachusetts, and a JD from the George Washington University, Cohen first worked for a life insurance company.[21] In 1989 he launched his health staffer career on the House of Representatives' Health Subcommittee in the Environment, Economy, and Trade Committee. He soon established himself as health counsel and then as chief health counsel. When the Republicans were in the minority and then the majority, Cohen was part of the Republican team of staffers that fiercely opposed the Clinton plan when it was passing through Congress. In this context, with his colleague Gail Wilensky, he cowrote an article for Republican think tank the Heritage Foundation criticizing the health policy advocated by the Clinton administration.[22]. In 1999 Cohen left Congress to take up a career as a lobbyist for the Greenberg Traurig legal firm (1999–2001) and then as director of his own company, HC Associates Inc. (2001–2010). While merging his activities as an advocate for pharmaceutical, insurance, and private health clinics groups' interests, he worked with David Abernethy on the bipartisan efforts of the Alliance for Health Reform. In 2011, disappointed with the direction taken by the Obama reform, Cohen returned to the House of Representatives as head of the legal health advisers at the Energy and Trade Committee to help the Republican majority obstruct the process of implementing the Affordable Care Act.

Finally, the portrait of Charles "Chuck" Clapton illustrates the social background and career path of a technocratic translator who moved across the two houses of Congress.[23] With a history BA from Boston University, Clapton worked as a paralegal in a Massachusetts law firm from 1990 to 1992. Then, to launch his career as a congressional staffer, in 1995 Clapton completed his legal training with a juris doctor from Columbus School of Law at the Catholic University of America. He then pursued a career as a committee staffer and held a post as a legislative aide to Senator Arlen Specter (1995–1996) before moving to the House of Representatives. There, Clapton held posts as health legal adviser, senior adviser to Congressman Harris Fawell and then as counsel and chief health counsel for the Energy and Trade Committee. At the start of George W. Bush's administration, Clapton became involved in the MMA (2003), which made "the system more competitive by structuring it according to the mechanisms of the market in order to deliver quality health care while at the same time managing cost efficiency."[24] Acknowledged as one of the best Republican health staffers in Congress and extremely well connected to his Democratic colleagues, he was recruited as a health policy adviser by Dennis Hastert, who at that time was the Republican Speaker of the House of Representatives (2006–2007). Clapton went on to follow Hastert when he returned to the Ways and Means Committee in the wake of the Democrats' majority win in the elections to the 110th Congress (2007–2008). When President Obama took office and a new health coverage reform project emerged, Clapton returned to the Senate to apply his detailed knowledge of the legal health process in both Houses for the benefit of Republican Senator Mike Enzi, who was close to Democrat Ted Kennedy and to members of the "Gang of Six" senators who backed the bipartisan approach to reform. When the Republican members of Congress changed tack, however, Clapton found himself opposing the ACA, even taking part in preparing an appeal for the Supreme Court against the draft bill.

The examples studied in this section clearly show that the career paths of Republican technocratic translators resemble that of their Democrat peers, the Clinton plan veterans. Notably, Republican technocratic translators' penchant to gravitate toward interest groups was not systematic, in contrast with Republican institutional migrants. Technocratic translators longing for professional appointments to think tanks was genuine, however. Moreover, their ability to specialize in policy issues arose in a fairly similar way as it had for the Clinton plan veterans. This in part explains their decision to take a bipartisan approach to reform with the "Gang of Six" at the end of George W. Bush's presidency. This was clearly the case for Mark Hayes and his work with Senators Snowe and Grassley, and Chuck Clapton's work with Senator Enzi.

Policy Bureaucrats Moving Prematurely
to Interest Groups

Although Republican policy bureaucrats' portraits resembled those of the Clinton plan veterans of the same type, they differed in terms of how their career paths ended. It seems that after twenty years spent in policy formulation, Republicans chose earlier and more systematically to move into the private sector. Having identified within the population of health coverage policy elites thirty-odd examples that illustrate this type, we will next outline the most significant cases.[25]

Roland "Guy" King's portrait constitutes an exemplary career path as a Republican senior bureaucrat at the head of the financial administration of HHS. In 2009 King was described in the Washington press as "a former chief actuary for Medicare and Medicaid, with almost forty years of experience preparing cost estimates for federal health care programs."[26] Indeed, for sixteen years King would hold the post of chief of actuaries at the HCFA; in some ways, he was the counterpart of Democrat Rick Forster (see chapter 4). Having trained at the US Naval Academy, where he obtained his BA in mathematics and engineering sciences, King then took part in active duty in the Navy; he then obtained his master's in mathematics from the University of Virginia in 1972. The director of administration for the actuaries for Medicare and Social Security recruited King when he was only twenty-two years old, prompting him to ask himself: "What is an actuary?"[27] After six years with this agency, King mastered all the codes of this profession, whose cardinal values include probity and impartiality. King acceded to the post of chief of actuaries at the HCFA; in this role that ended in 1994, he came into conflict with the CBO regarding the issue of overestimating the costs of the medical legislation known as the Medicare Catastrophic Coverage Act (1988). Afterward, King worked on the Clinton task force as a public finance specialist. He then came into conflict with the Democratic advisers to the White House regarding his underestimate of the costs of this reform project. After this long period in charge, King left health administration to set up his own private consulting firm (King Associates). Although he was on the periphery of government, King remained very involved with debates during the 2000s concerning the central issue of how to finance the future health care system and the need to control costs. With this in mind, he wrote numerous articles, including some that were published by the Republican AEI think tank in collaboration with Joe Antos, the Republican institutional migrant.

Ann Agnew's portrait reflects a different facet of the Republican policy bureaucrat's career path.[28] With a BA and an MA in political science from the Virginia Polytechnic Institute and State University, Agnew started doctoral research in international relations at the University of South Carolina (ABD, or all but dissertation)[29] before returning to Washington, DC, to work for the Republican Party's national committee from 1977 to 1981. After her initial experience in the defense policy sector at the Pentagon during George H. W. Bush's presidency, Agnew followed her department director, Connie Horner, when the latter was appointed assistant director at HHS. Agnew was then appointed to Horner's office (1991–1992). Following Bill Clinton's victory, she joined the health administration for the State of Wisconsin, where she headed the insurance sector (1993–2000). When President G. W. Bush first took office, as one of the health policy experts with a Republican leaning, Agnew was given the opportunity to "choose her job in the new federal government," which she proceeded to do by selecting the post of executive secretary at HHS. In explaining her choice, she allows us to consider the practical role of the policy bureaucrat: "I don't enjoy playing a public role. I like to be behind the scenes in public policy, and the executive secretary, when it is structured properly, it's a staff of about thirty-seven people, and it is the central—think of it as the switching station for all the engines and trains. Nothing goes to the secretary that has not gone through that office, so [that includes] any decision memorandum, any policy papers, and most importantly, any regulations."[30] Agnew would hold this gatekeeper post monitoring all HHS programs during both George W. Bush terms (2000–2008). When the Democrats returned to power, Agnew moved to the private sector to work for McConnell International as a consultant for partnerships between private companies and the federal government. It is interesting to note that recently Agnew was the one and only Republican long-term insider from George W.

Bush's administration who returned to work on this issue while President Trump was in office, during which time she held the post of executive secretary to HHS starting on March 27, 2017.[31]

During one of our interviews, a Democratic Clinton plan veteran explained their differences from the Republicans: "Republican staff don't stay very long. They stay and then they work there, they get a reputation, they get contacts, a network, and then they go downtown and make a lot of money. And then sometimes they will come back [to government], get back involved again, and go back downtown. And that is a normal career path for them, to go from working for Congress to working for pharmaceutical companies, to working for HHS, to working for insurance companies, back and forth, [so] that it is industry intertwined with government."[32] Our study of different portraits of Republican long-term insiders' social backgrounds and career paths highlights certain aspects of this observation. For example, choosing an undergraduate degree or later holding the post of associate professor in a school of public policy or public health was uncommon among Republicans, but common among Democrats. On the other hand, it seems that career paths in the back offices of government, whether in Congress or in the executive, require the same skill in health governance among Republicans and Democrats.

These elites' circulation to and from prestigious health subcommittees (such as the Ways and Means Committee and the Finance Committee), or even the executive in the HCFA or CMS and the OMB, shows that, among Republicans, awareness of cost-containment issues was a heavy burden—one that was also prevalent among Democratic insiders. Moreover, for some of them, especially the technocratic translators, their involvement with the work of the Alliance for Health Reform shows that the bipartisan approach to health insurance reform was a reality. But unlike the Clinton plan veterans who, once they left policy formulation, opted for work in the private sector, a majority of Republican long-term insiders preferred to work for lobbyists and sector-based interest groups.

Democratic Newcomers: In the Clinton Plan Veterans' Footsteps

Here we will look at the portraits of the Democratic long-term insiders we dubbed the "newcomers"—those in the back offices from 1994 to 2010.[33] These are the individuals who moved into health governance positions in Congress or the executive branch after the failure of the Clinton reform.

These individuals spent a minimum of six years in a position of power. They were in charge after the defeat and during the second Clinton term. They were committed neither to formulating the programmatic orientations nor to the Clinton plan battle (chapter 6 and 7). During George W. Bush's terms from 2000 to 2008, most of the newcomers moved into the private sector, often to the nonprofit sector (including NGOs, foundations, and think tanks). Our study of their social backgrounds and career paths will enable us to ascertain whether the newcomers targeted the same positions of power as the Clinton plan veterans in Congress and within the executive (HCFA [CMS], ASPE, OMB). It will also allow us to highlight the convergence of their career paths toward the reform forums in Washington (the Bipartisan Policy Center, the Hamilton Project, the Health Policy Consensus Group, the Center on Budget and Policy Priorities, the Alliance for Health Reform), and we will identify the forums Clinton plan veterans and Republican insiders shared.

The analysis of sociological features will confirm or invalidate the hypothesis that the newcomers had the same social background and career path as their predecessors. At this stage of the programmatic elite framework, we will highlight the development of professional appointments within those institutions controlling the costs of health policies. The way that these long-term insiders internalized the necessity to devise a reform project based on cost containment, bringing the market on board, and based on the quest for a bipartisan consensus will be examined through the lens of our study of the Democratic newcomers' portraits.

Circulation between Two Branches of Power Replicated

The study of the institutional migrants' career paths among the Democrat newcomers will enable us to discuss the changing role of the custodians of health coverage policy. Moreover, this will confirm that the newcomers tended to move into the back offices of government the same way the Clinton plan veterans did. The study of health coverage reforms in France has already shown a strong interdependence between two generations of social insurance policy elites, who developed the role of custodians of state policies by promoting the "great social security" program (i.e., universal health coverage and increased state control) from 1990 to 2020 (Genieys, 2010; Genieys & Darviche, 2023). In the case of the US, it will be necessary to verify empirically whether the newcomers follow the same subtype of career paths as the Clinton plan veterans (chapter 4). The cases of Peter R. Orszag, Elizabeth (hereafter Liz) Fowler, and Cybele Bjorklund illustrate this perfectly—in their career paths and significant roles in both the executive branch and Congress during the Obama administration.[34]

Peter R. Orszag's portrait reveals how a brilliant young economist, specializing in fiscal policy, emerged as the "craftsman" on health care financing issues for President Obama. In moving from Congress to the White House, Orszag established himself as the craftsman of the budgetary issue for the health coverage reform project.[35] Son of a mathematics professor at Yale University, Orszag was a brilliant economics student at Princeton University, where he received a BA, and the London School of Economics, where he received an MSc and a PhD. As a young economist, Orszag first joined the White House during the Clinton administration, initially as a senior economist and adviser, then as the president's special adviser for economic policy (1995–1998). Close with economist and Treasury Secretary Robert Rubin, Orszag was at that time a budget policy specialist. When the Republicans came to power, he went to the University of California, Berkeley, for two years to work as a lecturer and to collaborate with Joseph Stiglitz, the Nobel Prize–winning economist. In 2001 Orszag took up a post as a senior fellow at the Brookings Institution in Washington, DC. Orszag once again established his career path on the margins of governmental affairs and re-oriented his research toward health insurance budgetary policy issues. Orszag and Jason Furman, another young economist from Harvard University, then cofounded a Washington-based initiative called the Hamilton Project.[36] Its aim was to generate innovative ideas that would have an immediate impact on "policy-making circles" regarding economic security, energy, and health. The Hamilton Project, in which the young Democratic senator from the state of Illinois, Barack Obama, was involved, was launched on April 5, 2006.[37] This working group enabled Orszag to meet certain Clinton plan veterans such as Judy Feder, as well as some other rising stars among the newcomers, such as Jeanne Lambrew (see below). When a Democratic majority returned to the House of Representatives, Orszag was appointed director of the CBO in December 2006, at age thirty-eight, after being proposed by Speaker of the House Nancy Pelosi and President pro tempore of the Senate Joe Biden (Joyce, 2011: 132).

Within the CBO, Orszag developed the notion of "fiscal responsibility" and justified the need to institute grand health insurance reform by regulating its entire cost over the long-term (McDonough, 2011: 32–33). During his time in Congress, he became known as the budget "guru," able to provide strong arguments to Democratic health coverage policy elites as they considered the formulation of a new reform bill.[38] As soon as he was appointed CBO director in January 2007, Orszag increased the number of experts from twenty to fifty people working on health budget issues. With this staffers "armada," he published a "mammoth report" of more than 1,500 pages on the future options for health policy in the United States (Starr, 2013: 190). Fortified by this legitimacy acquired on health budgetary issues in Washington's power circles, he was appointed in November 2008 by President Obama to head the OMB at the White House (Starr, 2013: 193; Hacker, 2010: 870). His recognition in Congress and his genuine professional expertise in fiscal and budgetary issues would be crucial during negotiations with the health sector's various stakeholders when the finishing touches were put to the draft bill (Brill, 2015: 393).

The career path of institutional migrant Cybele Bjorklund illustrates the case of a newcomer circulating from health administration to

Congress and then within Congress between the two chambers at the time of the Obama reform.[39] A journalist by training, with a BA from the University of Oregon, it was when reporting on the defeated Clinton reform that Bjorklund realized she was "tired of talking about what people do in health policy." She chose to enroll in the school of public health at Johns Hopkins University in 1994. Soon after the failed Clinton plan, she worked as a young expert on the health policy services of the HCFA at HHS. Following this administrative experience, she focused her professional trajectory on Congress and held posts as a legislative aide on health policy and aging for Senator Tom Daschle on the Finance Committee (1995–1997). Bjorklund then became Senator Ted Kennedy's deputy director of staff in charge of health policy on the Health, Education, Labor and Pensions Committee (1998–2001). In 2003 Bjorklund became a committee staffer in the House of Representatives, taking the post of staff director on the Health Subcommittee of the Ways and Means Committee, where she stayed for twelve years. In this role, she worked with Democrat Liz Fowler (see below) and Republican Mark Hayes (see above) on formulating the bipartisan reform known as the MMA (2003) during the George W. Bush administration. It was in this political context that she befriended Liz Fowler.[40] Fortified by this experience and her knowledge of the legislative process, Bjorklund became involved "night and day" in the House during the debates on the draft Affordable Health Care for America Act—namely by leading the "Tri-Com" alongside Clinton plan veteran Karen Nelson (McDonough, 2011: 72). After the Affordable Care Act was passed, Bjorklund regularly explained the new legal framework of the reform to the Centers for Medicare and Medicaid Services (CMS, formerly HCFA), which was part of HHS, because, as Bjorklund explained, "several colleagues have left the Hill for the CMS to implement the 2010 health care overhaul." One of those colleagues was her friend Liz Fowler.

Conversely, our study of Liz Fowler's portrait shows how the newcomers, after a long career in Congress's Health Committee until the Obama reform, then moved toward HHS to contribute to implementing the reform.[41] As a young graduate with a JD of the University of

Minnesota Law School, Fowler went to Washington, DC, to practice as a lawyer. Finding this profession "very boring," Fowler did a PhD in economics at Johns Hopkins University. At the same time, she began work as a committee staffer in the Senate, first as a Medicare counsel for Democratic Senator Daniel Patrick Moynihan and then as chief health counsel for the Senate Finance Committee (1999–2005). In 2003, during the George W. Bush administration and when Republicans were in the majority in the 106th Congress, Fowler played a key role with Cybele Bjorklund, who was then at the House of Representatives, and with the Republican Senate technocratic translator Mark Hayes (see above) in elaborating a bipartisan reform strategy around the draft bill of the MMA. Fowler then went into the private sector as a consultant, first working for Health Policy Alternatives Inc. alongside Clinton plan veteran Mike Hash and then as vice president in charge of public policy at WellPoint Inc., a major private insurance company.

Some authors have sometimes noted this professional detour and deduced that afterward, when highly committed, Fowler would plead for a reform project on health care coverage to be founded on bringing private insurers on board in the care-cost reimbursement mechanism (Brill, 2015). We will discuss further on the uncertain basis of this type of causal deduction (chapter 8). At this stage, however, it seems more important to highlight that despite working in the private sector, Fowler remained very involved in the work of reform forums such as the Alliance for Health Reform. In March 2008, a few months before Obama was elected, she took up once again her role as chief health counsel, this time for Senator Max Baucus, so that she could take part in developing the new health care insurance reform project (McDonough, 2011: 65). It was in Congress with the Clinton plan veterans—David Nexon (with Senator Kennedy), Wendell Primus (with House Speaker Pelosi), and Karen Nelson (with Congressman Waxman)—the Republican Senate technocratic translator Mark Hayes (with Senator Grassley), as well as the newcomers David Bowen (with Senator Kennedy) and Cybele Bjorklund (on the Ways and Means Committee), that Fowler was involved in the collective work of drafting the text of the reform.[42] None of these people, however, had any personal proximity or professional relationship with the world of private insurance. After the Affordable Care Act was passed, Fowler was appointed to HHS from 2010 to 2011 on the National Economic Council as special adviser to the president on health matters. Unlike some of her colleagues, however, who had similarly migrated from one institution to another, Fowler acknowledged that, for her, the key moment had been when "I was 'in charge' in my role as a policy person, [and] I worked on drafting the bill. . . . On the other hand, the routine work in the Department of Health and Human Services, consisting of putting into place the new policy, turned out to be much less compelling."[43] This comment is a reminder of the various professional qualities needed throughout the reform process, and the importance of "the right people implementing" the policy.

Technocratic Translators Asserting Their Preference for Reform Consensus

In the population of health coverage policy elites, there was a small number of Democratic newcomers with a technocratic translator career-path profile. This can be explained by several logical reasons linked to the criterion of the length of the insiders' career paths. Unlike the institutional migrants, the technocratic translators, by circulating through Congress and the executive during their long careers, had the capacity to attenuate the effects of a majority change in political power by transferring from one power to the other. On the other hand, empirically the technocratic translators can be defined by their long career paths in one of the two branches of power, a subtle activity owing to the reduction on offer of the number of posts available to Democrats during a period of "absolute" government when the Republicans ruled both the presidency and Congress from 2000 to 2007. To illustrate empirically this type of career path, our presentation will limit itself to studying a single representative portrait per branch of power.

The exemplary cases of Jeanne M. Lambrew (in the executive) and David Bowen (in Congress)[44] will show whether and how the career paths of the technocratic translator newcomers converged or diverged from those of the Clinton plan veterans. Lambrew's path, typical of the technocratic translator in its newcomer's version, is interesting in several ways.[45] Indeed, while researchers in the field of American politics acknowledge the centrality of the technocratic translators' role in placing health care coverage reform on the policy agenda (including Nancy-Ann DeParle, Karen Pollitz, Mike Hash, and Phil Schiliro, alongside the Clinton plan veterans), some scholars reproached the technocratic translators, such as Liz Fowler, for having impeded its culmination in a more ambitious reform and so paving the way for a public-private project that advantaged the private insurance lobby (McDonough, 2011; Marmor, 2012; Starr, 2013; Brill, 2015). It is true that Lambrew's cowriting with Senator Tom Daschle (Daschle, Lambrew & Greenberg, 2008) of a book calling for the development of a complex public-private partnership with strong regulation of the health-insurance market to anchor the reform project could lead to this form of speculation. But it seems bold to reduce such a political result to the action of one or two individuals, even if it was based on a tacit agreement. On the other hand, by enlisting private interests, in this case the insurance companies, the frantic search for a consensus agenda supported by a majority of Clinton plan veterans and newcomers allows them to maximize the chances of passing legislation despite the checks-and-balances game. In the long term, it would be more difficult to challenge a reform around which many interests have coalesced (chapter 9).

With her academic background—a master's and PhD from the school of public health at the University of North Carolina at Chapel Hill, Lambrew took the post of assistant professor in public policy at Georgetown University in Washington, DC. She appears far from a typical figure, not having participated in the genesis of the Clinton reform project; rather, she worked in roles in the back offices of executive power "on the fringes" a few months before the reform failed.[46] More precisely, in October 1993 when the Clinton reform was being challenged, Lambrew joined a small team of Clinton plan veterans who, with First Lady Hillary Clinton and Ira Magaziner, tried to find a counterargument within the executive branch of power against that of Congress. According to Judy Feder, "the ascension of Jeanne Lambrew in the Clinton administration" occurred after the draft bill's defeat.[47] This experience enabled Lambrew to make lasting contacts with the Clinton plan veterans, with whom she shared a desire for revenge for this defeat. In 1997, late in the Clinton presidency, Lambrew worked as PAD in charge of programs and health budgets at the OMB at the White House, like the Clinton plan veteran Nancy-Ann DeParle, and subsequently she developed the same type of career path.[48] At the OMB, Lambrew stood out by playing the role of architect in preparing the bipartisan reform, the State Children's Health Insurance Program (SCHIP), along with other Clinton plan veterans, Chris Jennings and Neera Tanden. When the Republicans returned to power, Lambrew took up an academic post again, first as associate professor at the school of public health at the George Washington University before moving to the University of Texas at Austin as associate professor at the Lyndon B. Johnson School of Public Affairs. At the same time, Lambrew held a post as senior fellow, alongside Neera Tanden, at the Democrat think tank the Center for American Progress and another post at the Bipartisan Policy Center.

During this time, Lambrew also published several articles pleading for a project that would extend health care insurance based on strong regulation of the private insurance market.[49] In parallel, she worked with the Clinton plan veterans drawing up an inventory of the strategic errors that had led to the eponymous project failing, and she suggested several avenues to avoid repetition of these errors—namely, by getting involved in the Alliance for Health Reform forum (chapter 8). Lambrew's career path followed in Nancy-Ann DeParle's footsteps and confirms the persistence of the technocratic translator's type of career path among the Democratic newcomers. This explains why with renewed awareness of the issues at stake after their spell at the OMB, together they would cleverly wield the cost-containment argument during negotiations with interest groups and Congress on the Obama reform project. Indeed, as they succeeded each other in the same top positions in the OMB in the wake of the Clinton defeat, they knew owing to their personal experience more than anyone about the effects of the debate on cost containment when the issue of reforming the health care coverage system arose.

In order not to replicate the errors that had led to the Clinton defeat, these two long-term insiders pleaded for a bipartisan approach to reform that would inevitably bring the interest groups into the fold. It was certainly for all these reasons that, three months after having appointed Nancy-Ann DeParle to the White House, in April 2009 President Obama chose Lambrew as policy director of the Office for Consumer Information and Insurance Oversight (OCIIO) at HHS, the position in charge of driving through the reform (McDonough, 2011: 89). In 2011 Lambrew joined the National Economic Council at the White House as special adviser on health issues with Nancy-Ann DeParle.[50] Indeed Lambrew and DeParle were the two "masterminds" for the president who, along with other Clinton plan veterans, would work day and night during the decision-making process.

Newcomer David Bowen was a young neurobiology researcher when he changed careers to become a committee staffer—embarking on a career path reminiscent of that of the congressional technocratic translators.[51] A brilliant individual, Bowen simultaneously obtained a bachelor of arts and a bachelor of science from Brown University before, in 1995, accepting a National Science Foundation scholarship to do a PhD in neurobiology at the University of California, San Francisco. As a young postdoc, Bowen did research on receptive genes before a brief detour to work in a lab for a biotech company. Wishing "to set aside his microscope and refocus his energy to a profession reliant on human interaction," he obtained a grant in 1999 from the American Association for the Advancement of Science that led him to work as one of Senator Ted Kennedy's staff advisers on the Senate's Health, Education, Labor, and Pensions (HELP) Committee. Overqualified with so many degrees in biomedicine, Bowen epitomizes the profile of the young staffer sought by Clinton plan veteran David Nexon, who was then in charge of reinvigorating the team of advisers to Ted Kennedy, the "Old Lion" of health policy in the Senate (Littlefield & Nexon, 2015). While still learning the ropes of his new profession, Bowen quickly scaled all the echelons of the committee staffer's career path. He soon acceded to the post of Senator Kennedy's associate director of staff before going on to succeed Nexon.

In 2008, while Kennedy was ill, Bowen took on these new responsibilities with the support of another Clinton plan veteran, Michael J. Meyers, who was then chief counsel of the same staff; Bowen also worked with newcomer Liz Fowler from Senator Max Baucus's staff (on the Finance Committee) to draft the Senate bill known as the Affordable Health Choice Act.[52] This Senate bill differed from that of the House of Representatives' bill on the issue of the "public option"[53] (chapter 9); the Senate bill contained most of the main arguments taken up again in the final version of the Patient Protection and Affordable Care Act (Brill, 2015: 91). During this intense period of work, Bowen orchestrated more than fifteen meetings to draw up a reform project that would be as consensual as possible in Congress with the Clinton plan veteran staffers, the newcomers in the House of Representatives, and some Republican long-term insiders who shared this bipartisan approach (McDonough, 2011).

Our study of the sociological portraits of Democratic newcomers establishes not only the replication of career paths of the Clinton plan veterans but also the replication of strong interpersonal bonds. Like the Clinton plan veterans, most of the Democratic newcomers had a social background in public health policy and often temporarily redeployed themselves to schools of public policy or public health in universities in the Washington, DC, area when there was a political change of power. Similarly, apart from a handful of exceptions, we can ascertain that among the Democratic health coverage policy elites, the unquestionable tendency on the whole was to move toward the private nonprofit sector. In addition, their career paths reveal that not only have the newcomers moved between the executive and legislative branches, but they also coopted one another, often forming groups yet never a clique, and maintained amiable relationships that transcended generation gaps. These were certainly the reasons why they took advantage of the revolving-door system by succeeding one another in key positions when formulating health care coverage reform. It is also clear that the sociological study of these career paths shows that the traditional SI elites' career paths focused on the Social Security Administration is obsolete (chapter 2). The latter has ceded its place to career paths at the apex of government, integrating movement across Congress and the executive branch. Similarly, a spell in Congress (on the Ways and Means Committee, the Finance Committee, or in the CBO) or in the executive (at the OMB, HCFA [later CMS], or as finance director) seemed to constitute another distinctive characteristic among the new career paths of these long-term insiders. Further on, we will see that their shared longing for devising cost-contained health coverage policy would not be without consequences in terms of their overwhelming support for the most consensual version of the reform project underwritten by the Senate Finance Committee and to the detriment of that defended by the House of Representatives (chapter 9). The process of professional learning regarding the challenges and future of a health care coverage system occurred on the margins of government, in think tanks inside the Beltway and in Washington's reforming forums (Lepont, 2014). Indeed, it was in this unusual setting that the Clinton plan veterans became aware of the causes of their failure, including the central issue of the cost at stake with any reform project and the lack of bipartisan consensus.

Some Insights on the Government of Insiders

To conclude, our programmatic elite framework devoted to the empirical study of the social backgrounds and career paths of health coverage policy elites highlights the sociological characteristics of a group of long-term insiders. Identifying Democratic and Republican long-term insiders' career paths confirms the end of the power of "doctors and reformers" in the government of health affairs (Derthick, 1979; Oberlander, 2003; Lepont, 2014). On the other hand, Larry Brown's intuition (1983a,b) concerning the making of a new unelected governmental elite characterized by a mastery of technical knowledge linked to policies (e.g., the cost-containment issue) seems to be confirmed, and this applies to both the executive branch and to Congress. These insiders' awareness of being in charge in their professional "policy person" role was clearly a value they collectively shared.[54] It enabled them symbolically to differentiate themselves from all the other individuals, the short-timers, acting in an ephemeral or even episodic way in the decision-making process, such as the policy entrepreneurs who were emblematic of the "birds of passage" figure. For this reason, the long-term insiders were determined to differentiate themselves from academics such as Alain Enthoven and Jacob Hacker, who in the name of the "big pictures" they promoted often defended reform projects that were extremely difficult to translate and to formulate into legal and consensual processes. These insiders are in charge in government back offices to translate ideas into laws and render them operational, thus making them politically (despite partisan negotiations and interest groups' involvement) and financially (considering the OMB and the CBO) workable.

In terms of the executive branch, our in-depth study of long-term insiders' career paths built in the back offices of power (at HHS and the White House) makes improbable the idea of a government of strangers (Heclo, 1977). In the particular cases of the health care insurance reform projects being researched here—the Clinton plan and the ACA—policy formulation by "strangers" was rejected by insiders' mobilization. Whether they included our interviewee Ira Magaziner or great academic public health figures such as Alain Enthoven, Paul Starr, Theodor Marmor, or Jacob Hacker, these "strangers" would fail in their attempt to see their project of comprehensive reform take hold (chapters 7 and 9). Moreover, identifying long-term insiders' subtypes career paths within Congress allows us to revisit David Whiteman's assertions (1987): on the basis of his study of health staffers, he demonstrated how connected (based on strong friendship ties) and informed they were, and how inside Congress they were seen as the "health experts;" nevertheless, they themselves did not have the impression of forming a "health community." And so it seems that in the space of two decades, circumstances profoundly changed, as attested by the Clinton plan veterans' career paths (institutional migrants or technocratic translators) and those of the newcomers who maintained their networks with reform-oriented Washington think tanks and with the Alliance for Health Reform forums.

Moreover, our analysis of insider's career paths reflects the merit of exploring policy formulation not only in the executive and legislative branches but also in the circulating movement across these two branches of government. This allowed us to measure the importance of acquiring two kinds of professional knowledge in health policy work: (1) knowledge about how to adapt and translate ideas into law and (2) knowledge about how to master the political procedures of policy-formulation work during the decision-making process. In addition, our study of the three career-path subtypes (institutional migrant, technocratic translator, and policy bureaucrat) puts the thesis of the divided Democratic health elites under the Clinton administration in a new perspective (Johnson & Broder, 1996). By analytically separating the Clinton plan veterans' career paths from those of the elites who arrived in government health affairs later on, one can observe processes of continuity and discontinuity not only in career paths but also in the health coverage policy formulation process. Evidence can be observed through the lens of homogenous career paths shaped by the development of a means of "reproduction" within certain key positions in the executive branch and Congress (table 5.1). Identifying a strong equivalence between the Clinton plan veterans' career paths and those of Democratic newcomers attests to the rise of long-term insiders.

These insiders, with social backgrounds based in Washington, DC, were often educated in schools of public policy or public health policy; they built their career paths in the back offices of government and outside these offices (with a mobility toward the nonprofit private sector) thanks to their dual set of professional skills and knowledge on policy-formulation issues. The Clinton plan veterans, with their unique experience in earlier struggles between the executive and legislative branches when the health care coverage reform project was aborted (the Pepper Commission, the Clinton task force, etc.), initiated an original career-path mobility between the two branches of power. This type of circulation is shared by the Democratic newcomers and Republican health insiders (i.e., the institutional migrant type). The shaping of this kind of career by targeting specific power posts cannot, owing to patterns noted over time, be considered the random result of chance (table 5.1). Regarding the executive, these roles included those of ASPE, administrator or deputy administrator within the HCFA at HHS, or PAD at the OMB.

Likewise, in Congress, career staffer posts on health subcommittees in the House of Representatives and the Senate charged with overseeing financial or budgetary issues, as well as in the CBO, were targeted. Researching the technocratic translators' career paths and those of the policy bureaucrats confirms the rise in power of financial organizations regulating health coverage policy. Identifying new career paths that combined policy formulation and cost containment cannot be considered as a random outcome. It reveals the development of elective affinities with a policy issue that played an important role in the Clinton plan's defeat. Further on, we will show how the issue of cost containment became one of the pillars of the programmatic orientation collectively driven forward by the long-term insiders. It is equally clear that one can observe similarities in the choice of career-path types when the long-term insiders, often due to a change in political majority in the executive branch or Congress, moved back and forth to the private sector while remaining firmly based in the Washington, DC, area. On this point, the Clinton plan veterans and the newcomers opted in most cases for a post in nonprofit organizations, thus avoiding any complicity with powerful sector-based interest groups. Most of these insiders have chosen academic posts, such as associate professor in public health, in one of the many schools of public policy or public health in the Washington, DC, area, including the George Washington University, Georgetown University, and Johns Hopkins University (Baltimore and Washington campuses).[55] The other element typical of their paths was their collective involvement, during the George W. Bush administration, with reforming forums such as the Center for American Progress, the Bipartisan Policy Center, and the Center on Budget and Policy Priorities. Indeed, it was in these settings that the Clinton plan veterans would carry out a thorough inventory appraising the reasons for their defeat (notably with the Alliance for Health Reform). In parallel, these veterans would collectively create a veritable road map to maximize the next health care coverage reform project's chances of succeeding.

Comparing Democratic and Republican insiders' career paths shows similarities as well as notable differences. While the main outlines of different types of career paths were clearly identifiable, especially mobility across the executive and legislative branches and specialization in health coverage policy issues, a certain number of differences should be highlighted. The length of time Republican insiders spent in roles in charge was often shorter than Democratic insiders spent. Republicans' high level of qualifications was less Washington, DC–focused, and their background wasn't so frequently in schools of public policy or public health; their most preferred qualification was a juris doctor from a law school. It is certainly for this reason that very few Republican long-term insiders have opted for a position as associate professor in public health at a university. Many of them chose to serve sectoral interest groups (lobbies, insurance companies, hospitals, etc.) after their time in government.

On the other hand—and this is what they had in common with the Democrats—a number of Republicans became involved in the reform-oriented Washington, DC, forums to devise a bipartisan health insurance project, and closely advised the "Gang of Six" Republican senators. It is in this sense that one should understand Jeanne Lambrew's comments on the role of these people: "We were able to encourage the career people, who had ideas on making programs work better, to push through those ideas. We were able to improve the daily operation of health insurance programs for eighty-five million Americans . . . We are able to do I think a lot of quality work there, so you wouldn't just have decent policies at the top level . . . That's the story!"[56]

More generally, the study of Washington long-term insiders brings to the fore a set of clues which attest to the transformation of elites' social backgrounds and career paths that govern health care insurance policy-making (table 5.1). Our study of the Democratic health coverage policy elites' lengthy career paths reveals that despite their comings and goings in and out of the private sector with changes in political power, they often returned to top key policy-making positions. This finding tends to conjure an image of an elites' policy-making process very different from the ruling elite described by William Domhoff (1990, 1996) or more recently by Janine Wedel using the term "shadow elite" (2009). Our study of the health coverage policy elites career paths shows that Clinton veterans and Democratic newcomers tend, when they leave office, to opt for work in the private sector, most of the time for nonprofit organizations and for a relatively short period. As a result, their career paths make them relatively autonomous from influential health care

TABLE 5.1. Comparison of long-term insiders' career-path subtypes

Career-path subtype	Institutional migrant	Technocratic translator	Policy bureaucrat
Early occupation	Think tanks (Brookings, Urban Institute), universities, foundations (Kaiser Family)	Lawyer or assistant professor	Administrator, actuary, Inspector General's office
First post to Congress or the executive branch	Congressional staffer (legislative assistant), assistant director (HHS), budgetary adviser (OMB, CBO)	Congress: staffer on subcommittee Executive branch: health administration, state or federal	Office of the Actuaries, Office of the General Counsel (HHS); OMB; chief tax counsel on Ways and Means Committee
Targeted position in career paths	ASPE or budget director in HCFA (later CMS), OMB, or CBO; chief health counsel or legislative director on subcommittee in Congress	Executive branch: ASPE or budget director in HCFA, HHS, or OMB Congress: committee staff director, or general counsel in Congress	SES status; specialization in financial control and inspection bodies (chief counsel)
Revolving-door effect (Democrats and Republicans)	Democrats: nonprofit organizations (Robert Wood Johnson, Kaiser Family Foundation, Center on Budget and Policy Priorities) Republicans: interest groups (HIAA, HIP, FAH)	Democrats, executive branch: schools of public health (universities), nonprofit organizations Democrats, Congress: schools of public health (universities), nonprofit organizations Republicans: interest groups	Does not apply. Remains overwhelmingly in the same agency
Positions occupied during the ACA reform	Executive branch: White House (EOP), OMB, ASPE Congress: senior policy adviser for Speaker of the House or committee staff director	Executive branch: White House (EOP), OMB, ASPE Congress: senior policy adviser for Speaker of the House or committee staff director	Remains in the same position for a long time (20 to 30 years on average), possible OMB mobility

Reform project experience (1): Clinton plan veterans (before 1994)	Pepper Commission, Clinton task force, bipartisan organizations	Pepper Commission, Clinton task force, bipartisan organizations	Clinton task force
Reform project experience (2): Clinton plan veterans and newcomers (after 1994)	Bipartisan list: Alliance for Health Reform, Bipartisan Policy Center, Democratic list: Center on Budget and Policy, Priority Health Policy Consensus Group, Hamilton Project Republican list: HOPE project	Bipartisan list: Alliance for Health Reform, Bipartisan Policy Center, Democratic list: Center on Budget and Policy, Priority Health Policy Consensus Group, Hamilton Project Republican list: HOPE project	Alliance for Health Reform or Bipartisan Policy Center
Exit strategies from health governance	Democrats: universities, think tanks, foundations Republicans: lobby groups	Democrats: universities, think tanks, foundations Republicans: lobby groups	Democrats: universities, think tanks, foundations Republicans: lobby groups

SOURCE: OPERA Research Program

interest groups. In sum, the programmatic elite framework reveals the uniqueness in both social background and career path of Democratic health coverage policy elites in Washington, DC. The Clinton plan veterans and Democratic newcomers working within government and on its margins would collectively strive to assert the role of custodian of state policies. It is incumbent upon us to show how and why the long-term insiders shaped the formulation of a far-reaching reform by seeking political consensus and bringing market forces on board, while at the same time addressing the issue of budgetary constraints.

PART III

The Hidden Origins of the Affordable Care Act

Elite Configurations and Programmatic Changes

The second aspect of our programmatic elite framework focuses on the correlation between the transformation of the elites' structure with the change in reformist programmatic orientations. The Clinton plan and the program initiated by President Obama constitute the "big" reform projects selected to test this approach. We will study the link between the configuration of elites and the different programmatic orientations that confronted each other during the two reforms. As we have already shown (in part II), these battles pit insiders and outsiders (i.e., policy entrepreneurs) against one another. We will test the hypothesis of the making of a new configuration of elites dominated by the insiders—the Clinton plan veterans and the Democratic "newcomers"—who shaped over time a consensual reform project centered on the integration of market forces and the issue of cost containment. Moreover, we will show how these insiders have reactivated the role of custodians of state policies to promote this new programmatic orientation.

On the face of it, there is little interest in revisiting President Clinton's health insurance plan, as the reasons for its failure have been widely discussed (Starr, 1994; Aaron, 1996; Johnson & Broder, 1996; Skopcol,

1996; Glied, 1997; Hacker, 1997). The discussion is now in the hands of historians eager to mine the presidential archives and who, by bringing to light countless details and facts about the past that went unnoticed by researchers in American politics at the time, may shed additional light on this model of a political fiasco. Some scholars of public health have already drawn attention to the likely links between the failure of the Clinton plan and the success of the reform bill initiated by the Obama administration (Oberlander, 2007a,b; Hacker, 2010; McDonough, 2011; Starr, 2013). This work has referred to the supposed role of Clinton plan veterans without providing convincing sociological evidence, however (Donnelly & Rochefort, 2012; Genieys, Darviche & Epperson, 2022).

With the benefit of hindsight and historical reassessment, and steeped in our knowledge of insiders' career paths, we can establish continuity in the structure of the elites across these two administrations. We will point out the Clinton plan veterans' strategy in the process of socializing the newcomers to act as custodians of state policies. The Clinton plan veterans and newcomers developed a consensual programmatic orientation to reform the health insurance system. We will show that Democratic health coverage policy elites learned lessons from the failure of the Clinton plan and used them to formulate a new reform proposal that would result in the ACA. The key difference between these two initiatives (Clinton and Obama) lies in the effects of the transformation of social backgrounds and career paths of Democratic insiders on the decision to abandon advocacy for comprehensive reform and for a more consensual project of far-reaching reform.

We want to show that these unelected governmental elites' understanding of the lessons to be learned from their failure reverberated particularly loudly within the back offices where policies were formulated during the Obama administration. As a reminder, at the start of the 1990s when President Clinton began the process of reforming the health care system, every favorable political condition prevailed (a Democratic majority in Congress and a Democratic president); and this would be the case again twenty years later when the Obama reform project was launched during the prolonged ongoing financial crisis that followed the 2008 subprime crash. The challenge here is to illuminate the sociological mechanisms that led divided Clinton-era unelected governmental elites to opt for a consensual programmatic orientation fifteen years later during the Obama administration.

This detour through the Clinton era will thus allow us to link the divided elite configuration with the fragmentation of the reform program offered by the Democratic camp. The growing opposition at the apex of health government between two groups—insiders versus "strangers"— will serve as a departure point for our study. The long-term insiders, drawing on their career paths rooted in Washington at the heart of government (in Congress and the executive) and yet equally close to its margins (think tanks, foundations, universities), would fiercely contest ideas of a comprehensive reform proposed by those they considered as strangers—Heclo's "birds of passage" with their policy entrepreneur profiles. In this fratricidal dispute, the future Clinton plan veterans contrasted their own programmatic option, the "play-or-pay" model with that supported by the strangers, the "single payer" model and the "managed competition" option (chapter 6).

Correlating the change in the structure of the Democratic health policy elites with the different programmatic orientations in competition for reform will shed light on the making of a political conflict between insiders and strangers. In this context, the fragmentation between the single-payer option and the "play-or-pay" option, once the reform was on the institutional agenda, gave way to a reform project based on "managed competition" in the health care system (chapter 7). This political choice made by President Clinton and his close advisers has favored a divided elites' configuration. The clumsy management of the balance of power (between Congress and an executive-branch task force) was then amplified by the professional rivalries emerging within the Democratic reform camp between Washington's long-term insiders and the policy entrepreneurs.

The effects of the long-term insiders' circulation into the private sector during George W. Bush's administrations will be addressed to show where and how a new programmatic orientation was shaped. It was inside certain think tanks, such as the Center for American Progress, the Bipartisan Policy Center, and the Center on Budget and Policy Priorities, as well as several foundations, such as the Robert Wood Johnson Foundation, the Kaiser Family Foundation, and the Alliance for Health Reform (a communications forum), that the task of defining a consensual reform project that integrated market forces and cost containment was achieved (chapter 8). The notion that "the stars aligned" as negotiations were conducted behind closed doors and led to the success of the Patient Protection and Affordable Care Act will be reconsidered on the basis of the growing role of the insiders as new custodians of state policies (chapter 9). Did the return to the back offices of government by the Democratic health coverage policy elites with their homogenous career paths (Clinton plan veterans and newcomers) reflect the victory of these insiders who claimed to formulate domestic policies? Does this genuine strategy of colonizing the key decision-making posts within the executive, as well as in Congress, explain the reform's success? Beyond a common political learning, their professional savoir faire in formulating policy as much as their interchangeability in these positions of government led a group of insiders to act as custodians of state policies in the decision-making process. Based on their collective past experience, they opposed the intervention of "strangers" and chose a policy of accommodation. Despite the tensions within Congress between defenders of the public option (in the House of Representatives) and those partial to a mixed public-private approach, these people succeeded in driving through a far-reaching reform of the American health insurance system.

CHAPTER 6

The Clinton Plan

Programmatic Fragmentation and Divided Elites

THE FAILURE of Clinton's project to reform health coverage—the Health Security Act, which was presented to Congress in November 1993 and finally abandoned in September 1994—is our starting point for reflecting on the effects of the transformation of the social backgrounds and career paths of the unelected governmental health coverage policy elites. At first it might seem rather incongruous to imagine anything positive might emerge from this classic instance of a resounding political failure. Yet the in-depth analysis of long-term insiders' career paths links Clinton plan veterans to the success of the ACA. It is important to keep in mind that prior to its failure, the Clinton reform project met several significant political and social expectations. Health economist Sherry Glied stresses that the project's aim to offer insurance coverage for the uninsured and controlled costs for the already insured proved immensely popular (Glied, 1997: 7). According to sociologist Paul Starr, there was a consensus among the American middle class to sever the link between employment and access to health coverage, as well as a willingness to consider introducing universal health coverage (Starr, 1992, 1994). Starr highlights the notion of "negative consensus" in order to show how during the 1990s, 90% of American citizens were in favor of a comprehensive reform of their health care system (rather than gradual or incremental reform); even the journal of the American Medical Association (AMA) deemed it "inevitable," according to its editor (Starr, 2007: 14). Nevertheless, the history of the Health Security Act shows that the principle of "good policy may make a good compromise" was far from being put into practice (Starr, 1994: 77).

In their book *The System*, journalists Johnson and Broder interpreted in almost microscopic fashion all the conflicts that led to the disintegration of the Democratic front, thereby destroying the chances for the reform's success (1996). For Theda Skocpol, the fault lay with the various pundits and policy planners who aired their disagreements "on television, and in newspaper and magazine editorials and opinion pieces" (1996: 9). Moreover, there were many divisions between the reformers in the Social Security Administration—bureaucrats at HHS who managed the Medicare and Medicaid programs and backed the idea of gradually adjusting these policies—and Washington health elites and some policy entrepreneurs who promoted a comprehensive reform. These divisions explain why there are so many factors to take into account when explaining how the programmatic offer came to fragment (Starr, 1994; Glied, 1997; Hacker, 1997; Medvetz, 2012). In his study of the relationship between US presidents' political entourage and sector-based administrations, Michaels (1997: 284) points to the example of the Clinton plan to describe the formation of a "village of strangers." Drawing inspiration from Heclo's research on policy formulation, the political scientist Jacob Hacker attributes the way that the Democratic reform front fragmented to the policy entrepreneurs' and "health policy community's" stubborn attempts to curry favor with the powers that be (1997). As a consequence, their behavior led to the gradual loss of American society's support for the reform (Jacobs & Shapiro, 2000). The interplay between the various Washington cliques was held in check, however, either by very broad considerations (Johnson & Broder, 1996) or by the intervention of a binary reform vision, one facet of which was a plea to establish a public system, while the other advocated a mixed public-private initiative (Glied, 1997: 7).[1]

Our sociological analysis of elites' career paths during the Clinton administration highlights another type of divide: the political struggle between insiders and "strangers," and the fragmentation of a reform programmatic offer. The study of the tensions between the two groups (linked to the programmatic orientation) avoids the pitfall of reducing the conflict to one between individuals, who in this case shared similar sociological characteristics and were known either as "Washington group advisers" or as "Washington-based" (Starr, 1994; Glied 1997; Hacker, 1997). Therefore, it seems appropriate to establish correlations between results from the sociology of career paths with the three competing programmatic orientations at the time of Clinton's presidency, namely "single payer," "play-or-pay," and "managed competition."[2]

Furthermore, we will consider how the fragmentation of the programmatic orientation intersected with the sociological characteristics of health elites during the Clinton years. Was there any contradiction between the transformations affecting the social backgrounds and career paths of health coverage policy elites and the formulation of policy resulting from these three reform options? Can the traditional opposition between the government of insiders and "strangers" be reduced to the issue of rival playing fields in Washington, or even to the opposition between the public health coverage system versus the private market-led system? To what extent did the different conceptions of the role of the public sector (regulated by the government) constitute a divisive factor among the health elites? Finally, why did the programmatic orientations of a health coverage system based on strong regulation of private competition by the public sector hinder the project under Clinton while it was supported under Obama?

Rejecting the Canadian Single-Payer Model

Since the end of the 1970s, Democratic health experts have gradually been able to shape reform agendas with the goal of transforming the health coverage system because of the rising costs of public spending and the relative inefficiency of a private insurance–based system (Hacker,

1997). Eager to address the link between cost and efficiency of the system, and drawing on comparative research published in *Health Affairs* and the *Journal of Health Politics, Policy and Law*, Democratic health experts proclaimed the superiority of the Canadian single-payer model compared to the American model of public coverage. This single-payer model, with no one definition for researchers, was imposed as a mobile transferable programmatic orientation, which certain backers of a universal health coverage system initially supported (Sparer, Jacobs & Brown, 2009; Brown, 2019). In 1991 a report by Congress's General Accountability Office (GAO) carried out a benchmarking exercise by showing the lessons that the US could draw from the Canadian single-payer model, especially when it came to controlling public expenditures (United States General Accountability Office, 1991). The mere mention, however, of a national health insurance system overseen by the federal government drew a flurry of criticism based on the idea of "socialized medicine" (Tuohy, 2009). Nevertheless, from the early 1990s the idea that overhauling health coverage was necessary was shared by the vast majority of academic health policy experts—although some of them, like Len Nichols and others close to the Democratic Blue Dogs (a group of centrist Democrats), were skeptical about its feasibility.[3] Moreover, those who favored importing and adapting the Canadian single-payer model would rapidly face considerable opposition from the Democratic health insiders who pleaded to build a public-private system based on transformations of the existing health coverage programs (the play-or-pay model outlined below).

Some authors have attributed the fragmentation of the programmatic reform to a disciplinary rivalry between political scientists and health policy sociologists on the one hand and health economists on the other (Glied, 1987; Hacker, 2001). The health economists have blamed the political scientists and sociologists for underestimating the financial costs of this kind of reform. By looking at the transformation of social backgrounds and career paths as well as competing programmatic orientations, another divide emerges between those individuals with significant prior experience in the arenas of power (long-term insiders) and academic health experts who have little or no experience (policy entrepreneurs).

Advocates of the coverage system which incorporated the alternative single-payer model tended to be academics and researchers, health policy experts who rallied around the Health Care Study Group, an informal group of health policy specialists under the leadership of Ted Marmor and his young disciple, Jacob Hacker.[4] Their clearly stated intention was to design a public model that would provide coverage for all American citizens. These researchers then drew on international and institutional comparisons as well as OECD data to show how relevant the Canadian health coverage model was (Marmor & Mashaw, 1990; Marmor, 1994). For health economist Sherry Glied, this option brought to the fore a divide between the "medicalists," those who backed the single-payer model, and the "marketists," or health economists who upheld the role of the market.[5]

Despite its positive reception among some consumer organizations and a small group of doctors known as Physicians for a National Health Program, support for the single-payer model was limited to a circle of health policy experts (Rodwin, 1989). Indeed, the project hardly received any support among Democratic representatives, then in a minority in Congress (Skocpol, 1996). The same applied to the majority of governmental elites, such as the director of the CBO who, while receptive to the idea of a public health coverage system, made it clear that "it's not the best solution when it comes to cost saving. In Europe, they also face the funding problem."[6]

Some authors have interpreted the demise of the single-payer model as the defeat of political science by health economics. When the budget and cost issue was introduced, this certainly favored the approaches closest to economic theories, even market theories, at the expense of political scientists' perspectives. Therefore, the actual reason for this failure was linked to the opposition they encountered from the long-term health insiders. There were at least four reasons why these insiders did not support the single-payer option: (1) their strong commitment to cost containment when it came to public-sector financing of health coverage;

(2) the commitment to health insurance provision by employers for workers; (3) the government's dominant role in managing the system; and (4) their rejection of socialized medicine. So, the backers of the single-payer model were proposing a program incapable of rallying "Washington-based health policy advisers" to its cause; and as these advisers were on the whole in charge, this made it difficult to bring to fruition a project of "national reform without a national bureaucracy" (Starr, 1994: xx). Moreover, the fear of opening up the anti–National Health Insurance system argument as propounded by private interest groups—namely, that of instituting socialized medicine—went against this programmatic orientation (Quadagno, 2004, 2005).

The analysis of the career paths of these future Clinton plan veterans sheds light on why they seemed so skeptical of a project that would undoubtedly lead to cost increases in the health coverage system; what we see is that most of them had already been sensitized to how the Health Care Financing Administration viewed policy costs (chapter 4). This is why long-term insiders developed their own reform project. Judy Feder, who for a time was close to Ted Marmor, reflected on why these insiders sought a more effective programmatic orientation: "I always felt [that the single-payer model] might never have been launched because the private sector is too powerful in our system. An approach combining the public and private had much more chance of succeeding."[7] Alice Rivlin, former ASPE, CBO director, and assistant director of the OMB during the reform in the Clinton years, stressed that American citizens "did not want to go towards a European kind of system [and its single-payer plan], but hoped to keep their employer-based insurance, which should be extended to people who don't have any."[8] On the other hand, Republican institutional migrant David Abernethy first claimed that "the health coverage reform was meant to be a bipartisan initiative, and so it was meant to go through at that time without anyone realizing that it was based on the Canadian model" and then said to a *New York Times* journalist, "I am not a closet single-payer advocate."[9] Furthermore, this model gave rise to a fear among Democrats of seeing Republican representatives in Congress denounce the possible constitution of a system of socialized medicine (i.e., the government pays for all care and employs the providers) if a Democrat won the 1992 presidential election.

Debates surrounding the single-payer model reveal two converging phenomena rich in useful lessons: firstly, how difficult it was to import a foreign model to the United States, which, despite the flaws that were acknowledged within its health care coverage system, remained tied to the history of its own institutions (Steinmo & Watts, 1995; Steinmo, 2010). And secondly, there was the fear of seeing the resurgence of the ghost of the failed 1930s National Health Insurance project defended by the "old" generation of SI custodians (chapter 2). Two more elements—a reassessment of the employer and insured person relationship, plus the alleged threat of "socialist medicine"—led the new Democratic health elites to look beyond single payer. Confident after their prior experience in the fractious world of policy formulation, especially with the Pepper Commission (1990) in Congress, the long-term insiders would go on to develop their own reform option: the play-or-pay model.[10]

The Washingtonians' Failed Attempt: The Play-or-Pay Model

The second reform option, known as "play-or-pay," was devised by long-term insiders described as future Clinton plan veterans (chapter 4). The programmatic elite framework highlights with great precision the correlation between career paths—either the institutional migrant type or the technocratic translator type—and preferences in health policy formulation (part II).

Scholars in American studies tend to agree that the play-or-pay programmatic orientation was devised as a "politically feasible" alternative aimed at replacing the single-payer model (Rich, 2004: 115). When it was introduced to the political agenda as early as December 1991 by Ronald Pollack, however, the project was presented as a result of the work of the Pepper Commission coordinated by Judy Feder and Ed Howard (Rockefeller, 1990). Developed based on research carried out by bipartisan representatives, with experts brought together by the Pepper

Commission, the aim of this reform project was to extend health coverage to the poorest citizens by compelling employers to insure their employees or else contribute to a public fund, thus allowing the ensuing Medicare coverage scheme to encompass the entire population. This reform option immediately encountered a triple opposition from interest groups, Republicans, as well as some Democrats who were wedded to the notion of the market (Starr, 1994; Skocpol, 1996; Glied, 1997). Thus, it came to be considered as the programmatic orientation favored by the "Washington advisory group" (Hacker, 1997: 103–109).

The sociological analysis of long-term insiders' career paths has highlighted the key role of the Pepper Commission in their learning process around a shared programmatic orientation of the reform (chapter 4).[11] Indeed, these insiders' first task was to define the play-or-pay reform in order to differentiate themselves from the single-payer and the managed-competition options that were being driven mainly by academic experts and policy entrepreneurs. As a reminder, the Pepper Commission, under the leadership of Democratic Senator Claude Pepper, had inspired some serious soul searching about catastrophic health insurance by bringing together representatives and their staffers from both chambers of Congress, as well as Republican members of the executive branch—including institutional migrant Thomas Scully (chapter 5)—to think through the prospect of long-term care (Feder, 2007: 3–5).[12]

Several committee hearings were held as well as a series of closed meetings in order to prepare a health care reform proposal. This is how Judy Feder, then executive codirector with Ed Howard of the Pepper Commission and future director of the Alliance for Health Reform, summarized the issues and the context of the debate during the Clinton administration: "There were major alternatives, and we focused on three. If I remember correctly, it would have been a Medicare expansion (1), a safety net model . . . And the other end of the spectrum was single payer, (2), Medicare for all. And then the middle option was, at that point, what we called 'play-or-pay' (3), which built on an employer-based system and had employers either contribute to a public plan or offer coverage themselves. And we did an analysis that showed that play-or-pay was the most likely to get universal coverage. And that—but it was quite contentious. The contention was really there were no specifics about how to fund it, how to pay for it."[13] Feder also mentioned the strong relationship that she had established at the time with an institutional migrant from Senator Kennedy's staff, David Nexon (Feder, 2007: 5).[14] It was on the basis of that new proposal that the Pepper Commission sidelined the single-payer option and prioritized a mixed system of medical coverage combining public and private elements, while at the same time taking into account preexisting health programs, the reach of which needed to be extended. Long-term insiders in office never supported the single-payer model because it could not gain political support in Congress.[15]

The other striking element to emerge from the interviews we conducted was that participating in the Pepper Commission for that young generation of staffers in Congress played a fundamental role in creating strong and long-lasting interpersonal ties among these future Clinton plan veterans. Institutional migrant Chris Jennings, then a young congressional staffer, explained that "this was an opportunity for me, not only to talk to congressmen, but also to develop long-standing relations with various actors involved in health care policy; with outside entities, like interest groups, with foundations, with think thanks like the Kaiser Family Foundation, the Robert Wood Johnson Foundation, the Commonwealth Fund, the Brookings Institution. I also developed relations with the White House people."[16] More than twenty years later, most of our interviewees agreed that the bipartisan and two-chambered Pepper Commission facilitated the creation of lasting friendships between congressional staffers and certain members of the executive branch.

Some recalled how their long-term collaboration enabled them to share knowledge about "small town" Washington, DC, based on a shared desire to reform the health care insurance system.[17] Judy Waxman, at that time a staffer, also said that these long-term ties were woven across "both sides of Capitol Hill."[18] Some members of this commission hoping to advance these ideas placed their trust in the executive branch of power at the start of the Clinton administration (1992–1993), thus launching the institutional migrant figure. Moreover, some of them who claimed they had worked during the presidential campaign "with a group of people in Washington ... by writing a memo every two weeks" explained they had worked for "people who were driving the reform [i.e., Judy Feder] and not for Clinton."[19] Other former members of the commission, such as Marilyn Moon, deliberately chose to remain on the outside of the new administration in order to better support the project in the media (such as with the *Washington Post*).

Despite the initial bipartisanship, just when the Clinton reform was launched, the play-or-pay project encountered opposition from sector-based interest groups, mainly among Republican members of Congress (Hacker, 1997). Republican David Abernethy, then director of staff on the Health Subcommittee in the Ways and Means Committee in the House of Representatives, attributed a certain merit to a public health insurance system that left room for choosing private insurance and asserted, "An approach where you must either 'play' or 'pay.' This means an employer must offer private insurance which meets certain minimum requirements, what is considered as 'playing the game' or else paying a tax contribution that in turn will go towards financing public insurance."[20] Abernethy went on to make the case that in the US, it is very difficult for "non-egalitarian political solutions" to gain political support when a reform is initiated in this way, as one often finds a representative to comment "Wait a minute! It's totally unequal the way it is, what are you talking about?"[21]

In fact, the play-or-pay model reconsidered the "employer mandate," thus potentially transferring the new tax burden onto the employer. The political cost of this programmatic orientation—namely, new taxes—did not win unanimous support among the Democratic representatives in Congress who were facing upcoming elections. For some Clinton plan veterans, the root of the reform's failure lay in the absence of political courage among congressmen as they cast off the initial bipartisan strategy (Feder, 2007: 8–10). In fact, it was owing to the refusal to increase taxes on the business sector that Ira Magaziner and other White House health advisers, such as Len Nichols,[22] decided to abandon the insiders' project in favor of the managed-competition[23] model deemed more open to the logic of the market. The play-or-pay project was later derided by its opponents as a "self-serving" strategy developed by a clique of Washington health elites eager to increase their power over policy.

And so, by correlating the programmatic orientation with the transformation of the social backgrounds and career paths of unelected governmental elites, we can better understand how rival visions of policy hardened the opposition, not only between insiders and "birds of passage" but also among Washington's core health elites responsible for formulating policy, where the decline of the SI elites corresponded with the rise of the new health coverage policy elites. The former, wedded to managing their program, preferred an incremental mode of reform that would gradually broaden Medicare's scope (chapter 2). Indeed, after weathering twelve years of Republican rule, career bureaucrats at the Social Security Administration (SSA), heirs of the SI elites, saw in this promising change a way to increase their influence in the sector by extending the program that they were in charge of formulating (Glied, 1997: 246–247).

In fact, Republican insider Roland E. King, whose career path is typical of a policy bureaucrat and who was then chief of actuaries within the HCFA, justified the need for an incremental reform by harnessing the budget argument. Another long-term insider—who had an institutional migrant profile and was an expert in finance matters (at the HCFA and the CBO)—underlined the fact that during the Clinton reform project, the internal debate among Democratic insiders pitted Social Security Administration bureaucrats, to whom the reformers passed the baton, against the insiders, who, while far from being antagonistic, espoused very different interests and policy visions.[24] In fact, while both sides advanced the argument of the cost of health insurance, for the former it was in the context of justifying the extension of Medicare, while for the latter it was about justifying the choice of a comprehensive reform. This internal division among insiders probably did contribute to their reform plan's demise. On the other hand, in the wake of the failed Clinton plan, perhaps this elite configuration favored the HCFA's rise in power and led to the Social Security Administration growing weaker in its implementation of health coverage policy (Berkowitz, 2002: 179–184). Lastly, the issue of the cost of health coverage reform constituted a political argument that the Washingtonian insiders would gradually reclaim and foreground as a key aspect of their future reform project (chapter 9).

The "Strangers" Programmatic Coup: The Managed-Competition Model

The managed-competition model was the third and most comprehensive health care insurance reform option. Studying the sociological characteristics of those policy entrepreneurs who defined the content of this programmatic orientation offers many useful lessons (chapter 2). For example, it reveals how a reform project devised by eminent health policy experts external to or on the margins of Washington's health elites in charge in Congress was added to the reform agenda during the presidential campaign (Hacker, 1997; Rich, 2004: 115). It was during the presidential campaign that Clinton declared his personal preference for the "managed competition without a budget" project in order to guarantee "universal coverage provided by the private sector and guaranteed by the public sector" (Starr & Zelman, 1993: 9). Most research attributes the success of this programmatic option to electoral considerations (Jacobs & Shapiro, 2000) or to the intellectual authority of the health experts who devised it (Glied, 1997; Lepont, 2014). Our aim here is to retrace the history of the managed-competition reform formulated by health policy entrepreneurs on the margins of Washington circles who tried during the Clinton administration to seize a political opportunity and impose their vision of a health coverage system. The study of long-term health insiders' career paths has already shown that these outsiders failed to establish themselves in charge over time on health governance (chapter 4).

Jacob Hacker has retraced the genesis of managed competition in a very enlightening way (1997: 52–56). Formulated over a long period by Alain Enthoven (1978, 1980, 1993), a Stanford economist, this project outlined a national system of coverage based on a health economics model. The reform project hoped to introduce a "public-private" health coverage system where strong regulation of "consumer choices" would entail limited health spending (Enthoven & Kronick, 1990). In the early 1990s, these ideas that had emerged from discussions in the 1970s were taken up by the Jackson Hole Group, a pro-market forum of reformers in Wyoming who organized regular seminars under the leadership of neuropediatrician Paul Ellwood, father of the HMO during the Nixon administration (Ellwood & Enthoven, 1995; Altman & Shactman, 2011: 71–76). Sector-based interest groups became associated with this comprehensive reform project—namely, by funding the seminars via the Washington Business Group on Health (Hacker, 1997: 54). Conservative Democrats (Blue Dogs) who were against the creation of a universal system that would require increased tax revenue were fairly receptive to the concept of managed competition (Hacker, 1997: 56–71). With this in mind, the Jackson Hole Group put forward the idea of creating Health Insurance Purchasing Cooperatives (HIPCs) (Nexon, 2007: 7–9). Alain Enthoven appeared clear-eyed when it came to the intricacies of the political road that lay ahead: "So Hillary came along, and I met with her. At the end, a lot of my ideas were included in the final bill but with a big problem. Many Democrats could not trust the market to control cost, and the bill became 'trop dirigiste' [in French in the interview]. She said, 'My husband will have to campaign for a second mandate in three years, and he has to show some progress in reducing costs—cost is rising too much over control.' . . . And then she worked in secret in her office with Ira Magaziner and . . . we didn't know what would go out."[25]

The main idea pursued thereafter concerned bolstering the health market by reinforcing competition among private providers so that overall costs would diminish, and then subsequently extending the coverage to citizens more broadly. Moderate Democrats recognized themselves in this programmatic orientation where a market-regulation rationale prevailed over the idea of direct financing from tax revenue. On the other hand, those future Clinton plan veterans, partial to a more interventionist notion of government, would go on to reject this programmatic orientation that was alien to their vision of health coverage policy. In opposition, the promoters of managed competition "thought competition, if constructed in the right way, could work in a reform health care delivery system. That was their concept."[26] Similarly, a few single-payer supporters argued that their easier-to-grasp reform project was preferable to managed competition (Starr, 2013: 126). Eventually, this comprehensive reform project would unite against it the liberal Democrats disappointed by the abandonment of a great national single-payer system, the moderate Democrats in the "Washington advisory group" who backed play-or-pay, and the Republican health administration left over from President George H. W. Bush's term (Hacker, 1997).

The same applied to the Republican health experts: "Managed competition, to most of us—it was like our idea, but it was more regulatory and more controlled. We think [as Republicans] that managed competition is an oxymoron,"[27] and in no way consisted of a compromise. So Republican health experts again took up the traditional counterargument denouncing the advent of a socialist form of health care and reaffirmed the view that the federal government ought not to modify the health coverage system. Their crucial argument was that "establishing a state-based health system managed by Big Brother, even if it isn't true" would create a political alignment of Republican representatives, private interest groups (insurance companies, hospitals, etc.), and the American middle class.[28] If the Republicans' resistance can easily be understood in light of the political battle that traditionally pitted them against Democrats on the very concept of social welfare, the Democratic camp was divided between elite groups competing among themselves to design the best reform model.

While opposition to managed competition garnered a lot of comment, it seems appropriate to return to the opprobrium directed toward Alain Enthoven, the instigator in chief of this version of the reform—in fact the archetype of the policy entrepreneur[29]—who attracted considerable ad hominem criticism. As a member of the "Whiz Kids" at the Department of Defense under Robert McNamara in the 1960s,[30] Enthoven analyzed budget efficiency and cost-cutting measures in the defense sector (Enthoven & Smith, 1971). An economist from Stanford University, he would eventually specialize in health policy and public health; he was then recruited in 1972 to participate as a consultant in the health reform project launched by the Carter administration (the Consumer Choice Health Plan of 1977), which at that stage was aimed already at steering the American health coverage system toward managed competition in the private sector. Enthoven introduced a new and improved version of this plan to the 1992 reform agenda (Rich, 2004). For some, such as health economist Sherry Glied (at Columbia University and New York University), Enthoven was the "genius" who spurred on the reform mindset described as "marketist" following the 1974 Nixon plan and up until the Clinton plan.[31] Although Enthoven's intellectual authority as a towering figure in health economics who regularly published in the prestigious *New England Journal of Medicine* went unchallenged (Lepont, 2014), his involvement in the Clinton administration was considered by Washington's health elites as the hammer blow of a stranger wanting to leave his mark on the great health coverage reform (Medvetz, 2012: 40). The interviews that we conducted show how the individuals who worked in the back offices of government perceived their contribution to the reform process: "Enthoven never worked on the Hill, he was an adviser to President Clinton, he's the father of the managed-competition theory . . . I would say, he doesn't influence our work directly. We listened to him when we had the time. "[32] This point that "we listened to him when we had the time" reveals the conflict between those individuals who were directly involved in the matter and those who devised "big pictures." Rejection of a reform project initiated by an expert external to the Washington sphere of government would gradually evolve into real aversion by the time Bill Clinton and his White House–entrenched entourage opted for managed competition— with the aim of casting aside, once and for all, the play-or-pay option upheld by Washington insiders.[33]

Behind this fragmentation of programmatic orientations, one can clearly see that the conflict pitting insiders against strangers gradually slid toward rejecting the strangers' hold on health policy. The future Clinton plan veterans, whose career paths travelled across the executive and Congress, found themselves at odds with policy experts, those "birds of passage" such as Alain Enthoven, the sociologist Paul Starr (at Princeton University) and Ira Magaziner, director of the task force working on behalf of Hillary Clinton (chapter 7). One interviewee, an insider, involved in preparing the task force's reform described and denounced this phenomenon of policy formulation led by strangers: "The Clinton reform was a mixed experience. On the one hand, the basic ideas—that is the managed competition—came out from several very academic people and papers. And Ira Magaziner, who was in charge of it, relied heavily on them. I think most people would say that two of the reasons it failed is that political people were not heavily enough involved, and that academic ideas proved very difficult to put into operation, and to figure out how it would actually work. I think the reform needed to be more grounded and experienced—because many of the ideas had never been tried before—and secondly, that it needed more involvement by both the political world and the operation world, who actually delivered services."[34]

This rejection of intervening third-party reformers led the health insiders to develop a crucial argument that was relatively harsh toward managed competition. Institutional migrant Judy Feder, who although she was a member of the Clinton health team during the transition period (chapter 4), directly questioned the financial viability (cost containment) of this programmatic orientation: "It was managed care within a budget, competition within a budget, always."[35] It is interesting to note that the insiders, in their assault upon the outside reformers, harnessed the financial argument that had led to their play-or-pay project being sidelined. Indeed, while in the end it might seem banal to point out how the reformers were often divided among themselves when confronted with the realities in the political sphere, it was all the more important to identify sociological fault lines such as the distinction between competing professional groups responsible for policy formulation who, beyond intra-partisan political divides, were pitted against one another.

Furthermore, the various attempts to build a reform advocacy coalition of the different constituents of governmental health elites (experts, staffers, and bureaucrats) around a managed-competition project entailed the hardening of the socio-professional line dividing insiders from strangers when it came to putting policy into practice. Thus, when Princeton sociologist Paul Starr became involved with White House advisers to find "a bridge to compromise: competition under a budget" (Starr & Zelman, 1993), he reinforced the feeling of policy being formulated by third parties. Indeed, Starr, while partially determining the reform's financial scope, made a strategic mistake by suggesting that the Medicare program, which the bureaucratic elites in the Social Security Administration remained strongly wedded to, was not compatible with instituting managed competition (Hacker, 1997: 128). Thus, it seems that instead of establishing a relatively consensual reform front, what occurred was an alignment between various professional components of Washington's unelected governmental health elites—the long-term insiders and the Social Security Administration elites—against outside reformers.

On the basis of these observations, it is clear that the origins of the split in the reform front went further and deeper than those which Theda Skocpol imputed to the "pundits" (1996). The sociological analysis of health coverage policy elites' career paths illustrates how technical competence, as much as reputation within a field or even media savviness, tends to dissipate when the practical challenge of formulating policy appears on a reform agenda. Moreover, the decision to present these three programmatic orientations as competing options, each with their own occupational figurehead championing a particular health policy, reveals the bedrock of geographical and socio-professional divisions. Our study shows that beyond the antagonism over cherished ideas (or programmatic orientations) and socio-professional divisions (political scientists and sociologists versus health economists) looms another form of rivalry too often reduced to its territorial dimension (Washingtonian insiders versus strangers). Cross-referencing elite configurations with reform programs can show how geographical considerations cut across the struggle between professional groups competing to shape policy. During the Clinton administration, this took the form of rivalry between new health coverage policy elites, who developed career paths of long-term insiders, and eminent policy entrepreneurs, who wore the faded finery of policy formulation led by strangers.

In his analysis of the failure of the Clinton plan, Hugh Heclo pointed to the effects of the lack of learning from experience among reformers (1995). It was clear to him that the Republican era stretching from the end of the Carter administration to the early 1990s, did not foster this type of political learning. Our study of long-term insiders has enabled us to show that these lessons learned, mainly from Congress's studies carried out by the Pepper Commission, primarily affected those elites. For the insiders, however, the Clinton plan failure would turn out to be a key moment in terms of their collective political learning (chapter 8). The study over time of various types of career paths allows us to understand how these lessons shared among Clinton plan veterans would be methodically transmitted to the "newcomers" in order to maximize the chances of a new reform project succeeding. The final lesson to be drawn from the failed Clinton project concerns the effects of competing rival unelected governmental elites—namely, the insiders who wanted to initiate reforms from their positions of power within policy formulation and those strangers such as the policy entrepreneurs who tried to formulate policy from outside.

CHAPTER 7

The Impossible Government of "Strangers"

RESEARCH ON the Clinton plan pointed out that coalescing political and institutional factors could explain the failure of the health coverage reform project. It is quite probable that the development of multiple political conflicts during the early decision-making process encouraged American public opinion to turn against the health coverage reform (Blendon, Hyams & Benson, 1993; Johnson & Broder, 1996; Jacobs & Shapiro, 2000). Originally seen positively by Americans, it was nevertheless the notion of "a reform made by elites for elites" that would become entrenched by early 1993 (Hacker, 1997: 170). According to Theda Skocpol, the "pundits' arrogance" and the "Clintonian policy planners' choice" to promote a neoliberal approach to health care reform were to blame (1996: 9).[1] Skocpol reproached the former for having increased divisions among the reformers by letting them believe that a gradual and bipartisan reform would be adopted, and the latter for having succumbed to a "market-centered reform" (1996: 15). To what extent, in addition to the political conflict fomented by the Republican opposition, did the growing struggle between insiders and "strangers"—firstly among the executive and then within Congress—foster the reversal of public opinion?

The study of correlations between the structural elites' transformation and the programmatic-orientation changes of the reform highlights another type of explanation than that of the anti-reform "iron triangle" formed by interest groups, physicians, and insurance companies (Peterson, 1993). Traditionally, health sector reformers would bypass an advocacy coalition made up of doctors, insurers, and interest groups in order to maneuver particular institutional checks and balances to their own advantage (Steinmo & Watts, 1995). In the case of the Clinton plan, criticisms exchanged between rival reforming elites faced with their respective programmatic orientations resurfaced when the Republican opposition and various interest groups presented the draft reform bill to Congress (Jacobs & Shapiro, 2000: 88). The inability of Democratic insiders and strangers to share a common programmatic orientation appears to have helped the Republican Party, which, while focusing its electoral campaign on the threat of a future "socialized medicine," found itself in a favorable position during the midterm congressional elections (for the 104th legislature).

Henceforth, we will reconsider the stages of the decision-making process regarding the health coverage reform up until its demise at the end of September 1994 to show how transformation in the social backgrounds and career paths of health coverage policy elites exacerbated the conflict on programmatic orientations (chapter 4 and chapter 6). Appointing the duo of First Lady Hillary Clinton and adviser Ira Magaziner from the Clintons' inner circle would turn out to be a political misjudgment, the consequences of which have not been previously explored from this perspective. The way this duo put in place a task force at the heart of the executive in order to extricate the conflict-mired debate caught between the many programmatic orientations would, on the contrary, crystallize divisions between competing health insiders and strangers. The presentation of a 1,500-page draft bill to Congress, resulting from discussions with the task force led by strangers catalyzed this threat into reality. The defeat of the Washingtonian insiders who were driving the play-or-pay project was also the price payed under the Clinton administration. The multifaceted rebellion of all the congressional protagonists was tangible proof of this.

The development of the counterargument initiated by long-term insiders regarding the managed-competition option's lack of budgetary viability, which would be taken up again later in Congress by the Republican opposition and sector-based interest groups, reveals another effect of the insiders-versus-strangers struggle. Our focus on continuity here points to the searing lessons learned by those involved with the ill-fated Clinton plan. Rivalrous internal conflicts within the elites' Democratic reform front certainly constituted a key aspect of the collective memory upon which the identity of the future Clinton plan veterans would be built.

The "Strangers" in Charge: Hillary Clinton and Ira Magaziner

When President Bill Clinton designated First Lady Hillary Rodham Clinton and Ira Magaziner, a political assistant and old friend of the Clintons, as heads of the health care reform plan within the executive branch of power, this was deemed by their opponents as a grave error of misjudgment (Johnson & Broder, 1996). This period corresponds to the abandonment of the play-or-pay project—a project that had been the Washington health elites' preferred alternative to the managed-competition option defended by policy entrepreneur Alan Enthoven (Hacker, 1997). Our interviews carried out more than fifteen years later allowed us to revisit with some detachment the consequences of this political decision, which was experienced collectively by the long-term insiders as policy formulated by strangers.

Rather than reducing this issue, as Johnson and Broder suggest (1996), to a conflict between forceful personalities pitting Ira Magaziner, the political adviser, against the insider Judy Feder, this appointment goaded the insiders to rally together and wage trench warfare against the strangers. Far more than a struggle between egos and top decision makers, this deep antagonism rested upon internal professional rivalries among various unelected governmental elites competing with one another to formulate policy. This occurred behind the closed doors of power, where what was at stake was the substance of the reform as much as control over its future direction. Before elaborating further on this thought, it is worth dismantling the "Hillarycare" myth, which presented the first lady as the architect of the reform and, consequently, as the person responsible for the Clinton plan.

This argument was propounded in the media, and traces of the coverage can be found in the *Washington Post* (March 30, 1993) article "Who's on Hillary's List?," which looks at the task-force members entrusted with drafting the text of the reform. The article suggests that Hillary Clinton held a crucial role in selecting the health experts—just as much as she did in recruiting the task force's five hundred and fifty members. Ten years later, on the basis of facts and firsthand sources, sociologist Paul Starr, who participated in this task force as a health policy adviser at the White House, offered an account of Hillary Clinton's true role in the genesis of the health care reform project (2007). Starr declared that the first lady took part in debates orchestrated by Ira Magaziner because President Clinton wished to put forward two individuals whom he trusted to manage the conflict between the elites in HHS and those in the Treasury Department regarding the issue of the health care reform's cost (2007: 13). Moreover, Starr noted that despite the first lady's real involvement in the debates and work on the reform, she always spoke about "my husband's plan," insofar as the choice of the reform's orientation had already been established by President Clinton and the health advisers who were close to him during the 1992 presidential campaign (Starr, 2007: 15; 2013).

Interviews with Clinton veterans confirmed Hillary Clinton's limited role in finalizing the reform's contents. For Democratic institutional migrant David Nexon, Senator Ted Kennedy's staff director at the time, although the first lady had the title of "chair" of the task force, she only participated in a few meetings and was not in charge of either leading or coordinating the many working groups addressing different policy issues of the reform (Nexon, 2007: 5–7). This role fell to Ira Magaziner as the task force's director. Thus, it seems that Hillary Clinton's role was merely that of a guarantor providing a direct communication link to the White House. Indeed, Chris Jennings, an institutional migrant who, during the health care reform debate of 1993 to 1994 acted as a liaison with Congress and was "really working for Hillary Clinton," explained that a "first lady driving the reform effort was really unusual" and moreover "dangerous" in that she had little legitimacy on the health care coverage policy issue.[2] Alain Enthoven, the father of managed competition, eagerly denounced the way in which Hillary Clinton and Ira Magaziner "worked in secret."[3]

For those who were steering the reform project, their feeling of being excluded from Washingtonian health elites was exacerbated when Ira Magaziner was appointed to head the task force. In a lengthy interview we carried out for Bill Clinton's presidential archives, institutional migrant Chris Jennings drew attention to how unknown Ira Magaziner was within the circles of Washington health experts; thus, at the meeting when Magaziner first put the Clinton plan on the agenda, a shared question emerged among the advisory group: "Who is this guy?" (Jennings & Lambrew, 2003: 18). And so, although Magaziner was involved with Hillary Clinton's work, Jennings recognized that appointing Magaziner was a strategic error because, ever since the New Deal era, Congress had considered this sphere of social insurance policy to be its own "exclusive domain." Magaziner's appointment stemmed from his long friendship with President Clinton, stretching back to their time at Oxford University, where they were both Rhodes scholars. This political communications expert quickly gained the bad reputation of someone who knew nothing about health policy issues and "loathed Washington's political cliques" (Jennings & Lambrew, 2003: 15). In addition, despite being among the "brightest" and having graduated from one of the United States' best universities, Magaziner came from the world of consulting and political communications (Jacobs & Shapiro, 2000: 91). With his lack of experience in governmental back offices and health coverage policy, Magaziner epitomized the figure of the "stranger."

Comparing the many accounts about Magaziner that we gathered several years after the reform's defeat confirmed this idea. Alice Rivlin, another Clinton plan veteran at the OMB who experienced the task force from the inside, explained: "President Clinton put Hillary in charge of developing the health care reform and to gather the higher consultants. Ira Magaziner, who I have worked with before and who was a sort of business consultant—Ira set up a very [deliberate] process involving a lot of experts, inside and outside the government. I was one of those, but I was not in charge of it. This [rather deliberate] process began with a lot of meetings and decisions. For several months, the economic team within the administration was worried about that because we thought that it was rather over-deliberate. Not only the process was over-deliberate, but the plan was maybe too ambitious or too deliberate. But Ira and his team, and Hillary, had a pretty clear idea of what they wanted."[4]

Moreover, Karen Davis—former ASPE at the Department of Health during the Carter administration and a supporter of a public health coverage system who worked alongside Donna Shalala, the future secretary of HHS—remembered how Ira Magaziner had justified managing the reform process in January 1993, and why she later refused to join the task force: "Shalala disagreed with the fact that it was possible to plan a comprehensive health reform without recognizing that it would cost money and need taxes to increase. That's what Ira Magaziner said, and nobody believed him, nor the government. She [came back to New York and said] it's not my problem: they've got a crazy guy . . . So I went down when Shalala was asked to go down, but I was not part of this big task force headed by Ira Magaziner."[5] Another institutional migrant assigned to the task force, on behalf of Representative Henry Waxman, denounced Ira Magaziner's poor handling of the decision-making process and reproached him for "a year and a half talking inside the White House and inside HHS and inside academia, and, you know, just talking."[6]

These observations clearly illustrate how the health insiders reproached Magaziner for his lack of professional health policy knowledge, which made him unfit to spearhead the reform. Brian Biles was another institutional migrant who had recently joined HHS. In his interview, Biles emphasized that "the guy named Ira Magaziner" owed his appointment to his closeness to Bill Clinton—"he had been a Rhodes scholar with him in Oxford"—and that Magaziner "knew nothing about legislation in Washington and he knew nothing about health."[7] Biles went on to say that Magaziner was "a corporate consultant type" who knew how to organize a consultation, which he did around a very complex process (i.e., the task force) in order to draft the legislative proposal, thus proving that he did not understand a thing about how Congress works.[10]

Other Clinton veterans such as Judy Feder, whose friendship with Ira Magaziner went back to their opposition to the play-or-pay project (Johnson & Broder, 1996), reproached him for having claimed that when he set up the task force, he had initiated an innovative and open way of imagining the reform—a process that ultimately was brought to an end after "the drafting by a few hands and behind closed doors and amidst the greatest secrecy of the draft reform bill" (Feder, 2007: 11). A senior Republican career bureaucrat recalled, "The Democrats came in with a huge battery of experts from outside of government—consultants, professors, people who ran programs—and they put that—they installed that huge cadre of people to design the program."[8] Mirroring those presidential advisers described as czars, Magaziner was given the moniker Rasputin by Washington's health elites (Blumenthal & Morone, 2009: 375). From then on, once the decision-making process was launched and the task force set up by Ira Magaziner, a series of conflicts about the programmatic orientation were reignited: not merely the tension between insiders and strangers but also their professional rivalry with the health administration officials who were very wedded to the Medicare and Medicaid programs, and with the health staffers in Congress who were used to formulating these policies.

The Clinton Task Force: A One-of-a-Kind Institution

The creation from nothing of the health task force, entirely invented by Ira Magaziner, was considered a tour de force by government health elites. Created in January 1993, it was perceived to have given rise to the Health Security Act that President Bill Clinton presented to Congress on September 22, 1993. Innovative in form, the task force was an ad hoc group that included a vast number of health bureaucrats and health experts (around five hundred individuals); it was also seen as a new version of the government of strangers (Skocpol, 1996: 10). The interviews that we carried out nearly twenty years after its creation illuminate how the task force was considered to be the institutionalization of a government of strangers.

To begin with, the task force's institutional location was novel in that it was independent from both Congress and HHS; indeed, it was directly accountable to the White House (Starr, 2013). The way "its workload was organized was in a multitude of thematic 'clusters,' each addressing a different aspect of the plan," and thus, established patterns of working collectively to shape a policy reform were broken (Feder, 2007: 11; Glied, 1997: 10). In the eyes of some observers, Magaziner tried to introduce a very Oxford style of debate and put the finishing touches to the reform project's content by delegating the work to eight transversal cluster teams and thirty-four thematic working groups, all of whom needed to keep their deliberations secret (Blumenthal & Morone, 2009: 369). Others saw President Clinton's health advisers with Magaziner at the helm wanting to initiate opportunities for discussion among peers, as had occurred in "eighteenth-century intellectual salons" in order to devise "good public policy" together, which would transcend the divisions opposing the various health elite cliques regarding the reform's programmatic orientation (Jacobs & Shapiro, 2000: 81–82). To this end, the task force aimed to bring together the senior health bureaucrats of the outgoing Republican administrations (i.e., those of Ronald Reagan and George H. W. Bush), and some congressional health staffers and health policy experts, all the while including those recalcitrant Washington health insiders who objected to managed competition, and thus build a consensus around a responsible and non-statist project (which would be too public) (Jacobs & Shapiro, 2000: 85–86).

Sociologist Paul Starr, who worked on the task force, listed a catalog of tactical errors, such as giving decision-making powers to a select group of White House advisers, recruiting congressional health staffers late in the day as an afterthought, as well as awkwardly distinguishing between components of policy and those of politics (Starr, 2007; Hacker, 1997: 123). The wish to construct—by mustering this great armada[9]—an advocacy coalition on a consensual reform project capable of eventually rallying Congress and sector-based interest groups, even though they were not involved in the task force's blue-sky thinking (Starr, 2007: 15), would turn out to be an elusive utopia. In practice, the workings of this centralized structure dependent on the White House—as had been the case during President Franklin D. Roosevelt's tenure with the New Deal—gave rise to the feeling that only a small clique of mainly non-Washington-based presidential advisers surrounding Magaziner would be shaping the draft health care reform bill (Hacker, 1997: 124). Despite organizing more than a hundred seminars, the ideological gulf separating the insiders and the promoters of managed competition would continue to widen (Skocpol, 1996: 67; Starr, 2013: 94).

From this perspective, when Hugh Heclo diachronically compared the Clinton administration with the Kennedy-Johnson administration's War on Poverty reforms, and how socialization to its programmatic orientations had begun in the early 1960s, he pointed out that the task force did not incorporate the various lessons learned by the past (1995: 97). In the task force, Washington long-term insiders saw their professional authority on health policy diluted amid a cosmopolitan Areopagus made of Republican senior officials, bureaucrats, and academic experts.[10] Moreover, the insiders' ability to react collectively to the reform's programmatic orientation was limited by the small working groups method imposed by Magaziner. One institutional migrant who had taken part in the task force representing a congressman decried the poor working practices of the entire enterprise: "It was so slow to start. He convened this massive group of people, with Ira Magaziner . . . who advised the White House on what kind of health plan they should have, and rather than immediately going to Congress, they spent a year and half . . . almost a year and half talking inside the White House and inside HHS and inside academia, and you know, just talking."[11]

Even if some senior health administration bureaucrats did find the experience of collaborating in small theme-based working groups for three or four months "amusing," most agreed that "there was a core staff that was working with the White House to build the proposal, and they tried to convene the whole group to consider the options on all the different aspects."[12] One other senior health bureaucrat summarized the general feeling thus: "It's hard to say, because I worked on Hillary Clinton's task force, and the plan—the legislation that was submitted to Congress—was developed by bureaucrats really, with a few outside people, and this time we had no sort of participation in the design. It was all sort of staff, at the staff level."[13] Guy King, a Republican policy bureaucrat, referred to a frenetic work pace: "We would go to the White House in the evening and meet with Ira Magaziner, senior adviser to the president for policy development. We would brief him on the analyses that we had done that day and get our new assignment from him. We'd get home around midnight for a few hours of sleep and then get up early and do it all over again the next day. This went on for months" (King, 2007: 11–12).

Another long-term insider at the HCFA described the task force made up of "external experts, consultants, and professors," who with great authority outlined the parameters of the reform's scope, as the "biggest example" of a government of strangers.[14] This strategy had a dual negative effect: giving, on the one hand, the senior career bureaucrats of HHS the impression that they ought "only to manage and implement policies devised by others,"[15] while giving, on the other hand, the Washington insiders a merely peripheral and technical role (Jacobs & Shapiro, 2000: 81–82). This feeling was also shared by experts at the Brookings Institution who were seconded to the task force. One of them regretted that "I took a leave from Brookings and came to this group and became a temporary government employee for three or four months."[16] Indeed, Magaziner had organized the work of the task force by dividing it into small, loosely connected working groups. His goal was to ensure that the programmatic orientation of managed competition would not be questioned by the members of the task force.

Institutional migrant Chris Jennings, a task force member responsible for communication with Congress, reminded us that the problems encountered regarding the issue of integrating the health staffers was a warning sign of future conflicts that would emerge during the draft bill's passage through Congress (Jennings & Lambrew, 2003: 22–23). Integrating "a hundred congressional staffers" came late in the day after an opaque selection process. In addition, the method of working in theme-based workshops led to personal staff and committee staff being treated in undifferentiated ways, leading them to behave disloyally. Indeed, having traditionally had a firm grip on drafting reform bills, the committee staff found it difficult to share this role with both the best experts in the country and the executive's bureaucrats. From that point on, health staffers in Congress—namely, those who had not been recruited to the task force—had an arduous time trying to dissociate themselves from the ensuing outcome, even causing one of them to assert "After all, if I'm not part of it, it must be a joke or a plot" (Jennings & Lambrew, 2003: 23). David Nexon, an institutional migrant and Senator Kennedy's staff director, brought a little nuance by specifying that those members of Congress who wanted to take part were welcome, even though very few of them, apart from some of Waxman's staffers, took up the offer (Nexon, 2007: 5).

One policy bureaucrat interviewed confirmed that the leaders of Congress and their powerful health staffs had not been really involved with the process of drafting the reform bill behind closed doors: "Clinton didn't even consult with—I don't think he even had anybody from Congress working with him on his plan. They just had these experts all over the city drafting various sections of this health care bill that they were going to present to Congress as a fait accompli."[17] Compounding their poor integration in the task force was the symbolic blow suffered by congressional staffers when they saw it present an already completed reform project to Congress: "[They brought] a 1,500-page bill to Congress and said pass this, without recognizing that there are 435 people with ideas on the House side and 100 people with ideas on the Senate side, and they just brought it to Congress and said pass this."[18] Thereafter, Democratic representatives in Congress and their committee staffs, traditionally little inclined to follow the partisan line, would display a particular zeal in drafting amendments and counter-propositions. Those interest groups who were not linked to the task force's efforts benefited from the reform project's long gestation period, as they developed a strong counterargument thanks to the mediation of Republican health staffers and representatives. According to Kathleen Buto, a Democratic institutional migrant, "the criticism of the Clinton approach was there wasn't enough conversation with the stakeholders, for example, consumers, insurance companies [i.e., nonmembers of the task force]. The insurance companies mounted a campaign to defeat the health care bill, so there wasn't much interest in collaborating with them."[19]

Overall, the task force is still a one-of-a-kind institution, and the way it was staffed and managed by Magaziner created fissures within the reform front; and while these problems worsened, lobbyists and interest groups were able to gain support in Congress to defeat the reform (owing to its cost, the role of the private sector, etc.). From then on, as strangers formulated the reform while imposing their programmatic orientation (of managed competition), the plan found itself to be the butt of criticism from both long-term insiders and interest groups.

Congressional Rebellion against a Reform Project "Not Invented Here"

When the draft bill of more than a thousand pages was presented, the weakness of the budgetary framework and the determined effort of sector-based lobbyists supported by Republican representatives and their staffers would result in the reform being simply withdrawn at the end of September 1994.

Democratic institutional migrant Brian Biles remarked quite perceptively that the strategic error of those who were driving through the reform that emerged from the task force, and presenting it in full to Congress, was to have assumed that with "this 1,500-page bill, they went and found every problem in health care and solved it. . . . And the lesson is, for every problem you solve, you probably gain an opponent."[20] Technocratic translator Bruce Vladeck, HCFA administrator during the Clinton administration, reminded us that this strategic decision could only be imputed to Ira Magaziner (Vladeck, 2002: 185). Vladeck also referred to the task force director's two errors: first, suggesting that the amended version of the managed-competition option would lead to health care coverage being extended without any tax increases and, second, compiling a complicated and lengthy draft bill of which five hundred pages were devoted to how the reform would be funded.

The Washingtonian insiders' proposals in the executive illustrated the new financing culture of the health coverage policy elites who were in charge at the top posts in HHS. In fact, the services of the HCFA, whose budgetary hold over health coverage never ceased to increase after new regulatory and political tools were put in place, such as the HMO (Brown, 1983a; 1985), were found to be at complete odds with a reform whose costs and sustainable funding did not appear to be under control (Jacobs & Shapiro, 2000: 88). Among Democrats inside the Beltway, the issue of controlling the reform's costs magnified the divisions in the liberal camp, as well as between its liberal section and the conservative Blue Dogs who believed that only a gradual policy change would preclude increasing taxes (Johnson & Broder, 1996: 109). These divisions were underpinned by a great majority of health staffers in Congress who, despite their tardy and peripheral integration into the task force, remained on the whole attached to the programmatic orientation of play-or-pay that had emerged out of the Pepper Commission's work.

In addition, the Democratic insiders' reservations regarding the reform's cost, viewed through the lens of the programmatic option of managed competition, was manifest in the memorandum drafted by Judy Feder (and her group of colleagues), who by then occupied the post of assistant secretary for planning and evaluation at HHS. These insiders made a set of recommendations to prevent the future reform's budget from increasing by operating strict cost-control measures within the health coverage sector (Johnson & Broder, 1996: 109–111). President Clinton and Ira Magaziner then rejected the report's conclusions, written by these Washington Beltway experts who focused too greatly on increasing the government's power to intervene and too little on how to keep the costs of health care under control. Thereafter, the conflict between these insiders and the strangers, initially based on different visions of the government's role, would turn to the matter of the reform's financial issue in response to the criticism of it being a "reform without a budget."

Furthermore, the group of Democratic health insiders in Congress believed that formulating a draft bill exclusively within the executive branch proved to be a major tactical error. Here we should recall the fact that Hillary Clinton had recruited a number of young Washington health staffers, as seen in the hiring of institutional migrant Chris Jennings;

the purpose of this was to be able to defend the reform project before the powerful committees in both houses of Congress. In addition, as President Clinton had made a political commitment to limit the number of White House advisers, some of these staffers were appointed to posts within HHS. Indeed, Jerry Klepner, a former staff director on the Committee on Compensation and Employee Benefits in the House of Representatives, asserted that he had been appointed to HHS with a dual purpose: first, to "expurgate certain terms in the reform bill" and render it "saleable" to Congress and, second, to track its evolution in Congress's political agenda. This institutional migrant also mentioned that President Clinton had committed himself to reduce White House staff by a third, which he did. But in practice, he compensated for the decrease by moving staffers out of the agencies of HHS; these staffers then worked on his behalf. "So Clinton could say he cut the White House by a third, which he did, but the reality was, he was pulling people from HSS agencies to serve in the White House."[21]

The most significant example of this type of circulation among elites at that time was certainly that of Chris Jennings, who contributed to the Pepper Commission's work. This is how he recounted his experience: "I actually had a dual role. In 1993 I was formally staffed and paid by HHS. . . . But the reality was that I was working for the White House. At the same time, I was working on the Hill as a congressional liaison . . . I didn't even have an office in HHS. My office was in the Executive Office of the President. I was really working for Hillary Clinton. In this capacity, I prepared her for hundreds of meetings with members of Congress. I helped her understand the logic of Congress, the different priorities and the various concerns of every member. . . . It was a very intense time. At the conclusion of the health care debate, there were a lot of staff working on health care, so there was huge downsizing as the White House was moving to another issue."[22] For this institutional migrant, his negotiating work between the executive and legislative was a time of intensive learning and socialization insofar as he did not yet at that stage of his career path consider himself a "confirmed policy person."[23] But Jennings recognized that "the lessons we learned were that such a reform needed a strong investment from Congress. It needed to be supported by influential members. Back to 1993, the chair of the Finance Committee, Patrick Moynihan, hated the bill and hated the Clintons."[24]

Interestingly, there was also the case of Gary Claxton, an ex–health staffer who contributed to the Pepper Commission with institutional migrants Diane Rowland, Chris Jennings, and Judy Feder. Claxton remembers having been "appointed to an unusual post of staffer to Congress to work for the president with the aim of softening the rather negative view of the financial dimension of the reform, according to the influential Ways and Means [in the House of Representatives] and Finance [in the Senate] committees."[25] At that juncture, the task was to counter the CBO's argument, which was that the version of the reform project presented to Congress was financially unsustainable without a substantial increase in tax revenues (Joyce, 2011).

From that point, the battle shifted to a contest between the bodies controlling the budget within the two branches of power: the OMB and the CBO.[26] The CBO's mission was to provide a forward-looking analysis of the program's fiscal viability (Joyce, 2011: 157). Health economist Len Nichols, in charge at the OMB in the White House of assessing the cost of the reform before it was discussed at the CBO, drew our attention to the lengthy and conflict-ridden negotiations.[27] Between "the month of May 1993 and the end of August 1994," a fierce battle consumed these two evaluation bodies over technical issues and methods to be applied, in addition to the CBO's refusal to accept leadership within its own sphere of competence being taken over by its homologue in the executive branch. For Len Nichols, the CBO "was not friendly to Clinton," and its experts did everything in their power to "undo" the proposed reform's budgetary foundations.[28] Moreover, Paul Van de Water, then in charge at the CBO of reviewing health care budgets, underlined how owing to delayed communication about the Clinton plan reform in September 1993, the experts of this bipartisan congressional agency had drawn up ahead of time several scenarios, including the Managed Competition Act.[29]

Despite poor communication with the OMB and the financial administration wing of HHS—the Health Care Financing Administration (HCFA)—Van de Water claimed that these services worked closely together on this reform option—namely, on "understanding the language used to draft the bill which was unclear to us," especially the creation of new regulatory tools to control the health market, such as the health alliances (insurance cooperatives).[30] He recalled that the absence of individuals on the administrative side who could support the CBO officials made it awkward to devise reliable estimates. Moreover, unfortunate pressures placed by certain White House advisers upon the CBO director did not impede a report being published which revealed fierce disagreements on the Clinton administration's reform project when predicting its effects on the upcoming 1995–2000 federal budget (Joyce, 2011: 163–164). Another interviewee in a post at the CBO during these negotiations said that apart from the budgetary aspect, they understood little about the reform project's policy design when it was presented to Congress.[31]

Furthermore, the internal fragmentation of the reform front of the Democratic health elites opened up gaps into which the Republican health staffers ventured in order to undermine the Clinton plan and cut it off from the support it had received from a majority of American citizens (Skocpol, 1996: 133; Jacobs & Shapiro, 2000). Indeed, during the nine months of the project's gestation within the task force and the White House (from January 20, 1993, to September 15, 1993), the Republican opposition prepared its counterarguments with the upcoming legal battle in sight. Benefiting from the reform's long gestation period, sector-based interest groups (insurers, consumers, hospitals) developed a fierce opposition, alongside some renowned Republican insiders in Congress, such as institutional migrants Chip Kahn and David Abernethy. For example, David Abernethy, who was at that time staff director of a subcommittee of the Ways and Means Committee, and his team of staffers in the House of Representatives wrote eight volumes based on the congressional hearings conducted on the health care reform.[32] In a long section of our interview, Abernethy described in detail all the preparation work carried out by the Ways and Means Committee on the issue of health care coverage during the gestation of the Clinton plan. He also reminded us that "health policy is not something that a lot of people know. . . . It's a very esoteric area."[33] Thus, over nine months, they conducted hearings to help them prepare and debate aspects of the reform project.

From this Pandora's box, two arguments emerged encapsulating the Republicans' conservative rhetoric, which were targeted against any kind of project aimed at transforming the American health care coverage system: the first argument claimed that interfering with an individual's freedom of choice regarding their preferred health coverage plan would lead to "socialized medicine;" the second argument rejected any reform that would open the door to tax increases. Republican congresspeople from the House of Representatives filing behind their leader Newt Gingrich soon voiced the threat of central government increasing its power, and inevitably raising taxes, while referring to how President Clinton had committed himself during the campaign to reduce public spending (Joyce, 2011: 156–157). David Abernethy underlined the fact that the health care coverage reform project arrived late on the political agenda and right in the middle of the battle over reducing the federal deficit (Deficit Reduction Act, August 1993), which was a top political priority for the Clinton administration.[34] The Republicans, well aware of the conflicts regarding the programmatic orientation that divided the Democratic elites in Congress, worked in the CBO so that the principle of "pay as you go" (pricing based on use) would be applied as a golden budgetary rule and thus defy the reform project.[35]

Alongside all this, in order to discredit the version of managed competition introduced before Congress, private health interest groups (such as the AMA and the HIAA) had elaborated an argument propounding the threat of a new stage along the road to socialist medicine. Thus, when health alliances (insurance cooperatives) were set up as a regulatory tool to control competition between private groups—a key component of the final version of the reform—Republican health staffers retaliated. Both the pharmaceutical industry and the insurance lobby designed anti-Clinton plan advertising campaigns aimed at the general public on the theme of "the Clinton health reform was not going to be expanding things, it was going to take away what you had."[36]

The success of the "Harry and Louise" television advertisements[37] devised by Republican institutional migrant Chip Kahn, who was at that time employed by the private insurance lobby (HIAA), showed how those who were opposed to the reform project turned the criticism to their own advantage.[38] By putting onscreen a white middle-class American couple, Kahn was toying with citizens' attachment to private insurance schemes, which as a result of the new reform would be put in jeopardy. The political argument was straightforward: "Right, and people, politicians, particularly on the right, exploited that mercilessly. You know, Big Brother's taking over your health care, and that's the most surefire way to get Americans riled up, even if it's not true, I mean, it'll do it every single time."[39] The success of this strategy was recognized by Democratic insiders such as Judy Feder, who acknowledged that the ads "were very powerful. . . . It became a story in and of itself. Then there was an active campaign going to make it essentially safe for key members of Congress to oppose reform, and that was a big part of the fear strategy" (Feder, 2007: 17). Others such as institutional migrant Kathy Buto explained how sidelining the interest groups while the extension of Medicare coverage was being discussed constituted a strategic error that ought not to be repeated.[40] Faced with these multiple attacks, the Democrats in Congress withdrew the reform project on September 26, 1994, a few months before they lost the midterm elections for the 104th legislature.

Faced with the magnitude of their defeat, Democratic health coverage policy elites, a few of whom would remain in health administration during both of President Clinton's terms, or in Congress in a minority position, gradually embarked on drawing up an inventory of problems that had led to this collective failure. This task, carried out under the aegis of these insiders who had led some or all of the struggles over the choice of programmatic orientation, in addition to the in-fighting in the back offices of government, led these individuals to assert themselves as the veterans of the Clinton administration. It was the insiders who remained in charge despite the defeat; and for this reason, the burden of failure fell upon their shoulders (meaning, the feeling of accountability). With these considerations in mind, it is easier to understand why, after the Clinton plan collapsed and left nearly thirty million American citizens without health care coverage, the eponymous veterans who were tormented by a feeling of collective guilt[41] played a central role in political learning from their failure (chapter 8 and chapter 9). When the Republicans returned to power, these individuals, whose career paths had remained Washington-centered, would act collectively by recruiting Democratic newcomers and a few Republican insiders in order to reformulate a reform based on a shared programmatic orientation that would allow the contribution of the private sector, the consideration of budget constraints, and bipartisan political consensus-building.

CHAPTER 8

The George W. Bush Years

Clinton Plan Veterans Make the Next Reform Possible

FTER THEIR failure and until the end of the second Clinton presidential term, the Democratic health elites abandoned any desire to reform the health coverage system (Pierson, 2001). Apart from the fact that the wound from the Clinton plan failure was still raw, these elites had to face the aggressive behavior of Republicans who, holding a majority in Congress and inclined toward austerity policies, were trying to dismantle the programs already in force (Hacker, 2002; Pierson & Skocpol, 2007). In this conflict-ridden political context, what was at stake was the very survival of Medicare, a bipartisan and consensual health insurance program, which the Republicans under Newt Gingrich's leadership as Speaker of the House had attempted to privatize (Oberlander, 2003). Paradoxically, it was during George W. Bush's presidency that the idea of a new health coverage reform project, consensual and bipartisan, was shaped in Washington's health expert circles (Starr, 2013: 161). The ceaseless increase in the health insurance system's budget, and the bipartisan reform project devised and enacted in Massachusetts and led by Republican Governor Mitt Romney contributed to reinvigorating the reformers' front (Jacobs & Skocpol, 2010; McDonough, 2011). The programmatic elite framework shows how the long-term insiders who remained inside the Beltway during George W. Bush's presidency associated the invention of the new role of custodian of state policies with the formulation of a new consensual health coverage reform project.

From this perspective, we will revisit the political process that would lead to the Patient Protection and Affordable Care Act voted on by the 111th Congress on March 23, 2010, by looking specifically at the effects of long-term insiders' political learning (Hacker, 2010; Moronne, 2010; Oberlander, 2010). While the majority of US health researchers do refer to a link between the lessons learned from the ill-fated Clinton plan and the Obama reform (Donnelly & Rochefort, 2012), few of them have studied in-depth the effectiveness of this learning process (Lepont, 2014). Most research, with the exception of John McDonough (2011) and Jonathan Oberlander (2007a,b, 2010), neglects the correlation between the transformation of the elites' career-paths analysis and the formulation of a new reform agenda. Thus, drawing on Harold Lasswell's (1936) question—*Who Gets What, When, How?*—we will see how the Clinton plan veterans succeeded in getting newcomers on board with the next far-reaching reform project.

For Jonathan Oberlander (2007a), the Obama administration's triumph is the result of political learning that enabled the Democratic reformers to avoid the errors that led to the defeat of the Clinton plan. The effects of these lessons are seen in the choice of political strategy to pursue as well as the choice of programmatic orientations. This general observation is in fact shared by the great majority of health academics (Hacker, 2010; Jacobs & Skocpol, 2010; Morone, 2010). Historians Kevin Donnelly and David Rochefort, however, detect some retrospective reconstruction in these interpretations (2012). These authors point to how, during the reform process, certain recommendations emerging from the "supposed lessons learned," such as the president's weak intervention or the need for a bipartisan compromise, were abandoned. By studying the transformation of the health experts' career paths over time, Ulrike Lepont reveals that some Washington experts brought the lessons learned to bear on the adjustments they made to their reform strategy (2014). When seen through the lens of previous failures to find politically viable solutions, these learning processes can have various effects depending on the type of professional group involved (for example, elected politicians, congressional staffers, policy entrepreneurs, academics, and interest groups). Concurring with Daniel Béland, it is quite likely that the view of the "lessons to be retained" and the primacy of some over others vary according to experience and the degree of occupational commitment among these individuals in both their prior and future political battles (Béland, 2006). The analysis of long-term insiders' career paths has already revealed that the Clinton plan veterans were profoundly affected by this political defeat.

One question therefore arises: did the consequences of these lessons learned hold the same resonance and interest for the policy experts and the policy entrepreneurs—as they weighed up programmatic orientations while remaining on the margins of political infighting—as for the long-term insiders, who were trying for policy formulation in the back offices of government? Moreover, bureaucratic or political battles occurring in the back offices of government during decision-making (i.e., a reform) between individuals "in charge" are not comparable to and do not really have similar consequences as the controversies between policy experts and policy entrepreneurs regarding the programmatic orientations that surface in intellectual forums on the margins of government (i.e., think tanks). Returning to our empirical study, this observation allows us to put forward the idea that the defeat of the Clinton plan, including its legacy and the possible political lessons learned, did not have the same impact on the two types of elites (insiders versus strangers), both in terms of their career paths and their sense of group solidarity. History does not have the same meaning for, nor the same impact on, those participants who witnessed political battles inside the government, and who in this particular case experienced defeat after two years of struggle, as for those (academics and researchers) who, as external bystanders to the political arena, shape the intellectual framework of comprehensive reform.

It is precisely the distinction between insiders and strangers that we intend to highlight by examining how these lessons learned resulted from political work conducted by a group of individuals whose career paths matched those of insiders who, in these circumstances, donned the mantle of the Clinton plan veterans.[1] Behind their desire to use tried and tested recipes for reforming the health insurance system lay a hidden political commitment based on a narrative of the Clinton failure, the aim of which was to unite with the newcomers and then formulate a new project, while simultaneously marginalizing the strangers (i.e., the policy entrepreneurs). We explore how these veterans drew strength from sharing their behind-the-scenes policy-based experience of governmental battles during the Clinton administration, like ex-soldiers recalling their military exploits, in order to rally the Democratic newcomers to a shared conception of the role of custodian of state policies. Holding on to this common memory of defeat, they would shape the custodianship around a renewed programmatic orientation based on a consensual reform and a political strategy regarding policy design. Our aim will be to show how from inside the Beltway, until the Democrats returned to power, the Clinton plan veterans would redefine the role of custodian by shaping not only their programmatic orientation of the future health insurance system but, in addition, the means for inscribing it onto the political agenda. Their collective involvement in Washington's think tanks and philanthropic foundations to advance a bipartisan and consensual project of far-reaching reform of the health insurance system attests to this notion.

A Collective Political Learning: The Role of the Clinton Plan Veterans

First, let us be clear that although American political scientists have highlighted the effects of divisions among Democratic health elites on the failed Clinton plan (Starr, 2013), they do not outline any consequences from the defeat on the structure of career paths for the groups that formulate long-term policies. For Jacobs and Shapiro, the failed Clinton plan showed clearly how the idea of extending health care coverage to improve the lives of the poorest citizens, although popular to begin with, was gradually tarnished and replaced with the negative view of a reform designed by elites in order to satisfy those same elites (2000:

138). Certainly, the exacerbation of intra-elitist struggles concerning programmatic orientations (chapter 6), despite their justification of seeking a good policy, created the harmful image of a divided health leadership in government, leading inevitably to the reigniting of ongoing conflict in American political culture between the Washingtonians and American society. Although this political failure stemmed from interactions among all the health elites, its effects were most keenly felt, especially long-term, among the Democratic insiders. Indeed, some of them remained in charge in the Clinton administration (from 1994 to 2000) to manage the health insurance system, which was always at the breaking point, and faced a majority Republican Congress in opposition. While the policy entrepreneurs pursued academic debates, the Clinton plan veterans developed a strong sense of collective accountability regarding this defeat.

The sociological study of career paths illustrates how soon after the reform's defeat in September 1994, the Democratic long-term insiders with institutional migrant and technocratic translator career paths claimed all the positions of power, replacing the strangers in HHS and at the White House. Despite the Clinton plan's failure and the debacle that ensued, some individuals decided to protect the Medicare and Medicaid programs (Oberlander, 2003). Clinton plan veterans with an institutional migrant or technocratic translator profile stayed on in the administration in order to counter the majority Republicans' aggressive opposition after the midterm elections to Congress in November 1994 (chapter 4). The most significant examples of veterans are the institutional migrant Chris Jennings, who took Ira Magaziner's "birds of passage" place;[2] and the technocratic translators Nancy-Ann DeParle, who took over from Bruce Vladeck to head the HCFA, and Jeanne Lambrew, who took on the key post of PAD for budgetary health matters at the OMB. For Lambrew, it was clear that after the reform project unraveled, and following the Democrats' electoral defeat in 1994, the only people who would "survive" in their positions of power at HHS were the Washington governmental health policy elites, and they were the most professionally skilled to prevent the Republican majority in Congress from driving through their mission to dismantle the health care system (Jennings & Lambrew, 2003: 73).

Paradoxically, it was in this unusual context that the Democratic health coverage policy elites would set off in search of a bipartisan partnership with their Republican counterparts. On this matter, Len Nichols, a health economist at the OMB (from 1993 to 1994) during the Clinton administration, said that after the traumatizing "trench warfare" of the Health Security Act (the Clinton plan), seeking out a bipartisan compromise seemed necessary as an alternative tactic that the Clinton plan veterans would share with the Democratic newcomers and the Republican long-term insiders.[3] In 1997 it was in the context of the State Children's Health Insurance Program (SCHIP) and in support of the Balanced Budget Act (BBA), that Clinton plan veterans Chris Jennings and Nancy-Ann DeParle, and the newly arrived Jeanne Lambrew, instigated a bipartisan approach to health insurance policies. From late Clintonism to the George W. Bush era, the search for a bipartisan compromise was imposed by the majority of Democratic staffers in Congress as a prerequisite for launching the legislative process regarding health issues (Beaussier, 2016). Liz Fowler and Cybele Bjorklund, Democratic newcomers in a minority position in Congress—the former on the Senate's Finance Committee and the latter on the Ways and Means Committee in the House of Representatives—sensed that the understanding they shared with their Republican counterparts, Mark Hayes (on the Senate Finance Committee) and Chuck Clapton (on the House's Energy and Commerce Committee), favored the Medicare Prescription Drug, Improvement, and Modernization Act (2003) known as MMA being adopted, despite Republican Speaker Newt Gingrich's opposition.[4]

Other interviewees recalled that sections of the MMA covering health insurance were drafted in close collaboration with newcomers Fowler and Bjorklund and Clinton plan veterans from Henry Waxman's staff—Phil Schiliro, Karen Nelson, and Andy Schneider—as well as Republican staffers.[5] The example of these two bipartisan health acts—devised during the late Clintonism period and during George W. Bush's administration—by both Democratic and Republican insiders illustrates how the search for political consensus can limit the effects of a divisive policy formulation. It also shows that the first lesson learned from the Clinton defeat had actual consequences on the way in which some policy-makers tried to address health policy. Furthermore, one can see how in order to counter the "stupid institutional game" (Steinmo & Watts, 1995), the Clinton plan veterans perceived bipartisan consensus as an antidote to the programmatic fragmentation and divisions among the governmental health elites. Certainly, the reality of partisan political games and the rise in power of the Tea Party within the Republican party would render these efforts redundant.

Although some researchers investigating American politics have mentioned the role of the Clinton plan veterans in the Obama reform (McDonough, 2011; Starr, 2013), few have taken seriously the links between the learning of political lessons of history, the making of an elite group, and the development of a long-term collective-action strategy. If we take up Daniel Béland's invitation to reflect upon the effects of political lessons learned (2006), we can see that it is through the tension between ideas, and the strategies stemming from this, that we can measure these effects. The interviews conducted reveal the existence of a sense of collective responsibility for the failure of the reform rapidly spreading beyond the Clinton plan veterans' circles. Jeanne Lambrew recalled that the individuals constituting the "health policy community" believed that divisions among the elite front had prevented the "USA from being lifted into the closed circle of nations furnished with a system offering universal insurance" (Jennings & Lambrew, 2003: 77). In order to avoid the bias of retrospective reconstruction, it is important to point out that this long-term insider's 2003 comments were made in the context of assembling President Bill Clinton's archives.[6] Karen Davis, one of the insiders, spoke in a similar vein when she said: "I am very pragmatic, and it even made me angry that the purest wanted the perfect solution for decades, leaving people without coverage."[7] Seen from this angle, it is quite probable that the insiders, having been in charge in key positions in the back offices of government, did, looking back, feel responsible for the defeat more than anyone else. From the moment of defeat onward, the status of the Clinton plan veteran was inextricably linked to a political fiasco with severe consequences for the poorest American citizens. It is therefore very likely that this experience, accompanied by a feeling of responsibility if not guilt, favored the development of long-term career paths inside the Beltway—within think tanks, health policy schools, and not-for-profit sector-based organizations—thus keeping alive the hope of a replay of the reform once the opportunity arose.

Thereafter, these health insiders would work together to transform their social image by gradually asserting themselves in their role of bearers of memory. By organizing their political learning around "lessons" to be learned, they would explain "their defeat" by their lack of shared experience when the Clinton plan was launched (Heclo, 1995). One eminent Clinton plan veteran summarized the effects of the lessons learned from the defeat on the Obama reform: "Another lesson I learned during my career [responsible for relations between the White House and Congress during the Clinton plan] was that we are in politics, we are not in an academic environment, so to enact a reform, you have to make tradeoffs, you have to compromise on things you don't like. In the reform, some provisions are ugly. I think also some of them are really stupid, are bad policy." Later, reflecting on the effects during the Obama administration, the veteran had this to add: "But at least we did it, and we can reform the reform."[8]

One can also see in these comments a desire on the part of long-term insiders to distinguish themselves from policy entrepreneurs. Contrary to the latter, who approach policy as the continuation of academic conclusions, those who have been in charge over time during political battles vaunt their aptitude and willingness to reach compromises in order to devise viable health policy. It is clear that this aspect of the Clinton legacy left its mark among health experts when they began formulating their future programmatic orientation (Lepont, 2014). It is certainly owing to the search for political bipartisan consensus that the Clinton plan veterans, supported by the newcomers, collectively developed the role of custodian of state policies to diminish the short-timers' and policy entrepreneurs' influence during the process of drafting the new reform project. This new role fostered the formation of a group identity for insiders who rejected any return of a government of strangers and a divided elite configuration. Their political learning can be summarized as "divided we fail."

Moreover, one can imagine how the leitmotif "to reform the reform" had significant impact on the way the Clinton plan veterans approached the future reform project. It foreshadowed in Washington's many health think tanks the rise of individuals with a strong background in government affairs advocating for the development of a consensus-based programmatic platform that included the Republican insiders' cooperation. These veterans still believed that their quest for "good policy" had created conflicts leading inexorably to division and then to the failure of the reforming front (Oberlander, 2007a: 1678). Therefore, it is necessary to explore more precisely where and how, in practice, these individuals drew on memories of the Clinton plan failure and with what political objective in mind.

Inside the Beltway: Reform-Minded Think Tanks under Bipartisan Influence

As a reminder, it was during the first decade of the twenty-first century, in the midst of the Republicans' reign and during the transformation of power dynamics in the Democratic Party, that the idea of a new health coverage reform project emerged in the circles of insiders (Oberlander, 2007a,b). After the Democrats' midterm election victory on November 7, 2006, to the 110th Congress, and during the 2008 presidential election campaign, the outlines of the reform were gradually refined. Ulrike Lepont (2014) has underlined the key role the many forums of Washington health experts played. These include think tanks like the Center for American Progress (CAP), the Brookings Institution, the Bipartisan Policy Center (BPC), the Center on Budget and Policy Priorities (CBPP), and the Hamilton Project (at the Brookings Institution); these also include other foundations involved in public health such as the Commonwealth Fund (CWF), the Kaiser Family Foundation, and the Robert Wood Johnson Foundation (RWJF).[9] After studying the discussion favoring the ascent in power of the "pro-market" health experts within Washington's health circles, Lepont shows how the health experts' pronouncements from the left-leaning side of the Democratic Party were initially marginalized in the field of expertise and then discarded by the majority in Congress when the bill was being drafted.

The study of the insiders' career paths shows that many of them were involved in Washington's forums alongside the health policy experts when thinking through the new reform project (chapter 4 and chapter 5). One Clinton plan veteran whom we interviewed claimed that the preparatory work in the think tanks was particularly effective in the period leading up to President Obama's inauguration.[10] Getting involved in Washington's reform forums, whether in the think tanks or foundations, was a sociological characteristic that we have previously mentioned. This shows that during periods of circulation outside government, these individuals remained connected inside the Beltway while they debated the future of the health insurance system. It was in these forums that the Clinton plan veterans would apply the lessons learned from their collective failure and start to seek a bipartisan consensus, a necessity for any kind of attempt at reform. Bringing together several Republican insiders within these forums while the reform project's general programmatic orientations were gestating thus favored the newcomers who were coalescing around a strategy that some of them had already put into practice during the BBA (1997) and the MMA (2003). In the search for bipartisan rapprochement, the issue of health policy cost containment became the dominant issue. Consequently, the idea of a consensual and bipartisan reform within certain supportive think tanks (CAP and BPC) was inextricably tied to the issue of the future health insurance system's budgetary cost control (BPC and the Hamilton Project).

It was within CAP, a progressive Washington think tank founded in 2003 by John Podesta, formerly Bill Clinton's chief of staff (1993–2001), that on March 22, 2005, the Progressive Prescriptions for a Healthy America project was born. This report carried forth the main ideas developed by Jeanne Lambrew, Terry Shaw, and John Podesta, who sketched out the new programmatic orientation that would widen access to health coverage for the most in need.[11] As a reminder of the obstacles erected along the path of change following the Clinton defeat, this document proposed several avenues to reactivate the idea of a possible reform. Thus, the authors suggested imposing some limits on the new project of far-reaching reform by advocating consensual solutions that would, in principle, overcome the political obstacles that the Clinton plan veterans had encountered. The first avenue rested on the principle that it was politically less risky to build on what already existed than to try to change everything, which led them to propose extending the Medicaid program to create a health insurance system "for all." The second avenue consisted of making the reform project a lasting tool to tackle the increasing amount of public spending on health. The third avenue was a reminder that 75% of American citizens obtained health insurance from their employer and were attached to it. They associated this choice with the right to exercise their individual freedom, and this was where the idea of linking private and public coverage was born to make health coverage accessible to all (Lambrew, Podesta & Shaw, 2005: 128). The fourth avenue underlined the need to create a favorable political climate among all the actors in the system, including experts, researchers, interest groups, and media, as well as between the executive branch and Congress.

Hillary Clinton's close associate, Neera Tanden, who entered the back offices of government during the Clinton presidency, insisted that the new reform project introduced by 2005 predated the Massachusetts plan of 2006. She added that the former first lady had been shaken by personal attacks against her between "'93 and '94" and had become aware of the need for political consensus that went beyond the partisan divide long before Massachusetts first put a reform project to the test.[12] John McDonough, an academic as well as a health adviser to Senator Kennedy (from 2008 to 2010), moreover claimed that the 2005 plan from CAP was Hillary Clinton's main source of inspiration during the 2008 Democratic primaries, when her opponent was Barack Obama (2011: 58).

In March 2007, some senators, in order to progress along a route of bipartisan compromise, recruited the Clinton plan veteran Chris Jennings, who was close to Hillary Clinton, and the Republican long-term insider Mark McClellan, former director of the CMS during the George W. Bush administration, to set up and run the Bipartisan Policy Center for Health Reform (which was renamed the Bipartisan Policy Center after the vote on the ACA).[13] At the time of the Clinton plan, Senator George Mitchell was involved as Democratic Senate majority leader, and he said, "I bear a large share of responsibility for the '93–'94 failure. Don't repeat my errors" (McDonough, 2011: 57). The specter of the Clinton defeat acted as a red flag, leading reformers of all persuasions to transcend the political divide as they faced the health challenge. It was in order to conquer this challenge that in June 2009 these two insiders would publish the report *Crossing Our Lines: Working Together to Reform the US Health System*. According to one of these coauthors, the final text retained by Congress would resemble in many points the "detailed policy version" of the Bipartisan Policy Center project.[14] The report was published on December 1, 2008; it was cosigned by long-term insiders Jeanne Lambrew (a Democrat) and Joseph Antos (a Republican). Renamed *Health Insurance Design Choices: Issues and Options for Change*, it highlighted two crucial elements. The first was a warning against any return to the conflict between the elite cliques over the best policy formulation for the reform. The second element consisted of justifying the need to bring on board the public and private sectors so that the health coverage reform would be "affordable" for the greatest number of citizens, while leaving open the choice to the beneficiaries, to avoid another type of "Harry and Louise" advertising campaign (chapter 7). On this matter, Clinton plan veteran Chris Jennings contends that it was the ability to rally some of the insurers to this policy issue that convinced Barack Obama of the need to get the insurance groups interested in the reform. With all due respect to Donnelly and Rochefort (2012), these strategic prescriptions have their origins in the work of insiders who experienced the Clinton defeat and then examined the reasons for it.

The political lessons learned by the Clinton plan veterans and shared with the newcomers included cost-containment concerns. The Hamilton Project, which was set up by newcomers within the Brookings Institution, and the CBPP worked on the issue of budgetary sustainability to pave the way for a bipartisan compromise. The challenge was to develop a reform proposal that could be positively evaluated by the CBO. During the George W. Bush years, the debate would be launched inside the CBPP—a liberal but nonpartisan Washington think tank concerned with transforming US fiscal policy to improve redistribution to low-income citizens (Rich, 2004). It should be noted that this think tank also drew many insiders with a career background in the CBO and in powerful financial agencies such as the HCFA (table 5.1).[15]

To get beyond the issue of tax cuts advocated by Republicans, some veterans of the Clinton plan, such as institutional migrant Wendell Primus and technocratic translator Andy Schneider, would steer the CBPP toward a bipartisan approach. They were supported by two young economists: Jason Furman and Peter Orszag.[16] The CBPP experts would thus achieve an intellectual tour de force by linking the new reform project to reducing the federal health care budget deficit.[17] Clinton plan veteran Gary Claxton, at that time vice president of the Kaiser Family Foundation, recalls that under the Obama reform, "many people from the CBPP" worked behind closed doors on the financing issue with Senator Ted Kennedy's staffers on the Senate HELP Committee and Finance Committee.[18] This strategy of "budgetary legitimization" of the health insurance project was also advocated by the Hamilton Project working group's reports and publications. Launched on April 5, 2006, at the Brookings Institution, with the support of the young senator from Illinois, Barack Obama, this think tank included economists and health policy specialists such as insiders Judy Feder, Alice Rivlin, and Richard Franck, and public finance specialists, former treasury secretaries (Robert Rubin and Larry Summers), as well as corporate leaders (for example, from Google and Goldman Sachs).

Under the leadership of Democratic newcomers, the young economists Furman and Orszag, a third American way (Obamanomics) founded on a deft mixture of fiscal rigor and regulation of market forces was sketched out (Furman, 2008). When applied to the health system, for Jason Furman this new way translated into public policies that were limited by budget constraints and fit into a framework of controlling sector-based public spending.[19] In effect, this tactic resulted in the CBO being turned into an ally for the future reform project (Joyce, 2011: 199). It is interesting to note that Clinton plan veteran Judy Feder, a member of the Hamilton Project, drew on her experience with the disastrous effects of the controversies stemming from the budgetary sustainability of the different programmatic orientations between 1993 and 1994. For Feder, as for several other long-term insiders, everything proceeded as if internalizing the financial constraints constituted a prior condition for any new reform project: "Failure would serve as the ultimate judgment as to whether this effort was worth doing."[20]

Pursuing this perspective, the work of the Hamilton Project resulted in the elaboration of a budgetary counterargument showing how only a reform introducing a new state-regulated health insurance system would enable the spiraling federal deficit to be controlled. These recommendations quickly became a policy program with the appointment of newcomer Peter Orszag, first to head the CBO after the Democrats won a majority in the 110th Congress in 2007, and then at the OMB once President Obama initiated the reform process. Addressing budgetary constraints was seen by both Clinton plan veterans and newcomers as one of the conditions for the success of the future health coverage system.

The Alliance for Health Reform: "The Place to Be"

Despite being cast aside by American political scholars researching the Clinton administration's impact on the genesis of the new reform (Oberlander, 2007a, 2010; Hacker, 2010; Jacobs & Skocpol, 2010), foundations such as the Henry J. Kaiser Family Foundation and the RWJF played an important role in elaborating the new programmatic offer (Lepont, 2014). The study of the Democratic insiders' career paths has already shown that these nonprofit organizations were privileged places of temporary or permanent work when the insiders' exited governmental offices. Indeed, the Henry J. Kaiser Family Foundation was led by a Clinton plan veteran, Diane Rowland. The Alliance for Health Reform was not a think tank in the institutional sense of the term. It was a bipartisan forum dependent on the powerful RWJF, a philanthropic organization specialized in health issues where experts and health insiders came together to attend seminars, themed workshops, and roundtables devoted to the reform of the health care system. The Alliance for Health Reform promoted media dissemination of the new programmatic directions for reform advocated by the insiders.[21] Created in 1991 to prolong the Pepper Commission's work on the need to broaden health coverage, and led up until 2007 by former Democratic Senator John D. Jay Rockefeller IV, this bipartisan communications forum would play a vital role in promoting the political learning from failure carried out by the Clinton plan veterans.

While the Obama reform was gestating, particularly during the transition period of this administration, the Alliance for Health Reform played a unifying role by organizing several meetings and briefings regarding the need to build a consensual and bipartisan reform project.[22] One of our interviewees drew our attention to the unique role of these policy events, commenting, "That's really for the press. It's all televised." These events were also for Washington's "young and not so young health policy people" who concentrated on "the politics of issues."[23] In this context, the Republicans reasserted their attachment to the issues of cost control and the role interest groups played, while the Democrats fended off accusations of wanting the government to run the health insurance sector. It was unsurprising that most Washington insiders became regularly involved in the Alliance for Health Reform.[24] It was during one of these policy events between December 2007 and January 2008 that four Clinton plan veterans facilitated two seminars entitled *Lessons Learned: The Health Reform Debate of 1993–1994*. These veterans, all four of whom were institutional migrants, were selected as representatives of the branches of power and because of their "active [participation] in health issues on Capitol Hill during 1993 and 1994."[25]

Reassured by the shared feeling among Democrats and Republicans in the Alliance for Health Reform that this time reform was inevitable, the Clinton plan veterans drew on their personal experience to extract nine lessons from their collective failure.

Lesson 1: Carry out the reform in the first year following the presidential election (no task force).

Lesson 2: Find a speedy legislative procedure.

Lesson 3: Involve Congress and its powerful committees as soon as the process begins.

Lesson 4: Increase taxes without letting the middle class shoulder the burden while at the same time containing spending.

Lesson 5: Do not try to include everything in the bill.

Lesson 6: Be prepared to negotiate with one's opponents.

Lesson 7: Expect rejection.

Lesson 8: Listen to the opposition's arguments.

Lesson 9: Be aware of the impossibility of pleasing all parties. (See table 8.1.)

Brian Biles, a Clinton plan veteran with an institutional migrant career path, related the arguments put forward by linking them to his own experience of the earlier failure.[26] He explained: "No, no, we learned our lesson," and he and his colleagues would say, "You guys [in Congress] work it out." In the same vein, Alice Rivlin, CBO director from 1975 to 1983 and director of the OMB under Clinton from 1994 to 1996, confirmed that the Obama administration staff, whom we will show later on was made up of an overwhelming majority of Clinton plan veterans (chapter 9), were aware of this lesson and applied it by giving Congress a general context in a few pages, before handing over to the staffers in the powerful congressional committees the task of drafting the reform.[27] Another interviewee recalls about Obama that "he didn't want to make the same mistake that Clinton made" by prioritizing the administration to the detriment of Congress; moreover, this allowed for both houses to follow or not follow the public option route.[28] Brian Biles also pointed out that one of the main lessons was that it was better to integrate the Medicare program into the formulation of the reform project rather than try and integrate it into a system of managed competition, as the Clinton plan had intended. American citizens as much as the administrations that were driving through reform projects were very attached to the Medicare program, which was a unique part of the American health insurance system. Lastly, another Clinton administration veteran recalled that "Obama's advantage was to have in his team people like Nancy-Ann DeParle and Rahm Emanuel and others reflecting on their experience of defeat, in learning from their mistakes, and especially in their wish not to repeat these."[29] He then concluded by saying that "the advantage that Obama had over Clinton is that, whether it's Rahm Emanuel, whether it's Nancy-Ann DeParle, whether it's any one of a number of other people, they had the experience of the Clinton administration, and it was invaluable in terms of their strategy and implementation in the Obama administration."

As John McDonough indicated in his book on the Obama reform as seen from within, in April 2008, in the midst of the presidential campaign, the Clinton veterans rallied around an inventory exercise looking at the reasons for their defeat that would be exported beyond the shores of the Potomac River (2011: 1–4; 288–290). The author, who incidentally would work as health adviser to Senator Kennedy for a short period, recounted how during a conference held in Saint Paul, Minnesota, forty-odd former Democratic and Republican veterans of the Clinton presidency (elected officials, congressional staffers, and senior members of staff from the Clinton administration) discussed at length the reasons for the defeat. What emerged were "ten commandments" aimed at strengthening presidential leadership when launching the new reform project.[30] These ten commandments in many aspects resembled the lessons put forward in the Alliance for Health Reform's work (see below table 8.1): (1) that the president embody a political will; (2) that he communicate with the public about comprehensive reform; (3) that he choose good advisers; (4) that he involve Congress in the drafting of the bill; (5) that he manage the partisan issue; (6) that he master the short-term political agenda; (7) that he manage interest groups; (8) that he involve the states; (9) that he determine the terms of engagement; and (10) that he negotiate veto points with the leaders of Congress before launching the legislative work.

This type of seminar allowing both Democratic and Republican Clinton plan veterans to speak fits into a political learning process aimed at bipartisan compromise. We should also note that this political work occurred in peripheral political discussion forums rather than in typical Washington think tanks. Indeed, these forums functioned as fertile spaces where the Clinton plan veterans could induct the newcomers to policy formulation best practices, so as not to repeat previous political mistakes and setbacks.

TABLE 8.1. Comparison of Clinton plan veterans' recommendations

Nine lessons learned from the health reform debate of 1993–1994 Alliance for Health Reform. Washington, DC, March 2008	Ten commandments for presidential leadership on health reform Conference, Saint Paul, MN, April 2008
1. Carry out the reform in the first year following the presidential election (no task force).	1. The president must embody a political will.
2. Find a speedy procedure to get the bill through Congress.	2. He must communicate with the public about a comprehensive reform.
3. Involve Congress and its powerful committees as soon as the process begins.	3. He must choose good advisers.
4. Increase taxes without letting the middle class shoulder the burden; at the same time contain spending.	4. He must involve Congress in the drafting of the bill.
5. Do not try to include everything in the bill.	5. He must manage the partisan issue.
6. Be prepared to negotiate with opponents.	6. He must master the short-term political agenda.
7. Expect rejection.	7. He must manage interest groups.
8. Listen to the opposition's arguments.	8. He must involve the states.
9. Be aware of the impossibility of pleasing all parties.	9. He must determine the terms of engagement.
	10. He must negotiate veto points with the leaders of Congress.

SOURCE: OPERA Research Program

The political learning of the Clinton plan veterans resulted in a series of strategic recommendations for elected officials. The two recommendations put forward by the Clinton plan veterans, implicit during the ongoing presidential campaign, would become foundational factors once the Obama administration transition team[31] was in place in January 2009. The first recommendation stemmed from the search for a bipartisan consensus to bring the market on board in the reform project's design. The second recommendation, less visible at first glance, hides behind the call to the reforming elites to jointly own the matter of the reform's programmatic orientations. This led the head of the executive to appoint only "good people" in the back offices of government able to guarantee the unity of the reform front elite. How can one avoid seeing in this type of declaration as a sort of auto-promotion that would allow one a top position within the new administration once new posts were being filled? Clinton plan veteran Rahm Emanuel's strategic choice to appoint Nancy-Ann DeParle, another veteran, summarizes this state of mind, as described by historian Ed Berkowitz,[32] and is something we will return to. In a lecture given during the Clinton presidency, this argument consisted of a plea by some insiders to formulate policy themselves, thereby rejecting any attempt on the strangers' part to devise it.

The Massachusetts Plan: Chicken or Egg?

The Massachusetts plan of 2006 was the first reform achieved with bipartisan consensus to establish a system guaranteeing quasi-universal health insurance. It was perceived by the great majority of scholars researching the American health system as the "blueprint" for the Affordable Care Act (Jacobs & Skocpol, 2010; McDonough, 2011; Starr, 2013). Some authors, such as Jacob Hacker, outlined the general shape of the Massachusetts reform, deftly setting out both private interests and the public mechanism, that appealed to Obama and his campaign team (2010: 866–867). For Jill Quadagno, the Massachusetts health care plan was above all a syncretic reform that came to fruition in 2006 after six months of negotiations between Republican Governor Mitt Romney and Democratic Senator Ted Kennedy, a former single-payer supporter when he was dealing with the Nixon administration, and the Democratic leaders of the state legislature. On this occasion, Senator Kennedy had sided with the individual-mandate idea,[33] the political price for this bipartisan arrangement (2014: 45). And sociologist Paul Starr pointed to the national political connections existing between these northeast coast political leaders (i.e., Michael Dukakis, Ted Kennedy, John Kerry, and Mitt Romney) and Washington's policy-makers for ensuring the success of the Massachusetts plan template (2013:166–182). The fact that during his electoral campaign Barack Obama chose Jonathan Gruber, an MIT health economist known as the architect of the Massachusetts plan, as a technical consultant confirms this notion of people and ideas circulating between these two levels of the US government.

During a recent interview at Harvard University's school of public health with John McDonough, another "Bay State" health expert, Mc-

Donough pointed out that Gruber could influence Washington insiders because he had developed a policy instrument for financial analysis that met the Congressional Budget Office's requirements.[34] Paul Starr underlined how Clinton plan veterans Chris Jennings and Jeanne Lambrew, among others, as well as newcomer Neera Tanden (close to Hillary Clinton before joining Barack Obama's team), maneuvered in order to "cross-fertilize" the Massachusetts model with the Washingtonians' ideas. John McDonough, however, drew on his personal experience as adviser to Senator Ted Kennedy and approached this issue with the metaphor of "Massachusetts Avenue," which in substance consisted of a systemic transformation of the insurance market by combining the choice of an individual mandate to purchase one's insurance with some public aid, thereby making coverage affordable for the greatest number of people (2011: 35). Drawing on the efficient role played by the Senate's HELP Committee and inspired by the Bay State example in formulating the final text of the bill, McDonough lauded the model's practical influence on the reform's final formulation.

It is hard to argue with the fact that the Massachusetts health insurance reform influenced the Affordable Care Act; on the other hand, it seems unlikely, as some interviews suggest, that it was a blueprint serving as copy-and-paste material for the final version of Obamacare (Oberlander, 2010).[35] The Massachusetts model constitutes more of an argument underpinning the collective reform strategy initiated by the long-term insiders than a miraculous readymade solution that was transposed to the federal level. Our interviews with Clinton plan veterans and newcomers indicate that behind the facade of a consensual and bipartisan reform, the problem of controlling public spending, of rallying interest groups, in particular those powerful lobbies of the health insurance world, and the individual mandate were strong arguments that had already been put forward in the think tanks and Washington foundations prior to the Massachusetts health reform.[36] Behind this also lay hidden a powerful argument being prepared, one capable of giving insiders the means to rapidly win the struggle of ideas against their opponents always present in the health expertise sphere of public health insurance (Lepont, 2014).

With this in mind, one of our interviewees, a health economist who spent some time at the CBO, recalled that despite its defeat under the Clinton administration (chapter 6), the single payer model was still present in the minds of some progressive Democratic reformers. This influenced the long-term insiders who privileged "the new reform, which copies the Massachusetts reform, and gives a view of what was politically feasible in our system."[37] How can one forget the fact that it was the lack of consensus and compromise that was the principal reason for the great reform projects failing, as illustrated by congressional Democrats' inability to reach agreement with Republicans since 1974's failure of the Nixon plan for health care reform, despite Ted Kennedy's leadership.[38] For one interviewee, it was clear that the Clinton plan veterans and the newcomers, focused on the desire to take on this challenge, found in the Massachusetts example a historic event that legitimized their search for a compromise with the Republicans.[39]

Similarly, health economist Sherry Glied, author of the book *Chronic Condition* about the Clinton defeat (1997) and ASPE at HSS from 2010 to 2012 to implement the Affordable Care Act, believed that the Obamacare framework formed part of a spectrum where ideas held by both Democrats and Republicans, and set in motion during the Nixon project, came together and were formalized in the context of the Massachusetts plan.[40] Thereafter, as mentioned by a researcher at the Urban Institute who had to testify before a congressional committee on the state of Massachusetts's health reform issue, "beyond the issue of the reform's programmatic orientations, it's first and foremost all the groundwork linked to the bipartisan approach and the political consensus" which caught the interest of the congressmen—all the more so because everyone knew that this state was quite unique, being both "very wealthy" and "very progressive."[41] From this perspective, when the Senate's HELP Committee mentioned the Massachusetts plan, this had more to do with the bipartisan consensus model and a presumed similarity in the interplay among interest groups than a wish to import in full a model reform (McDonough, 2011).

This dimension was the object of scathing criticism from journalist Steven Brill in his book *America's Bitter Pill* (2015). To him, it was clear that the "Romneycare" model made it easier to abandon truly progressive alternatives such as single payer and Medicare for all. He denounced the role played by Liz Fowler, a health staffer on the Senate Finance Committee who, having worked alongside Max Baucus between 2006 and 2008 for the large health insurance company WellPoint, seemingly deployed her influence, "killing the public option" (Brill, 2015: 38–42). The point here is not to question this insider's role on the Senate Finance Committee in harnessing the Massachusetts model in order to outline the contours of the Affordable Care Act proposal put forward by the upper house of Congress and in large part pursued in the bill's final version. Nothing proves her influence on the death of the public option, which Brill believes was superior to that of the group of Clinton plan veterans with whom she worked when drafting the bill's contents. Moreover, although this type of negotiation occurred behind closed doors in Congress, we should not infer that the individual meant to act on behalf of insurance groups and had more influence than those with whom the decision was made (Dahl, 1958). In interviews with us over several years, Liz Fowler praised the diligence of and mentioned by name most of the colleagues with whom she had worked in practical terms while drafting the text of the reform. In the executive branch of power, this included Nancy-Ann DeParle and Peter Orszag; in the House of Representatives, Karen Nelson, Cybele Bjorklund, and Wendell Primus; and at the Senate, David Bowen (on the HELP Committee) and Republican staffer Mark Hayes (on the Finance Committee).[42]

The study of Liz Fowler's long-term career path (chapter 5) shows that her involvement in the private sector was just a short-lived career transition preceding a return to congressional affairs. This was the purpose of our argument; since the start of her work in the public sphere as an insider belonging to the generation of newcomers, Liz Fowler was enthusiastic, as were the Clinton plan veterans who helped establish the Alliance for Health Reform. Fowler stated in passing that "we learned a lot of lessons from 1993,"[43] (we focus on the fact that she was not at that stage involved in the public sector) and she worked to develop a bipartisan approach to health policy with a "more collaborative process of decision making."[44] Indeed, introducing the market by involving insurance companies was then considered by Clinton plan veterans as the price to be paid to maximize the chances of success for the reform. Furthermore, one can also explain interest groups' involvement in the reform as a practical consequence of the lessons learned in the wake of the Clinton defeat. Less obviously, it constituted an argument that enabled the insiders—once they were convinced of the pertinence of this political solution—to assert themselves in the role of custodians of health coverage policy. This role had developed with the ultimate goal of custodianship against possible further intrusions by the new strangers (i.e., policy entrepreneurs) in the decision-making process, as well as against any programmatic orientation that might rekindle the internal divisions of the reformers' front (chapter 9).

The book *Lion of the Senate* pays homage to Ted Kennedy and was written by two Clinton plan veteran staffers, Nick Littlefield and David Nexon. The book pursues this kind of hypothesis. For these authors, aware that in terms of the reform, the quest for perfection could well be the enemy of the good, the political leader of the HELP Committee deployed all his influence upon Obama so that the public-option idea would be discarded in favor of a model bringing the private insurers on board (2015: 447). Thereafter, the Massachusetts plan, with its comprehensive reform dimension, was merely an extra asset for the insiders intent on marginalizing their foes, while they boasted of their united reform front. Furthermore, as Mark Mizruchi surmised, the large health corporations were at that moment preoccupied with the effects of the subprime crisis in 2007 and needed reassurance about the impossibility of a new form of single payer–based reform (2013: 257). Rarely advocated by researchers of American politics exploring the genesis of the Affordable Care Act, the political learning carried out by the Clinton plan veterans regarding the reasons for their failure shows how they succeeded in rallying newcomers to a reassessment of the custodian role as a key player in future reform. From this perspective, one should recall that the political lessons learned had a dual purpose.

The first objective was, in a clear attempt at socialization, to share with Democratic newcomers a programmatic direction for reform by passing on their experience of past failures. The interviews we carried out with the newcomers who played a practical role in drafting the text of the reform confirm that the aim was attained. Whether it was David Bowen, Cybele Bjorklund, or Liz Fowler, newcomers in Congress with a technocratic translator's career path asserted, during the legislative battles between the two houses of Congress, that they had "the experience of defeat," although they were all far too young to have any high-level experience in the Clinton administration (chapter 5). This fact illustrates the transmission of a political learning between two generations of Democratic reformers. The second purpose of these lessons learned by the Clinton plan veterans was perhaps less visible yet significant: it consisted in marginalizing the strangers, bearers of operationally weak programmatic models, fairly unaccountable and politically irresponsible, by making them carry the responsibility of the fragmenting reform front (the divided elites). Indeed, raising the need to present a consensual programmatic orientation, the one the insiders adhered to, they denounced at the same time the influence of the strangers who had presented the idea of managed competition incubated within the executive and handed ready-made to Congress (chapters 6 and 7).

More generally, the results of these political lessons learned enabled the difference to be appreciated, in terms of professional roles and in the political finality of their action, between, on the one hand, those who aspired to concretely formulate health insurance policies in the long term—the insiders—and, on the other hand, the policy entrepreneurs and certain policy advisers with a short-timer's outlook who hoped to leave their intellectual mark on the programmatic orientations. Comparable to the generic figure of the unelected health governmental elite in the US or that of the custodian of state policies in France, the insiders acted in the back offices of government not only to attract the favors of the "prince" but also to impose their political authority by highlighting their knowledge and unique experience of the exercise of power.

On the basis of the sociological analysis of long-term insiders, we can ask ourselves whether, by asserting their role of custodian of state policies, these elites did not manage to confine their rivals in the role of "useful idiot" during the genesis of the Affordable Care Act. Indeed, aware of their singular status, they wanted to distinguish themselves from mere policy experts.[45] The fact of being in charge over a long period of time constituted a strong marker of collective identity. Very often, the role of custodian led them to prioritize an operational and consensual programmatic orientation to decision-making, facilitating their search for accommodation and political compromise. In this role, they collectively differentiated themselves from the academic experts who were drawn by a vision of health insurance policy in terms of "big pictures," which more often than not failed when confronted with the reality of conflicts endemic to the political arena. In Weberian terms, the role of custodian led the Clinton plan veterans to inscribe their logic of action in "an ethic of responsibility," whereas that of the health policy academic experts tended to be grounded in the realm of "an ethic of conviction." (Weber, 2004)

Rooted in their experience of previous struggles and lessons learned and shared after the Clinton plan defeat, the insiders developed a strategy of the "politically feasible" in the sense Richard Rose meant it (1991), where the aim is to rally together both elected political officials and interest groups. According to Chris Jennings, this resulted in conceptualizing four policy foundations upon which the new reform health project needed to be structured: (1) to guarantee access to the health insurance system without any discrimination; (2) to be assured that all individuals can access non-employer-based insurance; (3) to ensure that private insurance be affordable (i.e., financed from direct funding or taxes); and (4) to set up a cost-control mechanism so that the system is financially viable and sustainable over the long-term.[46] There must be complete political consensus regarding these four pillars of "good policy" which are non-negotiable; otherwise their chances of succeeding will be at risk. The means of putting them into practice, however, can be the object of compromise and political negotiation. These elements, as we shall see, constitute the hidden sociological underpinnings of the decision-making style that contributed to the advent of the Affordable Care Act.

CHAPTER 9

Behind the Congressional Votes

Custodianship and the Politics of Accommodation

AUNCHED BY President Barack Obama before Congress on February 24, 2009, the bill that was voted on in its first draft by the House of Representatives on November 7, 2009 (the Affordable Health Care for America Act), and voted on again in a new draft in the Senate on December 23, 2009 (the Affordable Health Choices Act), before being finally ratified by the head of the executive on March 23, 2010—the Patient Protection and Affordable Care Act (PPACA, or ACA)—has received a lot of attention from scholars of American politics (Hacker, 2010; Jacobs & Skocpol, 2010; Oberlander, 2010; Mc-Donough, 2011; Starr, 2013). Studies focusing either on institutional power games, partisan politicization, or the role of Congress's elected representatives highlight how, having opened the way to a far-reaching reform of the health coverage system, the decision-making process was littered with obstacles. Indeed, the consensual and bipartisan strategy that had slowly matured within certain think tanks in Washington, particularly under the guidance of the insiders, was gradually cast aside, especially when the election to the Senate of Republican Scott Brown, replacing Ted Kennedy after his death, reduced the Democratic majority to sixty seats and made a vote on the bill in its final phase uncertain.[1]

By studying this political situation through long-term changes within federal power, particularly the Republicans' entrenched polarization regarding health issues, Anne-Laure Beaussier has shown how an "unorthodox" legislative process led to this reform (2012). It is also by looking beyond the idea that the stars aligned for this political accomplishment that we will show how the Clinton plan veterans and the newcomers, despite the Republicans' political desertion, reinvented the role of custodian of state policies in order to endorse a consensual and accommodating impetus in the decision-making process.

Sociologist Paul Starr points out that reform took place in two distinct political spheres (2013: 190–193). The first sphere, or "outside game," illustrates how public opinion was won over. During the gestation period of the Affordable Care Act, journalists and experts, those whom Skocpol qualifies as "pundits," played their part in legitimizing the choice of a consensual programmatic orientation unlike the Clinton plan moment. The second sphere, or "inside game," allows us to observe how the political and institutional Washington game this time fostered the formation of grand consensual coalitions. Thus, Starr notes that the reform was supported by a coalition of "strange bedfellows," referring to the political leaders of Congress and the interest groups that ensured the reform was accomplished. Nevertheless, although Starr mentions the role of political networks, such as Obama's choice of health advisers and the House of Representatives' "long-time aides" (2013: 200), he never links them to the effects of the transformation of the social backgrounds and career paths of the unelected governmental health elites on the decision-making process. Yet clearly, according to Blumenthal and Morone's sociohistorical research on White House (2009) chiefs of staffs and Whipple's study of gatekeepers (2017), all of these issues combine to create the X factor that can sway the president's decision-making.

John McDonough has taken this type of interpretation the furthest (2011). His career path is dotted with specific appointments as a health adviser: first while the health reform was being designed in the state of Massachusetts and later when Senator Ted Kennedy recruited him to the HELP Committee (2008–2010). On the basis of his mobility in the back offices of government, where he witnessed the decision-making process at work, McDonough more than all other authors of American politics insists on how staffers in both chambers worked long hours, even 24-7, often behind closed doors on most policy issues to eventually deliver a consensual bill.[2] Philip Joyce agrees with him on this point, as his thought-provoking interpretation of the rise of the CBO delves into why many of these staffers, especially the health experts, smoothed the way for the health coverage reform (2011). For McDonough, by sharing the same policy-analysis culture and mastering a fiscal and budgetary policy language, these staffers easily gravitated toward the "big committees" in Congress and brought with them a "cost-containment" culture (Joyce, 2011: 226). Peter Orszag offers a staggering example of this kind of career path: he was a newcomer and an institutional migrant who from 2006 to 2008 went from CBO director to OMB director in order to further the decision-making process (chapter 5).

It is through a deeper study of the "inside game" that we will be able to pinpoint the effects of the transformation of the social backgrounds and career paths of governmental health elites on the policy decision-making process. To this end, we will revisit James Meisel's compelling metaphor of the three "Cs"—group consciousness, cohesion, and conspiracy (1958: 361)—and show how insiders, whose group consciousness and cohesion are reflected in their role as custodians, carry a consensual programmatic orientation to reform the health coverage system. The programmatic elite framework identifies Democratic institutional migrants and technocratic translators who opted to return to the back offices of health government once the decision-making process began (chapter 4 and 5). Moreover, this approach reveals how these insiders went from one prestigious government policy post to another both within the executive (ASPE, administrator of the HCFA, or PAD in the OMB) and the highly regarded congressional committees and subcommittees. It was by prolonging their career paths within forums outside government, where the orientation of these policies was devised, that these insiders developed their shared programmatic orientation of a future reform that prioritized a far-reaching reform (rather than a comprehensive reform) and included the roles played by market forces and the need for cost containment of public funds.

After setting out in the previous chapter how the Clinton plan veterans passed on their experience of failure to the newcomers in order to constitute a homogenous reform platform strong enough to withstand any strangers' influence (from policy entrepreneurs or short-timers), I will now study how the insiders conquered the key posts in the back offices of Congress before they went on to colonize those of the executive branch after Obama's election. This collective strategy of assuming power is linked to the sociological transformation of the unelected governmental health coverage policy elites in Washington and to the carrying of a consensual and bipartisan reform project. Boosted by their shared experience, the insiders would go on to assert themselves as custodians by marginalizing the more progressive public-option alternative, which was seen as more expensive, less consensual, and initiated by strangers. In addition, analysis of the political agenda for a reform bill, which would eventually be called the Patient Protection and Affordable Care Act (PPACA or ACA), will highlight the link between elites and the role of custodian in the decision-making process.

The Early Conquest of Congressional Committees

The study of health coverage policy elites' career paths shows that some insiders held key long-term positions in charge of health issues in congressional subcommittees. At the same time as the Clinton plan veterans were throwing themselves into a project to analyze the reasons for their failure while on the margins of power, some of them returned to the congressional back offices. This tactic, first limited to a few people during the Republican majority from 2000 to 2006, took off after the Democrats' victory in the elections for the 110th legislature. In contrast to the Clinton era, Congress hoped to return to its "normal" working practices and to prepare a necessary and feasible budget for a new health coverage reform project. Everything proceeded as if—following the lessons learned from recent history—political institutions needed to be reset by putting Congress back in its usual place. This choice would put the elected Democrats and congressional committee staffers, as well as the CBO experts, at the heart of the work to develop the new reform bill.

In order to illustrate the phenomenon of the long-term insiders' gradual conquest of congressional committees, it is worth mentioning some representative examples of Clinton plan veterans or newcomers who repositioned themselves. Firstly, the case of Clinton plan veteran Wendell Primus shows how the institutional migrant career path can shed light on this hidden dimension of the decision-making process. In 2003, with a career in a highly regarded congressional subcommittee (Ways and Means) and a stint as ASPE at HHS already under his belt, Primus joined Nancy Pelosi's staff when she was house minority leader as "chief adviser for health and budgetary issues." When Pelosi became Speaker of the House of Representatives after the Democrats' 2007 victory, Primus established himself as both architect and ardent defender of a far-reaching reform of the health coverage system. Primus had a heated exchange with President Obama's chief of staff Rahm Emanuel. After Republican Scott Brown's win of Senator Kennedy's vacant seat on February 4, 2010, Emanuel made Primus try to force the hand of congressional staffers so that they would abandon their project of far-reaching reform and take up instead a project of incremental change regarding the health insurance system.[3] This conflict was proof both of the political influence Primus wielded and of his intention to assert his role as custodian of health coverage policy.

Other examples of insiders with similar newcomer profiles include Cybele Bjorklund,[4] staff director of the Ways and Means' Health Subcommittee in the House of Representatives, and Liz Fowler at the Senate Finance Committee. Both of these individuals, after a post in the executive branch for Bjorklund and preceding an executive post for Fowler, would play a similar custodian role once they were spearheading the negotiations and drafting of the bill with the two chambers (McDonough, 2011: 72). Their circulation during the decision-making process shows how these career paths are inextricably linked to the development of a project of far-reaching reform. Our interviews confirm their willingness to participate in the collective development of a major piece of legislation to set the American health coverage system on a new course.

In order to see through a different lens how Democratic insiders took control of powerful congressional committees, it is appropriate to carefully study their mobility across the staffs of two political leaders who for many years were committed to the American health coverage reform project: Congressman Henry Waxman and Senator Ted Kennedy (chapter 4 and 5). Although Waxman sat for years on the House Committee on Energy and Commerce, it is important to note that from 2009 to 2011 he was chair of the House Committee on Oversight and Government Reform,[5] which enhanced his ability to recruit staffers. His case shows how his team of loyal staffers, made up exclusively of insiders—among others Karen Nelson and Ruth Katz—would progressively reestablish itself to prepare for future legislative battles. As a reminder, being a staff member for Waxman was the crucible through which many Clinton plan veterans passed, including Brian Biles, Philip Barnett, Howard Cohen, William Corr, Jack Ebeler, Michael Hash, Ruth Katz, Karen Nelson, Diane Rowland, Forbes Ripley, Phil Schiliro, Andy Schneider, and Tim Westmoreland. Most of these close advisers remained sensitive to the issue of extending health coverage to the majority of US citizens. Stigmatized in the press as the "Waxman Clan or the Waxman Gang,"[6] these staffers developed over time a strong sense of solidarity. One of them sums it up thus: "The other good thing for people working on Waxman's staff is knowing that you share the same ideology and beliefs. . . . Working in this staff group means working as a team [to] end up with a great progressive reform of the health system."[7] The staffer also reveals that on "the Waxman staff, no one ever leaves, and when we get fired, we stay friendly with each other. And we call on each other as a network, almost. I mean, we are—it's extraordinarily unusual, so don't form your thesis around this, but we are. And there have been some right-wing political commentators who have said that Henry controls a mafia of liberal policy people."[8]

After the Democrats won the 110th congressional elections, the insiders who remained in office included Karen Nelson and Philip Barnett, Clinton plan veterans with a technocratic translator profile, and Ruth Katz and Andy Schneider, who both left their posts as adjunct associate professors of public health at the George Washington University to return to governmental affairs—Katz as public health counsel in charge of legislative affairs on the Health Subcommittee of the Energy and

Commerce Committee and Schneider as head legislative health adviser on Medicaid on the Oversight and Government Reform Committee. Similarly, Tim Westmoreland, then associate professor at Georgetown University's law school, cut his workload to part-time to get involved once again in the health policy reform process.[9] Other Clinton plan veterans on Waxman's staff, such as Michael Hash and Phil Schiliro, also returned to governmental affairs by moving to the executive branch: Hash joined Obama's team of health advisers at the White House as Nancy-Ann DeParle's deputy director at the Office of Health Reform; Schiliro, after a brief stint on the Senate Finance Committee, returned in 2006 to reinforce Waxman's staff on the Oversight and Government Reform Committee before President Obama recruited him to the White House as health adviser in charge of health relations with Congress (Bai, 2009: 4).

Clearly, not only do Clinton plan veterans in this staff group get redeployed in congressional committees, but moreover two of them "migrated" in quite a strategic way toward the apex of government at the White House. Former director of the CBO and the OMB Alice Rivlin, an expert on this kind of mobility, explains that "it is true that there were a lot of people who were in the Obama administration who had been in the Clinton administration. Many were not in the same kind of job."[10] The mobility of institutional migrants across the two branches of power increased with President Obama's victory, when congressional staffers would be appointed to the White House or HHS. This circulation mainly concerned the career paths of long-term insiders and highlights their significant difference from Clinton-era insiders during the decision-making process.

The comparison with Senator Ted Kennedy's staff allows to ascertain whether the same phenomenon of long-term insiders conquering the health committees occurred in the upper house of Congress. In contrast to Waxman's staff, the Clinton plan veterans gradually recruited newcomers during the George W. Bush era. Indeed, Nick Littlefield and David Nexon, the two insiders who led Kennedy's staff for many decades, ceded their posts to other insiders: Michael Myers, who defected from immigration policy, and the young newcomer staffer David Bowen (chapter 5). The injection of new blood into this staff corresponded first to a preparation strategy for the reform project that drew on individuals with a high level of knowledge and skills regarding health policies—mirroring the recruitment of advisers such as short-timer John McDonough with his experience of the bipartisan Massachusetts reform—and second to the need to "naturally" replace career paths with more than thirty years of work behind them. In fact, David Nexon, known as the dean of health policy in the Senate, would set about recruiting his own newcomers with specific qualifications, such as a PhD or a master's in public policy.[11] In this vein, he recruited his future successor to lead the health staff of the HELP Committee, a brilliant neurobiologist seeking a new adventure in his career: David Bowen. Bowen credited learning the ropes for his new staffer job to several conversations with his predecessors. It is certainly owing to his proximity to Clinton plan veterans that he could reflect on the reasons for the failed 1993–1994 reform, which happened when he had not yet begun his postdoctoral work. Bowen declared that in 1993–1994, the problem was the lack of political learning—experience now acquired precisely because the failure of 1993–1994 occurred.[12] Thus in 2008, full of confidence, he initiated discussions on how to frame the future health coverage reform project, organizing more than fifteen bipartisan round tables that brought together staffers and stakeholders. Convinced that the Senate should quickly draft a bill, Bowen single-handedly began to write, in the name of his committee, a large part of the proposal published on July 15, 2009: the Affordable Health Choices Act (Jacobs & Skocpol, 2010: 13). John McDonough, then sitting on the HELP Committee, confirmed this, pointing out that Liz Fowler carried out similar work for the Senate Finance Committee (2011: 81, 89). The speed of drafting the bill reflects the lesson learned during the Clinton era: get the reform through Congress swiftly. Thus, the preparations for and discussions of the draft reform this time owed a lot to Congress, where the new Democratic majority played a significant role (Beaussier, 2012). More generally, Senator Ted Kennedy's staff's ability to harness its resources and champion the reform reveals the insiders' key role in ensuring the success of the decision-making process—especially because their leader, owing to serious ill health, would be absent from the political scene. In fact, about the reform, Bowen said, much like the Clinton plan veterans on this staff Nick Littlefield and David Nexon: "We owe it to Ted" (Littlefield & Nexon, 2015: 446).[13]

Finally, it is within the CBO where the process of colonization has been most remarkable (Joyce, 2011). It is quite likely that the Clinton plan veterans, owing to their resounding failure, were aware of the need to obtain more than anything else a high score on budgetary viability for any reform project under evaluation (chapter 7). Lawrence Jacobs and Theda Skocpol criticized the role of Congress's Budget Office: "Finally, we need to take note of some vital behind-the-scenes players, above all the interacting networks of experts and bean counters employed in the White House Office of Management and Budget and the Congressional Budget Office. . . . For some years, the fate of legislation in Washington, DC, politics has been heavily influenced by CBO 'scores' . . . because many fiscally cautious representatives and senators, including so-called Blue Dog Democrats, will not support a bill unless it 'costs out' in a way that does not blow up the federal deficit over the next ten to twenty years" (Jacobs & Skocpol, 2010: 64–65).

Other authors put forth a hypothesis stating the secretary of the treasury supported the health insurance reform project as an example of public-finance cost containment (Brill, 2015: 113–115). These individuals consider cost-containment policy as a central political issue, as evidenced by their assumption of leadership positions that bring them in line with these types of issues (such as in the HCFA, the CBO, and the OMB). The analysis of the career paths of long-term insiders shows that this is the result of the process of political learning about health coverage policy. The struggle between Treasury Department elites and health insiders belongs to a past era—the Clinton one. During the Obama administration, on the contrary, the custodians' argument was about how to develop a reform project for which the costs would be contained.

In December 2006, just a few months after setting up the working group the Hamilton Project at the Brookings Institution with his economist colleague Jason Furman, the economist Peter Orszag was named CBO director by Nancy Pelosi, the Democratic House Speaker—in the

early days of the subprime crisis (Joyce, 2011: 180).[14] One of our interviewees said that the prospective work of legitimizing a health coverage
reform occurred well beforehand: "It was before Hillary Clinton spoke
about reform. Reform came out in 2008 for the presidential campaign."
Among the intellectual "Obamanomics" descendants who refused the
hardline austerity policy, Orszag, a brilliant young macro-economist,
put forward—along with his Hamilton Project colleagues (including
Judy Feder and Jeanne Lambrew)—a "neo-regulationist" approach to
budgetary policies based on the notion of "fiscal responsibility." For
Orszag, this great reform project needed to be seen as "the key to our
fiscal future." As soon as he took the reins, Orszag increased the number of staffers in the CBO by 10% in order to draw up "a panel of economic advisers who are generally macro-economists" and thus began
to assess the wild trajectory of health system costs, before suggesting "innovative policy interventions" capable of taming them.[15]

One interviewee explained how important this change was by reminding us "that when it was implemented in the 1970s, only 6 out of
roughly 225 advisers were allocated to health issues, whereas in 2010
there were more than 40 people working on these issues full-time."[16]
With this strategy, not only did Orszag and his team upset the CBO's
working practices, but they encroached on the well-defined skill
set that was the agency's preserve—control of public programs. In
December 2008, following several attempts with Congress's Finance
Committee, the fruit of his labor emerged in an unusual two-volume
document aimed at the new administration and at the congressional
committees. In the document, Orszag set out the interplay between
budget costs and the need for health reform (Joyce, 2011: 182).[17] These
mammoth reports, which by comparing the costs with the budget's viability over time and within various programs, have legitimized the
programmatic orientation advanced by CBO for the upcoming reform
bill. Because of Orszag's initiative while he headed the CBO, Barack
Obama, as soon as he was elected president, made clear his intention to
name Orszag as OMB director to drive through the reform project's
budget. His appointment as OMB director was confirmed after Senate
hearings on January 13 and 14, 2009.

Clinton plan veteran Alice Rivlin examines Orszag's astounding ascent to the government's summit: "In the midterm [2006], he had been the CBO director, and he realized that health care was going to come back as an issue, and his staff in CBO did a lot of analytical work on options and alternatives, and so on, and hired very good people. So the CBO would be ready when the health care reform came. Then Peter Orszag went to OMB, taking with him a lot of analysis and knowledge that he had got when he was there."[18] It is precisely for this reason that it was "Peter Orszag and the OMB who played a key role behind the scenes."[19] Looking at Orszag's career path does confirm the high mobility across both branches of power in the political decision-making process. It also shows that the budgetary cost argument would have had an impact on the programmatic-orientation content. In addition, it also means that the famous "new policies create new politics" line can be updated to "new programmatic orientations create new politics."[20]

Overall, the process whereby Clinton plan veterans and newcomers took up key positions of power on congressional subcommittees and within Speaker and CBO staffs happened alongside diligent attempts to legitimize a great necessary reform. Moreover, it took place well before President Obama launched the legislative process (in February 2009). The other observation to note is the rise in congressional back offices of insiders such as Wendell Primus and Peter Orszag, who arrived with prior experience in government issues and knowledge of budgetary and health policies.

The Colonization at the Summit of the Executive Branch

The process within Congress observed above would have had only a relative effect had it not been followed by the colonization of key positions in the Obama administration by Clinton plan veterans and newcomers (chapters 4 and 5). Indeed, after having won their first battle, the insiders had to conquer the ever-more uncertain heights of power in the executive branch. A government of strangers was still possible because of the game of incumbent appointments by the newly elected president

(Heclo, 1977). In contrast to the Clinton administration, during which Washington's unelected governmental health elites were locked into a task force led by strangers (chapter 7), the long-term insiders would succeed in preempting and filling almost every strategic post created to underpin the reform, both in the White House as well as in HHS.

The study of career paths has already enabled us to identify a crucial number of typical pathways by contrasting those institutional migrants who moved from Congress to the executive (or vice versa) and those technocratic translators who returned in charge. Most authors in the field of American politics have noted how "health care policy advisers" and former employees in the executive branch of the Clinton administration were appointed to top positions in the Obama administration (McDonough, 2011; Starr, 2013). None of these authors, however, has studied the pattern of transformation in social backgrounds and career paths of the elites that this appointment process reveals. Finally, few of them have examined the way that the Clinton plan veterans benefited from this situation to establish their role as custodian of state policies.

This lack of previous study is why I will adopt *New York Times* journalist Matt Bai's "Taking the Hill" metaphor to show that this move to colonize the summit of the government is not the result of random political or politico-partisan appointments but rather the effect of a collective strategy (2009). President Clinton, in contrast, tried with his task force "to separate from politics. And they didn't work with Congress. Obama did exactly the reverse. He said, 'Congress should just put it [the legal text] together well.'"[21] Moreover, the new president's appointments favored the Clinton plan veterans with lengthy professional experience in formulating health coverage policy. President Obama's political appointments to the executive confirmed that "they are people who build their careers around problems of public policy" (Michaels, 1997: 105) while anticipating that in order to maximize the chances of a reform's success, "you can't separate personnel from policy" (Bonafede, 1987: 48). The health advisers whom President Obama and his chief of staff, Rahm Emanuel—a Clinton plan veteran and non–health specialist—recruited to the transition formed an insider's team (Whipple, 2017). Although he failed in his attempt to appoint Senator Tom Daschle as secretary of HHS, President Obama, unlike President Clinton, favored the Washingtonians (Bai, 2009). Matt Bai, for instance, mentions several long-term aides and congressional staffers, such as Jim Messina (with Senator Baucus on the Finance Committee), Phil Schiliro (with Representative Waxman), Peter Rouse (with Senator Daschle on the Finance Committee), Lisa Konwinski (with Senator Conrad on the Budget Committee), Melody Barnes (with Senator Kennedy on the HELP Committee), and Peter Orszag (head of the CBO). Although Matt Bai does not list all the appointments of influential insiders in President Obama's inner circle—such as the very "Waxmanian" Mike Hash (White House senior health adviser), Karen Pollitz from the Pepper Commission (and adviser to the director of the Office of Consumer Information and Insurance Oversight [OCIIO]), Jeanne Lambrew (who was close to Senator Daschle in HHS and at the OCIIO), and especially Nancy-Ann DeParle at the White House—he does show how these appointments helped to smooth political exchanges and negotiations between Congress and the executive branch. By following up on Matt Bai's intuition, it is clear that there was a definite intention to respect various Democratic sensibilities when selecting a staffer within each congressional committee who could influence the reform, thus ensuring the advantages of privileged ties with the legislative branch.

The study of long-term insiders' career paths allows us to assess the effects of President Obama's political appointments of Clinton plan veterans within the executive branch. The first consequence of this kind of appointment was the exclusion of individuals who were deemed strangers to the health policy world, such as Ira Magaziner and Hillary Clinton. Policy entrepreneurs like David Cutler, a health economist at Harvard University who was considered one of the Massachusetts plan's architects, were relegated to the rank of mere technical consultant when the administration's transition team was put in place after the presidential election victory (Brill, 2015: 69–72). The same applied to Jonathan Gruber, a health economist at MIT who sought remuneration for his skills in the private sector. This exit of strangers from governmental affairs can also be seen as resulting from personal conflict that pitted insiders against strangers. It also explains David Cutler's disappointment in remaining a "bird of passage" despite his desire to enter government back offices.[22]

It was the Clinton plan veterans' grip on all the key Obama administration posts that led to the doors closing on any kind of outsider-run intervention in the decision-making process. Appointing five Clinton plan veterans to top posts at the White House to ensure the reform's progress reveals the extent of their own power within the executive. Nancy-Ann DeParle (director of the Office for Health Reform), the "Waxmanian" Mike Hash (White House senior health adviser), and Phil Schiliro (adviser responsible for relations with Congress), as well as Jeanne Lambrew at HSS (policy director of the OCIIO) where she was later joined by Karen Pollitz, had all worked together during the Clinton administration. These insiders, two of whom enjoyed career paths as technocratic translators and three as institutional migrants, were appointed to important positions owing to their seniority or experience during the Clinton administration, as well as for their ability to run the policy-formulation process.

The interviews carried out for the OPERA survey, in addition to more recent interviews in 2018 for the ProAcTA survey, show that the strong relationships between these insiders dating back to both Clinton administrations (Lambrew successively occupied the same director posts as DeParle [PAD at the OMB], and Hash and Glied contributed to the task force) played a role in their appointments, while others were excluded. Their legitimacy as insiders came from a combination of technical know-how regarding health policy formulation and a tight social network spread across Washington's power circles. One former Clinton task force member who worked for Congress and HHS prior to becoming a private-sector consultant considered them to be "some incredibly bright people."[23] The consultant went on to say "At the beginning, I said, Judy Feder, Sara Rosenbaum, Bruce Vladeck, Nancy-Ann DeParle, Bob Berenson, Jeanne Lambrew, Chris Jennings—basically, [these were] the top health policy people in the Clinton administration with regard to health care."[24] One of Rahm Emanuel's goals during the presidential transition period was to recruit Nancy-Ann DeParle, a Clinton administration veteran, and no one else, to steer the "health reform decision" from the

White House, which perfectly illustrates this tendency to entrust leadership positions to veterans of the Clinton administration.[25]

For Alice Rivlin, OMB director during the Clinton administration, Nancy-Ann DeParle's appointment was justified based on her long experience: "She worked for me at the OMB in the Clinton administration. She was in the HCFA, but during the health care debate, she was one of my important people in this 'task force' thing. She is a very good health expert and very skilled person, and I'm thankful that she learned a lot both from that experience and from when she was administrator of Medicare and Medicaid in the Clinton administration. So she was an important part of the team."[26] Len Nichols, another Clinton plan veteran close to the Democratic Blue Dogs corroborated this assessment of DeParle: "[She is] the perfect person for where she was in the White House."[27] He then added that with her skills, DeParle could have drafted the reform bill in "thirty minutes," but because of her experience with the Clinton failure, she supported the new presidential strategy based on the dictum "you are Congress, so draft your own reform proposal."[28] The "health reform decision" briefing memo drafted by Nancy-Ann DeParle as soon as she arrived at the White House on April 21, 2009, revealed the program's general outline and the spirit in which it ought to be undertaken. It also showed how internalized lessons from the past opened the way to a reform process that would respect the role of institutions and establish the principle of seeking as broad a political consensus as possible.[29]

This political choice to appoint Clinton plan veterans to the head of the new administration articulated the specific political learning and the development of the role of custodian of policy. Appointing these Clinton-era veterans confirmed how significant this experience was, as another interviewee emphatically stated, "The advantage that Obama had over Clinton is that, whether it's Rahm Emanuel, whether it's Nancy-Ann DeParle, whether it's any one of a number of other people, they had the experience of seeing the missteps of the Clinton administration, and then learning from those missteps, [and trying] not to make the same mistakes. . . . The experience of the Clinton administration was invaluable in terms of their strategy and implementation in the Obama administration."[30] Health economist and Clinton plan veteran Sherry Glied, appointed as ASPE at HHS by President Obama in 2010 after the adoption of the bill, placed this activity in a wider context: "It's a very small world, and the people who were here already who had worked for Congress, the 'government in exile' people who were here the whole time, [they] had worked with me in the past [during the Clinton administration] . . . by the time you make all the intersecting circles."[31]

As they returned in force to the back offices of power, the Clinton plan veterans felt they belonged to the *grande famille* of Washington health policy elites. "I could say it is like a family of people working on health care."[32] Belonging to a community of health care policy-makers could lead some generalists in the field to want to leave the sector. Neera Tanden, for example, who was close to Hillary Clinton but joined the Obama-Biden ticket during the campaign and played a role in the future president's adoption of the bill with the individual-mandate idea, explained how she quickly ended her experience at HHS: "Even though it's big and complicated . . . it's still, like, health care. So there was a real—on our team, there were a bunch of people who were health care people, like Nancy-Ann DeParle was a health care person, Jeanne Lambrew was a health care person, you know, Mike Hash."[33] In a more critical frame of mind, a Republican former ASPE during the George W. Bush administration who cited several Clinton plan veterans by name considered them a "bunch of people" forming "part of a big group of people thinking a certain way."[34]

Evidently, this shared way of thinking of the health coverage policy elites was not driven by ideology but by pragmatism and a political learning along the lines of "let's get the reform done this time!" Shaping the reform—its content, the ideas underlying it, and especially its catchall nature—lay at the heart of the long-term insiders' collective and pragmatic program that motivated them in their relentless ascent to the summit of governmental power. Moreover, their early takeover of Congress's health committees, along with some insiders' migration to the White House, was followed by their capture of key positions in the Obama administration. As an almost unheard-of situation in the US, it is quite likely that this elite configuration affected the outcome of the decision-making process.

The Consecration of the Role of Custodian of State Policies

Following the observations above, it is worth revisiting Paul Starr's "inside game" notion (2013) in order to show how the insiders asserted themselves in the role of custodian of health coverage policy by steering the decision-making process. While the majority of studies on American politics do mention the presence of Clinton plan veterans, they tend to point out the political adeptness of the congressmen whom the veterans were advising or overestimate the role of President Obama and his chief of staff, Rahm Emanuel, who seemed to capitalize on a moment when the stars aligned (Jacobs & Skocpol, 2010; McDonough, 2011; Starr, 2013). Other researchers, such as Jonathan Oberlander, stress the intra-elite personal closeness that emerged from the rubble of the Clinton failure in order to explain the consensual nature of the reform, which was based on the search for a compromise with Republicans and interest groups (Oberlander, 2009, 2010). Only a few research studies have linked the bipartisan, consensus-based policy orientation supported by Washington health elites to the rejection of the alternative public-option model (Beaussier, 2012; Lepont, 2014). By examining the making of the custodian of state policies role to align with the executive and congressional perspectives, we will delve beyond this alignment of stars and explore what happened.

Our study of insiders' career paths shows the making in health governance of a new "iron triangle" formed by the White House, HHS, and some congressional committees (Adams, 1982; Peterson, 1993). This triangulation was based on two types of circulation of elites—horizontal (the institutional migrants) and vertical (the technocratic translators)—in the back offices of government and was deployed by both Clinton plan veterans and newcomers. Indeed, one interviewee implicitly confirmed these two types of circulation by describing the career paths of three individuals in the Clinton and Obama administrations.[35] First of all, he stated that "Nancy-Ann was in the OMB during the Clinton health reform, and then became the Obama health chief. She stayed within the administration all that time. She was never part of Congress." Then he described Wendell Primus's pathway: "The Pelosi staff person is an interesting story. It's a man who's named Wendell Primus. Wendell has been around for a very long time. He was never on the Waxman staff. He was always on staff—I think he was on the Budget and Ways and Means [Committees], and it would be a very interesting graph to see how people move around over time . . . but during the Clinton administration, he went over to HHS, where, among other things, he worked on our welfare program, cash assistance for poor people."[36] Later, this same interviewee described Jeanne Lambrew's long career: "Another person who was a player in several different ways along the way: Jeanne Lambrew. During the Clinton administration, Jeanne was first at the Council of Economic Advisers. . . . She's an economist, and then she was in the OMB [still during the Clinton administration] . . . . In the Obama administration when Senator Daschle was appointed to be our secretary of health [he withdrew his candidacy before his nomination went before the Senate], Jeanne was the principal person. . . . She works at HHS now."

Other interviewees also described the insiders' mobility as an elite group. This circulation led Phil Schiliro, an institutional migrant, to leave Waxman's staff to take up a position as liaison between Congress and the White House. In this role, he found himself leading negotiations with, among others, his former Waxman-staff colleagues in the House of Representatives, such as Karen Nelson, coordinator of the Tri-Comm (the Committees for Energy and Commerce, Ways and Means, and Education and the Workforce), and Andy Schneider (with the Oversight and Government Reform Committee), which gave them a certain mastery over discussions unfolding about the contents of the reform.[37] Schiliro also stressed that many of the people involved were "over sixty" years old; several of them had more than thirty years' experience in health policy and were able to lead discussions from "six in the morning to eleven o'clock at night." In addition to their seniority, these insiders had real authority in choosing the programmatic orientation for the reform.

Evidently, assumptions cannot be made about the impact of this triangulation on the decision-making process, solely on the basis of these examples. Our interviews lead us to believe, however, that the effects of triangulation played their role: indeed, the vast majority of negotiations to decide on the programmatic orientation of the reform took place in the context of debates driven by insiders behind closed doors, thus ensuring a strong relationship between the executive and Congress. At the White House, Nancy-Ann DeParle and Phil Schiliro, who was in charge of relations with Congress, ran the Office of Health Reform as a duo. Both these Clinton plan veterans followed the almost daily progress of projects devised simultaneously in both houses (McDonough, 2011: 72–73). According to journalist Peter Nicholas, based on a plan imagined by Schiliro, DeParle conducted one-on-one interviews with more than 135 congressional staffers and representatives; this was not to dictate the bill to Congress but simply to act as a guarantor of the political arrangements necessary for the reform's outcome, while insisting on the need not to increase the public debt. DeParle was seconded by Jeanne Lambrew, director of the Office of Health Reform at HHS, to ensure that the administration would loyally follow suit. This tactic initiated by a senior figure among Clinton plan veterans constituted a radical change of strategy directly arising from lessons learned from the previous failure. In order to make sense of this triangulation, it is important to note that President Obama made his political appointments with a particular agenda in mind, naming DeParle as director of the White House Office of Health Reform on March 3, 2009, at the same time as he appointed Kathleen Sebelius as health secretary. On May 11, 2009, the health secretary replicated the structure at the White House that was delivering the reform when she created an Office of Health Reform whose direction she gave to Jeanne Lambrew. From then on, it was clear how it was exclusively these Clinton plan veterans who monopolized the most important positions in the decision-making process.

Within Congress, in the House of Representatives, it was Wendell Primus, acting on behalf of Speaker Nancy Pelosi and long-term insider staffers from the Tri-Comm—such as Karen Nelson (with the Energy and Commerce Committee), Cibele Bjorklund (with the Ways and Means Committee), and Michele Varnhagen[38] (with the Education and Labor Committee)—who were tasked with drafting the bill. Michele Varnhagen, mentioned here for the first time, perfectly illustrates the career-path effect under scrutiny in this chapter. Varnhagen was a Clinton plan veteran who, during the eponymous reform initiative, was on Senator Ted Kennedy's staff (with the HELP Committee); then she spent some time at USAID (the US Agency for International Development) before returning in 1999 to work for George Miller on the Education and Labor Committee in the House of Representatives. More left-leaning staffers on the Tri-Comm, launched in June 2009, had to manage internal political tensions stemming from Republican representatives and Democratic Blue Dogs' systematic opposition (Beaussier, 2016: 174). Despite the slow pace of negotiations regarding the reform project's cost and putting a partial public option in place, the House insiders united behind Henry Waxman's political stance to promote the Affordable Health Care for America Act on November 7, 2009 (HR 3962) despite initial opposition during the "bill reconciliation" process (Starr, 2013: 209).

On the Senate side, Clinton plan veterans DeParle, Lambrew, and Hash also pursued negotiations between the Senate's Finance, Budget, and HELP Committees and the Labor and Pensions Committee. Here again, they worked closely with insiders Liz Fowler, Lisa Konwinski, and David Bowen on the draft bill. The bill mirrored the orientation of the program discussed at the Alliance for Health Reform. And it reflected the consensual bipartisan approach built around controlling budget costs and bringing private insurers on board. One Clinton plan veteran remembered being invited to participate in the HELP Committee's work with two colleagues, health policy and insurance market experts Karen Pollitz (an associate professor at Georgetown University) and Gary Claxton (vice president of the Kaiser Family Foundation).[39] Together they defended Peter Orszag's stance (at the CBO and OMB) on budgetary viability, while also pleading to bring private insurers on board and thus divide and neutralize opposition from interest groups.

Choosing this orientation for the program overlapped with the expectations of those Clinton plan veterans in posts within the executive, all the more so since DeParle would steer the negotiations with the health lobbies (McDonough, 2011: 76; Brill, 2015). Certainly this was why following a period of barely disguised support, in order to let both chambers of Congress take on their legislator role, DeParle indicated that moving forward with the Affordable Health Choices Act (voted on in the Senate on December 23, 2009) was the only way for the reform to pass. This was during the "bill reconciliation" process and after Senator Scott Brown's election (Beaussier, 2012). As a result of this strategy, President Obama came to ratify the bill known as the Patient Protection and Affordable Care Act on March 23, 2010. Unsurprisingly, the final version adopted resembled in many places the famous briefing memo written when President Obama took up his duties at the White House. Moreover, one Clinton plan veteran then working for Congress said, "Nancy-Ann DeParle really was the driving force of the process."[40]

The insiders' master stroke was to press President Obama into giving carte blanche to Congress to avoid repeating the error of a ready-to-go reform. As a result, everything went ahead as if Obama and his advisers had adopted the famous phrase that President Lyndon Johnson used when addressing Wilbur Mills, the Democratic leader of the Ways and Means Committee, in 1964 when the Great Society project was launched: "I am not trying to go into details" (Morone, 2010: 1097). Although President Obama left his advisers and congressional staffers to do their work, he could draw on ideas broached during the Democratic primaries and his race against Hillary Clinton, and show himself open to a convergence of approaches to the content of the reform. This is how one of the insiders subtly commented on the situation: "Mr. Obama's staff people—including my friend Mike Hash, who is deputy of the number-two person . . . in the White House health office now—had been working for Congress during Clinton's health reform. He saw how the collapse happened. Nancy-Ann DeParle, she was in a governor's office, but she saw how it happened, she was in the OBM during the Clinton administration. She saw Clinton, and they learned lessons, I think, a little too well, I think they learned a little too much. But we all learned from it. . . . Mr. Obama never had a plan. He didn't spend lots of time pulling people into the room and saying, 'What should I do?' He said, 'Let the Congress—I want—here's the goal that I want. I want to cover X million people. I want to contain costs.' And he never came up with a 1,500-page plan. I mean, we could never get him to come up with a 3-page plan [for Congress]. He just said, 'Oh, the House and the Senate will—they are smart people up there, they will work it out.'"[41]

Owing to the insiders' strong presence in the back offices of the two branches of government, the president could insinuate that he was not concerned with the "details" of the programmatic orientation, leaving that role up to Congress.[42] In fact, he never intervened directly in the debate between both houses regarding the public-option issue, letting his advisers sway the balance against it, behind closed doors. From then on, the Clinton plan veterans felt emboldened to ensure that the impulse toward reform would rely on unity and consensus: "The Democrats, this time, came together, and we did not fight with each other. The three major committees in the House all worked together, and the staffs all worked together to come up with one bill for all three committees, and for that I give both Nancy-Ann [DeParle] and Speaker Pelosi a lot of credit, because they said, 'We are not going to have a civil war this time. We are going to work together behind closed doors so that everyone negotiates about what they have to have, but we are not going to fight with each other.'"[43] Only the matter of budget viability, exacerbated by the 2008 economic crisis, seemed to draw a line that could not be crossed: "Mr. Obama and Congress decided [based on the CBO score] they would spend some money. We raised some taxes in this, we lowered spending in some other areas, but we raised some revenues to pay [for] some of this too."

It is important to note that other Clinton plan veterans such as Judy Feder, Diane Rowland, and Chris Jennings, who remained inside the Beltway yet outside the back offices of government when the reform process was launched, would promote the bipartisan and consensual approach to the reform collectively devised in Washington's think tanks. Thus, they participated in legitimizing the role of custodians endorsed by their colleagues then in power. The most emblematic case was that of Chris Jennings, an institutional migrant. Between 2008 and 2009 he remained in Washington and worked as president and founder of Jennings Policy Strategies. He had this to say about promoting the reform: "I did participate, but from the outside," namely, by acting as a "proponent of the health care reform act and by contributing to the environment that made it possible, that made people think that it was possible. In 2008–2009, I made speeches, wrote articles, trying to explain why this time, it is possible. . . . I also explained to each sector of stakeholders why it was in their best interest to support the reform. It was really hard, but at the end of the day, people from the White House, from the House of Representatives believed that it was possible."[44] Jennings recalled that "I had worked with [them] for six years during the Clinton administration." He also talked about his personal closeness to key actors, saying, "I am close to everybody who worked on the reform." These individuals included those from the executive such as "Rahm Emanuel, Nancy-Ann DeParle, Jeanne Lambrew, at that time, Kathleen Sebelius, the health secretary's right-hand woman." He mentioned in passing, "They know I have been in their seats," meaning that he'd also been in charge; as a show of support he'd given them policy brief "notes" to help them drive the political process efficiently. This work in the shadows undeniably contributed to creating a shared impression in Washington, DC, even among those interest groups most impervious to political change, "that this time, something was going to happen."[45] Apart from his involvement in communications work at the Alliance for Health Reform, Jennings wrote an article in the *Journal of Law, Medicine and Ethics* whose evocative title neatly summarized the Clinton plan veterans' collective intention: "Proving the Skeptics Wrong: Why Major Health Reform Can Happen Despite the Odds" (Jennings, 2008).

In contrast with the Clinton administration years, sector-based interest groups enjoyed either direct links to Washington's think tanks or indirect links via Republican insiders, some of whom had worked for private lobbies during the new reform's incubation period. In this sense, even before it was launched, most interest groups remained loyal to the reform's principle of consensus and bipartisanship (Beaussier, 2012). This was also the reason why a shared belief prevailed among the business community that the reform would come to fruition even before President Obama had initiated it. Moreover, conflict and attempts to derail the project diminished, replaced by a feeling of mutual trust which the insiders created when the orientation of the reform was being negotiated. We must point out, however, that the extent to which the many stakeholders endorsed the project varied significantly, including the insurers (AHIP), medical associations (AMA), hospital federations (AHA, FHA), and the pharmaceutical industry (Pharmaceutical Research and Manufacturers of America [PhRMA]). Afterward, while negotiations took place in Congress, interest groups progressively became divided when faced with different program options promoted in both houses (Quadagno, 2011, 2014). In fact, when the coalition of interest groups fragmented, despite their shared "divided we fall" strategy, it was because the executive this time around did not seemingly have a pre-established "plan" (Hacker, 2010: 865). President Obama and his advisers clearly conveyed that they were giving Congress the reins to devise the reform, leaving the door open to traditional interest-group-led lobbyists (Oberlander, 2009). Yet, during almost daily meetings held behind closed doors, the negotiation tactics did not favor the interest groups, despite White House advisers being present. On this matter, one Senate Finance Committee staffer said that contacts with "DeParle and her team took place every day" and that those with Orszag, the OMB director, were just as frequent.[46] This same staffer added that during the bill's drafting by competent committees, other than those White House advisers mentioned above, she also worked with two insiders at the House of Representatives: Cibele Bjorklund (on the Ways and Means Committee) and Karen Nelson (on the Energy and Commerce Committee). Indeed, as one of Nancy Pelosi's main advisers said: "Most of the negotiations occurred behind closed doors, before the bill emerged."[47] Once discrepancies between the two versions of the proposed reform were worked out by both houses, it is likely the elite triangulation seen among the Clinton plan veterans, who were fearful of losing the Democratic sixty-seat Senate majority, favored and perhaps clinched the success of a more consensual version envisaged by the Senate during the bill's earlier development.

Finally, this triangulation of power strengthened the cohesion of health coverage policy elites, which rendered the lobbyists' work more difficult: they were incapable of focusing their collective effort toward a shared target. The failure to reactivate the "Harry and Louise" TV ad campaign about the new health policy, instigated by pharmaceutical groups during the previous reform project, was clear evidence of this lack of focus (Brill, 2015: 177). Moreover, looking at Mizruchi's work on the fracturing of the corporate elites of the private insurance sector, one can understand why they were in weak positions to negotiate with the Obama administration (2013). Having learned the lesson from 1993 for the need to integrate interest groups when negotiating the reform's new orientations, the insiders asked them: "What do you want to support the bill?"[48] This invitation did not go unheeded; it prompted concrete negotiations with the PhRMA lobby, which, by accepting an $800 million tax increase, obtained in return the lifting of controlled medicine prices that would qualify under the new health insurance program. The lack of cohesion among the sector's lobbies contrasted with the insiders' unity: apart from their socio-professional homogeneity acquired over time, these Clinton plan veterans, more than anyone, were aware of the cost of dissent. The inversion of the power balance with interest groups clearly resulted from veterans DeParle, Schiliro, and Hash's experience during the Clinton administration (i.e., the lack of integration and negotiation with sectoral interest groups); thus, they benefited from the interest groups' loss of influence on Congress and the opportunity to keep final negotiations on the reform draft behind the closed doors of the White House.[49] In addition, the decision to negotiate individually and separately with sector-specific interest groups—at Senator Max Baucus and Nancy-Ann DeParle's behest—consolidated the reform supporters' power over that of their potential opponents.

When Democrats in Congress rallied around the desire to deliver a reform (Beaussier, 2012), to which was added the long-term insiders' determination and tactical skill, serious risks emerged for those interest groups wanting to oppose the reform impetus. From then on, the relative neutralization of the typical game that interest groups played could be explained by the triangulation of insiders, who at that time monopolized key positions in Congress, the White House (in the EOP and OMB) and HSS. Their shared vision of this programmatic orientation legitimized their collective action in political negotiations led behind closed doors. The most remarkable manifestation of this was their united front, established against any other competing orientation that might reduce the likelihood of political consensus.

The Foreclosure of the Government of Strangers

The public-option idea put forward by Helen Halpin, a public health specialist at UC Berkeley School of Public Health, and Jacob Hacker, a political scientist and health policy expert, was discussed and reworked into the draft bill of October 29, 2009, and supported by the House of Representatives. It was known as the Affordable Health Care for America Act (HR 3962) and was presented as the most progressive of all the reform projects (Jacobs & Skocpol, 2010: 188). It offered US citizens the choice between a public or private health coverage system. The vast majority of American political researchers have interpreted its failure as the ultimate abdication of Democratic progressive forces to the Blue Dogs as well as to Republicans (Hacker, 2010; Jacobs & Skocpol, 2010). Other researchers have pointed to the "invisible force" of interest groups controlled by a handful of Democratic staffers who rallied to their cause (Brasfield, 2011; Donnelly & Rochefort, 2012; Brill, 2015).

Nevertheless, few among these researchers have noted the feeble interest shown toward this version of the reform project by the vast majority of Clinton plan veterans because of the risk of fragmentation that this reforming elite faced (McDonough, 2011). Yet these insiders, thanks to the Clinton plan veterans who had analyzed their failure, had insisted upon aligning themselves behind the most consensual orientation of the program possible. For the insiders, this alignment was a necessary condition for a new reform project to succeed. Seeking a political arrangement around a far-reaching reform to ensure that health coverage would extend to citizens the most in need undoubtedly shaped the formulation of the new programmatic orientation. The cost of this collective strategy was the obligation to guard against any attempt to revive a reform project inspired by the mythical National Health Insurance model (the single-payer model) or by that of a comprehensive managed-competition kind of reform. Seen from this angle, one can understand why for the majority of Clinton plan veterans working then, the public option contained divisive elements that could fragment the reforming vanguard: those nefarious consequences on the reform's outcome had already been felt during the Clinton administration. Indeed, some insiders, especially those supporting the representatives in the House, felt some intellectual affinity for the progressive parts of the public-option model; these parts have been defended by representatives on the left of the Democratic Party over many years (and even today).

Their wish to reform, however, as much as their personal closeness to their colleagues speaking on behalf of the Obama administration, would compel them to support the text presented to the Senate during the "reconciliation bill" stage (Beaussier, 2012). The opposite choice would have simply caused the reform project to fail. In any case, for the majority of insiders, especially within the executive, who were then in charge of carrying the reform project, the public option was never considered as a politically viable alternative. For many of them, it revived the mirage of the single-payer model, as well as the threat of strangers formulating policy, and it was therefore synonymous with political failure. The public-option project was actually led by Hacker and Halpin, academics who had never benefited from any political appointment in the spheres of power (Lepont, 2014). It must be emphasized that the Clinton administration's managed-competition, single-payer, and public-option models were developed by policy entrepreneurs, in the sociological sense described above, and induced, fifteen years later, the same defiance among Washington's insiders. In its program content, however, the public option went much further than the single-payer model in developing a health coverage system based on a choice between a public or a private system of medical coverage. This was the reason why a minority of insiders, those close to Waxman and the Speaker of the House Nancy Pelosi, for a long time defended the ideas underpinning the public option.

According to Jacobs and Skocpol, this more left-leaning version of the reform proposal was seen as the one that was championed by the heirs of the single-payer model; at that time, they opposed the version advocated by the "mainstream reformer" that favored a reform based on a system inspired by the Massachusetts plan (2010: 67). This reading, steeped in the American political perspective, tends to minimize the conflict surrounding these two visions of the reform to a typical internal partisan split among Democratic representatives in Congress (liberals versus conservatives) and the joint intervention of interest groups and Republicans, thus ensuring the ensuing victory of the conservative approach (Pierson & Skocpol, 2007; Hacker & Pierson, 2010). Although typical, this kind of interpretation can be seen as incomplete insofar as it ignored the division or unity issue of the unelected governmental health elites. Certainly, the public-option model, as much as the single-payer model, was and has always been held in high esteem among American social scientists. The introduction of the public-option model in congressional debates, however, as well as in discussions that took place behind closed doors, was collectively perceived by new custodians as a factor that could reactivate a political configuration of divided elites.

Before returning to the public-option failure, we consider the factors that initially caused the majority of insiders to be skeptical (Brasfield, 2011). Let us compare two contrasting interpretations of the public option's rejection. The first interpretation suggests that some Washington insiders' conversion to mainstream thinking, incidentally closely connected to sector-based interest groups, explains the triumph of the Massachusetts model (Brill, 2015). Although seemingly satisfactory at first glance, this interpretation assumes that most Clinton plan veterans (such as Judy Feder, Chris Jennings, and Diane Rowland), having defended the progressive play-or-pay model, which resembled the public-option model, would several years later have been converted to a "mainstream" approach to the reform in order to support the consensual catch-all model of the Affordable Care Act.

A second interpretation emphasizes the choice to reject a version of the reform project that would be divisive and therefore doomed to failure. The vast majority of interviews, especially those conducted with Clinton plan veterans at a nine-year interval (in 2010 and 2019), confirm their collective conversion to promote the more consensual programmatic orientation. For this reason, Clinton plan veterans such as progressive Democrats Judy Feder and Chris Jennings and conservative Democrat Len Nichols together justified that as a policy matter, they were in the middle, and this led to a reform project, meaning, "we are using the private insurance market and private incentives, to create a mixed rather than a public health insurance system."[50] This strategic reversal arose from the creation of a homogenous elites group, the long-term insiders, who collectively devised a new orientation for the program aimed at delivering a reform built on elaborate political arrangements.

The public option was primarily debated within the House of Representatives, where progressive Democrats were in the majority, thus suggesting for a short time that it was a possible alternative (Brasfield, 2011). According to one of Speaker Nancy Pelosi's advisers, "the public-option issue was also very difficult to negotiate" before being partially introduced in the first version of the reform draft bill proposed by the House of Representatives.[51] It was later removed under combined pressure from the Republicans, the CBO, and the Senate (McDonough, 2011; Starr, 2013). Furthermore, James Brasfield has underlined the fact that the public option was initially perceived in the policy community as an innovative orientation for the program but found itself, during its passage through Congress, described by its detractors in the political arena as a Trojan horse meant to establish a reworked version of the single-payer model (2011). One Clinton plan veteran, present in the House committees where the topic was debated, pointed out: "Single payer never went anywhere. I think we had, during the Obama debates, we had a serious possibility of a new idea, which people really did adopt, which was called the 'public option,' which was, in addition to all the private insurance, that the government would run an insurance program, like Medicare. Perhaps—and people could choose—rather than buying private insurance . . . they would buy the government plan. There was an entirely new idea in this debate that was not there during the Clinton debate. . . . Some people, who in the past would have said the whole thing should be a single payer, this time chose the public option as their liberal alternative."[52] He then went on to assert that the draft of the Affordable Health Care for America Act, backed by the House of

Representatives (in October 2009), did not survive opposition from the Senate, where "the final death was caused by [Senator] Joseph Lieberman of Connecticut—and Connecticut is one of our biggest insurance-industry states. Lots of insurance companies have their headquarters in Connecticut, so many people thought he was just doing the home-state business by killing the public option." As a result, investigative journalist Steven Brill's argument (2015) that the private insurance lobbies were able to sway the orientation of the final program (the Senate's Affordable Health Choices Act), whose flaws were already mentioned above, was a persuasive one.

While it is undeniable that the public option prompted great interest among progressive Democrats in the House during discussions in the Tri-Comm and Committee on Oversight and Government Reform, one must also take into account that whatever its intrinsic merit, for several insiders, it was considered a "big picture" emanating from elsewhere. Indeed, the public option was neither incubated nor developed by the insiders committed to a consensual model but by two policy entrepreneurs who were outsiders. Moreover, the public option had the potential to split the reform vanguard, thus reawakening the specter of the Clinton failure (Oberlander, 2010). Also, the vast majority of Clinton plan veterans, whatever their political affiliation, internalized the realpolitik principle, according to which "You need sixty votes in the Senate, and it was clear that conservative Democrats in the Senate would never vote for that."[53] Plus, they knew very well that their ex-colleague Karen Ignagni,[54] who went to work for the private insurance lobbies in the wake of the Clinton failure, had imposed certain conditions in order to garner support, such as taking market forces into account and scaling down the possibility of an overly state-based reform (Altman & Shactman, 2011: 260–261). Ignagni and AHIP hoped to extend medical insurance while at the same time preserve the interests of the insurance industry. And the insiders hoped for support while not wanting to sacrifice anything or defend the government's interest, as Nancy-Ann DeParle's words hinted at: "the [insurance] industry puts their special interest ahead of the national interests here."[55] The custodian of state policies role led them to integrate these two dimensions in a reform project that advocated strong federal regulation of the private insurance market while at the same time enabling a larger number of citizens to access it.

All in all, Brasfield, like many academic experts, was surprised that an original good idea did not find the support it deserved among Washington's health decision-makers. Once again, the interplay of intra-partisan political divisions and interest groups' power of veto was highlighted to explain why this program option considered to be a "good" one by academic health experts (Lepont, 2014) was rejected. Steven Brill cites PowerPoint documents on the reform's cost containment presented by the president's advisers pushing the reform in White House meetings (such as DeParle and Orszag) to underscore that the Clinton plan veterans who had President Obama's ear never considered the public option to be a possible programmatic orientation for the reform (2015: 117). By taking up his academic health policy stance once again, Jacob Hacker agreed that the argument around the future reform's budgetary viability was used to undermine the public option (2010). On this point, the scoring process undertaken by the CBO estimated the cost over ten years to public finances for the Affordable Health Care for America Act to be $1.052 trillion. The estimated cost for the Affordable Health Choices Act advocated by the Senate came in at $870 billion.[56] These totals undeniably favored the reform project developed by the second chamber. Aware that this failure, equally his own, could not be reduced to the ideological dimension of competing programmatic orientations, or even to strictly budgetary stakes, Hacker invites us to return to Lasswell's question—who gets what, when, how?—in order to grapple with the interests and motivations of elite groups who confronted each other to ensure that their own policy formulation would hold sway (Hacker, 2010: 872).

Our study of insiders' commitment to a different more consensual program option, initially conceived as bipartisan, addresses Lasswell's question. It shows that the partisan split between progressives and conservatives cannot alone account for why insiders favored one programmatic orientation over another. Identified on the basis of their career paths, these insiders connected their custodial role to their shared vision of policy-making based on a notion of accountability. Their professional identities were often forged as they moved from one prestigious position of power within an agency (HCFA or CMS, OMB) or specialized congressional committee (such as the Ways and Means or Finance committees) to another (table 5.1). These movements back and forth between institutions responsible for the cost-containment issue in the health coverage system prompted them to internalize what was budgetarily feasible, a concern inexorably remote from the public option. With their shared experience of policy failure as Clinton plan veterans in Washington's reform arenas during the time between the two Democratic presidencies, the insiders knew better than anyone the political cost paid when the executive and legislative branches disagreed on the design of the best reform possible.

Thus, one can more easily understand why the public option did not convince the majority of this elite. Finally, we must acknowledge the resurfacing divisions already noted during the Clinton administration between those with prior policy-formulation experience typical of insiders and the policy entrepreneurs on the margins of the political arena (such as Marmor and Enthoven). When we asked one interviewee whether Jacob Hacker had obtained an appointment during the Obama administration, he pointed out Hacker's particular professional role: "No, he is just an academic economist. He was an adviser to the White House, but he was never employed by the White House."[57] More generally, when asked whether "academic people" influenced the insiders' way of approaching the decision-making process, one Clinton plan veteran said, "They don't influence our work directly," adding that "we listen to what they say when we have time" and when it felt necessary.[58]

The insiders intended to distinguish their role as custodian of state policies from that of policy entrepreneurs, and any type of strangers, as much through their effective involvement in the decision-making process as in their sense of accountability and responsiveness: "Another lesson I learned during my career within the back offices of government was that we are in politics, we are not in an academic environment, so to enact a reform, you have to make tradeoffs, you have to compromise on things you don't like. In the reform, some provisions are ugly. I think also some of them are really stupid, are bad policy. . . . But at least we did it, and we can reform the reform."[59] These words reveal the insiders' attachment to formulate policies from inside the back offices of government by seeking the most consensual solution possible. "To reform the reform" then became the leitmotif justifying those compromises necessary for the objective to be pursued; the end result would be the syncretic bill known as the Patient Protection and Affordable Care Act. Finally, more than being a moment when the stars aligned, the successful decision-making process showed that insiders were able to step out of their routine advisory role in order to commit themselves to the custodian role and achieve a far-reaching health coverage reform.

From there, it seems quite likely that the transformation of the social backgrounds and career paths of unelected governmental elites formulating policies—as much as their uniting behind a shared programmatic orientation—was in the end facilitated by the aligning of points of view held by Congress, the White House, and HHS. This alignment of stars in the back offices of government was not coincidental, nor was the external constraint imposed by interest groups (Mizruchi, 2013). On the contrary, the alignment can be explained by the specific new social backgrounds and career paths of the unelected governmental health elite and the triangulation that it favored. When the reform was placed on the decision-making agenda, the converging career paths of institutional migrants and technocratic translators prevented the elite reform vanguard from fragmenting; at the same time, it impelled an internal decision-making process which undeniably favored the reform of the health coverage system.

The government of insiders appears as further proof of the speciousness of the US state—that is to say, a "policy state," weak overall, but which can, depending on the balance of political power and the areas of action, act strongly. Indeed, the relative failure of the "revolution in military affairs" in the national defense sector during the George W. Bush years (Jensen, 2018) and the reversal undergone by the climate-change reform during the Obama administration (Starr, 2013: 235) illustrate that the effect of the insiders' power can strongly fluctuate from one sector of the federal government's activity to another. Other authors have also commented on how the administrative power of sector policy elites can vary according to which party is in power, as illustrated by the national defense sector during Republican-led governments (Jacobs, King & Milkis, 2019). The history and long-term development of sectors other than the US policy state also constitute factors that make the formation of this kind of elite configuration more or less probable. More generally, these insiders who were striving to reinforce the federal government's capacity to regulate health policy can be compared on a number of levels to those custodians of state policies who initiated similar reforms in France and Europe at the same moment (Genieys, 2010; Genieys & Hassenteufel, 2015; Genieys & Darviche, 2023).

Conclusion

TO CONCLUDE this study on the people who made the ACA possible, it is necessary to return to the issue of a government of insiders and their role as custodian of state policies. When considering the way in which American social science addresses the issue of governmental elites and policy formulation, however, it seems that the perspective adopted is always the Millsian view of the "power elite" omnipotence. This perspective focuses on the "one percent" who have influenced policies and thus "made the rich richer" (Hacker & Pierson, 2010). In contrast to this perspective, our elite approach to the long-term insiders aims to draw attention to a situation where another type of interpretation may prevail. In this regard, policy formulation advanced by insiders, while occurring "out of sight," shows that Robert Dahl's notion of pluralist democracy still has a future in US government.

Centered on the study of unelected governmental elites, our research revives a dimension, often forgotten, of Gaetano Mosca's theory of the ruling class: that of the key role of unelected governmental elites in the decision-making process. Let us not forget that the founder of European political science was inspired by his personal experience as secretary to the Italian Parliament's president at the end of the nineteenth century, when he developed his theory of the "ruling class" (Genieys, 2011). Nevertheless, for reasons previously explained elsewhere, Mosca's theory did not get the favor it deserved. On the contrary, at present, with the development of political populism, it is the criticism of the political power of technocrats that is at the heart of the success of "anti-elite" leaders in Western democracies (the US, the UK, Brazil, etc.). And yet, transformations in the social backgrounds and career paths of unelected elites who formulate policy out of sight have in the US favored the making of a far-reaching health insurance reform that opened the way for coverage to be extended to more than twenty million citizens who were previously excluded.

This clearly illustrates that there are some unelected governmental elites who, despite or because of their appropriation of the role of custodian of state policies, continue to defend the common good and interests of American citizens, even though consecutive conservative administrations have weakened the "policy state" (Orren & Skowroneck, 2017). Thus, in the United States as in France (Birnbaum, 2018; Genieys & Darviche, 2023), there are still unelected governmental elites capable of acting to promote or defend the common good. Some thinkers galvanized by the zeitgeist might well remark that these long-term insiders have no democratic legitimacy to act in such a way. Our study of these insiders, acting in anonymity, shows they have supported politicians in Congress and in the executive branch (the White House and HHS) by converting electoral promises into reforms while respecting the necessary distinction in democracy between "decision-making" (their work) and "decision-taking" (the work of the elected officials) (Giddens, 1972).

The long-term insiders in the two branches of power indeed played a decisive role in the process of co-constructing the content of the programmatic orientation which would eventually emerge as a bill. Our study highlights their political governmental work, often conducted in negotiations with stakeholders and held behind closed doors in Congress and at the White House. Through this behind-the-scenes political engagement, theses insiders facilitated the consensus policy solution necessary for the successful completion of a far-reaching reform of the health insurance system. This finding provides insight into change in the health coverage policy domain while enriching our understanding of how governmental elites help to reconfigure contemporary states (King & Le Galès, 2017).

With the programmatic elite framework, we studied transformations in the social backgrounds and career paths of health coverage policy elites that affected changes in programmatic orientations in the health insurance system since the 1990s. Before returning to this interpretation of these correlations, it is appropriate to point out the singular sociological characteristics of these elites—the long-time insiders—to show how they differ from those of "policy issue experts" or "policy entrepreneurs." Long-term insiders share with the latter a similar academic background in public policy and a relevant skill set specific to health policy issues. Long-term insiders differ from most other sectoral elites, however, by constituting a professional group with long-term career paths at the top of health care government.

An in-depth study of the long-term insiders' career paths has explored their circulation within the spheres of power. We have highlighted the singularity of insiders' career paths by identifying strategic positions in the decision-making process which these governmental elites aspired to occupy—and where they followed in one another's footsteps, sometimes even co-opting one another. Within Congress, there are committees and subcommittees assigned to health affairs (such as the Committee on Education and the Workforce and the Committee on Energy and Commerce in the House of Representatives, and the HELP Committee in the Senate). We can see the increasing power of the committees in charge of policy cost concerns (the Ways and Means Committee and the Budget Committee in the House, and the Finance and Budget Committees in the Senate). Within the executive, the trend for insiders to take up posts in these budgetary committees was even more noticeable. Being appointed to lead the HCFA (the CMS since 2001) or as PAD at the OMB in the White House, as well as holding the post of ASPE and that of the president's health czar, often featured in the insiders' career paths. Circulating inside and across these institutions, where they learned about the financial constraints on the health sector, led these individuals to internalize the necessity of devising cost-contained policies. The way they managed to control these financial issues, as revealed by their shared professional journeys, had obvious consequences when it came to expressing their preference for one programmatic orientation over another. This allows us to understand in part their ambivalence during the Obama administration when they were confronted with the public option that was deemed more expensive by the CBO.

The sociological study of long-term insiders' career paths also allows us to highlight the particularity of their circulation in the back offices of government. Indeed, they devised patterns of circulation between the two branches of power, in addition to within each branch itself, in order to strengthen their political role in the decision-making process. Studying the institutional migrants' career paths (their horizontal circulation across the executive branch and Congress) and that of the technocratic translators (their vertical circulation within the same branch of power) has allowed us to analyze why and how the insiders were drawn onward and upward to the top roles in health insurance decision-making when the newest reform project was launched. The change in political majority and the arrival of a new presidential administration accelerated the ascent of these types of career paths. Moreover, this internal career-path circulation increased the insiders' capacity to play a key role in daily political negotiations behind closed doors once a reform project was launched. While weakly in place during the Clinton administration, the effects of this kind of mobility, typical of long-term insiders, became apparent when the new health insurance reform project was launched in 2006, following the Democrats' victory in the congressional midterm elections. Thus, the Clinton plan veterans who had rallied the newcomers to their reform project first filled the key positions in the congressional subcommittees where health policies were discussed, and headed the CBO. Then, under the Obama administration, they colonized key advisory positions at the White House (OMB) and at HHS

Our study of long-term insiders' mobility into the private sector, while they were temporarily shut out from government, also yielded rich insights. Firstly, it highlighted how Democrats' career paths prioritized the nonprofit private sector and the many schools of policy or public health in the Washington, DC, area—a pattern in contrast to the career paths of Republicans, who were more drawn to working for interest-group lobbies. Secondly, it allows us to see that during the George W. Bush years, both Democrats and Republicans moved into think tanks and philanthropic foundations to relaunch a bipartisan idea of a far-reaching health insurance reform. The programmatic elite framework, by combining the analysis of the transformation of unelected governmental elites' career paths with the development of a new programmatic orientation, confirmed the elites' tendency to remain strongly connected to each other inside the Beltway, even when they were no longer acting within political institutions. Because of this proximity, the political learning of the Clinton plan veterans—supported by a few Republican insiders—was very successful with the Democratic newcomers. Moreover, these efforts promoted the idea that only a bipartisan reform project built on consensus would have a chance to succeed.

In order to understand how insiders were able to make their preferred programmatic orientation prevail with Democratic political leaders, it was necessary to examine another unique feature established over time—namely, the insiders' collective effort to delegitimize any form of government of "strangers" (Heclo, 1977). To this end, these insiders defined themselves primarily as "policy people in charge" of the decision-making process in order to better differentiate themselves from short-timers (policy entrepreneurs and other issue experts) (Mackenzie, 1987). In addition to their long-term presence within the government of health policy, the insiders differed from these "birds of passage" by seeking a negotiated political solution, whereas the latter tended to privilege the best policy design. Thus, to set themselves apart from their rivals, the insiders unwittingly rekindled Weber's famous distinction between the "ethics of responsibility" and the "ethics of conviction" (2004). Indeed, for them, being responsible means seeking political consensus. They criticize their rivals for being motivated by convictions (for example, the best policy design) that are often difficult to convert into a politically viable programmatic orientation. This is also the reason why the public option was never considered viable by the majority of insiders during the incubation of the health insurance reform.

Our study also confirms that in their historical role, the health coverage policy elites supplanted the traditional SI elites—those Social Security Administration bureaucrats who had driven the National Health Insurance project in the New Deal and then promoted and defended the Medicaid and Medicare programs. By establishing themselves at the apex of power, the health coverage policy elites also contributed to the reinvention of the role of custodian of state policies. They shared with their predecessors a strong attachment both to the government's ability to intervene in the health insurance domain and to the necessity of extending the scope of coverage to the most dispossessed. But in addition, as a result of their long career paths inside the decision-making process, their unique professional circulation (internal and external to the government), and their initial failure as reformers with the Clinton plan, they reinvented the role of custodian. This allowed these elites to shape an agreement on a far-reaching reform.

As a result of the balance of power in the United States, we have seen over time how the circulation of elites through the executive and legislative branches of government, particularly when the reform process was initiated, facilitated the development of political agreement on a consensual reform issue. Despite their circulation, the insiders acting together as custodians promoting and defending the action of the federal government were endowed, like their French counterparts, with real political power that could influence health coverage policies (Genieys, 2010; Genieys & Darviche, 2023). In the American context, the health coverage policy elites formulated a new programmatic orientation which favored the emergence of a consensual reform project that combined the marketplace with an expansion of government's capacity to regulate. In contrast to the policy entrepreneurs during the Clinton administration—who defended a comprehensive reform involving a grand public coverage system or creating a managed-competition system based on market forces in the health sector—the long-term insiders devised the idea of a far-reaching reform that would fit in the existing system but introduce new policy instruments. Bringing the private insurers and the market idea on board and recognizing freedom of choice in the health insurance system are perhaps the best examples of this. With this programmatic orientation, the insiders were poised to take over the back offices of health insurance government once the Democrats returned to power. As custodians of this programmatic orientation, which was enshrined in law with the Affordable Care Act, the health coverage policy elites played an important role in the recent process of reconfiguring the US policy state.

Studying the latter provides a critique of research attributing a central place to interest groups in the policy-making decision process (Domhoff, 1990, 1996; Wedel, 2009; Hacker & Pierson, 2010). Based on the assumption that the US government is susceptible to forces in civil society, these authors have claimed that the mere fact of being a paid employee of an interest group inevitably renders one an eternal servant to their cause. Yet the insiders' policy decision-making allows us to note the limits of these studies (Leca, 2012). Our research highlights that the "price" of policies (the supply) is not defined in a unilateral way by political parties at the service of an omnipotent financial oligarchy seeking to maximize its profits (Winters & Page, 2009). By studying insiders and policy decision-making at the time of health coverage reforms, we have shown that although these interest groups were helped by the fragmenting Democratic elites' reform front and were able to easily challenge the Clinton plan, they were also incapable of reproducing their success when faced with the Obama administration (Mizruchi, 2013). The explanation is a simple one: the interest groups found themselves facing a group of unelected governmental health elites endowed with superior political resources who, in the course of the decision-making process, played their new role of custodian by seeking a form of political accommodation.

The development of the role of custodian illustrates a new kind of commitment to governmental power among unelected elites pursuing long-term careers inside the American government. This observation supports Heclo's idea at the end of the 1980s when he detected, in the changes affecting the structure of Washington's elites, a noticeable parallel with their homologues in the old established European democracies (1987). Indeed, on the basis of our findings, one can observe that the health coverage policy elites abandoned the idea of the grand National

Health Insurance system defended by the SI elites. In order to reach this collective goal, the health coverage policy elites did not hesitate to turn to the ideas of the regulated market and contained costs, despite these being abhorred by their predecessors. Their decision to select a public-private partnership as a matrix for the Affordable Care Act reflects changes at work. Moreover, in the health coverage sector, the issue of the market has always been a hotly debated one within the Democratic camp and between Democrats and Republicans.

More generally, the making of insiders and their role as custodian of state policies lead us to examine certain assumptions inherent to historical neo-institutionalism and notions of the American political development. Regarding this first point, it is clear that Steinmo's metaphor of the "stupidity" of US political institutions as a factor explaining the defeat of successive grand attempts to reform the health insurance system deserves to be tempered. By pursuing the metaphor, we can say that the supposed "debility" of the institutional game can be compensated by the persistence and skill of a group of elites in government whose grand collective aspiration was to devise at any cost a far-reaching reform of health coverage. This was despite the American policy state lacking a constitutional and administrative structure favoring the institutionalization of an integrated and unified group of social insurance policy elites like in France (Genieys, 2010; Genieys & Darviche, 2023). Considering the elites and the role of custodian in policy domains other than health coverage will help us better understand the role's future changes. Far from being limited to health insurance, the development of the role of custodian of state policies by unelected governmental elites was equally noticeable in the defense sector, although less successfully, with the advent of the revolution in military affairs (Jensen, 2018). Yet within this sector, it was the Republican elites who drove forward the government's initiatives and reinforced the policy state's capacity to act (Jacobs, King & Milkis, 2019). On the other hand, some new sectors such as the environment have not benefited from the elites acting as mediators as observed in the health sector, a factor partly explaining the Obama administration's failed reform on climate change policies (Starr, 2013: 235). And so, it seems that everything in the United

States still occurs in the way that Theda Skocpol (1985, 1995) and her colleagues so deftly illuminated regarding the New Deal—that is, within distinct "strong state islets" and policy sectors whose "strength" varies according to the ability of insiders acting "behind closed doors" to shape policy.

Finally, our study of the people who made de ACA possible reminds us of Skocpol's significant contribution to revealing the crucial role played by women, such as in the mothers' pensions movement, in the development of the American social protection system (1995). Our elite approach to career paths during the Obama presidency confirms the arrival of a new generation of women in senior advisory and congressional staff positions who played a key role in reforming the Affordable Care Act. Some of them were directly involved in drafting the bill, while others introduced good governance as part of the reform process. This achieved a political equilibrium which, during any attempt to reform the health care system, can often be very precarious. According to some journalists, this result can be explained by President Obama's desire to increase the influence of women in government affairs in order to change "the way America works" (Newton-Small, 2016). For one interviewee, the success of the Affordable Care Act demonstrates that kind of change: "At least you can see that this reform is a major policy success for women. . . . Who knows, maybe this had an impact on the reform? They may have a different decision-making style."[1] This phenomenon has slipped under the radar of studies on American politics.

Here are some significant examples of women involved in the decision-making process: Kathleen Sibelius as health secretary; Nancy-Ann DeParle as health czar at the White House; Jeanne Lambrew at HHS; Liz Fowler as director of the Finance Committee; Lisa Konwinski as chief counsel for eleven years on the Budget Committee; Karen Nelson and Ruth Katz in top posts on the Energy and Commerce Committee; Michele Varnaghen on the Education, Labor, and Pensions Committee; and Cybele Bjorklund leading the influential Ways and Means Committee. These examples reveal how women were in charge when the decision-making process began. Speaker Nancy Pelosi[2] found a remarkable set of colleagues in these women when they monopolized almost every key congressional committee post, in addition to those at the top of the executive branch like DeParle and Lambrew (chapter 4 and 5). Maneuvering skillfully within the rules of the political game in order to advance their vision of reform, these women have had a strong influence on the decision-making process. They were drawn to a decision-making style based on negotiation and political accommodation; and this came as a result of their long careers in health public policy, of lessons learned from the Clinton defeat, and of an aspiration to a bipartisan reform strategy open to market forces and based on negotiation. More than many others, these women, who shared sociological characteristics as insiders, were aware that the Clinton administration's programmatic divisions had come with a price: that of excluding thirty-five million citizens from health coverage.

As he had signaled during his presidential campaign, after Donald Trump was elected president in 2016, he rallied Republicans in both houses of Congress behind a "repeal and replace" strategy toward the Affordable Care Act. This slogan had already been bandied about by Paul Ryan when he was the Republican House Speaker from 2015 to 2019. But without the benefit of support from a new generation of Republican health elites pushing a viable alternative to the Affordable Care Act, the replacement project was limited to the traditional and necessary call to introduce a tax cut. The early results from the PRoACTA research, which extends the mapping of Washington's health coverage policy elites performed in 2010 (OPERA) to include additional mapping in 2020, have tended to confirm the phenomenon explored in this book regarding the differences between Democratic and Republican long-term insiders. The study also shows that—except for Ann Agnew, executive secretary at HHS—Republican insiders with long experience in the sector during George W. Bush's presidency returned to work on the issue extremely rarely. In the absence of any all-encompassing and alternative programmatic orientation, the Republican health elites in office are attempting to advance the aim of unravelling the ACA. This was the reason why, along with his contempt for Donald Trump, Senator John McCain, despite being very ill, refused to contribute to the sixty Republican votes necessary for the "repeal and replace" plot to be successful.

Given the lack of any credible alternative, the repeal of a systematic and far-reaching reform like the Affordable Care Act, to which all the major interest groups of the American health care system—employers, insurers, pharmaceutical companies, hospitals, and doctors—had already adjusted their strategies, posed a series of challenges. A series of questions without any answers loomed for the beneficiaries of the new health care coverage: What would happen to the more than twenty million American citizens who had gained health coverage from the Affordable Care Act without needing to rely on an employer? What would happen to them if Medicaid's scope were extended because of changes to the eligibility criteria? Would they receive any help to obtain private insurance? Would there be subsidized private coverage available through health care exchanges? Simply put, if Obamacare were suddenly repealed, what would happen next? In addition to the questions affecting millions of American citizens, questions arose in the corporate world. What would happen to the lobby groups, such as private insurers, who benefited from the ACA? What financial losses would they incur? Furthermore, how could clear budgetary cuts be introduced to the ACA while the system rested on a complex fiscal regime founded on interdependence between different programs for individuals and employers?

All these issues point to how the people who made the ACA—by endorsing negotiation and accommodation between several parties (stakeholders, users, interest groups, etc.)—put in place a sustainable legal apparatus and created a lasting legacy. These arguments are also what brought together Jeanne Lambrew, commissioner of Maine's Department of Health and Human Services, Sherry Glied, dean of the Robert F. Wagner Graduate School of Public Service at New York University, and other Democratic ex-insiders to defend in the media the irreversibility of the ACA. More recently, the Democrats' midterm victory in 2018 and Joe Biden's ascension to the presidency in 2021 have ensured a brighter future for the ACA.

Methodology

A Programmatic Elite Framework

The empirical data used in this study derive from two research programs funded by the French National Research Agency (ANR). ANR is a public administrative institution under the authority of the French Ministry of Higher Education, Research, and Innovation.

The first program was OPERA ("Operationalizing Programmatic Elite Research in America [1988–2010]").[1] This program, with me as principal investigator (Sciences Po, CNRS; formerly at the Université de Montpellier), benefited from funding from the ANR (€250,000) and lasted for four years, from 2008 to 2012 (OPERA: ANR-08-BLAN-0032). The empirical study focused on the transformation of the social backgrounds and career paths of US policy elites in the health insurance and defense sectors from 1988 to 2010.

The second program, ProAcTA ("Programmatic Action in Times of Austerity: Elites' Competition and Health Sector Governance in France, Germany, the UK [England] and the US [2008–2018]"), was a Franco-German research program from 2018 to 2022 (ANR-DFG ProAcTA [ANR-17-FRAL-0008-01/DGF BA 1912/3-1]) on the conflicts between "custodians of health coverage policy" and fiscal-austerity advocates over the period 2007–2018 (with funding of €333,496).

The fieldwork was carried out by a research team that included both experienced and junior researchers. The senior members of the team were Saïd Darviche, Jean Joana, and Marc Smyrl (Université de Montpellier), and Sébastien Guignier (Sciences Po, Bordeaux). The junior members of the team included two postdoctoral researchers hired from the Centre d'Études Politiques et Sociales at Université de Montpellier, Ben Jensen (American University, Washington, DC) and Catherine Hoeffler (Sciences Po, Paris); two doctoral students at Université de Montpellier, Anne-Laure Beaussier[2] and Ulrike Lepont;[3] and one doctoral student at Sciences Po, Paris, Hugo Meijer.[4] These doctoral research students have since obtained their doctorates in political science and published numerous articles based on the OPERA research (see the bibliography).

The French research team benefited from the support of American political scientists and sociologists in order to "decode" and facilitate our fieldwork in Washington, DC. We organized several annual seminars at the Université de Montpellier with Gary Adams (American University, Washington, DC), Larry Brown (Columbia University, New York), John Higley (University of Texas at Austin), and Joseph White (Case Western Reserve University, Cleveland, Ohio). André Mach from the University of Lausanne (Switzerland) completed the team of experts in the research program.

The empirical data regarding the American unelected governmental elites gathered during our fieldwork are of two complementary types. I composed a biographical data bank of the positions of elites studied and of numerous in-depth interviews conducted in Washington, DC, the majority of which were done by the junior researchers (see the CEPEL website's OPERA Data Bank, where the biographical files and interviews are available: http://cepel.edu.umontpellier.fr/banques-de-donnees-opera-2/, using the ID Opera2008).

The production and collection of fieldwork data took place in the context of developing a programmatic elite framework. This empirical approach was designed to study the role of unelected governmental elites in policy change. Before our OPERA research, the framework was tested in the health and national-defense policy domains in a selection of Europe countries (Genieys & Smyrl, 2008a,b; Genieys, 2010; Hassenteufel et al, 2010; Genieys & Hassenteufel, 2015; Genieys & Joana, 2017). Originally devised for a study on the transformation of the apex of power in the French social state, the framework was later adapted and modified so that international comparisons could be made (Hassenteufel & Genieys, 2021; Genieys & Darviche, 2023). For the present volume, the programmatic elite framework has been applied to the structure of power in the United States—that of "checks and balances" (Congress and the executive branch)—in order to study those unelected governmental elites who are responsible for policy formulation and decision-making in the health policy sphere. The programmatic elite framework combines two convergent empirical research strategies (see table A.1).

1. Quantitative strategy: We identified a population of elites using a positional approach. The elites were selected from Congress or the executive branch according to their possible relationship with the process of health policy decision-making (see details of the positions, below). This initial population was purposely reduced during this first stage of research according to the criteria of length of elites' career paths in the position. In practice, we approached the length of sector-based career paths using two indicators: (1) holding their position of power for six years or longer and (2) having a career in the Washington, DC, area addressing the health policy issue for twenty years or longer.

2. Qualitative strategy: A snowballing campaign of in-depth interviews with key informants known to have played a crucial role in health reforms during the Clinton and Obama administrations allowed us to both confirm the positions being researched and to reintegrate in the population those individuals considered to be highly influential even though they had held neither long-term nor official positions of power.

The Framework

From Big *N* to Small *n* for an In-depth Sociographic Study of Social Backgrounds and Career Paths

This first stage of the programmatic elite framework required us to define a period during which the observations would take place (1988–2010) and to identify a number of positions of power within both branches of US power (the administration, and the White House and Congress) on the basis of which the elites would be identified. The population initially defined by the positions was then reduced using the duration criterion (six years).

For the OPERA study, we focused on the period 1988–2010. We selected this period for two reasons: first, this period corresponded to twenty years; and second, we wanted to ensure an equilibrium between the three Democratic and the three Republican administrations and the 100th to 111th legislatures. Thus, we studied three Republican administrations (George H. W. Bush's single term and George W. Bush's two terms) and three Democratic administrations (Bill Clinton's two terms and Barack Obama's first term). The Congress, however, corresponds to the 100th to the 111th Congress, thus twelve legislatures, five of which were midterms during which the president in power held a majority in both houses: Clinton during the 103rd Congress; George W. Bush during the 107th, 108th, and 109th; and Obama during the 111th. Indeed, the temporal division enabled us to examine the continuity and discontinuity of unelected governmental elite careers at the apex of the health sector in the US government. The numerous political changes of power also enabled us to measure the effects of this elite's circulation between the private and public sectors, as well as within a single sector (the in-and-outer system).

From this perspective, we defined a population of 944 individuals who held positions in the power structure (i.e., senior appointees of the executive and Congress staffers) from 1988 to 2010 in the health sector by restricting this category to key positions in the policy decision-making process. We were aware that the positions we focused on in both branches of power corresponded to types of unelected governmental elites acting in the back offices of power whose regulations governing career paths were not the same. This is because the senior appointees of the executive branch tend to circulate far more according to the changes in power affecting this branch of power, while the committee staffers' careers are more protected.

The first list of positions within both branches of power was established by consulting the *Congressional Directory*, which can be accessed on the LexisNexis database (http://www.gpo.gov/fdsys/browse/collection.action?collectionCode =CDIR).

1. For Congress, the positions selected as pertinent were those of career staffers (committee staffers) identified in the committees and subcommittees of the House of Representatives and Senate as contributing to matters relevant to health coverage (Education and Workforce, and Energy and Commerce in the House of Representatives; and Health, Education, Labor, and Pensions [HELP] in the Senate) and finance and budget (Ways and Means, and Budget in the House, and those of Finance and Budget in the Senate).

2. For the executive branch, the positions identified were related to health and health coverage matters: the president's advisers on health policy (Executive Office of the President [EOP] and the Office of Management and Budget [OMB]; the five hierarchical levels below the secretary of Health and Human Services [Department

TABLE A.1. Number of positions held for longer than six years: Population of health coverage policy elites, 1988–2010

	Baseline population	Long-term insiders	
	Big *N*	Small *n*	%
Senior appointees of the executive branch	538	88	16.3
Congressional staffers (House of Representatives and Senate)	406	63	15.5
Total	944	151	16

SOURCE: OPERA Research Program

of Health and Human Services]; and the directors of agencies concerned [equivalent to health minister, minister's private secretary]).

This choice led us to define a population of 944 individuals holding positions in the executive branch and Congress, thus 538 senior appointees[5] within the executive branch and 406 Congress staffers from 1988 to 2010 (see table A.1). We then applied the longevity variable (i.e., those individuals who held a post for at least six years) so that from this funnel effect we would select only those individuals who according to our criteria had enjoyed long-term careers, thus 151 individuals (16% of the initial population). These individuals break down in the following manner between both branches of power: 88 senior appointees for the executive branch (16.3% of the initial population) and 63 committee staffers for Congress (15.5% of the initial population).

On the basis of this new population of 151 individuals, we conducted in-depth biographical research on each individual in order to constitute the OPERA Data Bank.[6] In this context, we compiled for each individual a biographical file based on available data from several sources that we cross-referenced, including institutional Internet sites (White House, Department of Health and Human Services, Congress), *Who's Who in America*, Leadership Library (now Leadership Connect), *First Street*, Revolving Doors, SourceWatch, Wikipedia, LegiStorm, LinkedIn, and all other available Web sources.

Drawing on these biographical files, we were then able to answer the following questions: What was the gender balance in this group? What level of qualification had these individuals attained? What university degrees had they obtained, where did they study, and what fields were their early careers in? In what ways were their career paths in the institutions of power specific? What was the average length of their careers? Were they subject to particular pressures to circulate and move from one post to another? What professions would they enter if or when they left government employment? Could one devise a typology to map their institutional career paths? It was on the basis of this database that we answered these questions and developed the sociographic analyses of the population that we subsequently termed "unelected governmental health coverage policy elites" (chapter 3).

Mobilizing In-Depth Interviews Regarding Ideas of Reform and Policy Formulation: The Sociological Portraits

The second research strand linked to the empirical application of the programmatic elite framework fits into a more comprehensive pattern. Our aim was to capture the potential role played by the unelected governmental health coverage policy elites (i.e., to link their positions of power with their potential influence, based on interviews) when formulating the health reform projects. So the programmatic elite framework passed through a stage where we reconstructed individual career paths by cross-referencing the evolution of their career paths with ideas or visions of reform projects which they themselves championed, from which we drew sociological portraits of the elites. The aim in using our in-depth interviews and other empirical material (oral archives,[7] press documents, etc.) was to ascertain how embedded these elites were in the reform processes that we were investigating, as we presumed that this factor shaped their career paths while also producing a collective output. The programmatic elite framework then makes it possible to correlate elites' career paths to transformation in health policy formulation.

To this end, drawing on our exploratory interviews, we tested the pertinence of elite positions and the power to influence which they wielded. The interviews were conducted with key informants selected from both the public and private sectors based upon their presumed reputation. This first set of in-depth interviews with elites selected according to a reputational criterion, who were not necessarily part of the initial population, allowed us to pilot our interview schedule. These semi-structured interviews were carried out with a single schedule that was shared among members of the research team. The schedule included three sections of issues concerning (1) the individuals' personal social background, with a particular focus on their career paths, (2) the knowledge they shared with other members of the health elites, and (3) how embedded they were in the process of policy formulation, as well as any reform models uniting these individuals (ideas and methods advocated).

The analytical aim of the interviews was to collect information about their backgrounds and career paths (professional mobility), to add to the biographical files, and so reconstruct the dimensions and reform options which these elites agreed on. Taking into account the history of their career paths thus enabled us to show how these health elites could alter or adapt their programmatic orientation of certain future reforms according to any required collective representations. The idea was to correlate these career paths with participation or not in the two major health insurance reform projects by drawing sociological portraits of the elites. These two reform projects were the Clinton administration's defeated project, the Health Security Act, or the Clinton health care plan (1993–1994), and the reform project known as the Patient Protection and Affordable Care Act (ACA), proposed and enacted during President Barack Obama's first term (2008–2010).

Moreover, using the snowballing effect, we asked these individuals to point out other, in their eyes, important people to us so that we could gradually compile an additional list of elites whom their own peers considered as influencing the sector reforms that we were researching. By this means, the programmatic elite framework allowed us to qualitatively enrich the original population of positional elites who were developing long-term sector-based careers (lasting six years in positions of power or longer), including a dozen or so individual cases that did not fulfill these formal criteria even though they played a significant role during the reform projects. These individuals, however, were incorporated as additional cases that enhanced the fine-grained study of the health elite career paths (see chapter 4 and 5).

The ProAcTA research program provided the opportunity to conduct a new series of interviews with health care elites. So ten years later, between 2018 and 2019, I conducted ten additional interviews in Washington, DC. These interviews were conducted with individuals we had previously interviewed who had played a significant role at the time of the ACA. They made it possible to integrate a more historical dimension into the vision of the success of this reform.

Appendix 1

1. https://anr.fr/en/funded-projects-and-impact/funded-projects/project/funded
/project/b2d9d3668f92a3b9fbbf7866072501ef-225a638dd6/?tx_anrprojects_funded%5
Bcontroller%5D=Funded&cHash=0d6cc29c238b5cc021f9f6ae5d9fd04a

2. Anne-Laure Beaussier conducted ninety-six interviews with congressional health staffers and drew on these interviews for her doctoral dissertation, "Health Put to the Test of American Democracy: The Role of Congress in Health Insurance Policy," which she defended on June 29, 2012, at the Université de Montpellier. Today she works as a researcher at the CNRS at CSO at Sciences Po in Paris.

3. Ulrike Lepont defended her thesis, "Formulating Policy at the Margins of the Government: The Role of Experts in Health Insurance Reforms in the United States (1970–2010)," in December 2014 at the Université de Montpellier. As part of her doctoral research, she carried out seventy-five in-depth interviews with health sector policy experts. Today she works as a researcher at the CNRS at CEE at Sciences Po in Paris.

4. Hugo Meijer defended his thesis at Sciences Po in Paris, titled "Trading with the Enemy: The Making of US Export Control Policy toward the People's Republic of China" (2013, Institut d'Etudes Politiques, Paris). Today he works as a researcher at the CNRS at CERI at Sciences Po in Paris.

5. The term "senior appointee" does not correspond to any official category designating those employees working in the US federal administration (political appointee, career appointee, etc.). We invented it ourselves to refer to all the employees who were appointed to top positions in the American executive branch of power (see above for the relevant executive-branch posts).

6. The entire set of biographical files compiled by the OPERA research team can be found in a database on the CEPEL website at this address: http://cepel.edu.umontpellier
.fr/banques-de-donnees-opera-2/. All these data are also accessible on beQuali, the website of Sciences Po, at this address: http://www.bequali.fr/fr/les-enquetes/.

7. See the Centers for Medicare and Medicaid Services, CMS Oral History Project at https://www.cms.gov/About-CMS/Agency-Information/History/.

Interviews for the OPERA (2009–2012)
and PRoAcTA (2018–2021) Research Programs

OPERA Research Program: "Operationalizing Programmatic Elite Research in America (1988–2010)"

This research program was funded by the French National Research Agency, or ANR (ANR-08-BLAN-0032). To read the study abstract, visit the following page: https://anr.fr/en/funded-projects-and-impact/funded-projects/project/funded/project/b2d9d3668f92a3b9fbbf7866072501ef-225a638dd6/?tx_anrprojects_funded%5Bcontroller%5D=Funded&cHash=0d6cc29c238b5cc021f9f6ae5d9fd04a.

List of Interviews

Interview 1: Washington, DC, September 30, 2011
Interview 2: New York, NY, August 28, 2008
Interview 3: Washington, DC, June 8, 2010
Interview 4: Washington, DC, April 26, 2010
Interview 5: Washington, DC, November 28, 2011
Interview 6: Washington, DC, May (undated), 2009
Interview 7: Washington, DC, May 28, 2010
Interview 8: Washington, DC, May 5, 2010
Interview 9: Washington, DC, June 1, 2010
Interview 10: Washington, DC, May 24, 2010
Interview 11: Washington, DC, October 12, 2011
Interview 12: Washington, DC, August 28, 2008
Interview 13: Washington, DC, April 11, 2010
Interview 14: Washington, DC, November 14, 2011
Interview 15: Washington, DC, May 19, 2009
Interview 16: Washington, DC, March 31, 2010 (2nd interview)
Interview 17: Washington, DC, June 9, 2010
Interview 18: Washington, DC, May 27, 2010
Interview 19: Washington, DC, December 14, 2010
Interview 20: Washington, DC, May 27, 2010
Interview 21: Washington, DC, June 14, 2010
Interview 22: Washington, DC, December 12, 2010 (2nd interview)
Interview 23: Washington, DC, April 30, 2010
Interview 24: Washington, DC, March 9, 2008

Interview 25: Washington, DC, May 15, 2009 (2nd interview)
Interview 26: Washington, DC, June 2, 2010
Interview 27: Washington, DC, May 21, 2010
Interview 28: Washington, DC, May 19, 2010
Interview 29: Washington, DC, May 17, 2010
Interview 30: Washington, DC, March 9, 2008
Interview 31: Washington, DC, May 18, 2010
Interview 32: Washington, DC, December 12, 2010
Interview 33: Washington, DC, December 12, 2011
Interview 34: Washington, DC, April 28, 2010
Interview 35: Washington, DC, October 26, 2011
Interview 36: Washington, DC, May 8, 2009
Interview 37: Washington, DC, April 1, 2010
Interview 38: Washington, DC, April 16, 2009
Interview 39: Washington, DC, May 19, 2010
Interview 40: Washington, DC, May 20, 2010
Interview 41: Washington, DC, May 14, 2010
Interview 42: Washington, DC, May 21, 2010
Interview 43: Washington, DC, May 21, 2010
Interview 44: Washington, DC, April 17, 2009
Interview 45: Washington, DC, May 28, 2010
Interview 46: Washington, DC, April 27, 2010
Interview 47: Washington, DC, May 11, 2010
Interview 48: Washington, DC, November 14, 2011

These anonymized interviews can be consulted on the CEPEL website at the following address: https://cepel.edu.umontpellier.fr/banques-de-donnees-opera-2/health/ (with this ID: Opera2008). They are also available on beQuali at https://bequali.fr/fr/les-enquetes/.

ProAcTA Research Program: "Programmatic Action in Times of Austerity: Elites' Competition and Health Sector Governance in France, Germany, the UK (England) and the US (2008–2018)"

(ANR-17-FRAL-0008-01/DGF BA 1912/3-1)
To read a summary of the study, visit the following page: https://anr.fr/Project-ANR-17-FRAL-0008.

List of Interviews

Interview 1: Washington, DC, June 18, 2018
Interview 2: Washington, DC, June 19, 2018
Interview 3: Washington, DC, June 19, 2018 (2 people)
Interview 4: New York, NY, June 22, 2018

Interview 5: Boston, MA, November 1, 2018
Interview 6: Boston, MA, November 2, 2018
Interview 7: Washington, DC, February 14, 2019
Interview 8: Washington, DC, March 29, 2019
Interview 9: Washington, DC, April 19, 2019
Interview 10: Washington, DC, June 18, 2019

Introduction

1. The Patient Protection and Affordable Care Act is Public Law 111-148, signed into law March 23, 2010, 124 Stat. 119, codified at 42 USC chapter 157.

2. ProAcTA interview, Washington, DC, June 19, 2018.

3. These researchers highlight public opinion, the impact of partisan divides, and the complexity of balances of power between the presidency, its administration, and Congress, the political influence of interest groups, and the role of the governmental federal structure in order to interpret change. For the Clinton defeat, see Morone and Belkin (1994); and for the Obama reform, see the special issue "Critical Essays on Health Care Reform" in the *Journal of Health Politics, Policy and Law* (2011).

4. In the American academic tradition (Mills, Domhoff, Kahn), the "social background" of elites refers to their economic wealth, private-school attendance, and social-club membership. In our perspective, the term has three main elements: (1) attitudes, aptitudes, and orientation (in this case toward activism and reform); (2) education (where schooled, what studied); and (3) the socialization that derives from institutional settings.

5. We define "policy formulation" as "the activity of finding, devising, and defining problem solutions, [which] takes place once a problem has been recognized as warranting government attention" (Howlett & Muckherjee, 2017: 4).

6. Research on health care reforms known as "comprehensive reforms" includes studying, for example, failed projects such as the National Health Insurance (NHI) during the New Deal and the Clinton plan (the Health Security Act), whose systemic dimension radically altered the way that health care was organized. The Affordable Care Act (2010) is characterized by the creation of a new pathway, that of a far-reaching reform introducing a considerable widening of the scope of health insurance as well as integrating procedures and practices from the preexisting system (i.e., Medicare and Medicaid).

7. We will distinguish between elected officials (secretaries and congressmen), who are politically accountable to citizens and have formal decision-taking powers, and unelected governmental elites, whose role is to devise policy formulation and solutions to social issues and to recommend these in the government's policy and decision-making agenda (Giddens, 1972).

8. The Medicare program is run by the federal government and allocates health insurance to people over the age of sixty-five and to the disabled. The Medicaid program, which offers health insurance to individuals and families with low incomes, is

administered and co-funded by each state. Initially, childless families were excluded from its provision. With the Affordable Care Act reform, its scope was significantly broadened (Jacobs & Skocpol, 2010: 185–186).

9. This research is based on two earlier important and well-regarded empirical studies surveying the apex of power in the health insurance sector: "Operationalizing Programmatic Elite Research in America (1988–2010)," known as OPERA (ANR-08-BLAN-0032); and "Programmatic Action in Times of Austerity: Elites' Competition and Health Sector Governance in France, Germany, the UK (England) and the US (2008–2018)," known as ProAcTA (ANR-17-FRAL-0008-01 / DGF BA 1912/3-1) (appendix 1, Methodology).

10. For a description of the programmatic elite framework, see appendix 1, Methodology.

Chapter 1. A Government of Insiders

1. There are 285 schools of public policy in the United States, awarding more than 10,000 undergraduate and graduate degrees per year. See J. Pierson and N. Schaefer, "The Problem with Public Policy Schools," *Washington Post*, December 6, 2013.

2. Regarding the policy wonk: "The word was presumably taken to Washington by Harvard graduates and formed the basis for the modern term policy wonk, which . . . is where most of us encounter it. There it acquired the meaning of 'a policy expert, especially one who takes an obsessive interest in minor details of policy,' with a disparaging implication of someone immersed in detail and out of touch with the real world" (http://www.worldwidewords.org/qa/qa-pol1.htm). For Chris Jennings's description of the policy wonk role through the lens of his work in Washington, see chapter 4.

3. The term "czar" is an often-used informal way to designate the American president's advisers employed in the EOP. As a general rule, this is an adviser highly specialized in a particular realm of public policy who is appointed by the president. This adviser must oversee the relationship with the secretary and the administration, as well as with the committees in Congress that lie within their sphere of competence. A czar must be highly knowledgeable about the policy issues in their area and have an overview of policy formulation (Vaughn & Villalobos, 2015).

4. Until 1979 the agency was known as the Department of Health, Education, and Welfare (DHEW) but thereafter as the Department of Health and Human Services (HHS).

Chapter 2. Variations in the Custodian Role

1. This chapter is based on an article coauthored with Lawrence D. Brown (forthcoming).

2. "Arthur J. Altmeyer," Wikipedia, accessed September 15, 2021, https://en.wikipedia.org/wiki/Arthur_J._Altmeyer.

Part II. The Making of Long-Term Health Insiders

1. Our method of selecting positions of power and those individuals who occupied them in the executive (the White House and HHS) and in Congress (the House of Representatives and the Senate) is outlined in appendix 1, Methodology.

2. The sociological portrait is a non-deterministic analytical tool of our programmatic elite framework. To complete the sociological portraits, we will use the biographical data gathered and the contents of the hundred or so interviews accumulated in our three academic studies (see Genieys & Darviche, 2023).

3. Certain roles on congressional committees, such as chief or general counsel and clerk, require a law degree. In the United States, this corresponds to the juris doctor qualification (JD) obtained at law school.

4. OPERA Interview 45, Washington, DC, May 28, 2010: 30.

Chapter 3. Mapping the Health Coverage Policy Elites

1. Today the figure is around 30,000 if we include all the employees working for the legislative branch (Beaussier, 2012: 170).

2. In the US, a senior bureaucrat's sector-based career in the hierarchy generally tends to stop five levels beneath the level of secretary. For this reason, senior bureaucrats contribute to implementing policies but on the whole are excluded from the process of shaping policies. It is possible, however, for senior bureaucrats to receive a temporary and discretionary appointment by the head of the executive to a senior director's post. In this instance, they would obtain the classification and status of senior executive service, thus avoiding when their time ended having to bear the brunt of retaliatory measures on their administrative career (Aberbach, 2003).

3. Staffers, whose number has sharply increased over the last thirty years, are recruited by members of Congress and remunerated by Congress. The staffers support and work alongside the members in political activities at both the federal and state levels. They follow and control the legislative process. We need to distinguish between those staffers attached to a congressperson (personal staffers) and those attached to a congressional committee (committee staffers). The latter play an important role in devising bills and develop their careers over time (Fox & Hammond, 1977: 1–11).

4. The term "revolving door" has a negative connotation in the United States. It refers to the practice whereby individuals occupy successive posts in the administration, Congress, and the private sector. See the OpenSecrets website that illustrates the patterns of this phenomenon: https://www.opensecrets.org/revolving/.

5. The term "senior appointee" does not correspond to any official category designating staff employed in the US federal administration (as a political appointee, a career appointee, etc.). We invented it to describe the whole group of employees appointed to senior posts in the executive (see appendix 1, Methodology for the relevant levels).

6. Fischer notes that the average age when appointed varies depending on who the president is and the functions of the position: 42 for the chief legal officers, 45 for the assistant secretaries, and 53 for the cabinet secretaries (1987: 7).

7. Heinz and Laumann, in their study of lawyers in Chicago, insisted that the category of "business lawyer" in the US includes two distinct types: the lawyer, known as house counsel, working within a company; and the lawyer, known as a corporate lawyer, working for a large independent legal firm. These are two distinct professional roles. The house counsel lawyer is strongly tied to the interests of the company that they represent, and in this capacity they behave primarily as a lobbyist. By contrast, the

corporate lawyer often plays the role of mediator between the government and the interests that they are defending (Heinz & Laumann, 1982).

8. To ensure a successful transition for his administration, and to compensate for his team's potential lack of preparation, Ronald Reagan commissioned the John F. Kennedy School of Government at Harvard University to run a series of training seminars at the White House (involving the Office of Personnel Management). These seminars were intended to induct his team to the new program's approach to public policy wished for by the president (Pfiffner, 1987: 150).

9. In a book corroborating Heclo's thesis on a "government of strangers," Malek drew on his own personal experience and remarked that "most appointees enter government with only limited understanding of the complexities of government policy-making, the interaction with Congress, the role of the media, and the other differences between the government and the private sector" (cited by Pfiffner, 1987: 143).

10. The length of political appointees' careers is even shorter at the White House, where the president's advisers remain in a post on average for a year and a half (Michaels, 1997: 127).

11. As confirmed by G. Calvin Mackenzie's table (2001: 37), which draws on Paul C. Light's data (1999: 170–172); positions occupied were secretary, deputy secretary, undersecretary, assistant secretary, and deputy assistant secretary.

12. In Congress, mobility forms part of the culture of non-elected staff whose status over a period of between one and five years evolves from being that of an informal "novice" to that of a "veteran" (Romzek & Utter, 1996: 423).

13. Romzek and Utter summarize in four stages the career of a typical staffer who remains in a post in Congress, indicating that these stages include periods when exits always remain feasible (1996: 427–428). The first stage corresponds to being initiated to working in Congress under a senior manager's supervision (for six months). The second stage leads to greater autonomy based upon expertise in a particular field (the option to become a policy expert). The third stage involves managing a group of staffers in a specific area, and the fourth stage includes political and administrative responsibilities (i.e., as a chief of staff).

14. Salisbury and Shepsle also note that the staffers' careers are tied to those of the representatives. When the latter lose their mandate, their staff leave their posts in 66% of cases in the House and in 78% of cases in the Senate (1981: 392).

15. The "single payer" model is a comprehensive system where universal health care insurance coverage depends on a single unique payer. It was inspired by the health care insurance system managed by the public sector in Canada (Marmor & Mashaw, 1990; Marmor, 1994). In use since 1989, this model allows its advocates to free themselves from any negative references linked to the failure of the new dealers in their attempt to create a National Health Insurance system (Hacker, 1997: 83). Sparer, Brown, and Jacobs have explored the different incarnations of the single payer model that incorporates organizational elements specific to Canadian federalism, as well as some aspects of the more removed British NHS (2009). Lawrence Brown has emphasized the illusory dimension of this proposal in the case of the United States (2019).

16. Lawrence Jacobs and Theda Skocpol define the public option "as a policy promoted by the progressive Democrats to create a health care insurance system

managed by the government that individuals as much as companies could choose instead of a private insurance scheme" (2010: 188).

Chapter 4. The Clinton Plan Veterans

1. The study of the sociological portraits of long-term health coverage policy insiders is based on the analysis of their social backgrounds and career paths. This rich empirical material was collected by the team of OPERA researchers (see appendix 1, Methodology). In addition to the numerous interviews and their accompanying firsthand biographical details, we have gathered sociographic health data (SHD) for the entire sample of long-term health coverage policy insiders whom we studied. To review these SHD, see the list of biographical databases presented in the appendixes. The SHD will be referred to in footnotes as follows: OPERA Sociographic Health Data (SHD), followed by the subject's full name. This empirical material is available to the research community as accessible data from the CEPEL website, Data Bank OPERA: http://cepel .edu.umontpellier.fr/banques-de-donnees-opera-2/sante/.

2. Our exploratory interviews with "key informants," conducted by researchers on the OPERA team in Washington, DC, led us to supplement the initial sample of long-term insiders by including those who were often mentioned in the interviews as individuals who had played a significant role in the reforms that we studied. Some of them had not yet fulfilled the condition of having spent six years in a position of power, while others had held posts before or after the period under study. Nevertheless, they all shared the common experience of having pursued a "long career" in the health sector. These "key informants" include Joe Antos, Brian Biles, Gary Claxton, Judy Feder; Michael Hash, Karen Ignani, Michael Iskowitz, Chris Jennings, Jeanne Lambrew, Len Nichols, Alice Rivlin, Phil Schiliro, and Neera Tandem.

3. The "Washingtonization of training programs" refers to the fact that many long-term insiders completed and pursued their academic studies by following a further high-level course once they arrived in the federal capital. This either took the form of a specialized master's in public policy or health policy, or a juris doctor (JD) program in one of the numerous prestigious universities and law schools in the Washington, DC, area. This phenomenon was encouraged by Congress, known for its training policy and continuing professional development aimed at this specific staff. One interviewee regarding this point explained: "We had a whole set of fellows, and they were typically—I would say predominantly people with PhDs, some with a master's in public policy." OPERA Health Interview 30: Washington, DC, March 9, 2009: 2.

4. They included Judy Feder, Diane Rowland, Brian Biles, David Nexon, Tim Westmoreland, Irene Bueno, Michael Iskowitz, and Christine G. Williams. To consult their sociographic health data and the interviews conducted with these individuals as part of the OPERA study, see the CEPEL website, Data Bank OPERA: http://cepel.edu .umontpellier.fr/banques-de-donnees-opera-2/sante/.

5. Among the long-term insider population with a Clinton plan veteran profile, we identified eight portraits for Democratic institutional migrants who held posts within both branches of power during the Clinton and Obama administrations. They mainly held powerful and strategic posts but also played a gatekeeper role between the two branches of power. They included the following individuals: William V. Corr (House of

Representatives to Senate to HSS to Senate to HHS); John Cerda III (House of Representatives to EOP to Senate to EOP); Michael M. Hash (House of Representatives to HHS to HHS); Ellen Murray (HHS to Senate to HHS); Karen Nelson (OMB to House of Representatives); Karen Pollitz (Senate to HHS to HHS); Wendell Primus (House of Representatives to HHS to House of Representatives); Phil Schiliro (House of Representatives to Senate to White House).

6. OPERA Health Interview 12: Washington, DC, August 28, 2008: 1–2; and Interview 13: April 11, 2010.

7. Feder cowrote articles in specialist journals, namely *Health Policy,* with a number of luminaries in Washington's health policy circles, such as Brian Biles, Diane Rowland, David Cutler, Jeanne Lambrew, Gary Claxton, and William Scanlon.

8. OPERA Sociographic Health Data (SHD): Judy Feder: 1–10.

9. This informal group of liberal Democratic advisers, including among others Bruce Fried (lobbyist), Marilyn Moon (Urban Institute), and Ken Thorpe (health economist), organized a conference every Tuesday morning to promote their programmatic orientation of health insurance system reform (Johnson & Broder, 1996: 70).

10. The Alliance for Health Reform is a bipartisan forum of experts linked to the Robert Wood Johnson Foundation; it is involved in communications work with media and stakeholders regarding the issues and challenges in health policy. This foundation advocates for health insurance to be extended to all US citizens.

11. OPERA Health Interview 35: Washington, DC, October 26, 2011: 1.

12. In addition to our OPERA research program, we use interviews from the *William J. Clinton Presidential History Project,* Miller Center, University of Virginia.

13. According to the political scientist Jacob Hacker, these individuals form the "Washington advisory group" whose objective is to defend the "play-or-pay" version of the reform project (1997: 107).

14. OPERA Health Interview 35: Washington, DC, October 26, 2011: 3.

15. OPERA Sociographic Health Data (SHD): Brian Biles: 1–2.

16. OPERA Health Interview 6: Washington, DC, May 2009: 19.

17. OPERA Health Interview 30: Washington, DC, March 9, 2008: 3.

18. OPERA Sociographic Health Data (SHD): David Nexon: 1–2.

19. OPERA Sociographic Health Data (SHD): Tim Westmoreland: 2.

20. OPERA Health Interview 45: Washington, DC, May 28, 2010: 3.

21. There are other instances of some institutional migrants involved in the struggles arising from the Clinton plan who moved to the private sector, at times to nonprofits, at times to for-profit organizations, and later half-heartedly rallied together once the new reform project was devised. See OPERA Sociographic Health Data (SHD): Irene Bueno, Michael Iskowitz, Kathleen Buto, and Christine G. Williams.

22. After having participated on the margins of managing the ACA, Jennings was recalled in 2013 by President Obama at the start of his second term to be special health adviser at the White House in charge of implementing the reform. See https://www.washingtonpost.com/national/health-science/chris-jennings-white-house-adviser-on-health-care-steps-down/2014/01/23/bb1539e4-846b-11e3-bbe5-6a2a3141e3a9_story.html.

23. OPERA Health Interview 23: Washington, DC, April 30, 2010.

24. OPERA Sociographic Health Data (SHD): Chris Jennings: 1–8.

25. OPERA Health Interview 23: Washington, DC, April 30, 2010.

26. For the empirical data collected, see our online data bank; OPERA Sociographic Health Data (SHD): Wendell Primus, William V. Corr, Ellen Murray, Karen Pollitz, Michael J. Myers, Karen Nelson, Michael M. Hash, and Phil Schiliro. See chapter 9 for details about who held which post under the ACA.

27. OPERA Sociographic Health Data (SHD): Wendell Primus.

28. Mary Ann Akers, "In the Speaker's Office, a Quiet Liberal Lion: Wendell E. Primus," *Washington Post*, June 21, 2010.

29. OPERA Health Interview 45: Washington, DC, May 28, 2010: 17.

30. It was thanks to the intervention of his old friend Andy Schneider that Wendell Primus accorded us in less than twenty-four hours a research interview at Congress. ProAcTA Interview: Washington, DC, June 19, 2018: 9–10.

31. OPERA Sociographic Health Data (SHD): Wendell Primus: 4–5.

32. OPERA Sociographic Health Data (SHD): William V. Corr.

33. We can point to similar cases in the OPERA study: Ellen Murray, a graduate of the George Mason University's law school, after a ten-year career (1990–1999) in the Health Care Financing Administration at HHS, spent another ten years working for Senator Tom Harkin's staff (1999–2010) before being appointed again to the administration as assistant director of finance at HHS under President Obama (2010). And Michael J. Myers, a political science graduate from the Columbia University, joined Senator Ted Kennedy's staff in 1987 before being appointed to the Defense Department as director of the military program helping refugees (1993–1995). Between 1996 and 2009, he worked on Senator Kennedy's staff as staff director and chief counsel, and he backed Kennedy in his fight for health insurance reform (McDonough, 2012: 66). See OPERA Sociographic Health Data (SHD): Ellen Murray and Michael John Meyers.

34. OPERA Health Interview 29: Washington, DC, May 17, 2010: 5.

35. OPERA Sociographic Health Data (SHD): Judy Feder: 3.

36. OPERA Sociographic Health Data (SHD): Karen Nelson: 3.

37. OPERA Sociographic Health Data (SHD): Michael M. Hash.

38. OPERA Health Interview 16: Washington, DC, March 31, 2010: 6.

39. OPERA Sociographic Health Data (SHD): Phil Schiliro.

40. For the technocratic translator subtype, we will draw on the following empirical data: OPERA Sociographic Health Data (SHD): regarding Congress, those for Andy Schneider, Ruth J. Katz, Philip S. Barnett; and regarding the executive branch, those of Bruce C. Vladeck, Nancy-Ann (Min) DeParle, and Carolyn M. Clancy. See http://cepel.edu.umontpellier.fr/banques-de-donnees-opera-2/sante/. ID: Opera2008.

41. OPERA Health Interview 45: Washington DC, May 28, 2010: 10. For the long-term aspects of this friendship over the trials and tribulations of health insurance reforms, see also: Jocelyn Guyer, "Health Reform Update: The Varsity Team Is on the Field," Georgetown University, Health Policy Institute, 2009, http://ccf.georgetown.edu/2009/04/27/health_reform_update_-_the_varsity_team_is_on_the_field/.

42. OPERA Sociographic Health Data (SHD): Andy Schneider.

43. OPERA Health Interview 36: Washington, DC May 9, 2009; and Interview 37: April 1, 2010.

44. During the period of interviews with our key informants, Andy Schneider arranged an appointment for us in less than twenty-four hours with Wendell Primus when the latter worked as Nancy Pelosi's chief of staff in the House of Representatives.

45. OPERA Sociographic Health Data (SHD): Ruth Katz.

46. OPERA Sociographic Health Data (SHD): Philip Barnett.

47. The large sample of long-term insiders provided us with other examples of individuals who focused their career on Congress, including the following examples: Michele Varnhagen (JD), specialist on health cost containment for employers; Michael A. Stephen, director of the association of public health colleges, moved into the private sector following the Obama reform; Nick Littlefield and Marsha I. Simon, long-term staffers who worked for Senator Ted Kennedy and are now lobbyists; Drummond Faye, MPH, health and minorities specialist (see our OPERA Sociographic Health Data (SHD): http://cepel .edu.umontpellier.fr/banques-de-donnees-opera-2/sante/.

48. Judy Moore and David Smith, "Interview with Bruce Vladeck," July 7, 2002, *CMS Oral History Project*: 713.

49. OPERA Health Interview 23: Washington, DC, April 30, 2010: 2.

50. Since 2001 the Health Care Financing Administration has been known as the Centers for Medicare and Medicaid Services. This federal agency within HHS coordinates and implements the Medicare program and works in partnership with state governments on Medicaid programs and the Children's Health Insurance Program.

51. This program is particularly sought after by students from elite US universities. Known as Rhodes scholars, they receive a scholarship to study for a second BA at Balliol College at the University of Oxford. President Bill Clinton (in 1968) and his adviser Ira Magaziner (in 1969), later director of the Clinton task force, both benefited from this program (see List of Rhodes Scholars, https://en.wikipedia.org/wiki/List_of_Rhodes _Scholars); see OPERA Sociographic Health Data (SHD): Nancy A. DeParle.

52. Program associate director (PAD): "OMB has a director, a deputy director, and then there are five PADs, who are the associate directors." See Edward Berkowitz, "Interview with Nancy-Ann Min DeParle": 197.

53. National Academy of Social Insurance, "Interview with Nancy-Ann Min DeParle," Washington, DC, April 2, 2015, interviewed by Edward Berkowitz.

54. Nancy-Ann DeParle, *Subject: Health Reform Decisions, Briefing Memo, The White House*, Washington, DC, April 21, 2009, http://www.documentcloud.org /documents/328161-health-care-memo.html.

55. Regarding this point, see a recent book devoted to the "czar" of different US presidents which refers to DeParle as "Obama's Health Czar" (Vaughn & Villalobos, 2015: 161–162).

56. OPERA Health Interview 45: Washington, DC, May 28, 2010.

57. OPERA Health Interview19: Washington, DC, December 14, 2010: 2; and more recently: ProAcTA Interview 4: New York, June 22, 2018.

58. Within the sample of long-term health policy insiders, I identified a total of thirty-eight individuals whose career path resembles that of the Democratic policy

bureaucrat type. For the examples presented in our argument, see OPERA Sociographic Health Data (SHD): Richard (Rick) S. Foster, June Gibbs Brown, Lewis (Lew) Morris, Andrew D. Hyman, David S. Cade, Barry Clendenin, Thomas G. Monford, Janice A. May, Maria Curpill, Carol C. Mitchell, Adrienne Hallet, Peter H. Rutledge, and Erik Fatemi.

59. The exact title is "chief of the Office of the Actuary, Health Care Financing Administration HHS" (until 2001) and then "Centers for Medicare and Medicaid Services HHS" (CMS since 2001).

60. OPERA Health Interview33: Washington, DC, December 12, 2011: 5.

61. OPERA Sociographic Health Data (SHD): Richard (Rick) S. Foster: 2.

62. The status of senior executive service was created in 1978 for senior civil servants who during their careers are appointed to posts affording them discretionary political power (Aberbach, 2003).

63. OPERA Sociographic Health Data (SHD): Andrew Hyman: 4.

64. OPERA Sociographic Health Data (SHD): Janice May: 1–6.

65. OPERA Sociographic Health Data (SHD): Janice May: 2–3.

66. OPERA Health Interview 47: Washington, DC, May 11, 2010: 2–3.

Chapter 5. From Late Clintonism to Obama

1. The Republican Party held the majority in the House of Representatives and the Senate during the 104th (1995–1997), 105th (1997–1999), 106th (1999–2001), 107th (2001–2003), 108th (2003–2005), and 109th (2005–2007) legislatures.

2. OPERA Health Interview 3: Washington DC, June 8, 2010.

3. Here is a non-exhaustive list of the main forums in Washington, DC: the Henry J. Kaiser Foundation, the Alliance for Health Care Reform, the Bipartisan Policy Center for Health Reform, the Center on Budget and Policy Priorities, and the Hamilton Project (chapter 8).

4. For an overview of all the Republican long-term health insiders' career paths of the institutional migrant type, see the following OPERA Sociographic Health Data (SHD): Joe Antos (White House to HSS to House of Representatives); David Abernethy (House of Representatives to New York Department of Health to House of Representatives); Charles "Chip" Kahn III (Senate to House of Representatives to HHS); Thomas A. Scully (Senate to White House to HHS); Marshall Alan Gilbert (Senate to HHS to White House); Vincent J. Ventimiglia (Senate to HHS); James W. Dyer (White House to House of Representatives); Susan E. Quantius (White House to Senate to House of Representatives to HHS to House of Representatives); Kerry Weems (Senate to HHS); Linda E. Fischman (House of Representatives to HHS to Senate); S. Anthony McCann (Senate to HHS to House of Representatives to HHS). (http://cepel.edu.umontpellier.fr /banques-de-donnees-opera-2/sante/.)

5. OPERA Sociographic Health Data (SHD): Joe Antos: 1–2.

6. OPERA Sociographic Health Data (SHD): Joe Antos: 1.

7. OPERA Health Interview 4: Washington, DC, April 26, 2010: 1.

8. D. S. Abernethy and D. Pearson, *Regulating Hospital Costs: The Development of Public Policy* (Washington, DC: AUPHA Press, 1979).

9. OPERA Sociographic Health Data (SHD): David Abernethy: 1–6.

10. OPERA Health Interview 2: Washington, DC, August 28, 2008: 6–8.

11. Robert Pear, "The Health Care Debate: Behind the Scenes," *New York Times*, August 6, 1994.

12. OPERA Sociographic Health Data (SHD): Chip Kahn: 1–7.

13. OPERA Health Interview 24: Washington, DC, March 9, 2008; and Interview 25: May 15, 2009.

14. OPERA Health Interview 24: Washington, DC, March 9, 2008; and Interview 25: May 15, 2009.

15. OPERA Sociographic Health Data (SHD): Thomas Scully: 1–5.

16. OPERA Health Interview 45: Washington, DC, May 28, 2010: 18.

17. For a broader overview of the Republican long-term insiders' career paths of the technocratic translator type, see the following OPERA Sociographic Health Data (SHD): Charles "Chuck" Clapton, Howard Cohen, Dean A. Rosen, Mark Hayes, Rodney Whitlock, Kimberly Barnes O'Connor, Aron Bishop, Gail Wilensky, Raynard S. Kingston, Lisa Simpson, Susan V. Ross, Edwin J. Gilroy, Robert L. Knisely, James A. Peretti Jr., Andrew Patzman, Edward D. Martin, Tevi David Troy, and Elias Zerhouni. (http://cepel.edu.umontpellier.fr/banques-de-donnees-opera-2/sante/.)

18. OPERA Health Interview 47: Washington, DC, May 11, 2010.

19. Gail Wilensky privileged the fact that "unlike some of the other people in the administration, I had a health policy research background. When I needed information, I had a broad reach." OPERA Health Interview 47: Washington, DC, May 11, 2010: 5.

20. OPERA Sociographic Health Data (SHD): Mark Hayes: 1–4.

21. OPERA Sociographic Health Data (SHD): Howard Cohen.

22. See the Heritage Foundation's website: http://www.heritage.org/research/lecture/a-high-price-prescription.

23. OPERA Sociographic Health Data (SHD): Charles "Chuck" Clapton: 1–3.

24. OPERA Sociographic Health Data (SHD): Charles "Chuck" Clapton: 1–3.

25. For a broader overview of all the Republican long-term health insiders' career paths of the policy bureaucrat type, see the following OPERA Sociographic Health Data (SHD): Roland "Guy" King, Ann Agnew, Richard P. Kusserow, Michael F. Mangano, Bettilou Taylor, Susan K. Hattant, and James J. Sourvine. (http://cepel.edu.umontpellier.fr/banques-de-donnees-opera-2/sante/. ID: Opera2008.)

26. OPERA Sociographic Health Data (SHD): Roland E. King: 4.

27. See King's interview in the specialist health magazine *Health Watch*: "Navigating New Horizons: An Interview with Guy King," September 2007: 11–12.

28. OPERA Sociographic Health Data (SHD): Ann Agnew: 1–2.

29. ABD is the qualification used in the US to refer to students whose doctoral research training has been validated but who have not completed their PhD dissertation nor had a viva.

30. OPERA Health Interview 3:Washington, DC, June 8, 2010: 5–6.

31. See details from ProPublica at https://projects.propublica.org/graphics/beachhead.

32. OPERA Health Interview 45: Washington, DC, May 28, 2010: 9.

33. The "newcomers" are individuals who had held subaltern entry-level posts before the final withdrawal of the Clinton health reform in September 1994. This

definition allows us to reduce the sample of Clinton plan veterans sociologically to just those individuals who held key posts in government during the political battle surrounding the health reform (chapter 4).

34. See the OPERA Sociographic Health Data (SHD): Peter Orszag, Cybele Bjorklund, and Elizabeth "Liz" Fowler. (http://cepel.edu.umontpellier.fr/banques-de -donnees-opera-2/sante/. ID: Opera2008.)

35. OPERA Sociographic Health Data (SHD): Peter Orszag: 1–24.

36. For more detail, visit https://en.wikipedia.org/wiki/Hamilton_Project.

37. OPERA Health Interview 17: Washington, DC, June 9, 2010.

38. Ezra Klein, "The-Number-Cruncher-in-Chief: Meet Obama's Budget Guru, Peter Orszag," *American Prospect*, December 11, 2008, http://prospect.org/article /number-cruncher-chief.

39. OPERA Sociographic Health Data (SHD): Cybele Bjorklund.

40. In our interviews, Cybele Bjorklund said that her friendship with Liz Fowler had a long history and was founded on a shared vision of the gestation of the Affordable Care Act. Their friendship continues to this day, and they regularly meet up for lunch or dinner. See ProAcTA Interview 1: Washington, DC, June 18, 2018.

41. OPERA Sociographic Health Data (SHD): Liz Fowler: 1–5.

42. OPERA Health Interview 14: Washington, DC, November 14, 2011.

43. ProAcTA Interview 1: Washington, DC, June 18, 2018: 9–10.

44. OPERA Sociographic Health Data (SHD): Jeanne M. Lambrew and David Bowen.

45. OPERA Sociographic Health Data (SHD): Jeanne Lambrew: 1–16.

46. Christopher Jennings and Jeanne Lambrew, Interview, April 17–18, 2003, *William J. Clinton Presidential History Project*, Miller Center, University of Virginia: 55.

47. OPERA Health Interview 13: Washington, DC, April 11, 2010: 2.

48. Jeanne Lambrew stressed how Nancy-Ann DeParle had helped her adjust to this new role and these new responsibilities, while some of the permanent staff at the OMB (career people) considered her to be a mere substitute career person. See OPERA Health Interview 13: Washington, DC, April 11, 2010: 98.

49. Jeanne M. Lambrew, John D. Podesta, and Teresa Shaw, "Change in Challenging and Improving Health Coverage," *Health Affairs*, March 23, 2005.

50. OPERA Sociographic Health Data (SHD): Jeanne Lambrew: 2.

51. OPERA Sociographic Health Data (SHD): David Bowen: 1–5.

52. OPERA Sociographic Health Data (SHD): Michael J. Meyers: 4.

53. Lawrence Jacobs and Theda Skocpol define the "public option" as "a policy advocated by the progressive Democrats that consisted in creating a health care insurance regime managed by the government which individuals and companies could choose instead of a private insurance scheme" (2010: 188).

54. In a more recent series of interviews conducted with top health policy advisers, we tried to examine in more depth the issue of how unique their professional role was. See ProAcTA Interview 1: Washington, DC, June 18, 2018; and Interview 2: June 19, 2018.

55. Insiders who took up posts at Johns Hopkins University's school of public health (Baltimore) include the following: D. Rowland and T. Morford, who were among the Clinton plan veterans; and C. Bjorklund and L. Fowler, who were among the newcomers. Those who worked for the health policy school at Georgetown University include

the following: J. Feder, B. Biles, W. Primus, K. Pollitz, and J. Lambrew. Those who took up posts with the school of public health at the George Washington University include A. Schneider, R. Katz, and C. Clancy.

56. Christopher Jennings and Jeanne Lambrew, Interview, April 17–18, 2003, *William J. Clinton Presidential History Project*, Miller Center, University of Virginia: 142.

Chapter 6. The Clinton Plan

1. Since the end of the 1970s, two new reforming programmatic orientations distinct from the NHI project were in competition with each other. The first option was formulated by Alice Rivlin, ASPE during the Johnson administration (1968–1969) and the CBO's first director (1975–1983) who, summarizing the liberal and progressive Democratic rationale in a *New York Times Magazine* article, called for the creation of a market-based health coverage system (see A. Rivlin, "Agreed: Here Comes National Health Insurance," *New York Times Magazine*, July 22, 1974, 46–50). The second option proposed strong regulation of competition and the market in order to reform the health coverage system. These ideas are set out in the memorandum "Consumer Choice Health Plan: A National Health Insurance Proposal" put forward by Alain Enthoven for HEW Secretary Joseph Califano on September 22, 1977, during President Carter's administration (Enthoven, 1978, 1993).

2. By programmatic offer, we mean the three different health reform options put forward by the Democrats that were part of the agenda setting as described by Andrew Rich: (1) managed competition, (2) play-or-play and (3) single payer (2004: 157).

3. OPERA Health Interview 31: Washington, DC, May 18, 2010: 3–4.

4. This group included the following academics and specialized health policy researchers: T. Marmor, J. White, C. Altenstetter, E. Richard Brown, Lawrence D. Brown, Robert Burt, C. Campbell, J. Creighton Campbell, P. Caper, D. Frankfor, W. A. Glaser, M. A. Goldberg, B. Gray, C. Grogan, P. Harvey, L. R. Jacobs, J. L. Mashaw, C. Massie, J. Roberts, V. Rodwin, A. Schick, M. Schlesinger, and D. Wilsford. See the report they cowrote: The Health Care Study Group, (1994).

5. Sherry Glied describes as "marketist" those public health experts who, whether or not they are economists, see reliance on the market as the solution for reforming the health system. "Medicalists" on the other hand reject a market-based approach, insisting that health must be seen as deserving of the most egalitarian treatment possible (1997: 17–35).

6. OPERA Health Interview 33: Washington, DC, December 12, 2011: 4.

7. OPERA Health Interview 12: Washington, DC, August 28, 2008: 4.

8. OPERA Health Interview 34: Washington, DC, April 28, 2010: 4.

9. Robert Pear, "The Health Care Debate: Behind the Scenes," *New York Times*, August 6, 1994.

10. The play-or-pay model was a health insurance option whereby the employer offered health coverage to their employees ("play") or contributed to financing a public fund ("pay") (Skocpol, 1996: 33–35).

11. The detailed study of long-term health insiders' career paths reveals that a number of prominent individuals, after having worked on the Pepper Commission,

went on to have long careers either as institutional migrants, such as Democrats like B. Biles, J. Feder, C. Jennings, K. Pollitz, D. Rowland, D. Nexon, and the Republican T. Scully, or as technocratic translators, such as R. Katz in Congress and G. Claxton in the executive branch (chapter 4).

12. Judy Feder has described the composition of the Pepper Commission as follows: "Two-thirds Democrat and one third Republican (representatives and staffers), as well as three of President H. W. Bush's presidential appointees" (Feder, 2007: 3–5). See Judy Feder, Interview by Janet Heininger, July 5, 2007, *Edward M. Kennedy Oral History Project*, Miller Center, University of Virginia: 3–5.

13. OPERA Health Interview 12: Washington, DC, August 28, 2008: 3–4.

14. Judy Feder, Interview by Janet Heininger, July 5, 2007, *Edward M. Kennedy Oral History Project*, Miller Center, University of Virginia: 5.

15. Christopher Jennings and Jeanne Lambrew, Interview, April 17–18, 2003, *William J. Clinton Presidential History Project*, Miller Center, University of Virginia: 12.

16. OPERA Health Interview 23: Washington, DC, April 30, 2010: 1.

17. OPERA Health Interview 29: Washington, DC, May 17, 2010: 4–5.

18. OPERA Health Interview: Washington, DC, May 12, 2010 (non-inventoried, OPERA Data Bank).

19. OPERA Health Interview 29: Washington, DC, May 17, 2010: 7.

20. OPERA Health Interview 2: New York, NY, August 28, 2008: 8.

21. OPERA Health Interview 2: New York, NY, August 28, 2008: 8.

22. OPERA Health Interview 31: Washington, DC, May 18, 2010: 3.

23. See David Nexon, Interview by Janet Heininger, June 27, 2007, *Edward M. Kennedy Oral History Project*, Miller Center, University of Virginia: 4–5.

24. OPERA Health Interview 8: Washington, DC, May 5, 2010: 9–10.

25. OPERA Health Interview 11: Washington, DC, October 12, 2011: 5.

26. Chris Jennings and Jeanne Lambrew, Interview, April 17–18, 2003, *William J. Clinton Presidential History Project*, Miller Center, University of Virginia: 7.

27. OPERA Health Interview 21: Washington, DC, June 14, 2010: 6.

28. OPERA Health Interview 2: Washington, DC, August 28, 2008: 7.

29. OPERA Health Interview 11: Washington, DC, October 12, 2011: 1–2.

30. "Whiz Kids" is the name given to a group of fifteen experts from the RAND Corporation who, during the 1960s, joined forces with Defense Secretary Robert McNamara to modernize the department. Among other things, they initiated the famous method of streamlining public finances known as the Planning, Programming, and Budgeting System (PPBS). See https://en.wikipedia.org/wiki/Whiz_Kids _(Department_of_Defense).

31. OPERA Health Interview 19: Washington, DC, December14, 2010: 9.

32. OPERA Health Interview 37: Washington, DC, April 1, 2010: 9.

33. Christopher Jennings and Jeanne Lambrew, Interview, April 17–18, 2003, *William J. Clinton Presidential History Project*, Miller Center, University of Virginia: 7.

34. OPERA Health Interview 46: Washington, DC, April 27, 2010: 6–7.

35. Judy Feder, Interview by Janet Heininger, July 5, 2007, *Edward M. Kennedy Oral History Project*: 12.

Chapter 7. The Impossible Government of "Strangers"

1. According to Theda Skocpol, "Instant judgments came above all from Washington insiders and members of the 'punditocracy' of the media commentators and policy experts who appear daily on television and in the editorial and op-ed pages of newspapers and magazines" (1996: 9).

2. OPERA Health Interview 23: Washington, DC, April 30, 2010: 1–2.

3. OPERA Health Interview 11: Washington, DC, October 12, 2011: 5.

4. OPERA Health Interview 34: Washington, DC, April 28, 2010: 2.

5. OPERA Health Interview 10: Washington, DC, May 24, 2010: 7.

6. OPERA Health Interview 45: Washington, DC, May 28, 2010: 15.

7. OPERA Health Interview 6: Washington, DC, May 2009: 19.

8. OPERA Health Interview 20: Washington, DC, May 27, 2010: 4.

9. Paul Starr described the sociological composition of the task force, whose five hundred members were appointed during his involvement, as follows: "mostly federal employees, many of them at the request of their departments, as well as some independent experts, congressional staff (Democrats only), and state health care officials (Republican as well as Democrat)" (2007: 15).

10. Within the sample population of 151 long-term health insiders, we studied the career paths of a group of twenty individuals whose career paths reflected their contribution to the work of the task force. On the Democratic side, these included Judy Feder, Michael Hash, Chris Jennings, Andy Schneider, David Nexon, Tim Westmoreland, M. Michael Iskowitz, Gary Claxton, Christine Williams, Karen Nelson, Ruth Katz, Bruce Vladeck, Nancy Ann DeParle, Sherry Glied, Rick Forster, David Cade, and Andrew Hyman. On the Republican side, these included: Tom Scully, Joe Antos, and Roland G. King (see chapters 4 and 5).

11. OPERA Health Interview 45: Washington, DC, May 28, 2010: 13.

12. OPERA Health Interview 43: Washington, DC, May 21, 2010: 7.

13. OPERA Health Interview 42: Washington, DC, May 21, 2010: 9.

14. OPERA Health Interview 20: Washington, DC, May 27, 2010: 4.

15. OPERA Health Interview 20: Washington, DC, May 27, 2010: 4.

16. OPERA Health Interview 46: Washington, DC, April 27, 2010: 5–6.

17. OPERA Health Interview 20: Washington, DC, May 27, 2010: 16.

18. OPERA Health Interview 45: Washington, DC, May 28, 2010: 14.

19. OPERA Health Interview 8: Washington, DC, May 5, 2010: 2.

20. OPERA Health Interview 6: Washington, DC, May 2009: 14.

21. OPERA Health Interview 27: Washington, DC, May 21, 2010: 3 and 8.

22. OPERA Health Interview 23: Washington, DC, April 30, 2010: 2.

23. OPERA Health Interview 23: Washington, DC, April 30, 2010: 2.

24. OPERA Health Interview 23: Washington, DC, April 30, 2010: 5.

25. OPERA Health Interview 48: Washington, DC, November 14, 2011: 2.

26. OPERA Health Interview 18: Washington, DC, May 27, 2010: 1–2.

27. OPERA Health Interview 31: Washington, DC, May 18, 2010: 3.

28. OPERA Health Interview 31: Washington, DC, May 18, 2010: 3.

29. OPERA Health Interview 41: Washington, DC, May 14, 2010: 2.

30. The health alliances were intended to create openings for around five thousand employees, yet how these positions would be financed was not clearly stated. This problem reinforced the very theoretical and costly dimension of this structural reform of the health coverage system.

31. OPERA Health Interview 18: Washington, DC, May 27, 2010: 5.

32. OPERA Health Interview 2: New York, NY, September 28, 2008: 3

33. OPERA Health Interview 2: New York, NY, September 28, 2008: 3

34. OPERA Health Interview 2: New York, NY, September 28, 2008: 5.

35. OPERA Health Interview 2: New York, NY, September 28, 2008: 6.

36. OPERA Health Interview 2: New York, NY, September 28, 2008: 14.

37. To watch these advertisements, visit https://www.youtube.com/watch?v=Dt31nhleeCg.

38. OPERA Health Interview 24: Washington, DC, March 9, 2008: 5.

39. OPERA Health Interview 2: New York, NY, August 28, 2008: 7.

40. OPERA Health Interview 8: Washington, DC, May 5, 2010: 5.

41. OPERA Health Interview 10: Washington, DC, May 24, 2010.

Chapter 8. The George W. Bush Years

1. Having already used the expression "Clinton plan veterans" (chapter 4) to designate those individuals enjoying careers as long-term insiders who took part in the eponymous reform project, we will expand its sociological definition by highlighting the key role they played when they applied their political experience to formulate a new reform project.

2. OPERA Sociographic Health Data (SHD): Judy Feder: 9.

3. OPERA Health Interview 31: Washington, DC, May 18, 2010: 7–8.

4. OPERA Health Interview 15: Washington, DC, March 19, 2010: 5.

5. OPERA Health Interview 28: Washington, DC, May 19, 2010: 22–24.

6. These comments were largely corroborated in the context of our OPERA 2008–2010 interviews. (To access all the interviews, visit http://cepel.edu.umontpellier.fr/banques-de-donnees-opera-2/sante/.)

7. OPERA Health Interview 10: Washington, DC, May 24, 2010: 6.

8. OPERA Health Interview 23: Washington, DC, April 30, 2010: 7.

9. This young researcher listed at least a dozen reform plans devised between 2003 and 2009: "Road Map to Coverage" from the Urban Institute (2003); "Progressive Prescriptions for a Healthy America" (J. Lambrew, T. Daschle, J. Podesta) from the Center for American Progress (2005); "Framework for a High Performance Health System for the US" (D. Blumenthal, K. Davis) from the Commonwealth Fund (2006); "Massachusetts Plan" (J. Gruber in 2006); "Hamilton Project" from the Brookings Institution (2006–2007); "A High Performance Health System for the US: An Ambitious Agenda for the Next President" (D. Blumenthal, K. Davis in 2007); "Critical: What We Can Do about the Health Care Crisis" (T. Daschle, J. Lambrew in 2008); "A Call to Action: White Paper on Health Reform" (Max Baucus, Liz Fowler in 2008); "Path to a High Performance US Health Care System" (K. Davis) from the Commonwealth Fund (2009); "Crossing Our Lines" (Chris Jennings, Mark McClellan) from the Bipartisan Policy Center (2009); and "A Modest Proposal for a Competing Public Health Plan" (Len

Nichols, John Bertko) from the New American Foundation (2009), see chapter 6: "The Involvement of Experts in the Obama Reform (2005–2010)" (Lepont, 2014: 393–468).

10. OPERA Health Interview 31: Washington, DC, May 18, 2010: 7.

11. This article was published in the *Health Affairs* journal, considered by health professionals in Washington, DC, to be "the bible of health policy" (Lambrew, Podesta & Shaw, 2005).

12. OPERA Health Interview 39: Washington, DC, May 19, 2010: 17–19.

13. The Bipartisan Policy Center was initiated by two Democratic senators, Tom Daschle and George Mitchell, and two Republican senators, Bob Dole and Howard Baker, in March 2007. Its aim was to devise a consensual health care insurance reform project that could be brought before Congress by both parties of government.

14. OPERA Health Interview 23: Washington, DC, April 30, 2010: 6.

15. Our career-path study shows three Clinton plan veterans who moved between the CBO and the CBPP: W. Primus, R. Reischauer (ex-director), and P. N. Van de Water. See OPERA Health Interview 41: Washington, DC, May 14, 2010: 1–3.

16. OPERA Health Interview 41: Washington, DC, May 14, 2010: 4.

17. James R. Horney and Paul N. Van de Water, *House-Passed and Senate Health Bills Reduce Deficit, Slow Health Care Costs, and Include Realistic Medicare Savings*, Center on Budget and Policy Priorities, December 4, 2009; Paul N. Van de Water and James R. Horney, *Health Reform Will Reduce the Deficit*, Center on Budget and Policy Priorities, March 25, 2010.

18. OPERA Health Interview 48: Washington, DC, November 14, 2011: 2.

19. ProAcTA Interview 6: Boston, MA, November 2, 2018.

20. OPERA Sociographic Health Data (SHD): Judy Feder: 9.

21. OPERA Health Interview 23: Washington, DC, April 30, 2010: 5.

22. See the About Us page at http://www.allhealthpolicy.org/about-us/.

23. OPERA Health Interview 28: Washington, DC, May 19, 2010: 16.

24. The Democratic long-term insiders were Brian Biles, Chris Jennings, Judy Feder, Karen Ignani, Karen Davis, Diane Rowland, David Nexon, Sherry Glied, Gary Claxton, Len Nichols, Alice Rivlin, Bruce Vladeck, Karen Pollitz, Michael Hash, Andy Schneider, Tim Westmoreland, Liz Fowler, and Peter Orszag. The Republican long-term insiders were David Abernethy, Joe Antos, Howard Cohen, Dean Rosen, Mark McClellan, and Gail Wilensky.

25. These were the four Clinton plan veterans with an institutional migrant profile: Brian Biles, Chris Jennings, David Nexon, and Karen Pollitz. See the following document: Alliance for Health Reform, *Lessons Learned: The Health Reform Debate of 1993–1994*, Robert Wood Johnson Foundation, April 2008.

26. OPERA Health Interview 6: Washington, DC, May 2009: 15 and 18–19.

27. OPERA Health Interview 34: Washington, DC, April 28, 2010: 6.

28. OPERA Health Interview 9: Washington, DC, June 1, 2010: 19.

29. OPERA Health Interview 27: Washington, DC, May 21, 2010: 5.

30. D. Durenberger, S. Bartlett Foote, and L. Nichols, *The Ten Commandments for Presidential Leadership on Health Reform*, Report System 2009, meeting in Saint Paul, Minnesota: 5–6.

31. The presidential transition period in the US is a fairly long one. It lasts roughly two and a half months, from the first Tuesday in November, the date of the election, until January 20 of the following year when the newly elected president is sworn in and takes up their post. During this period, the president's advisers—not yet officially in charge at this stage—prepare the ground for the administration to initiate its reforms.

32. National Academy of Social Insurance, Interview with Nancy-Ann Min DeParle, Washington, DC, on April 2, 2015, interviewed by Edward Berkowitz, https://www.nasi.org/wp-content/uploads/2016/04/Insights_from_the_Top.pdf.

33. The individual mandate is a policy instrument developed by Stuart Butler, a Republican health expert with the Heritage Foundation at the end of the 1980s. It aims to bring together freedom of choice and the extension of health care insurance. For Anne-Laure Beaussier, the individual mandate is "the obligation to enable most American citizens or residents to access health care insurance or to pay a fine to the federal government" (2016: 158).

34. ProAcTA Interview 5: Boston, MA, November 1, 2018.

35. OPERA Health Interview 20: Washington, DC, May 27, 2010: 8–9.

36. See these OPERA interviews among others: OPERA Health Interview 23: Washington, DC, April 30, 2010, and OPERA Health Interview 39: Washington, DC, May 19, 2010: 17.

37. OPERA Health Interview 18: Washington, DC, May 27, 2010: 7–8.

38. OPERA Health Interview 18: Washington, DC, May 27, 2010: 8.

39. OPERA Health Interview 18: Washington, DC, May 27, 2010: 8.

40. OPERA Health Interview 19: Washington, DC, December 14, 2010: 9.

41. OPERA Health Interview 43: Washington, DC, May 21, 2010: 2.

42. OPERA Health Interview 14: Washington, DC, November 14, 2010: 3; and more recently, ProAcTA Interview 1: Washington, DC, June 18, 2018.

43. ProAcTA Interview 1: Washington, DC, June 18, 2018: 4.

44. ProAcTA Interview 1: Washington, DC, June 18, 2018: 5.

45. ProAcTA Interview 4: New York, NY, June 22, 2018.

46. OPERA Health Interview 23: Washington, DC, April 30, 2010: 6.

Chapter 9. Behind the Congressional Votes

1. As a reminder, the congressional practice whereby the passing of a bill can be obstructed or slowed down known as "filibustering" can be launched within the Senate once the minority political party holds more than forty seats (Jacobs & Skocpol, 2010: 183).

2. With utmost precision, John McDonough sets out a list of some fifty-five staffers who, with all congressional committees taken into account, have played a role in the decision-making process (2011: 11–12). In this list, it is worth drawing attention to the presence of the following nine Clinton plan veterans: Karen Nelson, Andy Schneider, Ruth Katz, Tim Westmoreland, Jack Ebeler (with H. Waxman), Liz Murray (with T. Harkin), Michele Varnhagen (with G. Miller), Wendell Primus (with N. Pelosi), and Michael Myers (with T. Kennedy). The following four newcomers also played a role: Cybele Bjorklund (with C. Rangel), David Bowen (with T. Kennedy), Liz Fowler (with M. Baucus), and Jim Esquea (with K. Conrad). For more detail, see http://cepel.edu .umontpellier.fr/banques-de-donnees-opera-2/sante/.

3. Mary-Ann Akers, "In the Speaker's Office, a Quiet Liberal Lion: Wendell E. Primus," *Washington Post,* June 21, 2010.

4. One of our long-term insiders, who for more than twenty years was Ted Kennedy's chief of staff at the HELP Committee cites Cybele Bjorklund as an influential staffer on the Ways and Means Committee in the House of Representatives, while reminding us that she was his assistant at the Senate for several years. See OPERA Health Interview 30: Washington, DC, March 9, 2008: 21.

5. The Committee on Oversight and Government Reform is a committee of the House of Representatives exercising control on the executive branch of power, particularly by orchestrating hearings. In the context of a major reform launch, this can be a key role.

6. OPERA Health Interview 45: Washington, DC, May 28, 2010: 6–7.

7. OPERA Health Interview 45: Washington, DC, May 28, 2010: 6–7.

8. OPERA Health Interview 45: Washington, DC, May 28, 2010: 12–13.

9. OPERA Health Interview 44: Washington, DC, April 17, 2009; and OPERA Health Interview 45: Washington, DC, May 28, 2010: 5.

10. OPERA Health Interview 34: Washington, DC, April 28, 2010: 4.

11. OPERA Health Interview 30: Washington, DC, March 8, 2008: 2–3.

12. Daniel Libit, "David Bowen from the Microscope to the Big Pictures," *Politico,* 2011, 44.

13. Non-itemized interview, Data Bank OPERA, conducted by Anne-Laure Beaussier, Washington, DC, April 6, 2010.

14. The director of the CBO is named by the Speaker and the president of the Senate (i.e., the US vice president) following the appointment by the two congressional budgetary committees for a four-year mandate (McDonough, 2011: 32).

15. Ezra Klein, "The Number-Cruncher-in-Chief: Meet Obama's Budget Guru, Peter Orszag," *American Prospect*, December 11, 2008, http://prospect.org/article/number -cruncher-chief.

16. OPERA Health Interview 18: Washington, DC, May 27, 2010: 1–2.

17. See Congressional Budget Office, *Budget Volume 1: Health Care* (Washington, DC, GPO, December 2008) and Congressional Budget Office, *Keys Issues in Analyzing Major Health Insurance Proposals* (Washington, DC: GPO, December 2008).

18. OPERA Health Interview 34: Washington, DC, April 28, 2010: 5.

19. OPERA Health Interview unnumbered: Washington, DC, April 2, 2010.

20. In a monograph published by the Brookings Institution, Larry Brown updates and develops Schattschneider's notion according to which "new policies create new politics" (1935) by adapting it to the expansion of the American government during the 1980s. Brown emphasizes how (1) new government programs produce new problems; (2) the new problems inspire political efforts ("rationalizing politics") to find policy solutions ("rationalizing policies"); (3) these rationalizing politics grow increasingly prominent in the universe of political actions at times; (4) as they do so, they entail changes in political institutions' styles, changes that collectively constitute the new politics (thus the politics are ultimately explained by growth of government); and (5) finally, new politics generate new policies in their turn (1983b: 5).

21. OPERA Health Interview 10: Washington, DC, May 24, 2010: 8.

22. ProAcTA Interview 5: Boston, MA, November 1, 2018.

23. OPERA Health Interview 46: Washington, DC, April 27, 2010: 2.

24. OPERA Health Interview 46: Washington, DC, April 27, 2010: 2.

25. National Academy of Social Insurance, Interview with Nancy-Ann Min DeParle, Washington, DC, on April 2, 2015, interviewed by Edward Berkowitz, https://www.nasi .org/wp-content/uploads/2016/04/Insights_from_the_Top.pdf.

26. OPERA Health Interview 34: Washington, DC, April 28, 2010: 5.

27. OPERA Health Interview 31: Washington, DC, April 18, 2010: 7–8.

28. OPERA Health Interview 31: Washington, DC, April 18, 2010: 7–8.

29. Nancy-Ann DeParle, Subject: Health Reform Decisions, Briefing Memo, the White House, Washington, DC, April 21, 2009, http://www.documentcloud.org /documents/328161-health-care-memo.html.

30. OPERA Health Interview 27: Washington, DC, May 21, 2010: 5.

31. OPERA Health Interview 19: Washington, DC, December 14, 2010: 7.

32. OPERA Health Interview 18: Washington, DC, May 27, 2010: 2.

33. OPERA Health Interview 39: Washington, DC. May 19, 2010.

34. OPERA Health Interview 22: Washington, DC, December 12, 2010: 19.

35. OPERA Health Interview 45: Washington, DC, May 28, 2010: 15 and 22.

36. OPERA Health Interview 45: Washington, DC, May 28, 2010: 15 and 22.

37. OPERA Health Interview 28: Washington, DC, May 19, 2010: 23 and 24.

38. OPERA Sociographic Health Data (SHD): Michele Varnhagen: 1–3.

39. OPERA Health Interview 31: Washington, DC, May 18, 2010: 6.

40. OPERA Health Interview unnumbered: Washington, DC, April 2, 2010.

41. OPERA Health Interview 45: Washington, DC, May 28, 2010: 15.

42. OPERA Health Interview 9: Washington, DC, June 1, 2010: 16; and OPERA Health Interview 42: Washington, DC, May 21, 2010: 9–10.

43. OPERA Health Interview 45: Washington, DC, May 28, 2010: 16.

44. OPERA Health Interview 23: Washington, DC, April 30, 2010: 5.

45. OPERA Health Interview 25: Washington, DC, May 15, 2009.

46. OPERA Health Interview unnumbered: Washington, DC, March 31, 2010.

47. OPERA Health Interview unnumbered: Washington, DC, April 2, 2010.

48. OPERA Health Interview unnumbered: Washington, DC, March 31, 2010.

49. OPERA Health Interview 45: Washington, DC, May 28, 2010: 19.

50. OPERA Sociographic Health Data (SHD): Judy Feder: 10; and OPERA Health Interview 31: Washington, DC, May 18, 2010.

51. OPERA Health Interview unnumbered: Washington, DC, April 2, 2010.

52. OPERA Health Interview 45: Washington, DC, May 28, 2010: 21.

53. OPERA Health Interview 48: Washington, DC, November 14, 2011: 2.

54. "Karen Ignagni," Wikipedia, last modified January 24, 2023, https://en.wikipedia .org/wiki/Karen_Ignagni.

55. Interview with Nancy-Ann Min DeParle, Washington, DC, on April 2, 2015, interviewed by Edward Berkowitz, https://www.nasi.org/research/2016/insights-top -oral-history-medicare-medicaid.

56. OPERA Health Interview 37: Washington, DC, April 1, 2010: 3.

57. OPERA Health Interview 45: Washington, DC, May 28, 2010: 28.
58. OPERA Health Interview 37: Washington, DC, April 1, 2010: 9.
59. OPERA Health Interview 23: Washington, DC, April 30, 2010: 6.

Conclusion

1. ProAcTA Interview 3: Washington, DC, June 19, 2018: 7.
2. For more discussion on this, see Robert Draper, "Nancy Pelosi's Last Battle," *New York Times Magazine*, November 19, 2018, https://www.nytimes.com/2018/11/19/magazine/nancy-pelosi-house-democrats.html.

Sources of Biographical Information
OPERA Data Bank:
https://cepel.edu.umontpellier.fr/banques-de-donnees-opera-2/health/
ID: Opera2008

beQuali:
https://bequali.fr/fr/les-enquetes/

Bernan's Insider's Guide to Key Committee Staff of the US Congress
Bernan's The Almanac of the Unelected
Biography at WhoRunsGov.com by the *Washington Post*, https://www.whorunsgov.com
/Profiles/David_Price
CMS Oral History Series, edited by E. Berkowitz, https://www.ssa.gov/history/orallist
.html
Harvard University, John F. Kennedy School of Government, https://guides.library
.harvard.edu/hks/leadership/leadership_biographical_research
Insights from the Top: An Oral History of Medicare and Medicaid, published by the
National Academy of Social Insurance, March 2016, https://www.nasi.org
/research/medicare-health-policy/insights-from-the-top-an-oral-history-of
-medicare-and-medicaid/
Leadership Connect, https://www.leadershipconnect.io/
LegiStorm, https://www.legistorm.com/
LexisNexis, https://www.lexisnexis.com/en-us/products/nexis.page
LinkedIn, https://www.linkedin.com
Marquis Who's Who?, https://www.marquiswhoswho.com/
OpenSecrets, https://www.opensecrets.org/
Politico, https://www.politico.com/
SourceWatch, https://www.sourcewatch.org/index.php/SourceWatch
Wikipedia, https://www.wikipedia.org

Works Cited
Aaron, Henry J., ed. 1996. *The Problem That Won't Go Away: Reforming US Health Care
Financing.* Washington, DC: Brookings Institution Press.
Aberbach, Joel D. 2003. "The U.S. Federal Executive in an Era of Change." *Governance*
16 (3): 373–399.

Aberbach, Joel D., Robert D. Putnam, and Bert A. Rockman. 1981. *Bureaucrats and Politicians in Western Democracies.* Cambridge, MA: Harvard University Press.

Aberbach, Joel D., and Bert A. Rockman. 2000. *In the Web of Politics: Three Decades of the US Federal Executive.* Washington, DC: Brookings Institution Press.

Adams, Gordon. 1982. *The Politics of Defense Contracting: The Iron Triangle.* New Brunswick, NJ: Transaction Publishers.

Allison, T. Graham. 2006. "Emergence of Schools of Public Policy: Reflections by a Founding Dean." In *The Oxford Handbook of Public Policy,* edited by Michael Moran, Martin Rein, and Robert E. Goodin, 58–79. Oxford: Oxford University Press.

Altman, Stuart H., and David I. Shactman. 2011. *Power Politics and Universal Health Care.* Amherst, NY: Prometheus Books.

Arrow, Kenneth J. 1963. "Uncertainty and the Welfare Economics of Medical Care." *American Economic Review* 53 (5): 941–973.

Bai, Matt. 2009. "Taking the Hill." *New York Times Magazine,* June 7, 2009. www .nytimes.com/2009/06/07magazine.

Balogh, Brian. 2009. *A Government Out of Sight: The Mystery of National Authority in Nineteenth-Century America.* New York: Cambridge University Press.

Beaussier, Anne-Laure. 2012. "The Patient Protection and Affordable Care Act: The Victory of Unorthodox Lawmaking." *Journal of Health Politics, Policy and Law* 37 (5): 743–778.

Beaussier, Anne-Laure. 2016. *La Santé aux États-Unis: Une histoire politique.* Paris: Presses de Sciences Po.

Béland, Daniel. 2006. "The Politics of Social Learning: Finance Institutions and Pension Reform in the United States and Canada." *Governance* 19 (4): 559–583.

Belkin, Gary S. 1997. "The Technocratic Wish: Making Sense and Finding Power in the 'Managed' Medical Marketplace." *Journal of Health Politics, Policy and Law* 22 (2): 509–532.

Berkowitz, Edward, ed. *CMS Oral History Series.* www.ssa.gov/history/orallist.html.

Berkowitz, Edward D. 1995 *Mr. Social Security: The Life of Wilbur J. Cohen.* Lawrence: University Press of Kansas.

Berkowitz, Edward D. 1996. "Interview with Arthur Hess in Charlottesville." HCFA Oral History Interview, Social Security History. July 8, 1996. https://www.ssa.gov /history/HESS.html.

Berkowitz, Edward D. 2002. "Interview with Bruce Vladeck." *CMS Oral History Series.* New York. August 7, 2002: 167–187. https://www.cms.gov/files/document /cmsoralhistorymedicare-pdf.

Berkowitz, Edward D. 2002. "Interview with Wendell Primus." *CMS Oral History Series.* Washington, DC. August 14, 2002: 659–680. https://www.cms.gov/files /document/cmsoralhistorymedicare-pdf.

Berkowitz, Edward D. 2002. "Interview with Nancy-Ann Min DeParle." *CMS Oral History Series.* Washington, DC. August 22, 2002: 188–211. https://www.cms.gov /files/document/cmsoralhistorymedicare-pdf.

Berkowitz, Edward D. 2005. *Robert Ball and the Politics of Social Security.* Madison: University of Wisconsin Press.

Best, Heinrich and John Highley. 2018. "Introduction." In *The Palgrave Handbook of Political Elites*, edited by Heinrich Best and John Higley, 1–6. London: Palgrave-MacMillan.

Biles, Brian. 2008. "Health Reform Lessons Learned: Veterans of 1993–1994 Offer Advice to Today's Reformers." Alliance for Health Reform and Robert Wood Johnson Foundation. January 18, 2008. https://www.allhealthpolicy.org/wp -content/uploads/2017/01/HealthReformLessonsLearnedTranscript-1062.pdf.

Birnbaum, Pierre. 2001. *The Idea of France.* New York: Hill and Wang.

Birnbaum, Pierre. 2018. *Où va l'État? Essai sur les nouvelles élites du pouvoir.* Paris: Le Seuil.

Blendon, Robert J., Tracey S. Hyams, and John M. Benson. 1993. "Bridging the Gap between Expert and Policy Views on Health Care Reform: The Public versus the Experts." *The Public Perspective* (March–April): 13–15.

Blumenthal, David and James A. Morone. 2009. *The Hearth of Power: Health Politics in the Oval Office.* Berkeley: University of California Press.

Blyth, Mark McGann. 2001. "The Transformation of the Swedish Model: Economic Ideas, Distributional Conflict, and Institutional Change." *World Politics* 54: 1–26.

Blyth, Mark. 2013. *Austerity: History of a Dangerous Idea.* Oxford: Oxford University Press.

Bonafede, Dom. 1987. "The White House Personnel Office Room from Roosevelt to Reagan." In *The In-and-Outers: Presidential Appointees and Transient Government in Washington*, edited by G. Galvin Mckenzie, 30–59. Baltimore: Johns Hopkins University Press.

Brasfield, James. 2011. "The Politics of Ideas: Where Did the Public Option Come from and Where Is It Going?" *Journal of Health Politics, Policy and Law* 36 (3): 455–459.

Brill, Steven. 2015. *America's Bitter Pill: Money, Politics, Backroom Deals, and the Fight to Fix our Broken Healthcare System.* New York: Random House.

Brookes, Kevin. 2021. *Why Neo-Liberalism Failed in France: Political Sociology of the Spread of Neo-Liberal Ideas in France (1974–2012).* Cham, Switzerland: Springer International.

Brown, Lawrence D. 1983a. *Politics and Health Care Organization: HMOs as Federal Policy.* Washington, DC: Brookings Institution Press.

Brown, Lawrence D. 1983b. *New Policies, New Politics: Government's Response to Government's Growth.* Washington, DC: Brookings Institution Press.

Brown, Lawrence D. 1985. "Technocratic Corporatism and Administrative Reform in Medicare." *Journal of Health Politics, Policy and Law* 10 (3): 579–599.

Brown, Lawrence D. 2011. "The Elements of Surprise: How Health Reform Happened." *Journal of Health Politics, Policy and Law* 36 (3): 419–427.

Brown, Lawrence D. 2019. "Single-Payer Health Care in the United States: Feasible Solution or Grand Illusion? *American Journal of Public Health* 109 (11): 1506–1510.

Brown, Lawrence D. and William Genieys. Forthcoming. "Elites and Custodians of the State Policy Role: Evidence for the US Social Coverage System Development (from 1932 to 2022)."

Brown, Lawrence D., and Michael Sparer. 2003. "Poor Program's Progress: The Unanticipated Politics of Medicaid Policy." *Health Affairs* 22 (1): 31–44.

Brownlow, Louis. 1958. *A Passion for Anonymity: The Autobiography of Louis Brownlow.* Chicago: University of Chicago Press.

Burris, Val. 2004. "The Academic Caste System Prestige Hierarchies in PhD Exchange Networks." *American Sociological Review* 69 (2): 239–264.

Daalder, Hans. 1995. "Paths toward State Formation in Europe: Democratization, Bureaucratization, and Politicization." In *Essays in Honor of Juan J. Linz: Politics, Society, and Democracy, Comparative Studies,* edited by Houchang E. Chehabi and Alfred Stepan, 116–140. Boulder, CO: Westview Press.

Dahl, Robert A. 1958. "A Critique of the Ruling Elite Model." *American Political Science Review* 52 (2): 463–469.

Daschle, Tom A., Jeanne M. Lambrew, and Scott S. Greenberger. 2008. *Critical: What We Can Do About the Health Care Crisis?* New York: St. Martin's Press.

Derthick, Martha A. 1979. *Policymaking for Social Security.* Washington, DC: Brookings Institution Press.

Domhoff, William G. 1990. *The Power Elite and the State: How Policy Is Made in America.* Hawthorne, NY: Aldine de Gruyter.

Domhoff, William G. 1996, *State Autonomy or Class Dominance? Case Studies on Policy Making in America.* Hawthorne, NY: Aldine de Gruyter.

Donnelly, Kevin P., and David A. Rochefort. 2012. "The Lesson of 'Lesson Drawing:' How the Obama Administration Attempted to Learn from Failure of the Clinton Plan." *Journal of Policy History* 24 (2): 184–223.

Ellwood, Paul M., and Alain C. Enthoven. 1995. "Responsible Choice: The Jackson Hole Group Plan for Health Reform." *Health Affairs* 14 (2): 24–39.

Enthoven, Alain C. 1978. "Consumer Choice Health Plan: A National Health Insurance Proposal Based on Regulated Competition in the Private Sector," *New England Journal of Medicine* 298 (March 23; March 30): 650–658; 709–720.

Enthoven, Alain C. 1980. *Health Plan: The Only Practical Solution to the Soaring Costs of Medical Care.* Reading, MA: Addison-Wesley.

Enthoven, Alain C. 1993. "The History and Principles of Managed Competition." *Health Affairs* 12 (suppl. 1): 24–48.

Enthoven, Alain C., and Richard G. Kronick. 1990. "Consumer Choice Health Plan for the 1990s (part I and II)." *New England of Journal Medicine* 320 (January 5; January 12): 29–37; 94–101.

Enthoven, Alain C., and Wayne K. Smith. 1971. *How Much Is Enough? Shaping the Defense Program 1961–1969.* Santa Monica, CA: RAND Corporation.

Ertman, Thomas C. 2005. "Building States—Inherently a Long-Term Process? An Argument from Comparative History." In *States and Development: Historical Antecedents of Stagnation and Advance,* edited by Matthew Lange and Dietrich Rueschemeyer, 178–179. London: Palgrave-MacMillan.

Feder, Judith M. 1977. *Medicare: The Politics of Federal Hospital Insurance.* Lexington, MA: Lexington Books.

Feder, Judith M. 2007. "Judy Feder Oral History." Interview by Janet Heininger. *Edward M. Kennedy Oral History Project.* Miller Center, University of Virginia.

July 5, 2007. https://millercenter.org/the-presidency/presidential-oral-histories/judy-feder-oral-history.

Fischer, Linda L. 1987. "Fifty Years of Presidential Appointments." In *The In-and-Outers: Presidential Appointees and Transient Government in Washington,* edited by G. Calvin Mackenzie, 1–29. Baltimore: Johns Hopkins University Press.

Fourcade, Marion. 2009. *Economists and Societies: Discipline and Profession in the United States, Britain and France from 1890 to 1990.* Princeton: Princeton University Press.

Fox, Harrison, and Suzan W. Hammond. 1977. *Congressional Staff: The Invisible Force in American Law Making.* New York: Free Press.

Furman, Jason. 2008. "The Promise of Cost Conscientiousness in Health Care Reform." In *Who Has the Cure?: Hamilton Project Ideas on Health Care,* edited by Jason Furman, 175–226. Washington, DC: Brookings Institution Press.

Genieys, William. 2010. *The New Custodians of the State: Programmatic Elites in French Society.* New Brunswick, NJ: Transaction Books.

Genieys, William. 2011. *Sociologie politique des élites.* Paris: Armand Colin.

Genieys, William. 2015. "C. Wright Mills: The Power Elite." In *Oxford Handbook of the Classics of Public Policy and Administration,* edited by Steven Balla, Martin Lodge, and Edward Page, 69–79. Oxford: Oxford University Press.

Genieys, William, and Saïd M. Darviche. 2023. *Elites, Policies and State Reconfiguration: Transforming the French Welfare Regime.* Cham: Palgrave-MacMillan.

Genieys, William, Saïd M. Darviche and Brent Epperson. 2022. "New Policy Elites and the Affordable Care Act: The Making of Long-Term Insiders." *Journal of Policy History* 34 (1): 1–24.

Genieys, William, and Patrick Hassenteufel. 2015. "The Shaping of the New State Elites: Healthcare Policymaking in France since 1981." *Comparative Politics* 47 (3): 280–295.

Genieys, William, and Joana Jean. 2017. "The Custodians of the State Policies Dealing with the Financial Crisis: A Comparison between France and the US." *International Relations and Diplomacy* 5 (6): 322–341.

Genieys, William, and Marc Smyrl. 2008a. "Inside the Autonomous State: Programmatic Elites, in the Reform of French Health Policy." *Governance: An International Journal of Policy, Administration and Institutions* 21 (1): 187–210.

Genieys, William, and Marc Smyrl. 2008b. *Elites, Ideas and the Evolution of Public Policy.* London/New York: Palgrave.

Giddens, Anthony. 1972. "Elites in the British Class Structure." *Sociological Review* 20 (3): 345–372.

Glied, Sherry A. 1997. *Chronic Condition: Why Health Reform Fails.* Cambridge, MA: Harvard University Press.

Grupenhoff, John T. 1983. "Profile of Congressional Health Legislatives Aides." *Mount Sinai Journal of Medicine* 50 (1): 1–7.

Hacker, Jacob S. 1997. *The Road to Nowhere: The Genesis of President Clinton's Plan for Health Security.* Princeton: Princeton University Press.

Hacker, Jacob S. 2002. *The Divided Welfare State: The Battle over Public and Private Social Benefits in the United States.* Cambridge: Cambridge University Press.

Hacker, Jacob S. 2010. "The Road to Somewhere: Why Health Reform Happened." *Perspectives on Politics* 8 (3): 861–876.

Hacker, Jacob S., and Paul Pierson. 2010. *Winner-Take-All Politics*. New York: Simon and Schuster.

Hammond, Susan W. 1984. "Legislative Staff." *Legislative Studies Quarterly* 9 (2): 271–317.

Hassenteufel, Patrick, William Genieys, Marc Smyrl, and Javier Moreno. 2010. "Programmatic Actors and the Transformation of European Health Care States." *Journal of Health Politics, Policy and Law* 35 (4): 517–538.

Hassenteufel, Patrick, and William Genieys. 2021. "The Programmatic Action Framework: An Empirical Assessment." *European Policy Analysis* 7 (1): 28–47.

Health Care Study Group. 1994. "Report: Understanding the Choices in Health Care Reform." *Journal of Health Politics, Policy and Law* 19, no. 3: 499–541.

Heclo, Hugh. 1974. *Modern Social Politics in Britain and Sweden*. New Haven, CT: Yale University Press.

Heclo, Hugh. 1977. *The Government of Strangers: Executive Politics in Washington*. Washington, DC: Brookings Institution Press.

Heclo, Hugh. 1978. "Issues Networks and the Executive Establishment." In *The New American Political System,* edited by S. H. Beer and A. S. King, 87–124. Washington, DC: American Institute Enterprise.

Heclo, Hugh. 1984. "In Search of a Role: America's Higher Civil Service." In *Bureaucrats and Policy Making: A Comparative Overview,* edited by Ezra N. Suleiman, 8–34. New York: Holmes and Meier.

Heclo, Hugh. 1987. "The In-and-Outer System: A Critical Assessment." In *The In-and-Outers: Presidential Appointees and Transient Government in Washington,* edited by G. Calvin Mackenzie, 195–216. Baltimore: Johns Hopkins University Press.

Heclo, Hugh. 1995. "The Clinton Health Plan: Historical Perspective." *Health Affairs* (Spring 1995): 86–98.

Heinz, John P., and Edward O. Laumann. 1982. *Chicago Lawyers: The Social Structure of the Bar*. New York: Russell Sage Foundation.

Henschen, Beth M., and Edward I. Sidlow. 1986. "The Recruitment and Career Patterns of Congressional Committee Staffs: An Exploration." *Western Political Quarterly* 39 (4): 701–708.

Howlett, Michael, and Muckherjee Ishani. 2017. "Policy Formulation: Where Knowledge Meets Power in the Policy Process." In *Handbook of Policy Formulation,* edited by Michael Howlett and Ishani Muckherjee, 3–22. Northampton, MA: Edward Elgar.

Ingraham, Patricia W. 1995. *The Foundation of Merit: Public Service in American Democracy*. Baltimore: Johns Hopkins University Press.

Insights from the Top: An Oral History of Medicare and Medicaid. 2016. National Academy of Social Insurance. https://www.nasi.org/research/medicare-health-policy/insights-from-the-top-an-oral-history-of-medicare-and-medicaid/.

Jacobs, Lawrence R., and Robert Y. Shapiro. 2000. *Politicians Don't Pander: Political Manipulation and the Loss of Democratic Responsiveness*. Chicago: University of Chicago Press.

Jacobs, Lawrence R., and Theda Skocpol. 2010. *Health Care Reform and American Politics*. Oxford: Oxford University Press.

Jacobs, Nicolas, Desmond King, and Sidney M. Milkis. 2019. "Building a Conservative State: Partisan Polarization and the Redeployment of Administrative Power." *Perspectives on Politics* 17 (2): 453–469.

Jennings, Chris. 2008. "Proving the Skeptics Wrong: Why Major Health Reform Can Happen Despite the Odds." *Journal of Law, Medicine and Ethics* 36 (4): 728–730.

Jennings, Chris, and Jeanne Lambrew. 2003. "Chris Jennings and Jeanne Lambrew Oral History." *William J. Clinton Presidential History Project*. April 17 and 18, 2003. https://millercenter.org/the-presidency/presidential-oral-histories/chris-jennings -and-jeanne-lambrew-oral-history.

Jensen, Benjamin. 2018. "The Role of Ideas in Defense Planning: Revisiting the Revolution in Military Affairs." *Defense Studies* 18 (3): 302–317.

Johnson, Haynes, and David S. Broder. 1996. *The System: The American Way of Politics at the Breaking Point*. New York: Little Brown.

Journal of Health Politics, Policy and Law. 2011. "Critical Essays on Health Care Reform" (special issue) 36 (3).

Joyce, Philip G. 2011. *The Congressional Budget Office: Honest Numbers, Power, and Policymaking*. Washington, DC: Georgetown University Press.

King, Desmond. 2005. *The Liberty of Strangers: Making the American Nation*. Oxford: Oxford University Press.

King, Desmond, and Patrick Le Galès, eds. 2017. *Reconfiguring European States in Crisis*. Oxford: Oxford University Press.

King, Desmond, and Robert C. Lieberman. 2009. "Ironies of State Building: A Comparative Perspective on the American State." *World Politics* 61 (3): 547–588.

King, Guy. 2007. "Navigating New Horizons: An Interview with Guy King." *Health Watch*. September 2007: 11–12.

Kingdon, John W. 1981. *Congressmen's Voting Decisions*. Ann Arbor, MI: University of Michigan Press.

Kingdon, John W. 1984. *Agenda, Alternatives, and Public Policies*. Boston: Little Brown.

Lambrew, Jeanne M., John D. Podesta, and Teresa L. Shaw. 2005. "Changing in Challenging Times: A Plan for Extending and Improving Health Coverage." *Health Affairs* (online exclusive, March 23, 2005): W5-119–W5-132.

Lasswell, Harold D. 1936. *Politics: Who Gets What, When, How*. New York: McGraw-Hill.

Leca, Jean. 2012. "L'État entre politics, policies et polity: Ou peut-on sortir du triangle des Bermudes?" *Gouvernement et action publique* 1 (1): 59–82.

Leibovich, Mark. 2014. *This Town: Two Parties and a Funeral—Plus Plenty of Valet Parking in America's Gilded Capital*. New York: Blue Penguin Press.

Lepont, Ulrike. 2014. "Façonner les politiques aux marges de l'État: Le rôle des experts dans les réformes de la protection maladie aux États-Unis (1970–2010)." PhD diss., Université de Montpellier, France.

Lewis, David E. 2008. *The Politics of Presidential Appointments: Political Control and Bureaucratic Performance*. Princeton, NJ: Princeton University Press.

Lieberman, Robert C. 2002. "Weak State, Strong Policy: Paradoxes of Race Policy in the United States, Great Britain, and France." *Studies in American Political Development* 16 (2): 138–161.

Light, Paul C. 1987. "When Worlds Collide: The Political-Career Nexus." In *The In-and-Outers: Presidential Appointees and Transient Government in Washington,* edited by G. Calvin Mackenzie, 156–173. Baltimore: Johns Hopkins University Press.

Linz, Juan J. 2006. "Time and Regime Change." In *Political Sociology and the Future of Democracy,* edited by Roberto Michels, 81–113. New Brunswick, NJ: Transaction Publishers.

Littlefield, Nick, and David Nexon. 2015. *Lion of the Senate: When Ted Kennedy Rallied the Democrats in a GOP Congress.* New York: Simon and Schuster.

Mackenzie, G. Calvin, ed. 1987. *The In-and-Outers: Presidential Appointees and Transient Government in Washington.* Baltimore: Johns Hopkins University Press.

Mann, Michael. 1984. "The Autonomous Power of the State: Its Origins, Mechanisms and Results." *Archives Européennes de Sociologie* 25 (2): 185–213.

Mann, Michael. 1993. *The Sources of Social Power,* vol. 2: *The Rise of Classes and Nation States, 1760-1914.* Cambridge: Cambridge University Press.

Marmor, Ted R. 1970. *The Politics of Medicare.* New York: Aldine de Gruyter.

Marmor, Ted R. 1994 *Understanding Health-Care Reform.* New Haven, CT: Yale University Press.

Marmor, Ted R., and Jerry L. Mashaw. 1990. "Canada's Health Insurance and Ours: The Real Lessons, the Big Choices." *American Prospect* (Fall): 1–9.

McDonough, John E. 2011. *Inside National Health Reform.* Berkeley: University of California Press.

Medvetz, Thomas. 2012. *Think Tanks in America.* Chicago: University of Chicago Press.

Meisel, James H. 1958. *The Myth of the Ruling Class: Gaetano Mosca and the Elite.* Ann Arbor, MI: University of Michigan Press.

Michaels, Judith E. 1997. *The President's Call: Executive Leadership from FDR to George Bush.* Pittsburgh: University of Pittsburgh Press.

Mills, C. Wright. [1956] 2000. *The Power Elite.* Oxford: Oxford University Press.

Mintrom, Michael. 2019. "So You Want to Be a Policy Entrepreneur?" *Policy Design and Practice* 2 (4): 307–323.

Mizruchi, Mark S. 2013. *The Fracturing of the American Corporate Elite.* Cambridge, MA: Harvard University Press.

Morone, James A. 1993. "The Health Care Bureaucracy: Small Changes, Big Consequences." *Journal of Health Politics, Policy and Law* 18 (3): 723–739.

Morone, James A. 1994. "The Bureaucracy Empowered." In *The Politics of Health Care Reform: Lessons from the Past, Prospects for the Future,* edited by James A. Morone and Gary S. Belkin, 148–164. Durham, NC: Duke University Press.

Morone, James A. 2010. "Presidents and Health Reform: From Franklin D. Roosevelt to Barack Obama." *Health Affairs* 29 (6): 1096–1100.

Morone, James A. 2011 "Big Ideas, Broken Institutions, and the Wrath at the Grass Roots." *Journal of Health Politics, Policy and Law* 36 (3): 375–385.

Morone, James A., and Gary S. Belkin, eds. 1994. *The Politics of Health Care Reform: Lessons from the Past, Prospects for the Future.* Durham, NC: Duke University Press.

Mosca, Gaetano. 1939. *The Ruling Class.* New York: McGraw-Hill.

National Academy of Public Administration (NAPA). 1985. *Recruiting Presidential Appointees: A Conference of Former Presidential Personal Assistants*, Washington, DC.

Nexon, David. 2007. "David Nexon Oral History, Staffer of Edward Kennedy." Interview by Janet Heininger. *Edward M. Kennedy Oral History Project.* Miller Center, University of Virginia. July 5, 2007: 1–29. https://www.emkinstitute.org/resources /david-nexon-oral-history-staffer-edward-kennedy.

"News of Affiliated Associations and Regional Branches." *American Journal of Public Health* 58, no.7 (July 1, 1968).

Newton-Small, Jay. 2016. *Broad Influence: How Women Are Changing the Way America Works.* New York: Time Inc. Books.

Novak, William J. 2008. "The Myth of the 'Weak' American State." *American Historical Review* 113 (3): 752–772.

Oberlander, Jonathan. 2003. *The Political Life of Medicare.* Chicago: University of Chicago Press.

Oberlander, Jonathan. 2007a. "Learning from Failure in Health Care Reform." *New England Journal of Medicine* 357 (October 25): 1677–1679.

Oberlander, Jonathan. 2007b. "Presidential Politics and the Resurgence of Health Care Reform." *New England Journal of Medicine* 357 (November 22): 2010–2104.

Oberlander, Jonathan. 2009. "Great Expectation—The Obama Administration and Health Care Reform." *New England Journal of Medicine* 360 (January 22): 321–323.

Oberlander, Jonathan. 2010. "Long-Time Coming: Why Health Reform Finally Passed." *Health Affairs* 29 (6): 1112–1116.

Orloff, Ann-Shola. 1991. "Gender in Early US Social Policy." *Journal of Policy History* 3 (3): 249–281.

Orren, Karen, and Stephen Skowroneck. 2004. *The Search for American Political Development.* Cambridge: Cambridge University Press.

Orren, Karen, and Stephen Skowroneck. 2017. *The Policy State: An American Predicament.* Cambridge, MA: Harvard University Press.

Peterson, Mark A. 1993. "Political Influence in the 1990s: From Iron Triangles to Policy Networks." *Journal of Health Politics, Policy and Law* 18 (2): 395–438.

Pfiffner, James P. 1987. "Strangers in a Strange Land: Orienting New Presidential Appointees." In *The In-and-Outers: Presidential Appointees and Transient Government in Washington*, edited by G. Calvin Mackenzie, 141–156. Baltimore: Johns Hopkins University Press.

Pfiffner, James P. 2011. "Organizing the Obama White House." In *Obama in Office: The First Two Years*, edited by James Thurber, 75–88. Boulder, CO: Paradigm Publishers.

Pierson, Paul. 1994. *Dismantling the Welfare State? Reagan, Thatcher, and the Politics of Retrenchment.* Cambridge: Cambridge University Press.

Pierson, Paul, ed. 2001. *The New Politics of the Welfare State.* Oxford: Oxford University Press.

Pierson, Paul, and Theda Skocpol. 2007. *The Transformation of American Politics: Activist Government and the Rise of Conservatism*. Princeton: Princeton University Press.

Prasad, Monica. 2006. *The Politics of Free Markets: The Rise of Neoliberal Economic Policies in Britain, France, Germany and the United States*. Chicago: University of Chicago Press.

Price, David E. 1971. "Professionals and 'Entrepreneurs:' Staff Orientations and Policy Making on Three Senate Committees." *Journal of Politics* 33 (2): 316–336.

Price, David E. 1978. "Policy Making in Congressional Committees: The Impact of 'Environmental' Functions." *American Political Science Review* 72 (2): 548–574.

Prewitt, Kenneth, and William McAllister. 1976. "Change in the American Executive Elite 1930–1970." In *Elite Recruitment in Democratic Politics: Comparative Studies across Nations*, edited by Heinz Eulau and Moshe M. Czudnowski, 105–132. New York: Sage.

Putnam, Robert D. 1977 "Elite Transformation in Industrial Advanced Societies: An Empirical Assessment of the Theory of Technocracy." *Comparative Political Studies* 10 (3): 383–411.

Quadagno, Jill S. 2004. "Why the United States Has No National Health Insurance: Stakeholder Mobilization against the Welfare State, 1945–1996." *Journal of Health and Social Behavior* 45 (extra issue): 24–44.

Quadagno, Jill S. 2005. *One Nation, Uninsured: Why the US Has No National Health Insurance*. Oxford: Oxford University Press.

Quadagno, Jill S. 2011. "Interest-Group Influence on the Patient Protection and Affordability Act of 2010: Winners and Losers in the Health Care Reform Debate." *Journal of Health Politics, Policy and Law* 36 (3): 449–453.

Quadagno, Jill S. 2014. "Right-Wing Conspiracy? Socialist Plot? The Origins of the Patient Protection and Affordable Care Act." *Journal of Health Politics, Policy and Law* 39 (1): 35–56.

Rich, Andrew. 2004. *Think Tanks, Public Policy, and the Politics of Expertise*. Cambridge: Cambridge University Press.

Rockefeller, John D., IV. 1990. "The Pepper Commission Report on Comprehensive Health." *New England Journal of Medicine* 323, no. 14: 1005–1007.

Rodgers, Daniel T. 1998. *Atlantic Crossings: Social Politics in a Progressive Age*. Cambridge, MA: Harvard University Press.

Rodwin, Victor G. 1989. "Physician Payment Reform: Lesson from Abroad." *Health Affairs* 8 (4): 76–83.

Romzek, Barbara S., and Jennifer A. Utter. 1996. "Career Dynamics of Congressional Legislative Staff: Preliminary Profile and Research Questions." *Journal of Public Administration Research and Theory* 6 (3): 415–442.

Rose, Richard. 1991. "What Is Lesson-Drawing?" *Journal of Public Policy* 11 (1): 3–30.

Sabatier, Paul A. 1998. "An Advocacy Coalition Framework of Policy Change and the Role of Policy-Oriented Learning Therein." *Policy Sciences* 21 (2–3): 129–168.

Saiger, Aaron J. 2011. "Obama's 'Czars' for Domestic Policy and the Law of the White House Staff." *Fordham Law Review* 79 (6): 2577–2615.

Salisbury, Robert H., and Kenneth A. Shepsle. 1981. "Congressional Staff Turnover and the Ties-that-Blind." *American Political Science Review* 75: 381–396.

Sardell, Alice. 2014. *Ensuring Children's Health: Contentious Politics and Public Policy.* Boulder, CO: Lynne Rienner.

Schlesinger, Arthur, Jr. 1973. *The Imperial Presidency.* Boston: Houghton Mifflin.

Selznick, Philip. 1957. *Leadership in Administration: A Sociological Interpretation.* Berkeley: University of California Press.

Sheingate, Adam. 2009. "Why Can't Americans See the State?" *Forum* 7 (4): 1–14.

Skocpol, Theda. 1985. "Bringing the State Back In: Strategies of Analysis in Current Research." In *Bringing the State Back In,* edited by Peter Evans, Dietrich Rueschemeyer, and Theda Skocpol, 2–37. Cambridge: Cambridge University Press.

Skocpol, Theda. 1992. *Protecting Soldiers and Mothers: The Political Origins of Social Policy in the United Sates.* Cambridge, MA: Belknap Press of Harvard University Press.

Skocpol, Theda. 1995. *Social Policy in the United States.* Princeton, NJ: Princeton University Press.

Skocpol, Theda. 1996. *Boomerang: Health Care Reform and the Turn Against Government.* New York: W. W. Norton.

Skocpol, Theda, and Kenneth Finegold. 1982. "State and Economic Intervention in the Early New Deal." *Political Science Quarterly* 97 (2): 255–278.

Skocpol, Theda, and G. John Ikenberry. 1983. "The Formation of the American Welfare State in Historical and Comparative Perspective." *Comparative Social Research* 6: 87–148.

Skocpol, Theda, and Margaret M. Weir. 1985. "State Structures and the Possibilities for 'Keynesian' Reponses to the Great Depression in Sweden, Britain, and the United States." In *Bringing the State Back In,* edited by Peter Evans, Dietrich Rueschemeyer, and Theda Skocpol, 107–163. Cambridge: Cambridge University Press.

Smith, David G., and Judith D. Moore. 2008. *Medicaid Politics and Policy.* New Brunswick, NJ: Transaction.

Sparer, Michael S., Lawrence D. Brown, and Lawrence R. Jacobs. 2009. "Exploring the Concept of Single Payer." *Journal of Health Politics, Policy and Law* 34 (4): 447–451.

Stanley, David T., Dean Mann, and Jameson Doig. 1967. *Men Who Govern: A Biographical Profile of Federal Political Executives.* Washington, DC: Brookings Institution Press.

Stark, Jack. 1995. "The Wisconsin Idea: The University's Service to the State." In *State of Wisconsin Blue Book, 1995–1996.* Madison: State of Wisconsin.

Starr, Paul E. 1982. *Social Transformation of American Medicine.* New York: Basic Books.

Starr, Paul E. 1994. *The Logic of Health Care Reform: Why and How the President's Plan Will Work.* New York: Penguin Books.

Starr, Paul E. 2001. "What Happened to Health Care Reform?" *American Prospect.* November 19. www.prospect.org.

Starr, Paul E. 2007. "The Hillarycare Mythology." *American Prospect.* October 12–18. www.prospect.org.

Starr, Paul E. 2013. *Remedy and Reaction: The Peculiar American Struggle over Health Care Reform.* New Haven, CT: Yale University Press.

Starr, Paul E, and Walter A. Zelman. 1993. "A Bridge to Compromise: Competition under a Budget." *Health Affairs* (supplement): 7–23.

Steinmo, Sven H. 2010. *The Evolution of Modern States: Sweden, Japan, and the United States.* Cambridge: Cambridge University Press.

Steinmo, Sven H., Kathleen Thelen, and Frank Longstreth. 1992. *Structuring Politics: Historical Institutionalism in Comparative Analysis.* Cambridge: Cambridge University Press.

Steinmo, Sven, and Jon Watts. 1995. "It's the Institutions, Stupid! Why Comprehensive National Health Insurance Always Fails in America." *Journal of Health Politics, Policy and Law* 20 (2): 329–372.

Stevens, Robert, and Rosemary A. Stevens. 1974. *Welfare Medicine in America: A Case Study of Medicaid.* New York: Free Press.

Suleiman, Ezra N. 2003. *Dismantling Democratic States.* Princeton: Princeton University Press.

Tuohy, Carolyn H. 2009. "Single Payers, Multiple Systems: The Scope and Limits of Subnational Variation under a Federal Health Policy Framework." *Journal of Health Politics, Policy and Law* 34 (4): 453–496.

United States General Accountability Office (GAO). 1991. *Canadian Health Insurance: Lesson for the United States.* Report to the chairman, Committee on Government Operations, House of Representatives. Washington, DC. June 1991.

Vaughn, Justin S., and José D. Villalobos. 2015. *Czar in the White House: The Rise of Policy Czars as Presidential Management Tools.* Ann Arbor: University of Michigan Press.

Weber, Max. 2004. *The Vocations Lectures.* Indianapolis, IN: Hackett.

Wedel, Janine R. 2009. *Shadow Elite: How the World's New Power Brokers Undermine Democracy, Government and the Free Market.* New York: Basic Books.

Whipple, Chris. 2017. *The Gatekeepers: How the White House Chiefs of Staff Define Every Presidency.* New York: Penguin Random House.

Whiteman, David. 1987. "What Do They Know and When Do They Know It? Health Staff on the Hill." *PS: Political Science and Politics* 20 (2): 221–225.

Whiteman, David. 1995. *Communication in Congress: Members, Staff, and the Search for Information.* Lawrence: University Press of Kansas.

Wildavsky, Aaron. [1979] 2001. "The Once and Future School of Public Policy." In *Speaking Truth to Power: The Art and Craft of Policy Analysis,* edited by Aaron Wildavsky, xv–xxi. New Brunswick, NJ: Transaction Books.

Wildavsky, Aaron. 2001. *Budgeting and Governing.* New Brunswick, NJ: Transaction Books.

Winters, Jeffrey A., and Benjamin I. Page. 2009. "Oligarchy in the United States?" *Perspective on Politics* 7 (4):731–751.

Young, James S. 1966. *The Washington Community 1800–1828.* New York: Columbia University Press.

Aaron, Henry J., 43, 143

Aberbach, Joel D., 2, 15, 54, 57, 60, 63, 64, 66–69, 71, 74, 267n2, 273n62

Abernethy, David, 114

accommodation and custodianship of health coverage policy, 209–42

Adams, Gordon, 19, 225, 255

Affordable Care Act (ACA), ix, xix, 1, 4, 24, 25, 50, 64, 85, 89, 120, 128, 130, 143, 146, 185, 210, 229, 236, 250, 259, 265n1, 265n6, 266n8, 275n40, 286, 289, 294; bipartisan approach of, 119; and custodians of state policies, 212, 225–34, 240, 249; elite configuration and programmatic orientations during formulation of, 143–146; as far-reaching reform, 29, 92, 253; and foreclosure of "government of strangers," 234–42; and the Massachusetts Plan, 202–8; and women in charge, 251–52.

Affordable Health Care for America Act, 209, 228, 234–242

Affordable Health Choice Act, 134, 216, 229, 238, 239

age of congressional staffers and political appointees, 69–74

Alliance for Health Reform, 83, 85–88, 92, 94, 99, 120, 140–41, 146, 197–202, 231, 270n10, 273n3; and Bipartisan Policy Center, 83, 90, 95, 103; and Center on Budget and Policy Priorities, 83, 109; and Clinton Plan Veterans and, 92, 108, 113–14, 124–25, 136, 138, 197–98, 200–1, 228, 280n25; (democratic) newcomers, 132, 198, 205; and Pepper Commission, 93, 154. See also Robert Wood Johnson Foundation.

Allison, T. Graham, 15

Altman, Stuart H., 43, 159, 238

Altmeyer, Arthur J., 32–35

American Academy of Actuaries, 105

American Enterprise Institute (AEI), xix, 21, 38, 51, 113, 123

American Health Information Community Program, 116

American Health Insurance Portability and Accountability Act (1996), 101

American Hospital Association, 95, 232

American Medical Association (AMA), 34, 36, 37, 148, 232

Arrow, Kenneth J., 42

assistant secretary for planning and evaluation (ASPE), xi, xix, 21, 39, 43, 85, 92, 103, 109, 125, 137, 140–41, 152, 170, 177, 204, 211, 213, 224, 245, 276n1.

back offices (government), 1, 8, 14–15, 17–18, 23–24, 53–54, 56, 59, 64, 69, 74–76, 82–84, 87, 90, 96–97, 110, 124–26, 131, 136–37, 144, 146, 161, 169, 182, 186, 190, 194, 201, 207, 210–12, 219, 221, 224–25, 230, 240–41, 246, 248, 257.

Bai, Matt, 92, 215, 220–21

Balanced Budget Act (1997), 58, 90, 101–2, 115, 189

Ball, Robert, 34–36

Balogh, Brian, 9

Barnett, Philip, 97, 100

Baucus, Max, 129, 134, 205, 221, 233, 279n9, 281n2

Beaussier, Anne-Laure, 119, 189, 210, 216, 225, 228–29, 231–35, 255, 260n2, 267n1, 281n33, 282n13, 286

Béland, Daniel, 186, 190, 286

Belkin, Gary S., 265n3, 286, 293

Benson, John M., 165, 287

Berkowitz, Edward D., 32–35, 38, 91, 101, 102, 157, 202, 272n52, 281n32, 283, 283n25, 285, 287

Best, Heinrich, 4, 287

Biles, Brian, 86–88

bipartisanship: and Affordable Care Act, 108–9, 111–14, 116–17, 121, 124, 133–35, 139, 152, 183, 184, 190–96, 200–5, 209, 212, 216, 225, 228, 230–31, 239, 247, 252; legislation, 90, 98–99, 101, 119, 128–29, 132, 156, 165, 179, 184, 189, 270n10; and Pepper Commission, 82, 84, 155; and think tanks, 83, 92, 108, 125, 138, 141, 145, 198. *See also* Alliance for Health Reform; Bipartisan Policy Center (BPC); Center on Budget and Policy Priorities (CBPP)

Bipartisan Policy Center (BPC), xix, 83, 92, 95, 98, 192, 273n3, 279n9, 280n13; Clinton Plan veterans and, 108–9, 125, 138, 145, 195; long-term insiders and, 103, 132, 140–41. *See also* Alliance for Health Reform; Center on Budget and Policy Priorities (CBPP);

"birds of passage" (Heclo), 61, 75, 136

Birnbaum, Pierre, xv, 10, 244, 287

Bjorkland, Cybele, 127–28

Blendon, Robert J., 165, 287

"blueberry donut group," 81, 85

Blumenthal, David, 34, 42, 84, 116–18, 171–72, 210, 279n9

Blyth, Mark, 11, 27, 287

Bonafede, Dom, 220, 287

Bond, Christopher, 119

Bowen, David, 133–34

Brasfield, James, 234, 236, 239, 287

Brill, Steven, 96, 115, 127, 129, 131, 134, 204, 205, 217, 221, 229, 233, 234, 236, 238, 239, 287

Broder, David S., 81, 84, 114–16, 137, 143, 148, 165, 167, 171, 270n9, 291

Brookes, Kevin, 11, 27, 287

Brookings Institution, 21, 51, 63, 84, 140, 155, 174, 192, 279n9, 282n20; and the Hamilton project, 126, 195–96, 217

Brown, Lawrence D., xii, xv, 3, 15–16, 39, 40, 46, 101, 105, 111, 135, 150, 177, 255, 266n1, 268n15, 276n4, 282n20, 287–88

Brown, Scott (Senator), 209, 213, 229

Brownlow, Louis, 1, 288

Burris, Val, 66, 288

Bush, George H. W., 7, 44, 46–47, 53, 59, 109, 123, 160; administration, 63, 112, 116, 118, 172, 257, 277n12

Bush, George W., 7, 90, 105, 111, 113, 123, 125, 185, 189, 195, 215, 241, 247, 252; administration, 8, 19, 58, 88, 95, 106, 109, 112, 116, 118–19, 121, 124, 128–29, 139, 145, 184, 194, 224, 257; health coverage reform during administration of, 184–208; health coverage policy elites in administration of, 110–4. *See also* Medicare Prescription Drug, Improvement, and Modernization Act (MMA, 2003)

Canadian single-payer model, rejection of, 114, 149–53

career longevity of health coverage policy elites, 21, 53, 54, 274–80

career path (and social background) of elites, 3–7, 10, 17, 24, 50, 53, 54, 59–62, 81–82, 112, 120, 124–25, 134–35, 137, 142, 144, 147–48, 150, 157, 163, 210–12, 220, 244–47, 256–59; difference "short-timers" vs. "long-term insiders", 25, 30, 217; of institutional migrants, 55–56, 58, 83–97, 113–117, 124–130, 157, 178, 211, 213, 219–20, 241, 273n4, 280n25; of policy bureaucrats, 104–9, 116, 121–24, 157, 175, 274n25; of policy entrepreneurs, 44, 136, 151, 157, 161–62, 221; SI elites, 32–33, 53; of technocratic translators, 97–104, 176, 188, 196, 205, 207, 214, 216, 221, 241, 271n40, 274n17, 277n11; Washingtonians, 18–21, 23, 64, 69–80, 182, 185–88, 191, 193, 197, 199, 225, 239; and women in charge, 251–52. *See* "iron triangle"; *Programmatic Elites Framework* (PEF); social background; sociological portraits

Carter, Jimmy, 14, 20

Cato Institute, 37–38, 51

Center for American Progress (CAP), xix, 51, 132, 138, 145, 192–94, 279n9

Center for Health Affairs, Project Hope Foundation, 118

Center for Health Policy Studies, Georgetown University), 84

Center for Medicare and Medicaid Services (CMS), xx, 28, 50, 56, 96, 100, 105, 109,

124–25, 128, 135, 140, 194, 240, 245, 260n7, 272n48, 273n59, 285n, 286, 287. *See also* Health Care Financing Administration (HCFA)

Center on Budget and Policy Priorities (CBPP), xix, 83, 98, 103, 108, 125, 138, 140, 145, 192, 195–96, 273n3, 280n15. *See also* Alliance for Health Reform; Bipartisan Policy Center (BPC); Clinton plan veteran; long-term insiders

Chronic Condition: Why Health Reform Fails (Glied), 103

Clinton plan veterans, 57–58, 81–109, 110–11, 116–22, 124–29, 130–39, 141–42, 143–46, 147, 152–53, 155–56, 159, 161, 164, 171, 185–210, 212–25, 227–40, 246–47, 269n5, 275n33, 280n15, 281n2; definition, 279n1; and the role of custodian, 248. *See also* (democratic) newcomers; institutional migrants; long-term insiders; policy bureaucrats; technocratic translators

Clinton, Bill, 4–8, 18, 24–25, 29–30, 44–45, 49, 50–51, 57, 82, 95, 98, 100, 111, 114–15, 123, 128, 131, 138, 143–45, 147–164, 165–183, 184, 186, 188, 190–91, 195, 206, 208, 210, 225, 238, 248, 252, 256, 257, 265n3, 265n6, 270n21, 272n51; administration, 5, 12, 27–29, 43, 64, 81, 84–85, 91, 102, 106–9, 113, 116, 118, 120, 137, 200, 204, 207, 215, 217, 220, 222–23, 226, 231, 233, 235, 240, 246, 259, 274n33. *See also* Clinton task force and Plan; Hillary Rodham Clinton; Ira Magaziner; "managed competition" model

Clinton, Hillary Rodham: and insurance reform task force, 89, 131, 159, 161, 166–71, 173, 178, 194, 203, 218, 221, 224, 229, 296.

Cohen, Howard, 118, 120

Cohen, Wilbur J.: on Medicare, 38; as SI elites, 32–38, 286; "Wisconsin idea", 34. *See also* New Deal; Social Security Administration (SSA)

Commons, John R., and "Wisconsin idea", 34

Commonwealth Fund, xx, 51, 192, 279n9

comprehensive reform, 92, 94, 99, 107, 136, 144–45, 147–48, 157, 159, 170, 186, 200, 265n6; Clinton plan veterans

against, 200–2, 248; National Health Insurance project as, 34. *See also* managed-competition model; policy entrepreneurs; "single-payer" model

Congressional Budget Office (CBO), xix, 8, 28, 49, 50, 56, 92, 105, 113, 122, 127, 135–36, 138, 140, 151–52, 157, 179–81, 195–97, 199, 203–4, 211–12, 215, 217, 219, 221, 228, 230, 237, 239, 246, 276n1, 280n15, 282n17, 291. *See also* long-term insiders; Office of Management and Budget (OMB); Peter Orszag

congressional committees, 17–18, 22, 25, 55, 57, 69, 75, 82, 103, 189, 204, 211–13, 215, 218–19, 221, 225, 240, 246, 252, 267n3, 281n2

congressional staffers, 17, 20, 21, 54, 60–61, 69–71, 73, 76, 84, 120, 140–41, 174–75, 186, 202, 215, 221, 227, 229, 251, 258, 260n2, 278n9

cost-containment (as health policy issue), 27–28, 50, 56, 124, 132, 135, 177; and CBO, 211, 217; and custodian role, 195, 208, 240, 246

Council of Economic Advisers (CE), xix, 41–42, 113, 126, 130, 133, 140. *See also* Executive Office of the President (EOP); presidential advisers; program associate director [PAD] at the OMB

custodial role, defined xi–xii

custodians of state policies, 5–8, 13, 19, 22, 24, 27; custodianship, 9–11, 31, 35, 44–45, 47, 49, 209, 217; custodians of policy, 23, 26; in France, 5–6, 23, 25, 207; role of custodian of, 6–7, 27–28, 30, 33, 36, 51, 57, 74, 126, 142–44, 146, 185, 187, 191, 206, 208, 210–13, 220, 223, 225, 230, 236, 238–44, 248–50; SI elites and custodianship, 41, 48, 53, 153. *See also* policy state; unelected governmental elites

Daalder, Hans, 9–10, 268

Dahl, Robert A., 205, 243, 288

Danforth, John, 119

Darviche, Saïd M., xv, 6, 9, 16, 19, 23, 27, 31, 68, 126, 144, 242, 244, 248, 250, 255–56, 267n2, 289

Daschle, Tom A., 93, 96, 128, 131, 221, 226, 279n9, 280n13, 288

Davis, Carolyn, 43
Davis, Karen, 85
decision-making process, 1, 7, 14, 17–18,
  21, 54, 56, 73, 82, 165–66, 209, 216, 256;
  Clinton plan veterans and, 96, 101, 133,
  146, 186, 219, 222, 240; custodians of
  state policies role and, 23, 206, 208,
  210–13, 225; distinguished from decision-
  taking process, 5, 244, 265n7; programmatic elites framework, 24, 104, 257;
  role of women on, 64, 251–52; unelected
  governmental elites and, 5, 10, 16, 25,
  55, 80, 90, 94, 100, 135, 137, 170–72, 227,
  240–49, 281n2. See also Affordable Care
  Act; long-term insiders
DeParle, Nancy-Ann (Min), 101–3, 106,
  131–33, 189, 205, 271n40, 272n51, 272n52,
  272n53, 272n54, 272n55; in the Clinton
  task force, 116, 278n10; in Obama administration, 200, 202, 215, 221–24, 227–33,
  238–39, 252, 275n48, 281n32; at the OMB,
  106
Domhoff, William G., 2, 19, 220, 139, 265n4,
  288
Donnelly, Kevin P., 144, 185, 195, 234, 288
Durenberger, David, 115

Edelman, Marian Wright, 47
educational background of health coverage
  policy elites, 64–69
Eisenhower, Dwight, 35
elected officials, 2, 4, 18, 22, 186, 200–1, 208,
  209, 212, 265n7. See also elites; unelected
  governmental elites
elite(s) (political): circulation of, 50, 54–56,
  113, 124, 126, 145, 178, 193, 213, 215, 225–26,
  245–46, 248, 257; definition, 4; elite
  configurations, 5, 7–8, 24, 145, 157, 163,
  192, 224, 242; ruling elites, 2, 19, 139,
  243–44; "shadow elite", 2, 19, 22, 139;
  sociology of, 26; technocratic, 2, 15, 19.
  See also custodians of state policies;
  "iron triangle"; long-term insiders;
  Programmatic Elites Framework (PEF);
  Social Insurance (SI) elites; unelected
  governmental elites
Ellwood, Paul M., 39, 43, 79–80, 159,
  288
Ely, Richard: and "Wisconsin idea", 32.

Emanuel, Rahm: and Affordable Care Act
  (ACA), 213, 222–23, 231; as Clinton plan
  veteran, 92, 199, 200, 202, 220, 225.
Enthoven, Alain C., 12, 43, 44, 45, 79–80,
  90, 136, 158–61, 167, 169, 240, 276n11, 288.
  See also "managed competition"
Enzi, Mike, 121
Ertman, Thomas C., 10, 288
Ewing, Oscar, 34, 36, 36
Executive Office of the President (EOP), 16,
  18, 101, 116, 226, 266n3. See also presiden-
  tial (health) advisers; program associate
  director (PAD) at the OMB

Falk, Isidore S.: and the New Deal, 34–36.
  See also Social Insurance (SI) elites;
  Social Security Administration (SSA)
far-reaching reform (ACA as a), 5, 8, 29, 92,
  142, 144, 146, 185, 187, 194, 209, 211, 213,
  234, 241, 244, 247–48, 250, 253, 265n6.
  See also comprehensive reform
Feder, Judith M., 40, 84–86, 93, 101, 116,
  127, 131, 152–57, 162, 167, 171–72, 177–79,
  182, 196–97, 218, 222, 230, 236–37, 269n2,
  270n7, 270n8, 271n35, 276n55, 277n11,
  277n12, 277n14, 278n10, 279n2; and
  "play-or-pay" model, 153–57, 160–63,
  166–67, 171, 177, 270n13. See also Clinton
  plan veteran; long-term insiders
federal state or government, 26, 31, 34, 42,
  48–49, 54, 62, 72, 94, 123, 150, 160, 210,
  241, 242, 248, 265n3, 267n3, 281n33
Federation of American Hospitals (FAH),
  115–17, 232
fee-for-service delivery of health care, 39
Finegold, Kenneth, 2, 10, 13, 295
Fischer, Linda L., 19, 54, 61, 63, 67, 69,
  72–74, 267n6, 289
Forster, Richard, 104–5, 116–17
Fourcade, Marion, 11, 289
Fowler, Liz (Elizabeth), 95, 275n34; as
  (democratic) newcomers, 126, 129–31,
  207, 213, 228, 251, 280n24, 281n2; Medicare Prescription Drug, Improvement,
  and Modernization Act (MMA, 2003),
  119, 128, 189; and Senator Max Baucus,
  129, 134, 205, 216, 279n9.
Framework, 256–60. See also Programmatic
  Elites Framework (PEF)

France, custodian of state policy role in,
xii, 2, 6, 14, 19, 23, 25, 64, 68
Furman, Jason, 127, 196, 217, 267n2, 289

"Gang of Six" senators, 119, 121
gender balance in health coverage policy
formulation, 62–64 See also women in
health coverage policy.
General Accountability Office (GAO), xx,
56, 150, 296
Genieys, William, 2, 6, 9, 11, 14, 19, 23–27,
68, 126, 241, 244, 248, 250, 256, 289–90
Giddens, Anthony, 5, 244, 265n7, 289
Gingrich, Newt, 114
Glied, Sherry A., 81, 103, 144, 147–49, 151,
154, 157–58, 161, 172, 204, 276n5, 290; as
Clinton Plan veteran, 224; Clinton task
force, 222, 278n10; long-term insiders,
280n24.
Goldwater, Barry, 36
"government of strangers" (Heclo), 2, 5, 8,
14, 17–18, 20, 24–25, 30, 44, 51, 58, 136,
145–49, 158, 161–64, 165–67, 171–72, 174,
176–77, 186–88, 191, 202, 206–7, 212,
219–21, 234–35, 240, 247, 249, 268n9
Grassley, Charles, 119–21, 129, 139. See also
bipartisan approach
"Great Society" program, 2, 4, 15, 111, 126,
229; and President Johnson, 6, 37. See also
Medicaid program; Medicare program;
Social Insurance (SI) elites
Greenberger, Scott S., 288
Gruber, Jonathan, 79–80
Grupenhoff, John T., 59, 63, 290

Hacker, Jacob S., 3–4, 18, 20, 28, 79, 80–84,
118, 127, 136, 144, 148–51, 154–60, 163–67,
172–73, 184–85, 197, 202, 209, 232–43, 249,
268n15, 270n13, 290
Hamilton Project, 125, 127, 141, 192–93,
196–97, 218, 273n3, 275n36, 279n9; and
Brookings Institution, 192, 217, 289.
Hammond, Susan W., 65, 69, 267n3, 289,
290
"Harry and Louise" advertising campaign,
115, 181, 195, 233
Hash, Michael, 86, 94, 95–96, 99, 103
Hassenteufel, Patrick, xv, 27, 242, 256, 289,
290

Hastert, Dennis, 121
Havighurst, Clark, 43
Hayes, Mark, 117, 119
Health and Human Services, Department
of, xi, xx, 18, 56, 59, 60, 83, 91, 93, 94, 95,
105, 106, 117, 122–24, 130, 133, 136, 148, 168,
170, 172–74, 178, 188, 215, 220–22, 225–27,
241, 244, 246, 251–52, 270n5, 273n4; assistant secretary for planning evaluation
ASPE in the, 85, 87, 103, 109, 140, 213,
224; Health Care Financing Administration or CMS, 100–4, 116, 118, 128, 137, 177,
179, 271n33, 272n50, 273n59
Health Care Financing Administration
(HCFA), xi, xx, 28, 43–44, 49, 50, 56,
101–3, 109, 113, 116, 118, 122, 124, 125, 128,
135, 137, 140, 157, 174, 176–79, 188, 196, 211,
217, 223, 240, 245, 286. See also Center for
Medicare and Medicaid Services (CMS)
health coverage policy, 4–8, 25–26, 28–29,
30–32, 47–51, 53–55, 59–80, 81, 84, 98,
108–9, 110–13, 119, 122, 127, 130, 134–35,
137–42, 144, 146, 147, 149, 157, 163, 166,
176, 189, 210, 212, 224–25, 232, 240, 245,
248–50, 252, 258–59, 269n1. See also
Clinton plan veteran; (democratic) newcomers; long-term insiders; (political)
elite(s)
health coverage reform, 24, 58, 85, 90, 92,
102, 111–12, 119, 126, 127, 157, 161, 165–66,
184, 192, 195, 211–12, 214, 216, 218, 241.
See also Affordable Care Act (ACA);
health insurance reform; Health
Security Act
health economists, 41–45, 84, 85, 113, 127,
147, 150–51, 158, 163, 179, 189, 196, 210, 218,
221, 226, 240, 270n9; HMOs and, 80.
Health Insurance Association of America
(HIAA), xx, 115, 140, 182.
Health Insurance Portability and
Accountability Act, 115
health insurance reform, 1, 18, 96, 102, 104,
110, 124, 127, 217, 244, 246–47, 259, 271n33.
See also Affordable Care Act; Clinton
plan; health coverage reform; Health
Security Act
health maintenance organizations (HMOs),
xx, 3, 39, 40–41, 43–44, 80, 159, 177, 287;
43–44

health policy advisers, 14, 18, 41, 85, 88, 152, 156, 161–62, 166–68, 172–74, 194, 200, 203, 210, 214–16, 218, 220, 232, 275n54
Health Policy Alternatives (HPA), xx, 95, 129
Health Security Act. *See* Clinton Plan
Health, Education, and Welfare (1953 to 1979), Department of, xx, 38, 39, 40, 43, 85, 118, 276n1. *See also* Department of Health and Human Services (HHS 1979 to present)
Health, Education, Labor and Pensions (HELP), Senate committee on, xx, 133, 196, 203–6, 210, 216, 221, 228, 245, 257n1, 282n4. *See also* health policy advisers; long-term insiders; technocratic translator; Ted Kennedy; Veterans Clinton Plan
Heclo, Hugh, ix, 2, 14–16, 20–24, 30, 61, 74, 79–80, 136, 145, 148, 163, 173, 191, 220, 247–49, 268n9, 290
Heinz, John P., 267–68n7, 290, 294
Henschen, Beth M., 60, 290
Heritage Foundation, 21, 37, 120
Hess, Arthur, 38, 40, 286
Higley, John, xv, 4, 255, 287, 290
Hill-Burton Act, 31
Howlett, Michael, 265n5, 291

Ikenberry, G. John, 2, 295
Ingraham, Patricia W., 61, 291
insiders, government of. *See* Clinton plan veterans; (democratic) newcomers; health coverage policy elites; institutional migrants; long-term insiders; policy bureaucrats; Social Insurance (SI) elites; technocratic translators
institutional migrants, defined 56, 77, 131; and bipartisan approach of the reform, 117–21, 124, 152; circulation of across executive and legislative branches, 83–97; and Clinton plan, 162, 168, 170, 174–78, 181–82, 188, 196, 199; examples of, 84–97, 113–17, 124–30, 157, 211, 213, 273n4, 280n25; and Pepper Commission, 153–55; and technocratic translators, 83, 91, 98–99, 101, 108–9, 136–37, 153, 211, 220, 225. *See also* Clinton plan veterans; (democratic) newcomers; "iron triangle"; (republican) long-term insiders

invisibility of unelected governmental elites, 19–22
"iron triangle", 19, 166; elite circulation in new, 225.

Jacobs, Lawrence R., 4, 6, 82, 148–50, 158, 165–69, 172–74, 177, 180–87, 197, 202, 209, 216–17, 225, 234–35, 242, 250, 266n8, 268n15, 275n53, 276n4, 281n1, 291, 296
Jennings, Chris, 89–90, 95, 101, 168–69, 174–79, 188–90, 208, 266n2, 269n2, 271n24, 275n46, 276n56, 279n9. *and* Affordable Care Act, 91, 270n22; and Alliance for Health Reform, 89; and Hillary Clinton, 169; and Clinton plan veterans, 87–91, 101, 106, 132, 189, 195, 203, 222, 230, 236–37, 280nn24&25, 291; as institutional migrant, 155, 168, 174, 177, 188, 231, 277nn 11, 15, 26; as long-term insider, 278n10; and Pepper Commission, 86, 178–79; as "policy wonk" 90
Jensen, Benjamin, 241, 251, 291
Joana, Jean, xv, 6, 11, 27, 31, 255–56, 289
Johnson, Haynes, 81, 84, 115, 137, 143, 148, 165, 167, 171, 177, 270n9
Johnson, Kay, 47
Johnson, Lyndon B, 2, 6, 36–37, 41–42, 111, 115–16, 229; administration, 173, 276n1. *See also* "Great Society" program; Lyndon B. Johnson School of Public Affairs; Medicaid program; Medicare program
Joyce, Philip G., 28, 92, 105, 117, 127, 179–81, 196, 211, 217–18, 291

Kahn, Charles "Chip," III, 114–116, 117
Kaiser Commission on Medicaid and the Uninsured, 85
Kaiser Family Foundation (KFF), xx, 51, 88, 140, 196, 228; Alliance for Health Reform, 85, 92, 94, 99, 146, 197–202, 273n3; Commonwealth Fund, 192; Pepper Commission, 86; prepaid group practices (PGps), 39; and Robert Wood Johnson Foundation (RWJF), 90, 155, 192. *See also* Clinton plan veterans; think tanks
Katz, Ruth, 86, 97, 99

Kennedy, John F., 35–36; administration, 41–42, 59, 173; Harvard School of Government, 102, 268n8, 285

Kennedy, Edward M. 38, 97, 109, 121, 133, 209, 213, 292; congressional staffers of, 86, 87, 88, 128–29, 133–34, 155, 168, 175, 196, 200, 210, 215–16, 221, 228, 271n33, 272n47, 281n2, 293; and the Massachusetts Plan, 202–6; Oral History Project, 277n12, 277n14, 277n23, 277n35, 289.

Keynes, Maynard, 11, 13, 26–27

King, Desmond, 6, 10, 13, 24, 27, 242, 250, 291

King, Roland "Guy,' 122, 174, 274n25, 274n27, 291

Kingdon, John W., 39, 79, 101, 292

Kronick, Richard G., 158, 288

La Follette, Robert, and the "Wisconsin idea", 32

Lambrew, Jeanne M., 86, 89, 130–33, 139, 169, 174–75, 189, 193–94, 222, 251–53, 269n2, 270n2, 275n45, 275n46, 275n49, 275n50, 276n56, 277n15, 277n26, 279n9, 280n11, 288, 291–92; and Affordable Care Act (ACA), 224–28, 231; and Alliance for Health Reform; and Clinton plan veterans, 190, 203; and democratic newcomers, 103, 127; Hamilton project, 218; as long-term insider, 188–89, 195; as technocratic translator, 130–33, 188

Lasswell, Harold D., 185, 239, 292

Laumann, Edward O., 267–68n7, 290

Le Galès, Patrick, xv, 24, 27, 245, 295

Leavitt, Michael O., 116

Leca, Jean, 10, 249, 292

Leibovich, Mark, 51, 292

Lepont, Ulrike, 14, 81, 111–13, 119, 135, 158, 161, 185, 191–92, 203, 225, 235, 239, 255, 260n3, 280n9, 292

Lewis, David E., 59, 61, 292

Lieberman, Robert C., 3, 10, 13, 24, 291–92

Light, Paul C., 21, 268n11, 292

Linz, Juan J., 4, 288, 292

longevity of service, 23, 53, 74–80

Longstreth, Frank, 3, 296

long-term insiders (health): and Affordable Care Act, 212–13, 215, 217, 220–21, 224,

248; and bipartisan approach, 195, 197; Clinton plan veterans as, 81, 92, 98, 100, 103–4, 107–8, 147, 150–57, 186, 188–89, 269n1, 269n5, 276n11, 278n10, 279n1; conflicts with "the strangers", 167, 173–74, 176, 185, 191, 242, 247, 249; and custodians of state policies role, 25, 27, 207, 227, 233, 244; definition of, 4; democratic newcomers, 125–35, 205; Massachusetts plan, 203–4; population and features of, 7, 50, 135–42, 145, 163, 243, 245, 252, 255–60, 269n2, 272n58, 274n25, 280n24; republican as, 8, 110–17, 123–24, 194, 273n4, 274n17; typology of career paths (institutional migrant, technocratic translator, policy bureaucrat), 55–58, 61–62, 66–68, 73, 79–80, 82–83, 246.

Mackenzie, G. Galvin, 14, 24, 54, 61, 247, 268n11, 289, 290, 292, 294

Magaziner, Ira: and Clinton administration, 156; and Clinton task force, 102, 161–62, 168, 272n51; and "government of strangers, 136,' 167, 169–77, 188; Hillary Rodham Clinton, 159, 166, 221.

managed competition, 48, 207, 276n2; Clinton administration, 149, 158–64, 172, 179; and Clinton task force 172–76, 199. defined, 79; as programmatic orientation, 44–45

Mann, Dean, 63–64, 67, 72–73, 296

Mann, Michael, 2, 9, 292

market forces, 41, 49, 112

Marmor, Ted R., 4, 36, 79, 101, 240, 276n4, 292. See single payer model, 80, 151–52, 268n15

Mashaw, Jerry L., 151, 268n15, 276n4, 292

Massachusetts Plan, xi, 50, 194, 202–8, 216, 221, 279n9; as a historical model, 204, 236; as "Romneycrare," 205; and Senator Edward Kennedy, 202–3, 210

McAllister, William, 64, 294

McDonough, John E., 82, 90, 94, 99, 105, 115, 119, 127–29, 131, 133–34, 144, 185, 190, 194, 195, 200, 202–4, 210, 213, 216, 220, 225, 227, 229, 234, 237, 271n33, 281n2, 282n14, 292

means-tested programs, 30, 48, 49

Medicaid program, 6, 8; and custodian role, 48–51, 215; evaluation of, 118, 122, 128, 272n50; extension, 108, 148, 171, 194, 253, 265n6; as a "poor people's program", 37, 45–47, 63, 85, 87, 98–99, 288, 295, 296; protecting the, 188; SI elites, 46, 248. *See* Clinton plan veterans; Representative Waxman (Henry)

Medicare Catastrophic Coverage Act (1988), xx, 98, 122

Medicare Payment Advisory Commission (MedPAc), xx, 43, 118

Medicare Prescription Drug, Improvement, and Modernization Act (MMA, 2003), xx, 58; administration, 119–21; Clinton plan veterans, 129, 189–90; (democratic) newcomers and MMA, 119, 128, 189

Medicare program, 4, 6, 8, 11, 35, 84, 289, 292, 293; Affordable Care Act, 199, 265n6; Clinton plan veterans and, 87, 95, 98, 105–8, 184, 188, 237; (democratic) newcomers, 189; expansion, 154, 157, 171, 182; "Medicare for all" model, 205; Medicare Part A and B, 36; Medicare Part C, 39–40; (republican) long-term insiders, 113, 116–22; SI elites and Johnson Administration, 15, 35–51, 142, 248; Social Security Administration (SSA), 148, 162. *See* Centers for Medicare and Medicaid Services (CMS); "Great society" Program; Health Care Financing Administration (HCFA); Medicare Catastrophic Coverage Act (1988); Medicare Prescription Drug, Improvement, and Modernization Act (MMA, 2003)

Medvetz, Thomas, 16, 90, 148, 161, 292

Medvetz, Thomas, 90

Meisel, James H., 211, 292

Michaels, Judith E., 18, 20, 60, 64, 148, 220, 268n10, 293

Milkis, Sidney M., 6, 242, 250, 291

Miller, George, 47

Mills, C. Wright, 2, 19, 243, 265n4, 289, 293

Mills, Wilbur, 46, 229. *See also* Medicare program

Mizruchi, Mark S., 206, 233, 241, 249, 293

mobility of health coverage policy elites, 7, 54, 61, 74–80

Moore, Judith D., 47, 272, 295

Morone, James A., 34, 42, 84, 116, 118, 171–72, 185, 210, 229, 265n3, 287, 293

Moscan, Gaetano, 243–44

Mount Sinai School of Medicine, 101

National Bipartisan Commission on the Future of Medicine, 101

National Governors' Association, 47

National Health Insurance (NHI) project, 6, 11, 30–35, 150, 153, 235, 248–49, 265n6, 268n15, 276n1, 294, 296; anti—, 152.

National Institutes of Health, 31

Nelson, Karen, 86, 92, 94–95, 98

neoconservatives, 19

neoliberal revolutions, 27

New Deal (Roosevelt presidency), 1–2, 4, 6, 10, 13, 33–35 41, 111, 169, 173, 265n6, 268n15, 295; and custodian role, 33–35, 248; and weak state, 251.

newcomers (democratic): career path of, 58, 119, 125–31, 132, 134, 137–39, 142–44, 146, 216, 225, 246, 281n2; and custodian role, 191, 193, 195–97, 200, 203–7, 210, 212–13, 219, 247; definition, 274n33; as long-term insiders, 7–8, 103, 108, 110–11, 164, 183, 185, 187, 189. *See also* Clinton plan veterans; Elizabeth Fowler (Liz); institutional migrants; Jeanne Lambrew; Peter Orszag; policy bureaucrats; technocratic translators

Newton-Small, Jay, 251, 293

Nexon, David, 87–88, 133, 159, 206, 292–93, as Clinton plan veteran, 88, 129, 168, 269n4, 270n18, 280n25; and John E. McDonough; and Pepper Commission, 277n11; and Senate Committee on HELP, 216–17; and Senator Ted Kennedy, 88, 129, 155, 175, 215; task force 278n10

Obama, Barak, Administration, 5–8, 17–18, 28, 53, 57, 84–87, 92–94, 101–2, 126, 133, 144–45, 191, 199–202, 213, 215, 217, 220–27, 233, 235, 240–41, 246, 249, 250, 256n2, 269n5, 271n33; Affordable Care Act (reform), 27, 81–83, 89, 95, 98–99, 106, 109, 119–21, 128, 132, 143, 185, 190, 193–98, 209–10, 212, 219, 229–30, 232, 237, 239, 265n3, 270n22; and the Hamilton project,

127; and women in charge, 251–52. *See*
Affordable Care Act (ACA); Clinton plan
veterans; (democratic) newcomers
Oberlander, Jonathan, 4, 37, 101, 144,
184–85, 188, 192, 203, 209, 225, 238, 293
Office for Consumer Information and
Insurance Oversight (OCIIO), xix, 133,
221–22
Office of Health Reform (HHS), 95
Office of Management and Budget (OMB),
xxi, 28, 45, 50, 56, 72, 87, 84, 106, 124–25,
127, 135–38, 140, 169, 179, 189, 199, 211,
215, 234, 240, 246, 257n2, 270n5, 275n48;
Nancy-Ann Deparle, 222–23, 226; program associate director (PAD), 60, 100,
102–3, 109, 113, 116–17, 152, 188, 197, 245,
270n5, 272n52. *See also* Clinton plan
veterans; Congressional Budget Office
(CBO); Health Care Financing Administration (HCFA); Peter Orszag,
Office of the Actuary (HHS), 104
OPERA Research Program, xv, 30, 50, 55,
62–63, 65–70, 73–74, 76–79, 89, 95, 104,
136, 139, 141, 159, 161, 177, 180–81, 192,
201, 207–8, 222, 252, 255–58, 266, 269n1,
269n2; Appendix 2, 261–62. *See* ProAcTA
research program
Orloff, Ann-Shola, 62, 293
Orren, Karen, 4, 10, 13, 244, 294
Orszag, Peter: at the CBO, 127, 196–97, 211,
217–19, 221, 228, 282n15; as democratic
newcomer and institutional migrant,
103, 126, 127, 205, 239, 275n34, 275n35,
275n38, 280n24; at the OMB, 232.
Oversight and Government Reform
Committee, 96, 98–100, 226, 228, 282n5

Page, Benjamin I., 249, 297
Pelosi, Nancy (House speaker): and ACA,
230–32, 237, 251, 284n2; CBO Orszag
appointment, 127, 217; on staffers of,
91–92, 129, 213, 226, 227, 272n44, 281n2;
and Henry Waxman, 235
Pepper Commission, 82, 84, 86, 89, 93, 99,
116
Perkins, Frances, 32–33
Peterson, Mark A., 225, 294
Pfiffner, James P., 15, 17–18, 20–21, 64, 72,
268, 294

Physician Payment Review Commission,
xxi, 118, 295
Pierson, Paul, 3, 11, 20, 27, 44, 184, 236, 243,
249, 266, 290, 294
Planning, Programming, and Budgeting
System (PPBS), 12. *See also* Alain
Enthoven
"play-or-pay" as programmatic orientation, and Affordable Care Act, 236;
Clinton administration, 84, 145, 149–50,
153–57, 160–63, 166–67, 171, 177, 270n13;
defined, 7, 276n10. *See* Clinton plan
veterans; Feder (Judy); programmatic
orientation
pluralist stagnation (S. H. Beer), xii
Podesta, John D., 193, 194, 275, 279, 280,
292
policy advisers, 1, 14, 18, 21, 41, 56, 72, 88,
92–100, 119–22, 140, 168, 207, 257n2,
275n54; role, 80–81; "Washington based
health, 154–56, 220. *See* Clinton plan
veterans; (democratic) newcomers; long-
term insiders; policy entrepreneurs
policy bureaucrat as long-term insiders
career path subtype: features and definition, 55, 83, 104–9, 116, 121–24, 157, 175,
274n25
"policy czars," ix, 14, 109, 171, 295–96; defined, 16–17, 266n3; Nancy-Ann DeParle
as, 102, 245, 251, 272n55
policy elites. *See* Clinton plan veterans;
(democratic) newcomers; health coverage policy elites; long-term insiders
policy entrepreneur, 3, 5, 23, 39–41, 49, 51,
79–81, 103, 136, 143, 145, 148, 151, 154, 158,
163–64, 186–88, 191, 206–7, 212, 221, 235,
238, 245, 247–48, 293; Alain Enthoven as,
43–45, 160, 167, 240; as outsiders, 143,
158, 238; Paul Ellwood as, 39, 43, 79, 159.
See also government of strangers;
long-term insiders
policy state, 4–5, 10, 13, 24, 29, 30, 37, 41,
241–42, 244, 249–50. *See also* custodians
of state policies; state (theory)
"policy wonks", 14, 16, 90; defined, 266n2.
See also Chris Jennings; policy czars
Pollitz, Karen, 87, 93–94, 99
"power elite" (C. Wright Mills, 2
Prasad, Monica, 11, 27, 294

Prescription Drug, Improvement, and Modernization Act, 58
presidential (health) advisers, 18, 81, 91–92, 95–96, 102, 105, 116, 149, 152, 156, 161–62, 166–68, 171–74, 178, 180, 210, 215, 221–22, 229–30, 232, 239–40, 257n2, 266n3, 268n10, 272n51,281. *See also* Clinton plan veterans; long-term insiders
Prewitt, Kenneth, 67, 294
Price, David E., 18, 22, 294
Primus, Wendell, 91–92, 98
private sector employment, 71–74
ProAcTA research program, xx, 222, 252, 255, 260, 266n9; Appendix 2, 261. *See also* OPERA Research Program
program associate director (PAD) at the OMB, 60, 100, 102–3, 109, 113, 116–17, 132, 137, 152, 188, 197, 211, 222, 245, 272n52. *See also* Clinton plan veterans; Czar; (presidential) health policy advisers
Program Planning and Budgeting System (PPBS), xxi, 12, 277n30
Programmatic Elites Framework (PEF), 7, 24, 60, 104, 184, 266n10; Appendix 1: Methodology, 251–60; PEF and in-depth sociographic analysis, 53; PEF and programmatic orientations, 143, 211, 247; social background and career path, 125, 135, 142, 153, 245; sociological portraits, 82, 267n2. *See also* elites; institutional migrant; long-term insiders; policy bureaucrat; technocratic translator
programmatic orientation: Affordable Care Act and new, 185–87, 191, 193, 207, 210, 218, 230, 248, 252; Clinton plan veterans and, 85, 93, 96, 102, 104, 109, 117, 162, 173, 177, 182, 197, 201, 205, 239; cost-containment issue and, 27, 218, 246; and custodian role, 211, 249; (democratic) newcomers, 124, 138; elite types and, 18, 20, 23, 26, 64, 143, 145, 157, 161, 163, 166, 181, 183, 227, 234, 241, 244, 270n9, 276n1; features and content, 5, 8; long-term insiders and, 55–56, 117, 247; Massachusetts Plan and, 204; "play or pay" model as, 156; and Programmatic Elites Framework (PEF), 24, 259; SI elites and, 36, 48–49; "single payer" model as, 150, 152.

See also policy entrepreneurs;"public option" model
Progressive Era, 11, 30, 32–33
Prospective payment system, xxi, 43
"public option" as programmatic orientation, 80, 134, 146, 247, 287; defined, 79, House of Representatives and, 199, 235, 237; Senate Finance Committee and, 205, 228, 238–40. *See also* "single payer" model
public policy schools, 15–16, 26, 48, 65, 78, 134, 137–40, 246, 266n1, 286
Putnam, Robert D., 2, 14, 286, 294
Putnam, Robert, 2

Quadagno, Jill S., 3, 152, 202, 232, 294
Quayle, Dan, 115

revolving door effect, 54, 56, 60,74–80, 134
Rich, Andrew, 153, 158, 160, 196, 276n2, 295
Robert Wood Johnson Foundation (RWJF), xxi, 49, 88, 90, 101, 106, 140, 146, 155, 192, 270n10, 280n25, 287
Rochefort, David A., 144, 185, 195, 234, 288
Rockefeller IV, John D. (senator), 93, 153, 198, 295. *See also* Pepper Commission
Rockman, Bert A., 2, 60, 63–64, 66–69, 71, 286
Rodgers, Daniel T., 32–33, 35, 295
Rodwin, Victor G., 151, 276n4, 295
Romzek, Barbara S., 60–61, 65, 69, 71, 75, 268, 295
Roper, William, 43
Rose, Richard, 208, 295
Rosen, Dean, 87
Rosenbaum, Sara, 47
Rowland, Diane, 47, 85–86, 88
Roy, William, 86
Rubin, Robert, 21
"runaway spending," 37

Saiger, Aaron J., 17
Salisbury, Robert H, 61, 71, 75, 268n14, 295
Sardell, Alice, 45, 47, 63, 295
Schaeffer, Leonard, 43
Schiliro, Phil, 86, 94, 96, 103
Schlesinger Jr., Arthur., 17, 276n4, 295
Schneider, Andy, 47, 86, 92, 97–99 ,100

schools of public policy, 15–16, 26, 48, 65, 78, 134, 137–40, 246, 266n1, 286; or health policy, 26, 65, 78, 103, 108, 134, 137–40, 191, 246

Scully, Thomas A., 95, 105, 116–17

Selznick, Philip, 23–26, 295

senior executive service, 57, 104–9

Shactman, David I., 43, 159, 238, 286

"shadow elite" (Wedel), 2

Shapiro, Robert Y., 148, 158, 165–66, 169, 172, 174, 177, 180, 187, 291

Shaw, Teresa L., 193–94, 275n49, 280n11, 292

Sheingate, Adam, 9, 295

Shepsle, Kenneth A., 61, 71, 75, 268, 295

short-timers", 25, 61–62, 80, 135, 191, 200–1, 207, 216, 247, 268n10. See also "government of strangers"; policy entrepreneurs

Sidlow, Edward I., 60, 290

"single payer" as programmatic orientation: and Clinton administration, 145, 149, 153–54, 204–6, 276n2; definition, 79, 268n15, 296; and "public option" model, 237; and Ted Marmor, 80. See also "government of strangers"; policy entrepreneurs

Skocpol, Theda, 2, 4, 10, 13, 63, 79, 82, 84, 148, 151, 154, 163, 165, 171, 173, 180, 184–85, 197, 202, 209–10, 216–17, 225, 234–36, 251, 266n8, 268n16, 275n53, 276n10, 278n1, 281n1, 291, 294, 295

Skowroneck, Stephen, 4, 10, 244, 294

Smith, David G., 47, 295

Smith, Wayne K., 12, 160, 288

Smyrl, Marc, xv, 11, 26, 255–56, 286, 289–90

Snow, Olympia, 119–21, 129, 139

social background (and career path of elites, 3–4, 6–7, 10, 16, 24, 50, 53, 59, 62, 82, 112, 120, 124–25, 134–35, 137, 142, 144, 147–48, 150, 157, 210–11, 220, 244–45, 255–56, 259, 268n1; difference with American academic tradition, 265n4. See career path; long-term insiders; Programmatic Elite Framework; sociological portraits

Social Insurance (SI) elites, 31–33, 35–38, 40–41, 45–51, 53, 96, 111, 118, 134, 153, 157, 248, 250. See also custodians of state policies; elites; "Great Society" program;

Medicaid Program; Medicare Program; Social Security Administration (SSA)

Social Security Act, 32

Social Security Administration (SSA), xxi, 34–36. See also Social Insurance (SI) elites; Wilbur J. Cohen

socialism, 33, 115

sociological portraits (of elites), 55, 81–82, 109, 259, 267n2; of democratic institutional migrants, 84–94, 126–28, of republican institutional migrants, 113–17; of democratic long-term insiders, 110, 125; of democratic policy bureaucrats, 104–7, of republican policy bureaucrats, 122–24; of democratic technocratic translators, 97–101, 130–34, of republican technocratic translators, 119–20; social background and career path, 82, 267n2. See also Clinton plan veterans; programmatic elite framework

Sparer, Michael S., 46, 150, 268, 288, 296

Specter, Arlen, 120

Stanley, David T., 63–64, 67, 72–73, 296

Stark, Jack, 86, 296

Starr, Paul E., 4, 34, 80–81, 89, 127, 131, 136, 143–44, 147–49, 152, 154, 158–59, 161–62, 168, 172–73, 184, 187, 190, 202–3, 209–10, 220, 225, 228, 237, 241, 250, 278n9, 296

state (theory), 10–22; activities or capacities, 16; American state, 3–4, 16; authority, 27, 126, 200–1; elites of the state or state elites, 9–10; federal state, 30–33, 42, 45–46, 49, 73, 86, 114, 140; French, 6, 256n1; Keynesian, 26–27; reconfiguration, 9, 24, 48, 245; "strong state", 10, 13, 251; universities, 67–69, 118, 123, 169; "weak state", 13, 19, 22, 251; See also custodians of state policies; policy state

State Children's Health Insurance Program (SCHIP), 45–47, 90, 132, 189, 272n50. See also Medicaid program

Steinmo, Sven H., 3, 22, 153, 166, 190, 250, 296

Stevens, Robert, 46, 296

Stevens, Rosemary A., 46, 296

"strangers," struggle between insiders and, 165–83

"strong" policies and "weak" states, 10 13

Suleiman, Ezra N., xv, 27, 290, 296

Sweden, social-democratic model in, 11
Sydenstricker, Edgar, 33

task force (Clinton), 82, 85, 88–89, 93–95, 98, 99, 101, 102, 106, 108, 113, 116, 118, 122, 137, 141, 145, 179–80, 198, 201, 220, 222–23, 278n9; Clinton (Hillary Rodham), 166, 161, 168, 169; and Magaziner (Ira), 161, 166, 168, 169–77, 272n51. *See also* Clinton plan veterans; government of strangers
technocratic translators: features and definition, 55, 56, 57, 111, 140; examples of, 97–104, 176, 188, 196, 207, 214, 241, 271n40, 274n17, 277n11; and bipartisan approach of the reform, 117–21, 124; and institutional migrants, 76, 83, 91, 108–9, 136–37, 153, 211, 220, 225; and preference for Reform consensus, 130–33. *See also* Clinton plan veterans; democratic newcomers; "iron triangle"; republican long-term insiders
Thelen, Kathleen, 3, 296
think tanks, 8, 15–16, 19–21, 26, 37, 50, 51, 55, 56, 72, 73, 77, 82, 103, 108, 113, 121, 125, 135–36, 140–41, 145, 186–87, 191–93, 200, 203, 209, 230–31, 247. *See also* American Enterprise Institute (AEI); Bipartisan Policy Center; Brookings Institution; Center for American Progress; Center on Budget and Policy Priorities
third-party payments, 39, 42
Tri-Committee (House of Representatives): and ACA reform, 94, 129, 226, 228, 238. *See* Clinton plan veterans; (democratic) newcomers
Truman administration, 11
Truman, Harry S., 11, 35
Trump, Donald, 10, 124
Tuohy, Carolyn H., 150, 296

unelected governmental elites as subtype of political elites, 1–9, 256, 257, 259; as Clinton plan veterans, 82–109; and government of insiders, 11–22, 144, 145, 157, 164, 167, 243–44, 247, 249, 265n7; as health coverage policy elites, 59–80; as long-term insiders, 53–54, 59–80, 82–109, 110–42; and the role of custodians of state policies, 23–28, 250. *See also* elected

officials; institutional migrant; policy bureaucrat (as elites subtypes); technocratic translator
unelected officials. *See* long-term insiders; institutional migrant institutional; policy bureaucrat; technocratic translator; unelected governmental elites;
United Auto Workers, 36
United Hospital Fund of New York, 101
United States, xv, 1–2, 11, 13–14, 24, 27, 31–32, 39, 41, 49, 54, 60, 101, 127, 150, 153, 244, 248, 251, 260n3, 267n3
universities: Ivy league, 48, 50, 67–69; state, 67–69, 118, 123, 169; in Washington area, 48, 50, 51, 56, 64–69, 82, 87, 94, 103, 112, 120, 131, 132, 134, 137, 138, 247, 269n3, 276n55. *See also* schools of public policy or health policy
Urban Institute, 84, 118
"useful idiot" (Domhoff), 2
Utter, Jennifer A., 60–61, 65, 71, 75, 268n12, 295

Vaughn, Justin S., 2, 16, 266n3, 272n55, 296
veterans health, 118
Vietnam War, 37
Villalobos, José D., 2, 16, 266n3, 272n55, 296
Vladeck, Bruce: as Clinton plan veteran, 222, 280n24; and Health Care Financing Administration (HCFA), 100–2, 272n48, 286; on Task force (Clinton), 278n10; as technocratic translator, 100, 176, 188, 271n40, *Unloving Care*, 101.

Watts, John, 3, 22, 153, 166, 190, 296
Waxman, Henry (Representative): and the ACA, 228, 235; House committee on Energy and Commerce (staffers), 85–89, 92–100, 109, 129, 170, 175, 221–22, 226, 281n2; and Medicaid, 47, 108; and Medicare Prescription Drug, Improvement, and Modernization Act (2003), 189; "Waxman Clan or the Waxman Gang", 214–15. *See* Pelosi (Nancy); State Children's Health Insurance Program (SCHIP)
weak state, 10, 13, 14, 19, 22, 24
Weber, Max, 45, 208, 247, 296
Wedel, Janine R., 2, 19–20, 139, 249, 297

Weir, Margaret M., 2, 295
Westmoreland, Tim, 86, 87–88, 99
Whipple, Chris, 2, 17, 210, 297
Whiteman, David, 18, 22, 136, 297
Wildavsky, Aaron, 15, 297
Wilensky, Gail, 117, 118–19
"winner-take-all politics," 20
Winters, Jeffrey A., 249, 297
"Wisconsin idea", 6, 32, 34, 296

Witte, Edwin: and "Wisconsin idea",
32–34. *See also* Social Insurance (SI)
elites
women in health coverage policy, 7, 54,
62–64, 78, 251–52, 293.

Young, James S., 2, 10, 297

Zelman, Walter A., 158, 162, 296